From the Salem witchcraft trials of the 1690s to the Rodney King and O. J. Simpson trials of the 1990s, highly publicized court cases have both disclosed and shaped changes in American society. In this volume, Michael Grossberg examines the d'Hauteville child custody battle of 1840 to explore some timebound and timeless features of American legal culture. He recounts how marital woes led Ellen and Gonzalve d'Hauteville into what Alexis de Tocqueville called the "shadow of the law." Their bitter custody fight over their two-year-old son forced the pair to confront contradictions between their own ideas about justice and the realities of the law, as well as to endure the transformation of their domestic unhappiness into a public legal event with lawyers, judges, newspaper reporters, and a popular following.

The d'Hautevilles' multiple legal experiences culminated in an eagerly followed Philadelphia trial that sparked a national debate over the legal rights and duties of parents and spouses. The story of the d'Hauteville case explains why popular trials become "precedents of legal experience" – mediums for debates about highly contested social issues. It also demonstrates the ability of individual women and men to contribute to legal change by turning to the law to fight for what they want.

A Judgment for Solomon

CAMBRIDGE HISTORICAL STUDIES IN AMERICAN LAW AND SOCIETY

Editors

Arthur McEvoy   *University of Wisconsin Law School*
Christopher Tomlins   *American Bar Foundation*

To my Parents and my Sister

Solomon's Judgment

Then there came two women, that were harlots, unto the king, and stood before him.

And the one woman said, O my lord, I and this woman dwell in one house; and I was delivered of a child with her in the house.

And it came to pass the third day after that I was delivered, that this woman was delivered also: and we were together; there was no stranger with us in the house, save we two in the house.

And this woman's child died in the night; because she overlaid it.

And she arose at midnight, and took my son from beside me, while thine handmaid slept, and laid it in her bosom, and laid her dead child in my bosom.

And when I rose in the morning to give my child suck, behold, it was dead: but when I had considered it in the morning, behold, it was not my son, which I did bear.

And the other woman said, Nay; but the living son is my son, and the dead is thy son. And this said, No; but the dead is thy son, and the living is my son. Thus they spake before the king.

Then said the king, The one saith, This is my son that liveth, and thy son is the dead: and the other saith, Nay; but thy son is the dead, and my son is the living.

And the king said, Bring me a sword. And they brought a sword before the king.

And the king said, Divide the living child in two, and give half to the one, and half to the other.

Then spake the woman whose the living child was unto the king, for her bowels yearned upon her son, and she said, O my lord, give her the living child, and in no wise slay it. But the other said, Let it be neither mine nor thine, but divide it.

Then the king answered and said, Give her the living child, and in no wise slay it: she is the mother thereof.

And all Is'-ra-el heard of the judgment which the king had judged; and they feared the king: for they saw that the wisdom of God was in him, to do judgment.

I Kings 3:16–28

best interests of child
maternalism
love of the mother

what is being said about
the maternal role?

Contents

Preface

The d'Hauteville case is not the typical kind of case recovered from the legal dustbin and subjected to intensive study. It is simply not very important by orthodox legal standards. Its main event was a trial in a lowly municipal criminal court. And the case never reached an appellate tribunal, and thus did not become a binding precedent in the conventional sense of that word. Even its subject, a parental custody fight over a two-year-old boy, excludes it from the innumerable collections of great cases devoted as they are to crime, politics, and commerce. Yet the more I studied the d'Hauteville case, the more I realized that it had a particular importance.

As in innumerable legal contests from the Salem witchcraft trials of the 1690s to the Rodney King and O. J. Simpson trials of the 1990s, I discovered that the d'Hauteville case was not a single event in a courtroom but a set of multiple legal experiences that exposed timebound and timeless realities of American legal culture. The case began in an insular way, as a domestic drama must, with the rapid rise and equally fast fall of the d'Hauteville marriage. But as the fight for their son Frederick displaced their marriage as the central focus of Ellen and Gonzalve's relationship, the law assumed a greater and greater presence in their lives. The pair not only confronted contradictions between their own ideas about justice and the legal rules they had to learn, they also experienced the transformation of their domestic tragedy into a legal event with innumerable participants, from lawyers, judges, and legislators to courtroom spectators, newspaper reporters, and diarists. This startling metamorphosis raised the stakes of the case for the d'Hautevilles and everyone else drawn into their fight. As a result, the fierce battle Ellen and Gonzalve waged over Frederick led to numerous legal encounters that transformed their lives, while affecting the lives of many others; and it left a voluminous evidentiary record that can be used to recover the varied experiences that combined to create the d'Hauteville case.

Trying to interpret that record suggests that cases like this are very particular kinds of experiences. And experience is one of those

ix

troublesome words whose seemingly clear meaning masks confusion. I use the word as Raymond Williams did when he designated it one of the *keywords* of our language. To him, experience meant both the external influences to which people react and the interior consciousness of that reaction.[1] I want to add to his definition a recognition that the external and internal fuse to create individuals through their experiences. Using such a conception of experience underscores the reality that individuals are constituted through their experiences. Experience then becomes their history.[2] In other words, the evidence of experience includes records of both individual agency and the social systems that affect individual actions. As a result, trying to recapture legal experiences can bring an understanding of legal events not possible in any other way.

The d'Hauteville case became a legal experience worth recovering because of the relationship between the distinctive facts of the case and the particular setting in which it occurred. Two critical components of that setting are worth noting at the outset.

First, the d'Hautevilles fought over their son during an era of significant change in family life and gender roles. Years later, historians would look back at the bundle of changes occurring in late eighteenth- and early nineteenth-century households and announce that they had heralded the birth of the modern family.[3] At the time, however, conflict and confusion, not trend analysis, reigned in many North American and European homes. Most divisive were challenges to male power over households provoked by bourgeois visions of marriage as a companionate partnership and the family as a private refuge dedicated to child nurture and maternal authority. As the challenges rippled through families like the d'Hautevilles, countless conflicts broke out over how to construct new identities for spouses and parents. The struggles were so intense and the outcomes so unpredictable that battle after battle broke out between mothers and fathers, husbands and wives, and parents and children as well as between families and entrepreneurs, overseers of the poor, prosecutors, and other public and private agents. The debris of these troubled families offers the most revealing records of family change. In households like the d'Hautevilles', once silent assumptions about marriage, children, individual rights and duties, and all the other realities of daily life began to be voiced and defended. Challenges to existing power relations in the family had to be made plausible, as did their defense. The European and North American conviction that families constituted the bedrock institution of their societies made contests like the d'Hautevilles' even more troubling and momentous. Many Europeans and North Americans came to consider family conflict a telling indicator of *[handwritten margin note: still exist - family that the (alone) is goodness + morality - the society fiber of]*

their entire nation's well-being. What they found ignited hopes and fears that erupted into fierce debates about the very fate of the family. These debates continue into our own time.

Second, and equally – if not more important – for this study, Ellen and Gonzalve battled during a critical era in American legal history. Trial courts like the one in which the d'Hautevilles found themselves were the most visible symbols of a powerful postrevolutionary American legal system. For many early nineteenth-century Americans turning to law acted on beliefs and conventions already so deeply embedded in their culture that they were seen, when considered at all, as inevitable, indeed natural parts of their world. Since the Revolution, if not before in some provinces, law had tightened its stranglehold on American dispute resolution. As a result, while the disgruntled occasionally railed against particular statutes or specific judgments and attacks on lawyers might wax and wane, the American legal system wielded an immense power to frame and resolve many of the nation's most critical conflicts. Its power grew out of distinctive institutions, language, ideology, professionals, and rituals that somehow set the law apart from the rest of society as a distinct realm of experience and authority.[4]

[handwritten margin note: The Laws develops + strengthens since revolution]

Testaments to the newfound power of law proliferated during these years. Alexis de Tocqueville sailed across the Atlantic in 1831, surveyed the young nation, and then declared that in America every major issue eventually became a judicial question. Six years later, Abraham Lincoln, already seeking ways to bind together the contentious union, sermonized that law must be the nation's civil religion. Indeed becoming a lawyer proved so attractive that the growing number of attorneys easily outpaced the rate of American population growth at a time when it was the highest in the Western world. Lawyers not only seemed to multiply like locusts, law became the breeding ground for antebellum powerbrokers ranging from politicians like Lincoln and Daniel Webster, educational reformer Horace Mann, and even revivalist Charles Grandison Finney, to the innumerable mayors, land speculators, and other go-getters of the age. And countless other women and men affirmed the law's power year after year by pushing their way through courthouse doors as litigants, jurors, and spectators. Years later, historians would try to capture the growing power of law in these years with phrases like "formative period," "era of the release of energy," and "legal transformation." These labels suggest that much like the family changes of the period, those in law left an indelible imprint on the women and men who experienced them. They also suggest the emergence of debates over the place of law in American society that have continued to bedevil us as well.[5]

[handwritten margin note: power]

The d'Hautevilles' varied legal experiences illuminate their era's legal and family changes as well as the critical connections between them. They do so by reminding us that such changes were composed of innumerable individual experiences. Like so many others then and since, Gonzalve and Ellen discovered that going to law was not a neutral process. Translating problems like theirs into the language and forms of the law had a profound and often unpredictable impact not only on the outcome of a case but on all those drawn to it. The transformation of the fight for Frederick from a private quarrel into a public trial, with an avid following, bitterly contested legislative battles, and divisive public debates, thus documents not just the incendiary character of family conflict but also the lure of the law as a means of solving disputes.

As the rippling impact of the case suggests, when it is considered as a legal experience the d'Hauteville case appears not as a single event but a series of encounters, each of which spun multiple stories, meanings, and identities for Ellen and Gonzalve, their families, and their lawyers, and also for others beyond their immediate circle such as judges, legislators, courtroom audiences, newspaper readers in Philadelphia, New York, and Boston, and countless other cities and towns. These experiences were simultaneously distinct yet interwoven; and they cannot all be recovered. But looking at the case as a series of legal experiences is the best way to understand what the d'Hautevilles' fight for Frederick can tell us about the place of law in American society. It helps us understand how a case like this one becomes, as Richard Wightman Fox said of another highly publicized nineteenth-century family law drama, the Beecher/Tilton adultery trial, "a culture-shaping and culture-disclosing event."[6]

The dual reality of popular cases as cultural shapers and disclosers is best recovered from the past as a form of microhistory – the study of singular exemplary events. Microhistory traces structural changes in a society through stories of the struggles in individual lives.[7] Through such an approach controversial cases reveal aspects of a legal culture obscured in studies of a larger scope. They also reveal how individual legal experiences illuminates the past they had helped create.

Yet legal cases are problematic kinds of events to put under the historical microscope. Despite the tendency of most legal storytellers to turn popular cases into mirrors of society, such cases are not mere reflections of the broader culture at a particular moment. Rather, they are particular kinds of social dramas that illustrate the interactive reality of all legal experiences. In a trial, as in other crucial legal encounters, external beliefs, interests, and other forces are siphoned through the peculiar rules, practices, words, and institutions of the law. Inside the law office, the courtroom, and the legislative chamber, they acquire distinctive meanings that are then broadcast back to the public through client stories, lawyers' arguments, witness testimony, judges' verdicts, legislative debates, and statutes. These in turn help construct popular images of social relations. Interactively, legal events become thus active shapers of a culture, not merely its reflections. For that reason, microhistories like this one, which pay attention to the law as a site for both cultural revelation and cultural shaping, show how such cases enter popular and professional consciousness to become part of the process of social change.[8]

However, the d'Hauteville case is but one of many, from the Zenger trial to the Baby M contest, that have captivated the public. In it are the vices as well as the virtues of a single tale. And its record is inevitably incomplete. Not only are the principal actors long gone, so are other sources. Letters have been lost, diaries discarded, notes cast aside, documents destroyed, impassioned declarations have floated away in the wind, private thoughts have died with their authors. The participants in the d'Hauteville case had an understanding of the fight for Frederick knowable only to them. Yet enough remains to reconstruct the story of the case and to probe its meaning. Although a historian like myself can never fully recover a story from the past, I can arrange its many shards into a mosaic that none of its participants could ever have completed. I can bring to the tale a sense of their multiple experiences of the dispute, of the meaning of its occurrence at this particular time and place, even the story of the years since it ended that have added elements to the tale unknowable to any of its participants. Their understanding of the story and mine are both partial. Brought together they make reconstruction possible.

I have tried to capture the experiences of the d'Hauteville case through what David Hackett Fischer has called a braided narrative. By that I mean considering the case as a problem chain. Each problem leads to a resolution that creates the next problem in the story. I have divided the case into a chain of six storytelling problems, each of which occupies a chapter. The solution to each problem leads to the next chapter of the story.[9] Each chapter thus has twin goals. It tells the next episode of the case, while suggesting what that episode can show us about American legal practices and beliefs. In this way, I have tried to meld the obvious appeal of a narrative with recent insights about the distinctiveness of narrative constructions.

My single braided story of the d'Hauteville case is composed of three different kinds of narrative. In each chapter, I rely as much as possible on the words of the case's varied cast of characters to describe their legal experiences and explain the impact of those experiences on their lives. These personal stories, best understood as *ontological narratives,* reveal how Ellen, Gonzalve, their families, their lawyers, and innumerable members of their audience tried to make sense of the varied experiences spawned by the case. But because the actors in the d'Hauteville case, like those in all past events, cannot tell a complete story, I fill in the inevitable gaps in their tales with other evidence and my own inferences to place their legal experiences in a more comprehensive context. In particular, I have used legal periodicals, cases, statutes, newspapers, and other public records to recover the dominant stories used by groups of people in the era to understand cases like this. These *public narratives* formed a critical and changing part of the setting in which the actors in the case experienced the law. Finally, my own presentation of the case through a braided story can be understood as a *conceptual narrative.* In constructing an analytical method of telling the tale, I have woven my interpretation of the case into the chapters both in the way I have braided the links of the story and through direct observations of my own and others. My approach has stylistic implications as well. Rather than setting off passages as indented block quotes, I have melded the words from these narratives together into the paragraphs of the story. Each form of narrative is critical to reconstructing the d'Hauteville case. Taken together, they also show how narratives, like the lives and experiences they recount, must be understood to be cultural productions as well as structures of meaning and power.[10]

Through these narrative forms, I present the experiences of the d'Hauteville case in the order in which they were lived. The case was a series of legal experiences of specific individuals who made choices at particular times that had concrete consequences. A narrative like this one can uncover parts of past lives not retrievable in any other fashion. By doing so it provides a revealing glimpse of the operation of American legal culture at a particular moment in the past. Similarly, recalling the sequential way in which the cast of characters in the d'Hauteville case lived their lives and the intricate webs of relations through which they understood themselves and others returns a necessary uncertainty to their story and its meaning as a legal experience. As in most trials, the outcome remained uncertain until the very day of the verdict. And, as in most controversial trials, disagreement over the verdict immediately engulfed the case. These time-bound uncertainties and disagreements were critical parts of the case, and only a narrative can recover their significance and that of the other major legal events of the case.[11]

A braided narrative of the d'Hauteville case can serve another purpose as well. I want to use my story of Ellen and Gonzalve's fight for Frederick as an example of how to place popular cases and the varied legal experiences that constitute them in historical context. My intent is to present the d'Hauteville case as a model for contextualizing popular cases, and a brief for narratives as a way to probe the legal dynamics of social change. In particular, I want to argue that repeatedly in the past, as in the present, controversial cases like this one became symbolic contests that provoked and framed critical debates about social change. The d'Hauteville case allows me to do that through the medium of a dramatic narrative of one couple and their son. It offers a revealing example of how a dominant legal system collided with the actions of specific individuals and the press of timebound circumstances to ignite a legal conflict and kindle a series of revealing legal experiences. Such inherently particular and subjective stories from the past can begin to give us a legal history that recognizes the importance of the lived experiences of individual men, women, and children along with those of lawyers, judges, legislators, and legal writers.[12]

My goal is to bring the d'Hauteville case back to life and through it provide a glimpse of the legal culture in which it raged. I want to give readers a chance to experience this parental struggle as the maelstrom it was. Much of the power and social significance of a case like this comes from the way it forces every observer to identify with and judge the individuals at the bar of justice. I hope my narrative provokes similar reactions. In the end, only by reaching a verdict on Ellen and Gonzalve can the full meaning of their case be understood and the irresistible lure of the law be appreciated.[13]

Ultimately, the d'Hauteville case demanded the judgment of Solomon. Unable to divide Frederick in half, three Philadelphia trial judges had to decide whether Ellen or Gonzalve got the boy. The following pages try to tell why they had to make such a horrendous decision and to suggest the implications of their choice. It is a story at once bound to its own particular time and place, and yet also a tale of love, hate, and law that is universal and timeless.

Acknowledgments

When I stumbled across the d'Hauteville case several years ago, I realized it was an engrossing story. As I worked on telling it, I have been the fortunate recipient of numerous forms of support.

I began writing about the case while a Fellow at the National Humanities Center; and I completed much of the research and writing while holding fellowships at the Newberry Library and the American Bar Foundation. In between, I received timely research assistance from the Library Company of Philadelphia and the National Endowment for the Humanities. Archivists and librarians at the Library Company, Historical Society of Pennsylvania, Newberry Library, Massachusetts Historical Society, and Case Western Reserve University helped me locate crucial materials about the case. Law librarian Christine Corcos was particularly unstinting in her efforts to track down information. John Winthrop Sears also provided useful facts about his ancestor Ellen d'Hauteville. The research assistance of Christopher Cronin was invaluable. I would also like to thank the Massachusetts Historical Society for permission to reproduce pictures of the Searses. Unfortunately, I could not locate a likeness of Gonzalve d'Hauteville.

As I worked on the case, I received helpful comments from participants in seminars at the Newberry Library and the American Bar Foundation as well as at the law schools of the universities of Texas, Wisconsin, Michigan, Chicago, and Pennsylvania. Equally beneficial were responses to presentations on the case I gave at the Social Science History Association, Law & Society Association, and the American Anthropological Association. I am grateful as well to my former colleagues in the History Department at Case Western Reserve, especially Carroll Pursell and Angela Woollacott, who heard me talk about the d'Hauteville case time and again yet were always willing to discuss yet another issue. Several friends and colleagues also took the time to comment on various versions of this manuscript: Ann Warren, Carl Ubbelohde, and Dirk Hartog. Finally, I am indebted to the editors of the Cambridge Historical Studies in American Law and Society, Arthur McEvoy and Christopher Tomlins, and to Executive Editor Frank Smith. They encouraged the project during its transition from a rather convoluted initial version to its final published form. Chris, in particular, unselfishly lent his aid in the final stages of this project. His keen intellectual insights and thorough editorial commentary immensely improved my storytelling. Though I am, of course, responsible for all the judgments in this book, the aid of these colleagues has not only improved my story but taught me another lesson about the importance of collegial exchange.

Writing about past families inevitably places a burden on present ones. Tina, Matt, and Ben have suffered through this project for too many years. But their support has been unwavering. I could not have completed this book without it nor would I understand its subject as well as I do.

I dedicate this book to my parents and my sister Gail. Through our experiences together, we bring our own understanding of family troubles and family law to the tangled tale of Ellen, Gonzalve, and Frederick d'Hauteville.

A Judgment for Solomon

What are the twin
failures that lead (E+G)
them to court?

1.) marriage fails

Caught between
Period of negotiated
marriage + romantic
marriage

E + G's ideas of
marriage differed

Federalism
complicates the issue

" SOCIETY IS IN FLUX "
  (R.H.)

(1st married women's
  property law in US
  1837 in Mississippi)

Who do they hire as
lawyers? What does
it say about availability
of money?

1

Entering the Law's Shadow

Thursday, July 16, 1840, would be the first of many vexing days that summer and fall for Presiding Judge George Washington Barton of the Philadelphia Court of General Sessions. He huddled with his fellow judges Robert T. Conrad and Joseph M. Doran not knowing quite what to do. The case had seemed like a routine parental fight over a little boy, but complications quickly set in. The judges found themselves forced to decide between the clashing claims of a young, beautiful daughter of a Boston Brahmin and a youthful Swiss count. They faced five of the most eminent lawyers of the state. As usual in such delicate cases, they had decided to handle the dispute privately behind the closed doors of their chambers. But word of the case had leaked and spread around the city. A crowd demanded to be let in, and the parents differed over the wisdom of doing so. Perplexed, Barton called a recess.

Two days later, the presiding judge regretfully ruled: "After a careful consideration of the circumstances of the case, we think it our duty to sit in public. The affair has already gotten into the newspapers, and, by a private hearing, great injustice would probably be done to one party, if not to both. Perfect privacy or entire publicity is desirable. The former being out of the question, we must decide upon the latter. It is with pain and reluctance we make this decision, but nothing else is left us."[1] By throwing open the courthouse doors, Barton made the custody contest between Ellen Sears d'Hauteville and Paul Daniel Gonzalve Grand d'Hauteville a public event.

Twin failures had led Ellen and Gonzalve to Barton's courtroom. First their marriage unraveled; then their private bargaining over what to do about their failed union collapsed. As their marital problems worsened and a resolution remained elusive, turning to the law seemed the only way to resolve their problems. Like most people, though, the estranged spouses were reluctant legal combatants. They entered the courtroom only after experiencing the first of a seemingly unending series of encounters with the law.

The d'Hautevilles' first encounter with the law occurred outside

1

the courtroom. Slowly but surely, legal ideas and words began to dominate their dispute and their lives. These initial legal experiences are best understood through an image of American law penned a few years before their trial by that famous visitor to America, Alexis de Tocqueville. In his survey of American mores, *Democracy in America,* the French commentator expressed amazement at the authority ceded law and lawyers in the new republic. In words that have retained their explanatory power ever since, he described the breadth of the law's power by asserting that in America every major social and economic question eventually became a judicial question. But to understand the d'Hautevilles' initial legal experiences, Tocqueville's keenest insight about American law comes from his attempt to sketch a word picture of its hold over the republic: "The authority which is accorded to the intervention of courts of justice by the general opinion of mankind is so great, that it clings even to the mere formalities of justice, and gives bodily influence to the mere *shadow of the law.*"[2]

Tocqueville's arresting metaphor is a phrase from the d'Hautevilles' own time that can be employed to understand how they experienced the legalization of their dispute. The shadow of the law suggests how they, like all others drawn into its realm, came to feel the law's power over them. Critical to the metaphor is the insight that black letter legal rules applied in formal law making and law enforcing institutions like legislatures, courts, and administrative agencies are not the only forms of American legalism. On the contrary, Tocqueville's shadow of the law identifies how the formal legal order combined with popular legal ideology and customary practices to influence individual consciousness. It asserts the existence of a conscious sense of legal entitlement that encourages individuals and groups to use legal beliefs in disputes about their status, rights, duties, and problems. Finally, like so many of his insights, Tocqueville's shadow of the law not only explains the legal experiences he observed in America at the time of his visit, but also those in the years since his journey.

Of course, not all problems fall under the shadow of the law. In the past and present, conflicts are often solved by other forms of dispute resolution. But the d'Hautevilles and countless Americans caught up in disputes both petty and profound have found themselves in the law's shadow. From consumers who began to think of themselves as creditors not buyers when a merchant threatened bankruptcy to injured workers who began to consider themselves litigants not employees when felled by an industrial accident, the shadow of the law provides a means of conceptualizing the power of law to order individual consciousness. At the same time, the shadow metaphor also gives us a sense of the breadth of American legal

beliefs and actions. In the l   s asserted claims
that ranged from vague req   · equal treatment
by their former owners to   :cused felons for
due process rights. The leganzauon ~·   utevilles' marital
problems is a revealing example of why people enter this shadowy
realm and what happens to them once they are trapped there.[3]

Thinking of the law metaphorically in terms of its ability to cast a
shadow strong enough to be felt by warring couples like the
d'Hautevilles also implies a critical corollary of Tocqueville's insight.
The law could cast a shadow because it existed as a somewhat separate realm within American society. That is, the legal system was a
relatively autonomous system of authority because it created rules
and practices internally while at the same time those creations were
influenced by social currents, political developments, economic
changes, and other forces in the larger society.[4] Tocqueville discovered this interactive reality between law and society. He recognized
that the American legal order dominated dispute resolution in the
republic through its distinctive language, values, and institutions,
but also that these forms of legalism were never completely divorced
from the passions of the day.

Tocqueville's shadow metaphor thus presumes that individuals
like Gonzalve and Ellen experience the law's relative autonomy in
their own way and with their own recognition and reaction. And
their experiences, in turn, illuminate the distinctive realm he discovered. Consequently, examining how and why the d'Hautevilles
entered the law's shadow reveals that the legalization of a dispute
like theirs is neither a neutral nor a unilateral process. As their dispute became more and more legalistic, the estranged spouses un-
derwent individual transformations. They began to think of their
problems in legal terms and consider themselves legal actors. As
they did, the law began to dominate their lives and their consciousness long before they entered a Philadelphia courtroom. Even so,
Ellen and Gonzalve did not become legal automatons. The range of
beliefs and actions available to them in the law's shadow gave each
spouse a set of choices that made them active agents in their legal
struggles. Their experiences demonstrate that they, like others
trapped in that realm, are both creatures and makers of law. Nevertheless, the d'Hautevilles also discovered just how difficult it was to
leave the law's shadow once they had entered.

Stumbling Toward the Altar

Love, of course, preceded law. Just three years before their trial a
more joyous, yet in its own way ambiguous, public event had created the marriage that now crumbled in the courthouse. On August

22, 1837, Ellen ⬚ Swiss church. Their wedding ended a tumult⬚ on in the ballrooms and salons of Paris th⬚ nter and spring. Barely had the wedding be⬚ fore acrimony began tearing the couple apar⬚ ip problems not only undermined the d'Hautevilles' chance for marital happiness, they provided evidence eventually used to judge their clashing legal claims. And so to understand the d'Hauteville case, the romance that began it must be reconstructed.

Yet recovering the d'Hautevilles' courtship is no easy matter. As their conflicting tales of marital woes began to transfix the judges and spectators in Philadelphia, it became clear that their brief union could not be understood as a single story. Quite the contrary, their stories illustrate that troubled marriages, like all other bitter disputes, produce not two sides of the same story but two quite different stories. These tales intersect time and again, but they always remain distinct stories.[5] The single "true" story of the d'Hauteville's marriage, if indeed such a tale ever existed, can never be recovered from its scattered debris. Instead those who heard tales like the ones Gonzalve and Ellen told had to determine their own version of the story out of the conflicting reports given in the courtroom. The pair's contradictory tales inevitably followed a pattern of charge and countercharge as the pair told clashing versions of the same events. The d'Hautevilles' courtroom stories blended the couples' recollection of events with letters written by each of them, members of their families, and other intermediaries. It is from those stories recorded in the transcript of their trial that the couple's courtship can be reconstructed.

Both of their stories begin at a Paris ball. Ellen attended the dance because in the summer of 1836 her parents, David and Miriam Sears, had decided to take their family on a grand European tour. Family wealth made the trip possible. David was one of the richest men in Boston. Tracing his pedigree back to Pilgrim forefather Richard Sears, his family had prospered in the new world. Upon coming of age in the 1790s he inherited "the largest estate which had descended to any young man in Boston, amounting to some eight hundred thousand dollars."[6] After graduating from Harvard College in 1807 and a brief stint studying law in the office of Harrison Gray Otis, David increased his fortune through timely investments in land and New England manufacturing companies. By 1846 the author of *Our First Men*, a survey of the wealthiest Bostonians, credited him with holdings of $1,500,000.[7] In 1809 David had married Miriam Mason, daughter of leading Bay State lawyer and politician Jeremiah Mason and herself the descendant of an old, wealthy Puritan family. The Searses eventually sired four daughters and four sons. Like so many other elite Americans, the lure of European travel brought them to the continent, and Ellen to the ball.

Though she would later insinuate that her father's pocketbook captivated Gonzalve, the eighteen-year-old Ellen must have also caught his eye as she had so many others during that Parisian season. Her beauty was renowned. During a memorial to her father in 1871, a relative would take the occasion to pay tribute to Ellen: "There are still handsome women in Boston, both in the Sears family and elsewhere; but to those of us who were old enough to recall the late Mrs. d'Hauteville in the zenith of her attractions, the mention of no other can better suggest those well-known lines of Byron:

> The light of love, the purity of grace,
> The mind, the music breathing from her face,
> The heart whose softness harmonized the whole,
> And oh! that eye was in itself a soul.[8]

Gonzalve came to the ball while in Paris for the social season. As the elder of two sons, he would inherit Hauteville, his family's ancestral home in the Francophone, Protestant Swiss Canton of Vaud, and the customary title of count.[9] Besides yearly service as a militia officer, Gonzalve's future lay as a landed country gentleman like his father, Eric Magnus Louis Grand d'Hauteville. Though Gonzalve's family resources could not match the wealth of the Searses, the Hautevilles held a position of power and influence in their community. The elder d'Hauteville had been a lieutenant-colonel in Vaud's militia, a judge of the district court of Vevey, an official of the Commune of St. Legier and la Chiesay, and a member of the Grand Council of the Canton de Vaud, the Canton's highest governing body in the National Reformed Church. At twenty-five, Gonzalve was in the market for a bride to share his land and title. His model, perhaps, was his mother, Aimée Philippine Marie, herself the daughter of a leading Swiss family.

However shrouded in the mists of their memories and revised for courtroom combat, Ellen and Gonzalve both recalled beginning the rituals of courtship in the spring of 1837. By early June, he received the Searses' permission to speak to their daughter of matrimony. The match promised to be an alliance pleasing to both families. The Searses as members of an always socially insecure American upper class would gain the much valued cachet of a titled aristocrat in the family; the d'Hautevilles with their treasured pedigree and more constrained finances would gain kinship with an American family of immense wealth.

Ellen Sears d'Hauteville (above) and Miriam Mason Sears (below)

David Sears

But the road to the altar proved particularly rocky for Gonzalve and Ellen. Three major obstacles had to be overcome. These same obstructions would reemerge in the courtroom as contested sources of the pair's conduct before and after their marriage. They also illustrate the class dynamics of the d'Hauteville case. As elites, Ellen and Gonzalve occupied privileged places in their respective societies. Even so, the pair shared many values with women and men of the middling and lower classes. The combination of elitism and commonalty would permeate their case as it did their lives. Men and women of all classes would identify with the claims and charges Ellen and Gonzalve hurled at each because the couple voiced gender and legal beliefs that transcended class lines; at the same time, the d'Hautevilles' wealth and status made their stories unusually appealing as exposes of the lives of the wealthy.[10]

The first problem Ellen and Gonzalve faced, as did so many courting couples, was monetary. Their financial differences emerged

The Sears Mansion, Beacon Street, Boston

as David and Magnus tried to negotiate the marital alliance. The prenuptial bartering proved particularly difficult for David. He was caught between changing marriage regimes. Like many other fathers in the period, David reacted ambivalently to the new marital mores of his age. He accepted the right of his children to make their own marriage choices as demanded by the new regime of romantic love and nuptial individualism coming to govern courtship, but he also clung to the traditional patriarchal responsibility of protecting his children's financial interests and his family's standing. Particularly for men of wealth like himself, the separation of marital choice from questions of lineage and economic advantage would never be as complete as it might be for those of other classes or as the new demands of romantic love seemed to require. Boston Brahmin customary practices reinforced those concerns by treating marriages as capital investments and kinship networks as means of perpetuating family wealth and power. No doubt like many other elite fathers in the period, Sears resolved the conflicting pressures he felt between the dictates of romantic love and the patriarchal duty of arranging

So Coll...
but I'm a
romantic

marriages by trying to influence   dren in
a subtle rather than dictatorial f   s would
learn to their dismay, this tactic al   r confusion and indecision.[11] Magnus seemed to suffer no such problems.
He fought for the best financial arrangement confident in Gonzalve's choice and in his son's willingness to accept whatever arrangement he could work out. Perhaps his negotiating stance also
represented the very different paternal responsibilities owed a
courting son rather than a daughter. Magnus may well have felt less
need to supervise Gonzalve's nuptial decisions than David assumed
he must exert over Ellen.

The negotiations proved difficult because of the Searses' concerns
about Gonzalve's wealth. David asked for a financial accounting and
was distressed to learn that his would-be son-in-law had far less resources than Ellen had been led to believe. In terms of actual funds,
the Searses had assumed Gonzalve would receive about 12,500
francs a year. David planned that Ellen's marital contribution would
add another 8,000 francs to that sum. However, he learned that
Gonzalve could only count on 8,000 francs a year and would not
have his own separate residence until he inherited Hauteville. The
financial shortfall, David feared, meant that the Swiss suitor would
not be able to support Ellen in the style to which she had grown
accustomed while living in his household. He cited the need to rent
residences in various European capitals and the costs of servants,
coaches, and the other necessities of elite life. When the count suggested that David contribute a larger marriage gift to make up the
difference, the Bostonian balked and the negotiations stalled amid
charges and countercharges of false dealing.[12]

As the fathers bargained, a second nuptial obstacle arose. Ellen
began to reconsider her decision. Gonzalve believed then and later
that he had won her heart. She, however, claimed he had only secured her consent to be his bride, and that it had been given very
reluctantly. Almost immediately after accepting his proposal, Ellen
recalled, she began to harbor doubts about a life in Europe away
from her family. She later said that her affection for Gonzalve was
not strong enough to quiet those fears. But his persistent requests
for her hand overcame her resistance, and she had agreed to marry.
Her equivocations heightened the couple's courtship tensions and
turned Gonzalve into a supplicant repeatedly forced to plead that
his fiancée keep her promise and join him at the altar.

The stalled financial talks seemed to offer Ellen a graceful way
out of the engagement. David decided to break off the match and
take her on a quick trip to England so she could forget the whole
affair. But the journey had far different results.

Ellen recalled feeling trapped. Despite thinking that Gonzalve

had sec⋯ fully disclosing his financial cir-
cumstan⋯ of violating my word, when once
given, u⋯arily released by him to whom it
had bee⋯ deeply concerned, that my father
should ⋯ I had accepted him. Young, and
imbued with the sentiments ordinarily entertained at that age, I was
peculiarly sensitive upon the subject of my duty to keep my word in
this respect, and until freely released, considered it nearly as binding as the marriage contract. My experience had since then taught
me to know and to feel, even that solemn contract can admit of
being severed." She worried about her reputation as well as her
honor, fearing that she would be thought a mercenary for turning
her Swiss suitor down only upon hearing that his fortune had not
met her expectations.[13]

Ellen's fears disclose one of many instances in which her experiences with Gonzalve led her to voice concerns common to many
other women of the time. Honor was hardly a male monopoly. Ellen's feminine sense of honor matched the intensity and seriousness
of the much more visible masculine code of honorable behavior. For
her, like other women, honor produced a finely honed sense of duty
and manners. Keeping promises headed the list. And no promise
was more important than a pledge to marry. Breaking such a pledge
was the most serious transgression a woman could commit. It had
not been that long ago since custom as well as law sanctioned law
suits against women who jilted their fiancées.[14] Promise keeping
constituted a central virtue in a society more and more committed to contractualism and to self-regulated behavior. Indeed, for
nineteenth-century Americans of all classes promise keeping was a
critical duty demanded by a new set of manners. Like other compulsory social rules, it had to be adhered to with a law-like fidelity evident in Edmund Burke's frequently cited dictum: "Manners are of
more importance than laws. Upon these in a great measure the law
depends."[15] Accordingly, Ellen's sense of honor fed worries that her
promises to Gonzalve had gone too far. Her honor and reputation
were now at stake. And for her, like so many women and men of
her era, honor had to be protected at all costs.

Yet Ellen had to balance concerns about tarnished honor with
equally frightening fears about making the wrong marriage choice.
Her experience of "marital trauma" revealed the emotional consequences of the new system of individual courtship system. The
"freedom" to choose a mate for life made these courtship dilemmas
difficult for all suitors, particularly women. Admonished by the new
rules of romantic love to disregard property, status, or influence as
crassly materialistic concerns, the more elusive feelings of affection,
respect, and potential happiness had to be pondered by women of

all classes. Her father's reluctance to arrange her marriage reinforced the dilemma. Ellen worried about the implications of her
choice as courtship for her, like so many others, became a lonely
period of deep introspection.[16]

Caught between fears of lost honor and a poor nuptial choice,
Ellen unburdened herself to her father during their coach ride to
the French coast. Though she would later say he misunderstood
what she had said, her words convinced David that she really
wanted to marry Gonzalve. When his illness forced an immediate
return to Paris, David resumed the prenuptial negotiations.[17] This
dramatic turn of events, of course, spawned different stories. Gonzalve would speak of the triumph of love; Ellen the demands of
duty. Both, though, agreed that like their financial disagreements
Ellen's willingness to marry was a critical issue in understanding
their stories.

As their fathers resumed the antenuptial haggling, wealth and
leisure precipitated a third and final nuptial obstacle. Ellen and her
parents wanted assurances about "visits to A.[merica], whenever it
may suit the convenience of the parties, and at any and at all
times."[18] Such trips emerged as an issue in the matriarchal negotiations that accompanied the bargaining between David and Magnus.
Miriam Sears pleaded that her daughter's family ties were too
strong and her affection for Gonzalve too weak to withstand permanent exile. If not allowed frequent trips back to Boston, Miriam
feared that even "such a delightful abode as Hauteville" would "become a prison house to her!" Aimée d'Hauteville parried these requests. She offered vague assurances of at least a single trip to
America and promised to treat Ellen like a daughter and make her
feel that Hauteville was her home. The countess explained her response by reminding Miriam that the American mother had "eight
children, and that we have but two, of which the eldest ought to
remain the head of the family, in his country, and on the estate of his
fathers, that he has not the thought or the possibility of quitting."
Nevertheless, both the mothers and the betrothed couple continued
discussing the issue without a clear resolution leaving the problem
to smolder and the participants to draw their own conclusions.[19]

Finally late in June, David and Magnus hammered out what Ellen
would call "a treaty of marriage." Both had compromised. The elder d'Hauteville agreed to supplement his son's income; conversely,
the senior Sears doubled his daughter's marriage portion and increased her annual allowance until 1850, when Ellen's trust fund
would yield a comparable income. The antenuptial contract itself
ran to several pages and included innumerable clauses besides the
income guarantees. It assured the couple's right to stay at Hauteville, Ellen's right to retain legal control of her clothes, jewels, and

like this, tell not giving it all to husband

other personal property owned at the time of marriage, her right
to use but not own the ancestral d'Hauteville diamonds and pearls,
and granted the bride 3,000 francs a year in pin, or personal spending, money. David also ensured that his daughter controlled her
trust fund.[20]

However, the nuptial treaty did not end Ellen and Gonzalve's
courtship battles. Tension and distrust continued up until the very
day they wed. With the finances settled, the couple and their families continued to wrangle over trips to America and Ellen's actual
willingness to leave her family and join Gonzalve's. The acrimony
wounded both bride and groom and further undermined their confidence in each other.[21]

Vevey became the site of final acts of Ellen and Gonzalve's tor-
tured courtship. Located in the southern reaches of the Canton of
Vaud in an area that hugged Lake Geneva, bordered France, and
had inspired Rousseau's *Heloise* and Byron's poetry, just a few years
before the couple's wedding a visit to the picturesque village and its
surrounding countryside led touring American author James Feni-
more Cooper to declare: "I shall not affirm that this was the finest
view we had yet seen in Switzerland, but I do think it was the most
exquisite. It was Goethe compared to Schiller; Milton to Shake-
speare; Racine to Corneille. Other places had a grander nature,
more awful principals, and altogether sublimer features; but I cannot recall one, in which the elements, of themselves noble and imposing, were so admirably blended with extensive, delicate, and
faultlessly fine details."[22] Amidst vineyards, sloping hillsides, and
panoramic lake views, Ellen and Gonzalve suffered through one last
courtship crisis.

By the time the Searses arrived from Paris in late August, Ellen
and Gonzalve's banns had been posted and no one reading them
had come forward to object to the marriage. Yet as the wedding
day approached, Ellen continued to brood. She recalled her feelings
starkly: "My affection for Gonzalve was not strong enough to allevi-
ate the sacrifices, which, in an evil hour, I had inconsiderately bound
myself to make. My heart yearned more and more to return to my
native country; but I felt myself too far committed to recede with
honour, unless I should be released from my engagement by Gonzalve, of his own free will and accord, and without any movement
on my part to obtain my discharge." Her obvious melancholy forced
Gonzalve to grant such a release. But he prayed that time and freedom to choose would send her back to him, "If you return to me,
my Ellen, oh! shall I be most happy!! If a frightful misfortune await
me, I shall repeat, that I have done my duty. Oh that God might
restore you to me and bless you."[23]

She was restored to him. Once again, though, their versions of the reconciliation diverged dramatically. Ellen explained that Magnus's description of his son's wretchedness made her realize that Gonzalve's release had not been genuine. The would-be bride recalled feeling trapped yet again. She finally decided that her personal code of honor and responsibility demanded that her nuptial pledge be fulfilled. Gonzalve's release had not been heartfelt, instead it seemed "to be a case of a reluctant and constrained sacrifice to duty, made by him for her sake, against his own will, and under circumstances calculated to occasion him lasting unhappiness. It also appeared, that, with the fullest knowledge of her repugnance to the marriage, he was still desirous of the fulfillment of her engagement. In a word, the release was not an act of free will on his part, and he desired to recall it." Ellen would remember being moved by feelings of sympathy and justice. She had "suffered the affair to proceed to that extremity, and after having given full notice of the state of her own feelings, it was her duty, if the happiness of one of them must be sacrificed, to make her own the offering, by becoming his wife." Gonzalve told a quite different story. He recalled that his father had reluctantly described the dejected state into which Ellen's hesitancy had cast him. Claiming that his release had been genuine, and heartened by the news of Ellen's change of heart, Gonzalve concluded that love had triumphed.[24]

Having surmounted every obstacle in their path to the altar, Gonzalve and Ellen wed on Tuesday, August 22, 1837, in the village church at Montreux on the shores of Lake Geneva. After exchanging vows, the newlyweds and their families returned to Hauteville for a wedding feast and ball.[25]

A rocky courtship, of course, did not doom a marriage. Countless grooms and brides endured such traumas and created successful marriages. Many other American women besides Ellen "vacillated and wavered as they took the last steps to the altar." They did so because of the immensity of the changes marriage wrought in women's lives. For most brides, a wedding ceremony not only imposed new duties on them, but led to their first break from home.[26] And so, despite their tumultuous courtship, like other newlyweds, Ellen and Gonzalve surely assumed that love would ripen into marital bliss. Whatever the future of other couples, a far different fate awaited them as they took up residence at Hauteville as husband and wife. Their courtship problems lay buried all around them like landmines ready to explode at the slightest touch. Writing from faraway Boston, Ellen's older sister Anna Amory had sensed the problems that lay ahead. After reading letters about the wedding, she wrote to her mother, "I am pursued by a strange feeling of dread, with regard to all that is taking place among you, but try my best to get you out of my head and heart."[27]

A Marriage Unravels

As Ellen and Gonzalve d'Hauteville entered what would be their only season together, the doubts and disagreements of their troubled courtship festered through the fall and winter of 1837–8 and then burst out in the spring. Their problems persisted because the pair could not successfully negotiate the transition from court- ing couple to husband and wife. Many, if not most, newlyweds found the adjustment difficult. Indeed Karen Lystra contends that "Victorians conceived of marriage in terms of love and personal choice. Yet spousal roles were largely defined as compulsory obliga- tions. An act of self-determined choice, Victorian marriage none- theless imposed a set of mandatory sex-role specific duties upon husband and wife. This contradiction was at the heart of the nineteenth-century middle-to upper-class conception of marriage." It was a contradiction Ellen and Gonzalve could not resolve. Their growing troubles exposed another common marital dilemma: "[N]ineteenth century companionate marriage was based upon an atomistic ideal of two individuals mysteriously but permanently bonded by romantic love; yet Victorian marriage was also an institu- tion steeped in the traditional obligations of husband and wife."[28] Again, most couples surmounted these problems; the d'Hautevilles could not. Instead, their brief life together turned into a power struggle between two strong-willed individuals over whose matri- monial vision would prevail.[29]

Events at Hauteville immediately after the wedding sent the couple's marriage on a downward spiral. The setting seemed inap- propriate for the tragedy. Hauteville's one hundred and fifty hilltop acres with its lush vineyards, beautiful gardens, imposing chateau, and deferential peasants seemed like an inviting locale for a wistful fairy tale.[30] Instead its grounds became the site for a dark story of multiple meanings, more like those crafted by the brothers Grimm.

As they told their stories in court, each d'Hauteville blamed the other for destroying their marriage. Ellen looked back and charged Gonzalve with marital tyranny. She claimed that disappointment over the size of her dowry exposed her husband's latent character flaws. In particular, she recalled noticing a yawning gap between his kind words and his treacherous deeds. Equally troubling to the new bride was a "dominant fault of his character" that she labeled "a species of jealousy, not of the ordinary sort, not a morbid feeling, the result of excessive affection, or of sensitive suspicion, but that jealousy, which arises from a desire of exclusive appropriation of every thing to self, and a consequent unwillingness to permit the most harmless and innocent association with others."[31] From these character flaws, Ellen claimed, came the tyranny that destroyed their marriage. Like many other American wives trapped in troubled marriages, she believed that "[t]yranny was not to be condoned in public or private life, and marriage was now to be considered a republican contract between wives and husbands, a contract based on mutual affection."[32]

Ellen offered three examples as proof of her charge of marital tyranny. First, she charged that once her father left for his return to Boston, Gonzalve and his family revealed a deep-seated antipathy toward Americans. Her husband refused to let her speak of her home or visit travelers from the United States. Instead he wanted her to made a swift conversion and become a Swiss. The unceasing anti-Americanism stoked her homesickness and outraged her nationalistic sentiments.

Her next example was a frequent source of conflict in troubled American marriages and one that plagued this transatlantic union as well: fights over feminine autonomy.[33] Ellen demanded a mutuality in their marriage that her husband resisted. She refused to accept Gonzalve's "ideas of the necessity of female subjection to the discipline of the more powerful sex." Ellen accused her husband of even using the Bible as a tool of conjugal subjugation. During their first week of marital life, he selected particular passages for her to read. The selections always stressed wifely submission and obedience. She recalled four examples:

1 Corinthian, xi:

3d. But I would have you know that the head of every man is Christ, and the head of the woman is the man, and the head of Christ is God

8th. For the man is not of the woman, but the woman of the man.

9th. Neither was the man created for the woman, but the woman for the man.

11th. Nevertheless, neither is the man without the woman, neither the woman without the man, in the Lord.

Ephesians, v. 24

Therefore as the church is subject unto Christ, so let the wives be to their own husbands in every thing.

1 Timothy, ii

11th. Let the woman learn in silence with all subjection.

12th. But I suffer not a woman to teach, nor to usurp authority over the man, but to be in silence.

13th. For Adam was first formed, then Eve.

14th. And Adam was not deceived, but the woman being deceived was in the transgression.

1 *Peter,* iii

5th. For after this manner in the old time, the holy women also, who trusted in God, adorned themselves, being in subjection unto their own husbands.

6th. Even as Sarah obeyed Abraham, calling him Lord; whose daughters ye are, as long as ye do well, and are not afraid with any amazement.

Ellen also remembered studying these passages with the desire of adapting "her conduct toward her husband to the standard of the true religion and of Scripture morality," and yet chafing at their use and thinking that Gonzalve quoted "these sacred rules, as though they had been prescribed in favour of the man for *his own* sake, and for the promotion of *his* happiness and welfare *upon earth,* rather of my own temporal and eternal welfare."[34]

Lastly, Ellen accused her husband of mistreating her mother. Miriam had agreed to stay with the newlyweds for the first year of marriage. Ellen claimed that out of groundless jealousy Gonzalve treated Miriam rudely and tried to keep mother and daughter apart at all times. He excluded her from his family's social activities, banned Ellen from entering her chambers or accompanying her on carriage rides, and consistently spoke to her in a cold and haughty manner. Gonzalve even ordered his mother-in-law not to share letters from her family and friends in Boston with Ellen. In treating Miriam coldly, Gonzalve struck at one of his wife's most vulnerable flanks. Her bitter denunciation of his conduct suggested that for Ellen, perhaps even more than for most American brides, the "mother–daughter relationship was the traditional focus for fear of separation that marriage aroused."[35] All the more so, because kinship ties were particularly strong among Boston Brahmin families and women were charged with maintaining them. Equally important, while she accused Gonzalve of victimizing her mother, Ellen also recalled growing concerns about Gonzalve's attachment to *his* mother. She remembered thinking that he seemed unable to free himself from his domineering mother and gain the personal autonomy a man needed to be a husband. Recalling that Gonzalve "stood in a degree of awe" toward Madam d'Hauteville, she concluded that "although I had myself been educated in filial piety, and in the observance of all the duties of a child to a parent," her husband's deference to both his parents, but especially his mother, was, "to my mind, altogether unaccountable." The woeful result, Ellen claimed, was that Gonzalve tried his best to deprive her "of the solace of even conversing with my mother," while, "what was far worse, not only

did nothing to prevent the slights and insults which my mother received from the rest of his family, but was, if not himself the author
and originator of them, a full participant and abettor of them."[36] In
framing her charges in these gendered terms, Ellen attacked the
most vulnerable flank of a Victorian man, his masculinity.

As her complaints accumulated, Ellen remembered growing increasingly despondent. What she would label a "succession of petty
tyrannies and capricious jealousies" plagued the "two months which
followed this inauspicious marriage." Sifting through the ashes of
her marriage, she would say that the marital tyranny that surfaced
in their first months together further undermined her faith in Gonzalve and prevented her from successfully adapting to a new life at
Hauteville. It left her "weary of life, and my health and strength
failed me."[37]

In the courtroom, Gonzalve also dated the couples' marital woes
from their first few months together as man and wife. And he too
attributed them to struggles over marital responsibilities. Yet he
identified a very different marital criminal: not himself, but his
mother-in-law. He charged Miriam Sears with purposely undermining his marriage. Unable to account for her conduct beyond observ-
ing that "[h]uman action often defies all reasoning as to motive," he
could only assume that "Mrs. Sears urged or consented to the marriage of her daughter to a foreigner, when she knew or suspected
her affections were not engaged," and then endeavored to make
her new son-in-law "subservient to her will, and failing in that, to
plant dissension, and induce separation between husband and
wife." Her plan, he had "no doubt," was either to compel the couple
"to live near her in New England" or "to take her daughter back."
And, he would insist, "it was not vague suspicion or idle jealousy
which induces this belief; the whole course of her conduct at Hauteville explains it."[38] Whatever the motive, Gonzalve traced the unraveling of his marriage to the scheming hand of Miriam Sears.

The dejected Swiss spouse claimed that Miriam's intrigues prevented his young bride from making the transition from daughter
to wife. He recalled with bitterness one incident that seemed to uncover the plot destroying his marriage. Local villagers had come for
a ball at Hauteville and Ellen gaily danced with one of the men. A
family friend, noting the bride's enjoyment, remarked to Miriam
that Ellen was "learning to become a Swiss." In rapid reply, the
friend would tell Gonzalve, came the tart declaration: "No, never:
my daughter never will, nor can become a Swiss."[39] In those words,
Gonzalve found both the source of the growing marital rift he had
experienced in the trying first months of his marriage, and reason
enough at the time to question Ellen's willingness to assume the
duties of a wife if they came at the expense of those of a daughter.

After explaining in their separate ways the tensions of their first few married months, the d'Hautevilles chronicled the final European acts of their marital tragedy. They occurred in Paris, where the pair and Miriam returned in the winter of 1838. While in the French capital a critical event occurred that would push them a bit farther down the path toward the Philadelphia courtroom. In a typically elliptical statement of the era, Ellen would tell the court of "discovering my situation." She was pregnant. The discovery, coupled with the tensions of her marriage and her mother's decision to "abandon her original intention of remaining a year with her, and to return to the United States," provoked a crisis. Ellen decided that she must go back to America for the birth. She requested Gonzalve's permission to "return with her mother, and pass the period of my confinement in Boston."[40]

Once again the pair would tell different stories of the tumultuous events that followed. This time, though, they explained their versions of the escalating conflict in terms of clashing rights claims. From their initial courtship problems to this crisis, both Ellen and Gonzalve had defined themselves as holders of particular rights and duties. Their intensifying conflict forced them to articulate their consciousness of those rights in ever greater detail.

Ellen recalled that her husband "gave her the leave, which she requested for herself as a matter of right, conformably to his promises before marriage, saying he considered it his duty to let her go." She was adamant that Gonzalve could not deny her the right to return to Boston for the birth of her child. The only question was whether he would accompany her or not. Nevertheless, in her retelling, after giving his approval, Gonzalve immediately started backpedalling. When illness struck his father, he rushed back to Hauteville and wrote Ellen expressing doubts about the wisdom of his making a long trip to America. Ellen would later contend that he exaggerated the seriousness of his father's illness as an excuse for not accompanying her. More important at the time, though, Gonzalve withdrew his permission for her voyage as well. In a letter to him at Hauteville, the distraught mother-to-be begged that he "put no difficulties in my way, but let me return *quietly* home. Think, *for once,* of my happiness, and not of your own; it is hard that I should have so great a mistrust of *you,* to whom I ought to be able to look for affection and sympathy in the sorrows and troubles which have unhappily fallen upon me. I do not mean to reproach you, for your own conscience will be the judge if you have acted rightly towards me, and if your own feelings for me do not prompt you to do differently, why then it is to my sorrow that I must know it now." Already three months pregnant in an era in which child-

birth was often a life-threatening experience, she pleaded with him:
"*Do not* let me feel that when the time comes that I shall be away
from my own relations, that I am *alone* and *unbefriended* in the
world." But her husband rejected her pleas; he told her that he
would shortly return to Paris with a traveling coach to bring her
back to Hauteville.[41]

[margin note: keeps her in Switz]

Gonzalve, of course, refuted Ellen's charges of treachery, deception, and broken promises. He claimed that the crisis was purposely
instigated as a direct challenge to his right to govern his family as
he saw fit. Looking back on the confrontation, he concluded that
his wife suffered from delusions induced by Miriam's scheming. He
was enraged that Ellen should have "persuaded herself" that "the
serious illness under which my father laboured . . . and on account
of which I was induced to change my mind as to my visit to America,
was feigned, and part of a design cunningly framed to detain her in
Europe." Gonzalve denied it all, and responded in kind by charging
that Ellen cast aside his "expressions of mingled tenderness for her,
and solicitude for my suffering parent" in her single-minded "determination to go to America." His wife, he contended, broke her
promise to seek a separation only when reasonable and violated her
wifely duties to remain with her husband. Sadly, he would recall,
Ellen "yielded to the morbid influence of which I believe she was
the victim, and took the last and most fatal step."[42]

As Gonzalve intimated, the next event in their marital tragedy
proved lethal. And, of course, it would be recounted differently by
each spouse. Ellen would charge trickery; Gonzalve would plead
misunderstanding. Both agreed, though, that Gonzalve's decision
to return to Paris and fetch Ellen set the ruinous events in motion.

Ellen charged that immediately after sending the letter withdraw-
ing permission for her voyage home, Gonzalve snuck into Paris. He
then spent a day and night in the French capital without telling her
of his arrival. By chance, a servant spotted him at his tailor's and
reported his presence in the city to his astonished wife. Foiled in
what Ellen charged was a plan to whisk her away with little interference, he immediately wrote her and told her to be ready to leave.
Terrified that he would "tear her from her mother's house,"
she petitioned the American minister to France, Lewis Cass, for
asylum.[43]

[margin note: permission to go... was this within relationship, social or semi-legal]

Gonzalve claimed that it was not his actions but Miriam's that
forced Ellen to flee. The minute his presence in Paris had become
known, he charged, "every circumstance of exaggeration as to probable motives and designs, was conveyed through the various servants." He later concluded that the flight to the Cass residence was
"the accomplishment of a design, by this very publicity and its

natural exasperation, to place an insuperable barrier between him and his wife."[44]

Cass, a veteran of the Midwestern Indian wars and a former Michigan governor, had been appointed to the French ministry by President Andrew Jackson. He soon became a popular and powerful figure in the French court. The New England-bred politician, destined to be the Democratic presidential nominee in 1844, had hammered out numerous political compacts. Now he turned his diplomatic skills to the d'Hautevilles' marital conflict, as with many of his other negotiations, he could achieve only a temporary truce.[45]

The minister convened a meeting of the principals and arranged for the couple to confer alone. Their conference produced clashing rights claims. Ellen reported that Gonzalve demanded that she accede to his husbandly commands and return to Switzerland. She refused and insisted that Gonzalve fulfill his nuptial pledge to let her return home. Finally he relented and allowed her to go. They agreed he would come to America and retrieve her after a year. Gonzalve, however, recalled the meeting as consisting of "a short interview, a few words of kindness and affection, when no one was by to interpose offices of unkindness, to produce a reconciliation, I still aver, the most complete."[46]

Both d'Hautevilles agreed that thanks to Cass's mediation a complete marital break-up had been averted. Ellen claimed that she consented only after Gonzalve repeated his promises in front of the American minister.[47] Perhaps in response to those pledges and the events that had provoked them, Cass had offered the Swiss husband his first glimpse of the legal ideas that lingered in the shadows of America. The minister's faith in the law was clear: "With us, the laws may be said to uphold themselves. It is their moral, not their physical force, which ensures the obedience of society. It is the habit of submission which we are all taught in early life, that gives to a little piece of paper, the effect of a magical wand to break down all opposition."[48]

The reconciled couple spent their last days living together as husband and wife in Paris. For Gonzalve these were seven weeks when kind feelings toward each other returned; for Ellen they were a time of further trials. She claimed that Gonzalve continued to treat her mother rudely and to demand that she subject herself to him completely. Despite his promise, he constantly tried to talk her out of returning home. A year of courtship and marriage with Gonzalve had reduced her from a healthy, cheerful young woman, to an invalid, who had "become pale, feeble, apathetic, nervous, and low spirited, to an extent that threatened my intellectual faculties." Only the intervention of her uncle, Dr. John C. Warren, a founder of

Massachusetts General Hospital and eminent Boston physician, finally convinced Gonzalve that her health was indeed imperiled,   *wants*
Touring the continent with his own family, Warren told the Swiss   *to go*
husband that Ellen suffered from the malady "nostalgia," or "*mala-*   *home*
die du pays." The doctor described it as a disease stemming from a
morbid desire to see home, and explained that it produced a deep
despair with dangerous physical consequences. Perhaps he even
told Gonzalve that, ironically, the disease had been first diagnosed
among Swiss expatriates who longed for their homeland. In any
event, Warren warned that resistance to Ellen's voyage threatened
her life because the malady led to headaches, sleeplessness, loss of
appetite, and even heart problems, stupor, and fever. Only then did
Gonzalve grudgingly grant his full consent for his wife to sail
home.[49]

Gonzalve accepted Ellen's claim that during these weeks she suffered mentally and physically. Yet he traced her problems, not to
his actions, but to the "struggles of an affectionate sense of duty, not
then extinct in my young wife's bosom, against a moral disease
which was preying on her constitution, and wasting her enfeebled
frame, and against the influences which never were applied to sooth
it, were quite sufficient to produce the misery" that Ellen reported.
He recognized her struggle as an "agonizing one," between her
longing for her home and her marital vows. Gonzalve also admitted
that the negotiations at the Cass residence had not allayed his fears
about her trip nor prevented him from expressing his displeasure.
On the contrary, he realized that "I had become, without any agency
of mine, the object of her mother's aversion, and I feared to trust
my wife away from me under that mother's control." He was convinced at the time that Miriam had poisoned Ellen's mind against
him, and alarmed by what he would recall as an only too true "apprehension of future and unknown unhappiness, which I could
scarcely define, but which never approached, in form or degree, the
wretchedness I had been made to suffer." He also feared for Ellen's
health on a dangerous sea journey. So he pressed her to change her
mind, but out of love not jealousy.[50] Failing, the dispirited husband
accompanied his wife to her ship at Le Harve for its May 16th departure.   *Letters*

As an ocean grew between them, letters served as the d'Hautevilles' primary medium of communication. For the estranged couple, perhaps even more than for many other American and European couples at the time, letters were not mere "artifacts of a
relationship; in many cases they were, for a time, the relationship
itself." And their words not only influenced their actions, they were
actions. As such, the letters exchanged between Ellen and Gonzalve

reveal the emotional power each spouse held over the other. Like other lovers' letters, the d'Hautevilles' words demonstrate that to "be able to inflict pain, to be vulnerable to intense misery, or to experience intense joy with another is to wield some interpersonal power. The dynamics of romantic love created interpersonal power through the pleasures and satisfactions as well as the vulnerability of a shared identity."[51]

As they put pen to paper, the couple faced the major challenge of effective letter writing: to express their feelings "with a warmth and sincerity that brought the written words to life." Countless letter-writing manuals of the day counseled the sentimental ideal of expressing true feelings and "the importance of sincerity in emotional self-expression." With their salutations of "My Friend" and organization that proceeded from general statements of sincerity to concrete issues and then back to the general, Ellen and Gonzalve conformed to the letter-writing rules of their age; and their words spoke with the fervent "mutual sincerity" that was "the substance of the romantic contract" of those years as well.[52] Within these prescribed social rules, the pair carried on their marital struggles by post.

Ellen's first two letters from America became critical events in the d'Hauteville marriage and trial. Upon arriving in New York and settling in at the Astor House on June 12th, she wrote her faraway husband describing how quick and invigorating the voyage had been. She expressed joy at being back in her homeland and impatience to receive his first letter.[53] Just a couple weeks later, however, she sent a very different letter. It laid out her conditions for returning to him.

"I feel that the time is arrived when we must understand each other," Ellen told Gonzalve, "and, now, under the protection of my father's roof, and no longer restrained from expressing my sentiments, by the fear that further opposition would still be made to prevent my return to my own country, I wish you to remain no longer in ignorance of my intentions." Charging that his conduct had "deeply wounded her" and that his "entire disregard of my wishes and feelings has often caused me to doubt the sincerity of the affection you expressed," the putative Swiss wife wrote emphatically: "I am decided that I never can return to Hauteville." Broken promises and mistreatment by Gonzalve and his family had made her hate Gonzalve's ancestral home. They forced her to assert a right of self-determination. She made her intentions quite clear: "I do not feel it is my duty to return, when I could neither promote your pleasures, or find life supportable. I have made many sacrifices for you, and in return I looked for kindness, sympathy, and protection from every sorrow and trouble which you could avert. I have been disappointed – still I do not intend to reproach you. It is true my health has sunk beneath the shock. My happiness has gone; but, believe me, it is under the influence of no angry or excited feelings against you, that I take this step." Instead, she wrote, that as the object of cruel treatment she had no choice but to act. She urged him to remain at Hauteville until mutually acceptable arrangements could be made. Pleading with him to think about what she had written very seriously, she bid him "to decide upon our future destiny."[54]

Gonzalve would express astonishment at the change in tone between the letter his wife wrote from the Astor House and this declaration of reproach from Boston. He attributed the shift to the final, fatal unfolding of the plot against his marriage. At the time, though, he continued writing and pleading his case. As he had during their courtship, once more Gonzalve assumed the role of supplicant. Writing in August, he implored, "Can it be, at the moment when God has made us the most beautiful of his gifts, that which sanctifies, which, if possible, renders still more sacred the act of marriage – that act which binds a man in the bands of God, and which he has no longer the power to recede from or dissolve – that we can speak of each other in a harsh and painful manner!" He pleaded that she retract her words, reconsider her demands, and resume her wifely duties.

Anticipating the impending birth of his child, Gonzalve gave Ellen other instructions that also became fodder for their trial. He had chosen his brother Leonces as godfather, and suggested that she select one of her sisters as godmother. As tokens of respect for his parents, he wanted to add either Eric or Aimée to the child's name. Adhering to traditional gender customs, he instructed that if Ellen bore a son, he wanted the boy named Alois, "a name dear to every citizen of Switzerland"; and that she should choose the name for a daughter. If illness threatened the infant, he urged a quick baptism in David's presence and "by the Presbyterian Church, of course."[55].

In other letters to Ellen and to David Sears, Gonzalve continued to seek both reconciliation and recognition of his family rights. A critical letter to David made both goals clear. After defending his actions, the Swiss husband penned a spirited and lengthy declaration of his husbandly responsibilities: "I am now responsible before God for the happiness and conduct of my wife, and I assure you, sir, that I think it my duty to blame her, so long as she will not live for her husband above every thing else. I regard her as culpable, so long as she does not devote herself entirely to my happiness. It is a principle with me, that a woman who opposes herself to the opinions dictated by the heart of her husband, conducts herself ill with regard to him, acts in opposition to a tender conscience and to God; that she does not fulfil her vow made at the altar, to place the delicacy of her husband in security . . . [she] must declare that those friends who seek her happiness and her pleasure, to the detriment of her duty, render her a poor service, which will not reach the end they propose." Explaining that he wrote not in anger but to inform David of his position, Gonzalve wanted to know when he would be able to bring Ellen back to Hauteville. "It is important," he declared, "to be master in my own house."[56]

masculinity is getting in the way

The Swiss husband's words exposed the yawning gap between his wife's conviction that a marriage must be one of mutuality and his equally fervent belief that a husband must have complete mastery of his home and its dependents. Ellen defended her beliefs and actions in a letter to her father not Gonzalve. She refused to rely any longer on her husband's "affection, or put faith in his promises," because he "preserves in his course and his letters evince the same spirit which he already knows drove me almost to insanity when in Paris." Gonzalve knew very well, she claimed, that "I did not marry him so much from affection, as from a sense of duty, and to save him and his family from distress; and my recompense for the sacrifice has been misery to myself, and mortification to you and my mother." Driven to these declarations by a marriage of just a year, the distraught mother-to-be exclaimed: "When I think of what my future life must be, if forced to return to him, I am terrified at the prospect, and I implore you to save me from it. . . . Let me remain with you, I beg of you, and give your aid and advice in my distress."[57] David offered Ellen his full protection.

goes against all of husbands wishes

On September 27, 1838, just seven days after she made that plea, Ellen gave birth to a son. Contrary to Gonzalve's explicit instructions, she named him Frederick Sears Grand d'Hauteville, after her brother, and a month later had the Reverend John Stone, Rector of St. Paul's Episcopal Church, baptize the infant. Across the ocean in Switzerland, the day after the baptism Gonzalve plaintively wrote: "Your silence, my dear friend, convinces me that you have not written to me again before your confinement. Oh, Ellen, can this be possible!"[58]

His doleful words revealed the deep division between the d'Hautevilles. During their brief months of marriage, they had failed completely to agree on their new duties as husband and wife. Like others caught in troubled marriages, Ellen and Gonzalve had tried to overcome their problems by instructing each other about how to be a good spouse. But those lessons too had failed. Ellen would not be the submissive and obedient wife Gonzalve wanted; and he would not temper his authority and be an equal partner as she demanded. As a result of their failures to meet each other's expectations, the d'Hautevilles' marriage had become a fatal contest of domestic power that left both spouses emotionally battered yet also defiant. Frederick's birth intensified these struggles and provoked the final unraveling of their marriage.

The Shadow Falls

As their marriage ties frayed, Ellen and Gonzalve pondered what to do. The options seemed clear: either reconciliation or separation. Their respective choices were equally distinct. Gonzalve fought to keep the marriage intact; Ellen searched for a marital exit. In the end, both choices led the d'Hautevilles to the law as their actions completed the legalization of their marital conflict.

Just four days before Frederick's birth, Ellen took the first step toward the law's shadow without realizing where it was taking her. She had her father begin negotiations for a permanent separation. David did so in a letter to Frederic Couvreu, a syndic, or civil magistrate, of Vevey. As the curator Ellen's Swiss interests, Couvreu also had the responsibility of overseeing Gonzalve's disposition of her dowry and other financial contributions to the marriage. In writing to the Swiss official, David acted on the paternal assumption that a lone woman, especially one as young as Ellen, seeking legal redress must obtain a male protector as her public advocate. An expression of the subordinate legal status of women, especially married women, the legal custom assumed that women could not act effectively at law by themselves and that feminine sensibilities would be violated by the rough and tumble of private bargaining. Women, in other words, ought to be recipients of male legal largesse, not active legal combatants. Though individual women challenged this legal paternalism in increasing numbers, Ellen, like most other women, relied on male advocates at this and other critical points in her fight with Gonzalve. David assumed that role with the emphatic declaration: "I shall defend my child to the extent of my power, and the rights which the law gives me."[59]

David turned to Couvreu hoping that the old family friend of the d'Hautevilles would convince Gonzalve "to make an amicable and quiet settlement, and allow his wife to remain with me unmolested." Whatever the specific details of the final arrangements, David relayed Ellen's one nonnegotiable demand: "I hold, however, but to this – that my daughter and her child, if she should have one, may be rid of . . . her husband and his family." Ellen and her family also feared scandal, so David pleaded that "this affair may be arranged with the least possible publicity." Though he used conciliatory language and hoped to free his daughter without intervening authorities or the glare of publicity, David became the first actor in the d'Hauteville case to invoke the law. He turned to it as a weapon to back up his requests with the threat of direct action. The Bostonian warned that if a private arrangement could not be worked out and Gonzalve tried to retrieve his wife and child, "*you will* THEN please to inform him, that we shall, on the day of his arrival here, commence an action and *demand a separation in our Supreme Judicial Court.*"[60]

From the day that Sears penned those fighting words, the law cast an ever-darkening shadow over the d'Hautevilles. David's threat of legal action displayed both the lure of law as a powerful weapon to those enmeshed in bitter disputes and the role of individual decisions in the legalization of private disputes. By throwing down their legal challenge the Searses fundamentally redefined the d'Hauteville's marital conflict. However blinded they were by the law's attractions and however limited they thought the alternatives might have been, the Searses' decision to frame the dispute as a legal contest ensured that Ellen and Gonzalve, like others who turned to the law to solve their problems, would enter the law's shadow.[61]

In a series of letters from the early fall of 1838 to the early spring of 1839, David doggedly pursued a private separation for his daughter. He tried to convince Couvreu of the legitimacy of Ellen's request and the futility of trying to keep the d'Hautevilles together. As in the past – and so often in the future – Ellen's champion portrayed her as the innocent victim of domestic strife. "Nothing short of necessity could impel my daughter to her present stand," he assured the Swiss official. "It places her in a mortifying position before her family and friends: it is in opposition to much of what we all hold dear – to her hopes in life, and to her chance of happiness; and deep indeed must be the wound, and sore the pain, which have forced her to speak out." In a flash of chauvinism that too would recur in the coming months, the Boston father also contended that Gonzalve's cruelties violated American sensibilities as well as, he intimated, American law. He did so by injecting charges of mental cruelty into the dispute.

Like many others who entered the law's shadows, David's assertion revealed how lay legal beliefs could foster legal claims. For David and countless other Americans, lay legal ideas about everything from marital rules to property rights served as a foundation for private claims. However, such popular legal beliefs did not always correspond with formal legal rules. Nevertheless, even though

lay people and even professionals may misunderstand the exact letter of the law, they still conceived of it as an external force that could ↙
be used to wage disputes. As a result, lay beliefs and formal rules
could both be found in uneasy existence in the law's shadows. The
discrepancy between them only became critical when private bargaining failed and disputants had to seek a formal resolution of
their conflict. And then differences between existing rules and individual demands could help frame public contests over the proper
meaning of the law. It would do so in the d'Hauteville case.

As Ellen's advocate, David contended, incorrectly as he and his
daughter soon learned, that mental as well as physical cruelty justified a marital separation under American domestic relations law: "I
know not what would constitute ill-treatment in Switzerland. Perhaps there the severity of manners may require a corporeal infliction as the proof. But here it is different; and, with us, that moral
tyranny which strikes its blows upon the mind, until it totters, is
thought fully equivalent to all that the body can be brought to suffer.
That this has been the fact, in my daughter's case, there is abundant
evidence before me." With words like these, David justified his
moral and legal absolution of Ellen. He also launched a legal challenge that would surface again and again in the case. At the time,
though, thinking himself on solid legal ground, David made clear
his paternal responsibilities by pledging that "while I have a shelter
to give, it will not be denied to my daughter." Insisting that he had
no wish to wound the feelings of the d'Hautevilles, David implored
the Swiss syndic to make them accept a separation.[62]

Across the Atlantic, Couvreu, who very reluctantly assumed the
role of marital bargainer, refuted all of David's claims and resisted
his request for an informal separation. He denied the need for a
separation: "Nothing, in my eyes, justifies it; and, shall I own it to
you, sir? none of the arguments alleged in your letter, seem to me
of a nature to demand it." On the contrary, rallying to Gonzalve's
defense, he portrayed the estranged husband as a gentle and affectionate man brought low by his father's illness, his wife's cruelty,
and his mother-in-law's scheming. The syndic also refuted Ellen's
claim that Gonzalve and his parents had agreed to American trips,
especially so early in the marriage. Instead he charged her with
breaking her vow to return to Europe. Before she sailed home,
Gonzalve had requested written assurances, but "both she and Mrs.
Sears were revolted at the idea, that the solemn though verbal
promises which she had made her husband could be doubted." Yet
upon "arriving at Boston, all this is forgotten. They do not even
admit the possibility of Gonzalve's coming there. They refuse him
all access to them: with threats they banish him from his child, and

to conclude, they demand a separation." Couvreu rejected out of hand the proposition that the young couple might live apart for an indefinite time with the vast Atlantic between them. Not only did Gonzalve refuse to consider the proposal, the Swiss syndic demonstrated that he too could use law as a weapon by issuing his own not-so-veiled legal threat: "An arrangement of this kind, which is equivalent to a separation, is not consistent with our customs, and is, in my opinion, immoral. As a Christian, and as a magistrate, I could not consent to its being concluded through my interposition." Instead, he pleaded that David try and work out a reconciliation.[63]

Amidst this bargaining, Ellen and Gonzalve tried to circumvent the negotiators and forge their own bargain. Ellen refused to rely completely on her father. Once more she used her pen to try and convince Gonzalve that reconciliation was impossible. Repeating charges of marital tyranny and broken promises, she hoped a firm expression of her determination to remain in America would force Gonzalve to accept a separation.

Significantly, while seeking the status of a husbandless wife, she added a new voice to her declarations. Ellen began to speak as a mother as well as a wronged wife. It was a critical expansion not merely in voice but also in self-perception. Maternal duties not spousal relations became the theme of her bargaining. "My child will, henceforth, be the greatest source of happiness that remains to me," Ellen asserted. "I have borne him in sorrow and trouble, and have never left him from the hour of his birth. You know nothing of him – your heart or your affections never warmed towards him. My determination is a decided one; nothing shall induce me to alter it . . . nothing shall induce me to live with any one, where every tie of affection has been severed by conduct such as yours. I accepted you with the best of the intentions; the world can judge of the sacrifices I made, had I been ever so much attached to you." The world would, indeed, make such judgments very soon, but first Ellen continued her efforts at private bargaining. Like her father, she issued a warning backed, she assumed, by legal force: "Any effort to force the return of myself or my child, I assure you, will be useless. I should not desire life upon the terms which you offer it, and your own expressions can never be retracted." After wishing him a happiness now forever denied her, Ellen pleaded: "Try to dismiss me and my unfortunate fate from your mind, and believe that in sorrow, more than in anger, I bid you farewell."[64]

Gonzalve refused to accept Ellen's dismissal just as he rejected her indictment. But her words wounded him. Forced yet again to be the supplicant, he had the difficult task of refuting her charges while at the same time trying to persuade her to change her mind and

return. Gonzalve's negotiating difficulties illustrate the gender dynamics visible at this stage of the d'Hauteville case. Romantic love
gave women like Ellen "some emotional power over men. Men
gained a similar advantage, but women's greater economic vulnerability and powerlessness in public meant that the emotional power
of love was more important to them."[65] Ellen's withdrawal of
affection surely cut Gonzalve to the quick and demonstrated her
power over this phase of the negotiations. All he could do was plead
his case and beg that she return.[66]

By the spring of 1839, compromise had eluded all of the negotiators. Positions had hardened; neither Gonzalve nor Ellen would
budge. With the Atlantic between them, Ellen and her father assumed that the now nearly year-long informal separation would
continue indefinitely. Couvreu, however, cautioned that Gonzalve
would "not rest, with folded arms, on this refusal of his wife to join
him, or give up his child to him."[67]

Just as the Swiss syndic predicted, when the winter of 1839
turned to spring Gonzalve acted. He set sail for America to retrieve
his wife and child. His voyage ignited yet another controversy because he traveled under the name Daniel rather than Gonzalve.
Ellen would charge that he sailed "under an assumed name" in a
clandestine effort to spirit her and Frederick back to Hauteville
much as he had attempted to do in Paris.[68] In response, Gonzalve
explained that he "used the name of Daniel, one of the names I
bear," because he "had every reason to apprehend, from the temper
of the previous correspondence . . . that if my arrival were publicly
known, my wife and child might be secreted or withdrawn from
me." Already feeling himself being drawn into the law's shadow by
David's legal threats, he avoided using his ordinary name because,
"being a stranger to the laws of the United States," he feared the
"the mysterious terrors 'of the Supreme Judicial Court of Massachusetts,' with which . . . Mr. Sears had threaten me in case I ventured
to follow my wife and child to the United States."[69]

Whatever the motive, the plan failed. Soon after his landing in
New York, an acquaintance of the Searses' spotted Gonzalve on a
Manhattan street and word quickly reached Ellen. Meanwhile, Gonzalve had presented himself to Henry C. De Rham, the Swiss coun-
sul in New York and a family friend. De Rham, a prominent New
York lawyer, would henceforth serve as Gonzalve's principal legal
advisor and oversee a growing legion of attorneys. De Rham and
his other lawyers began blending their professional counsel with
Gonzalve's increasingly well-developed sense of his legal rights as a
husband and father.

After considering his options, Gonzalve set off for Boston. He

tried to find her first at the Searses' Beacon Street mansion and
then at their summer home at Nahant on Boston's north shore. But
Ellen and Frederick eluded him. The minute she had heard of his
arrival, the distraught mother had fled into hiding. Claiming that
she feared Gonzalve would try to abduct her, Ellen kept her where-
abouts from her parents so that they could not be forced into revealing her refuge. Unable to find his wife and child, Gonzalve holed
up in a suite at the Tremont Hotel. Surrounded by the luxury of
America's finest hotel, he wrote Ellen yet another plea for reconciliation and waited for her to respond.[70]

Ellen and Frederick stayed in hiding. But Gonzalve's arrival
threw the Searses into crisis. They realized that their efforts at
reaching an informal understanding and their threats had failed.
They worried about what Gonzalve would do next.

What he did was retain a local lawyer, Peleg Sprague. The decision displayed the Swiss visitor's growing reliance on the law. Law
had become an appealing way to defend his claims and a seemingly
unavoidable response to the threats lodged against him. He found
a suitable champion in Sprague, a leading Boston attorney who had
graduated from Harvard College and attended Litchfield Law
School, the premier private legal academy of its day. Having entered the bar in 1815, like many lawyers Sprague mixed legal practice with stints in politics, including a few terms in Congress.[71]
Sprague certainly moved in the Searses' commercial and political
circles, if not their social ones. The Searses responded by obtaining
their own lawyer, Samuel D. Parker, who had married one of Miriam's sisters and had achieved local legal prominence as the Suffolk
County Attorney, represented David and Miriam while Ellen hid.[72]
Henceforth, lawyers would counsel all of the participants in the
d'Hauteville case. Their presence lengthened the shadow of the law
over the d'Hautevilles by reinforcing the reliance on law to frame
the dispute.

Sprague and Parker sparred through late July. Gonzalve's lawyer
wanted to negotiate Ellen's return directly with David. Parker rebuffed him arguing that neither David nor Miriam knew Ellen's hiding place. Sprague threatened to seek a search warrant. But it all
came to naught, and another round of negotiations stalled.[73]

In the meantime, Ellen sent a terse, combative message to Gonzalve. Refusing to see him or even show the father his child, once
more she defiantly rejected his plea for reconciliation. The em-
battled wife tried to convince her husband that his long journey had
been in vain. Clothing her defiance in claims of maternal responsibilities, she expressed a firm "determination to remain where I am,
unless torn away by force; and I would sooner part with life itself,

than to be separated from my child." Ellen beseeched him to pack his bags and return home.[74]

Stymied by Ellen and her parents, Gonzalve and his lawyer had to design a new strategy. As they did so, the frustrated husband and father must have begun to appreciate not only the steely determination of his wife but also the power of the man he now challenged. Just as Ellen had undergone her own Swiss education, so now Gonzalve began to learn about America. Back in Europe, he had been dazzled by the Searses' wealth. Yet in the antenuptial contract, which had trumpeted the civic and military honors of Gonzalve's father and grandfather, David had been described as but "a land owner (proprietaire) of the county of Suffolk."[75] Holed up in his suite at the decade-old Tremont, amidst technological innovations that included indoor plumbing and gas-lit public rooms, as well a reading room stocked with newspapers from around the globe, Gonzalve may have begun to recognize how much that simple description omitted.[76]

As he brooded, Gonzalve must have begun to appreciate the Searses' power and to understand why they assumed he would buckle under their threats. His stay in Boston may have given him a clearer feeling for the mix of "wealth, family, education, occupation, social connections, political and religious views, morality, and cultivation [that] merged to define the 'gentleman'" in the strange city.[77] Perhaps his fruitless visit to the Searses' Beacon Street mansion trying to find Ellen had awakened his sense of the family's standing in Boston. Constructed in 1820, the house was located among the residences of the social and economic elite of New England at a time of the region's economic ascendency over the new nation's burgeoning capitalist industries. Recognized as one of the city's most luxurious homes and reputed to be its first hewn granite dwelling, Gonzalve would have noted with special interest the houses for the Searses' sons-in-law that flanked the patriarchal manse.[78] He was doubtless told that David was considered one of the city's leading merchants and investors, having joined with Nathan Appleton, Francis Lowell, and other wealthy Bostonians in an investment group called the Fifty Associates. The Associates had taken the lead in developing the region's thriving manufacturing industries. David had also helped finance the construction of the India Wharf to receive goods from around the world. Perhaps the Swiss visitor even learned that the Searses had raised funds to build the very Episcopal church in which Frederick had been baptized against his wishes.[79]

As a European sojourner, Gonzalve may also have gained a sense of what Americans meant by calling Boston's elite like David Sears

Brahmins. Another European resident of the city, Viennese immigrant Francis Grund, had just published some biting commentaries
on American society that help explain the situation in which Gonzalve found himself. Grund satirized what he called the young republic's national vanity, a "feeling which is totally distinct from pa-
triotism – [and] exists in no part of the United States to the extent as
in New England, and especially in Boston, whose inhabitants think
themselves not only vastly superior to many people in Europe, but
also infinitely more enlightened, especially as regards politics, than
the rest of their countrymen." Shrewdly he recognized a chink in
the Brahmins' armor: The fear of publicity that had already surfaced in David's requests for an informal separation. "I have heard
it seriously asserted in America," Grund reported, "that there are
no better policemen than the ordinary run of Bostonians; and that,
as long as their natural inquisitiveness remained, there was no need
of a secret tribunal; every citizen taking upon himself the several
offices of spy, juryman, justice and – vide Lynch law – executioner.
This is by some called the wholesome restraint of public opinion:
but, in order that public opinion may be just, it must not be biased
by the particular faith of a coterie: and there are transactions in
private life of which the public ought never to be made the judge."
Grund's insights indicate why the Searses so devoutly wished that
the d'Hautevilles' marital strife would never be subjected to public
judgments.[80] Whatever the extent of his American education, Gonzalve once again found himself the supplicant pleading with Ellen
to return.

By early August 1839, the d'Hautevilles' negotiations had
reached an impasse that ensured that law would dominate their dispute. Gonzalve's decision to sail to America had not altered either
spouse's view of their marriage or their bargaining goals. Ellen still
considered their differences irreconcilable; Gonzalve continued to
believe that they could be worked out. And Ellen still insisted on
an informal arrangement that guaranteed her freedom from the
d'Hautevilles and possession of Frederick, while Gonzalve continued to demand that his wife and son return with him to their home
at Hauteville. Nevertheless, by showing up in Boston, he had called
the Searses' bluff. As as he waited in the Tremont, the Swiss visitor
expected a summons from lawyers carrying out David's threatened
suit for separation. It never came. Instead it was Gonzalve who decided to turn to that "mysterious" legal system that had been bran-
dished to threaten him into remaining at Hauteville. Its appeal became irresistible to the Swiss visitor as he tried to find a way to force
Ellen's hand. Later in the Philadelphia courtroom he would recall
his decision as a courageous act born of righteous indignation: "[r]e-

gardless of the threat of judicial prosecution, the first community I visited was her own Massachusetts, where her parents and family were high in position and respectability; strong too, as I had a right to infer, from Mr. Sears's apparent familiarity with the pains and penalties of the law, in the protection of the laws by which the wife, if injured, could be saved from a husband if a wrong-doer." But Gonzalve, not Ellen or David, "sought, reluctantly, redress from the laws of Massachusetts, my wife's native state, and the process was eluded or defied in the privacy of some secure retreat. The Supreme Judicial Court of Massachusetts, with whose penalties I had been threatened by Ellen's father was avoided as if its unfavourable decrees were surely anticipated."[81]

The legalization of the d'Hautevilles' marital conflict was now complete. David's threats, Ellen's assertion of spousal and maternal rights, Gonzalve's claims of patriarchal rights, and their common refusal to compromise had heightened the law's appeal and led them all into its shadow. Now they had to learn more about the shadowy realm they had decided to enter.

2

Bargaining in the Shadow of the Law

The d'Hautevilles now faced the consequences of the legalization of their marital struggle. From the late summer of 1839 through the winter of 1840 their legal experiences deepened through two more fateful encounters with the law. First, Ellen and Gonzalve learned more about the law itself. They discovered formal legal rules that, despite critical uncertainties, had implications as welcome for Gonzalve as they were ominous for Ellen. Legal knowledge transformed their bargaining and led directly to their next legal encounter. In a crucial reversal, the estranged pair exchanged roles as they resumed negotiating: Gonzalve issued dogmatic demands, and Ellen pleaded for compromise. In their new roles, they both experienced the law's increasing domination of their dispute as their understanding of legal rules dictated what they said and what they did. Together these next two crucial legal encounters taught Gonzalve and Ellen what it meant to bargain in the shadow of the law. Their experiences can be reconstructed as revealing illustrations of the power as well as the limits of law to influence individual consciousness and to order private bargaining.

Chronicling the d'Hautevilles' bargaining demonstrates the importance of timing and context in legal disputes. Trapped in the law's shadow, external realities had as profound an impact on the d'Hautevilles as did their dawning understanding of internal legal rules and procedures. Ellen and Gonzalve did not act in a temporal vacuum. On the contrary, as they would learn, their family troubles were hardly unique. The social landscape of North America and Western Europe was fast becoming littered with the debris of failed marriages. For decades countless couples like Gonzalve and Ellen had not only found themselves in troubled marriages, but had tried to bargain their way out. Indeed these years constituted a critical period in the history of the Western European family. New family forms and new family beliefs upset existing household arrangements and engendered countless controversies. Most importantly for understanding the d'Hauteville case, new conceptions of marital individualism and parental care raised the expectations and responsibilities of numerous spouses and parents and, consequently, increased the sources of domestic discord. The resulting conflict and change made both private and public governance of the family hotly contested issues.[1]

Changing family attitudes and practices influenced the d'Hauteville case directly and indirectly. They produced the larger climate of opinion into which it would be thrust, as well as the specific disputes that became precedents against which it would be judged. As a result, the case reveals the complex interaction of internal and external forces that combined to create significant legal experiences. Most importantly, the d'Hautevilles found themselves in the shadow of the law because in America law offices, courtrooms, and legislative chambers had become primary sites for the escalating conflicts over marriage and parenthood. In these legal arenas, men and women like Ellen and Gonzalve were caught up in local, national, and international debates over the roles, responsibilities, and rights of husbands and wives, mothers and fathers.

Yet the interactive reality of law in shadows also demonstrates the power of individual choice and action to influence legal change. Though bounded by the ideas and practices of their moment in time, women and men like Ellen and Gonzalve were not passive respondents either to external social change or internal legal processes. Quite the contrary, they were active agents constructing the relationship between internal and external forces as they acted upon the choices available to them. The d'Hautevilles did so through a series of legal lessons interspersed with spates of bargaining. As Ellen and Gonzalve studied and bargained, they also gained a clearer sense of what it would mean if their bargaining failed and they had to leave the law's shadows and enter the glaring light of the courtroom.

Legal Lessons

Gonzalve's futile trip to Boston to retrieve Ellen and Frederick forced the couple into lawyers' offices to learn the law. Their legal education can be reconstructed from their words and deeds. Like all clients, Gonzalve and Ellen wanted to know their options, and especially what would happen to them if they ended up in a courtroom. The answers they received in the summer and fall of 1839 came in series of lessons about marital separations, divorce, and child custody. Unbeknownst to them, these would be but the first of many sessions with lawyers during the next months and years. Being clients became part of their private and public identities as consciousness of the law increasingly defined who they were and what they could do.[2]

It was from their lawyers that Ellen and Gonzalve began to understand the connections between their private problems and the numerous public controversies over the family swirling about them. But their legal education not only made them conscious of change, it changed their consciousness. The d'Hautevilles brought to their counseling sessions their own sense of the law. Legal lessons forced each spouse to compare those convictions with the rules and procedures being explained to them. Like all clients, they learned that law was far less certain than they had imagined. The pair came to understand that in many ways law was neither a clear set of statutory directives nor "what judges say in the reports, but what lawyers say – to one another and to clients – in their offices."[3] From their lawyers, Ellen and Gonzalve learned law as a particular language, whose combination of fixed guidelines and contested rules increasingly framed their dispute and forced each of them to make a variety of tactical decisions.[4]

The d'Hautevilles' legal education occurred while they continued bargaining. Ellen negotiated from her hiding place, Gonzalve first from Boston and then New York City, which became his base of operations as he continued to rely on attorney and Swiss consul Henry C. De Rham. As the pair's lessons intensified, an anguished sense of lost love and dashed expectations continued to fill their letters, but expressions borrowed from the law increasingly drowned out those sentiments. The law now provided a script that stage-managed their bargaining. Though Gonzalve and Ellen had very different responses to their common legal lessons, each soon realized that they had more control over their fate by bargaining privately rather than subjecting themselves to the uncertainties of the courtroom. And so the star-crossed couple entered into one final round of negotiations.

Gonzalve took up his pen first. For the first time, he mixed thinly veiled threats of legal action with his continued appeal for reconciliation. Quickly legal rights became his dominant theme. He repeated the words of other husbands who had experienced the collapse of their marriages. For all of these men, an "angry and frustrated insistence on 'my rights' and the absence of 'your pretended rights,' became the standard refrain of correspondence from husbands to their separated wives."[5] Characteristically, Gonzalve cautioned his wife, "We have the opportunity of being reconciled, I pray you, my dear Ellen, to think much of it, and to pray much before you shut the door, and force me to act – before you make us both miserable for life, and prepare sorrows for our dear child." Writing with a new assurance, he confidently staked his claim to Frederick and asserted his masculine responsibilities: "I wish to have you freely and amicably. I do not seek to have you otherwise; but to abandon my son, my dear friend, no! such is not my duty. I love him too; he is my heir. I hope myself to make a Christian of him, and I put my happiness in it, to see him grow up, and to raise him in his own country – happy if this can be in concert with you." He also made his bargaining tactics and goals explicit: "I shall cruelly regret that you force me to separate you from him. I wish to have him, and that you should follow me, and pray from the bottom of my heart that thus it may be."[6]

Gonzalve's newfound confidence sprang from lessons he and Ellen received in the law of separation and divorce. The lawyers made both of them consider Ellen's flight from Hauteville as a legal act not merely one of wifely defiance. In doing so, they learned what marital wrongs warranted a legal exit and, more menacingly for Ellen, what ones did not. Those lessons form the backdrop of this phase of the d'Hautevilles' bargaining.   *women problems*

The lawyers had to begin their instruction with a few words about American federalism. The states had jurisdiction over most domestic relations, and set the terms for entering and leaving a marriage. Differing family policies had made the law of separation and divorce a patchwork of common and conflicting rules. As a resident of Vaud, which had similar jurisdictional power within the Swiss confederation, this knowledge would not have been startling to Gonzalve. But one of the major implications of federalism became clearer to both d'Hautevilles: They could each go forum shopping. Federalism freed them to find the state, or canton, with the most favorable combination of statutes, common law rules, and customary practices for their claims. To arm the pair with this potent legal weapon, their lawyers would have had to explain both general American rules of separation and divorce as well as its major variations.

However the d'Hautevilles received their lesson, one major point would have been made very clear to them. An antipathy to private marital separations had been deeply embedded in American and European law. The searing condemnation of informal separations by English jurist Lord Kenyon expressed the common sentiment; they created, he declared, the "undefined and dangerous position of a wife without a husband and a husband without a wife."[7] Yet Ellen sought precisely that position. She wanted to be a wife without the presence, and especially the residence and family, of her husband. But her demand for an informal separation was legally tenuous and might well be controversial. Despite the increasing intrusion of contractualism and its commitment to marital freedom and equality, indissolubility remained the basic organizing principle of American and European marriage law. Entrenched legal and religious opposition to informal separations undermined Ellen's legal position, while buttressing Gonzalve's even as it echoed the stance he and Syndic Frederic Couvreu had taken the previous winter.

Massachusetts, the site of their first lessons, was a case in point. Like all American states, as well as Vaud, it had a formal method of granting separations. Since the days of Ellen's forefather, Richard the Pilgrim, Massachusetts had authorized separations as well as divorces. Influenced by Swiss theologian John Calvin, among others, colonial Pilgrims and Puritans had dismissed Catholic and Anglican opposition to divorce as an ill-advised attempt to keep warring couples together. So despite official English policy against divorce, they made it an option early in the seventeenth century. Disgruntled spouses had two formal legal exits: divorces *a vinculo matrimonii*, or absolute divorces with the right to remarry; and divorces *a mensa et thoro*, or separations from bed and board. Though uncommon, enough Massachusetts spouses had tried to get out of their marriages, particularly through separations, that they had launched a debate over how to end marriages that continued in the law offices of 1839.[8]

Over the years Massachusetts legislators and judges had created general policies governing separations. The statutes had been revised but four years earlier amidst a general overhaul of the state code. Husbands and wives could obtain bed and board separations on the grounds of "extreme cruelty," and since 1811 wives had been able to seek such a separation if a husband "shall utterly desert" or refused to provide for his spouse.[9] A court-ordered separation required proof that one of the two parties had breached a fundamental marital obligation. Legal sanction was critical because a separation did not fully release a couple from their matrimonial bonds. Instead judges set the terms of maintenance, inheritance, residence, and child custody while the couple lived apart. In the absence of such an agreement, all marital obligations continued.

As an alternative to a formal separation, couples could also make private contracts to live apart. In these agreements they could divide property in the form of separate maintenance agreements and make arrangements for child custody. The private pacts were subject to equity law because the common law refused to accept contracts between husbands and wives. Often such contracts took the form of postnuptial trusts that required the participation of third parties. The agreements, though, demanded joint participation. Outside the law, of course, couples could always separate without formal contracts, third parties, or any other trappings of the law.

But such agreements could not be enforced. Knowing when separation was both proper and possible in Massachusetts, as in most jurisdictions, remained a tricky business for lawyers and their clients.[10]

Federalism offered a timely lesson in the law's uncertainties. Assuming, quite rightly it would turn out, that Gonzalve would return to Manhattan if his search in Boston proved fruitless, New York became a possible site for further legal combat. Yet its laws offered Ellen little more encouragement than those of her home state. An 1827–8 code revision empowered a married woman to seek a "separation from bed and board forever thereafter, or for a limited, time, as shall seem just and reasonable," only when her husband had been proven guilty of either cruel and inhumane punishment, or such conduct "as may render it unsafe and improper for her to cohabit with him," or when he abandoned her and neglected or refused to provide for her support. The code had strict residency requirements, however, making separation available only when the marriage had been solemnized in New York or the offenses had occurred in the state and parties had lived in the state for a year. New York equity courts also accepted private separation agreements made through the medium of trustees.[11]

Rogers v. Rogers illustrated the problems Ellen faced. Decided but five years before, a New York chancellor had refused to accept a separation agreement between a husband and wife without the intervention of a third party. His opinion not only reiterated the traditional antipathy to private separations, he relied on the primal family law principle of coverture to legitimate his argument. Coverture was the legal label for the status of a married woman. A wife was, in Anglo-American law's Norman French, a *"feme covert"* – a woman covered by her husband. As a matter of conventional legal theory in America as in Europe, a married woman had no separate legal identity. By the time Ellen and Gonzalve learned its meaning, coverture had long been one of the most powerful paradigms in Anglo-American law and Western political theory. It institutionalized the assumptions that wives were naturally subordinated to their husbands, like children to their parents, and that marriages could not be egalitarian because domestic sovereignty could not be divided. As a formal legal designation of a wife's status at common law, coverture placed a married woman and her property, as well as her children, under the protection and control of her husband. It made her economically dependent and legally invisible. And it spawned subsidiary doctrines, most significantly marital unity. A legal translation of the one-flesh doctrine of Christianity, the great compiler of English law, Sir William Blackstone had authored its most influential Anglo-American phrasing: "[T]he very being or existence of the woman is suspended during the marriage, or, at least, is incorporated and consolidated into that of the husband."[12] Marital unity had even been reduced to a pithy declaration: The husband and wife are one person, that person is the husband. Though under assault, coverture and marital unity remained the dominant public narratives of domestic relations as the *Rogers* case demonstrated. The New York chancellor relied on those primary story lines to denounce the right of couples to separate at will by arguing that it was "impossible for a *feme covert* to make any valid agreement with her husband to separate from him, in violation of the marriage contract and of the duties which she owes to society, except under the sanction of the court; and in a case where the conduct of the husband has been such as to entitle her to a decree for a separation. The law does not authorize or sanction a voluntary agreement between husband and wife. It merely tolerates such agreements when made in such a manner that they can be enforced by or against a third party acting in behalf of the wife."[13]

The chancellor's invocation of coverture revealed the problems Ellen faced. Coverture expressed the legal implications of the marriage vows she had recited in the village church at Montreux. In the wedding ceremony Ellen had exchanged legal dependence on her father for dependence on Gonzalve. It was precisely this transfer of male power over her that she now sought to reverse. Coverture rose as a massive legal roadblock in her way. No matter what rights and powers she believed to be hers, her status as a married woman barred a variety of independent legal actions. Coverture circumscribed her ability to retain, use, or bequeath property as well as to dissolve her marriage and or even retain custody of Frederick. Every action she might contemplate to free herself from Gonzalve fell under its sway. Being the daughter of a wealthy and prestigious family Ellen discovered, perhaps for the first time in her life, did not protect her from being classified with other married women as a legally invisible spousal dependent – a *feme covert*. Her sex threatened to overwhelm her class. Ellen's first legal lessons sharpened her sense of victimization, while offering only faint hope for redress.[14]

Gonzalve's response was quite different. Though he had probably not known the precise Anglo-American legal translations, he recognized and endorsed the concept of coverture. No doubt he was taken aback when he learned despite the powers it invested in husbands, they still had no legal authority to command that fleeing wives return. If Ellen chose to stay away from him, the law would not force her back. She must return voluntarily. Nevertheless, coverture and its ancillary doctrines like marital unity perfectly expressed his own vision of matrimony, and echoed his understanding of the proper relationship between husband and wife. It must have been gratifying for him to learn that American law offered the same basic instructions he had been trying to give his misguided wife. He may have even recalled the lines he used from *Genesis* in one of his letters to Ellen: "For this man shall leave his father and his mother and cleave to his wife, and they shall be as one flesh."[15] Legal learning seemed to justify everything he had done from his disposition of Ellen's property to his refusal to let her, or, worse yet, her mother, dictate their residence. Coverture lent legal support to his sense of outrage at Ellen's challenges to his authority. Her defiance had not only struck at the manly sense of honor that formed the core of his identity as a husband, now he saw it as a violation of the unity of man and wife dictated by the law. His letters had failed to convince Ellen that in marriage she occupied a subordinate place subject to his direction, perhaps the law would succeed where his pen had failed.

Conversely, lessons in the law of separation heightened Ellen's panic. She now recognized in the language of the law that her goal had become an informal separation. But her demand for Frederick complicated the negotiations and underscored the legal lesson she was learning: A separation guaranteeing that she kept her son could only be arranged with Gonzalve's assent. Yet he had adamantly refused to give it. As long as he did, only one marital exit remained: divorce.

Learning about divorce offered Ellen little more comfort. In Switzerland and America permanently dissolving a marriage remained controversial and rare despite the growing popular and legal conviction that some circumstances justified an absolute divorce. Embedded in Western European law was the conviction that divorce must not confer public sanction on the private agreement of a husband and wife to shed their marital obligations. Only sexual radicals championed divorce as a necessary remedy for failed marriages. Most Americans and Europeans accepted it only as a punishment for a serious matrimonial crime. Consequently, a couple would be divorced only when one of them convinced officials that a legally recognized marital wrong had been committed.[16]

In yet another lesson in American federalism, the couple would also have been told that since the Revolution divorce had become widely available in states around the republic. Not only had it spread geographically, but over the last couple of decades, like so much else in American family law, divorce had become the primary domain of judges. Around the republic, legislators were ceding their traditional rights to intervene directly in family disputes through private legislation in favor of general statutes granting courts the authority to adjudicate conflicts like the d'Hautevilles'. Judicial discretion and a body of state cases had emerged to vie with statutory guidelines as guardians of marital exits.[17] The question for Ellen became whether or not a divorce petition from her could win judicial endorsement.

A lawyerly survey of Massachusetts divorce law would not have been encouraging. Since casting off the British yoke, legislators and judges had gradually widened access to divorce until the recent 1835 code revision authorized that husbands or wives could obtain divorces only by proving their spouses guilty of adultery, impotence, desertion, or even a criminal conviction carrying a prison sentence of seven years. Just the year before, legislators had added malicious desertion for five years by either spouse to the roster of matrimonial crimes.[18] But none of the misdeeds seemed to fit Ellen's charges. And the possibilities seemed even dimmer in New York. Since 1787 an absolute divorce had been available from the chancery courts only for adultery. Though quite long, her list of Gonzalve's marital crimes did not include adultery.[19]

These lessons in American divorce law did not surprise Gonzalve. The United States was only one flank in trans-Atlantic skirmishes over marital permanence. Controls on marital exits had been eased throughout Western Europe. Divorce in America was anomalous only because of its divergent state policies and its growing reliance on judicially created rules. More specifically, Gonzalve learned that he had three options: defend himself in an American court if Ellen tried to divorce him; try to establish residency in an American state and sue her for divorce; or return to Vaud and initiate proceedings there. He knew that the last option was a very real one. Like his estranged wife, he too had inherited a divorce tradition that highlighted matrimonial fault and justified dissolving marriages only when one spouse was proven guilty of a marital crime and the other clearly innocent. Alone at Hauteville the winter before, he had pondered the possibility of divorcing Ellen. Like much else in Vaud, debate over divorce ran back to the years when Calvin and other leaders of the Reformation overthrew the Catholic idea of marriage as a sacrament. Like Ellen's Pilgrim ancestors, the acceptance of marriage as a civil contract by Gonzalve's Calvinist forefathers had opened the possibility of divorce. But the deep-seated popular and legal aversion to divorce that animated American law and custom also persisted within the Calvinist tradition. Through his own rejection of David's bid for an informal separation and repeated efforts at reconciliation, Gonzalve had voiced his own conviction that marriage remained a permanent, spiritual bond. The Swiss husband agreed with Calvin's declaration: "God ties them in an indissoluble knot from which they may not freely depart." He also shared the Calvinist view that attention to duty, not divorce, was the proper remedy for marital unhappiness: "When they were tempted to divorce one another, or to be incensed against one another, the right way to subdue all wicked passions was to have an eye to the pledge of the spiritual union between Lord Jesus Christ and us."[20]

Nevertheless, Gonzalve's lawyers told him that he very well might succeed in having Ellen convicted as a marital criminal. A divorce might be granted on grounds of desertion in Vaud, and perhaps, if he could establish residency, in Massachusetts or most other American states. In each jurisdiction, desertion ranked second only to adultery as a matrimonial crime. Gonzalve, as the abandoned spouse, could charge his wife with forsaking her primary marital duty: cohabitation. His pleas for her return could be entered as evidence of his innocence. With a divorce decree against Ellen would surely come custody of Frederick.[21] Customary practice strengthened his hand. In Switzerland as in America, women tended to sue for desertion, men for adultery. Ellen's flight from Hauteville ran afoul of traditional practice, making her a marital rebel. According to American and European gender beliefs, husbands deserted not wives. That is, of course, unless a wife fled for just cause.

Trying to figure out the just causes for leaving a marriage thrust Ellen and Gonzalve into the thicket of trans-Atlantic debates over marriage and law. Ellen explained to her lawyers that Gonzalve had forced her to flee. Like most clients, she cast herself as the victim of the story. Yet Ellen's claims that Gonzalve's marital sins justified her flight voiced a standard of marital expectations at odds with the law. David's emphatic declaration to Couvreu the year before that in Massachusetts, if not Vaud, marital tyranny justified a divorce, expressed popular rather than legal grounds for leaving a marriage.[22] Despite the Searses' convictions, American states did not recognize incompatibility, the essence of Ellen's charges, as a legitimate ground for divorce. As evidence, the lawyers could have cited the emphatic 1816 declaration of the Vermont Supreme Court: "A bill of divorce will not be granted where the only cause proved is a total alienation of the affections of one or both of the parties."[23]

Instead a charge of marital cruelty seemed Ellen's only possible divorce claim. Indeed she devoutly believed that Gonzalve had been a cruel husband. As she had told him time and again, his mistreatment had forced her flight and sealed her resolve never to return. Many other wives had done the same thing. Like her, their marital expectations had been dashed by their marital experiences. They too argued that harsh treatment instead of affection and respect had

driven them from their homes. Like Ellen, these women had assumed that their husbands would disavow mental as well as physical
cruelty. They too had been disappointed and, rather than accept
such treatment were willing to fight in courtrooms and legislatures
to make male conduct, indeed manhood itself, a legal issue. Nevertheless, though the word cruelty defined their experiences, it did
not express the law. Instead, by making such charges, Ellen and
other women challenged legal rules and institutional practices that
rejected their claims and dismissed their goals.

The distraught wife confronted the words of English jurist Lord
Stowell. In 1790 he had delivered what fifty years later remained
the leading Anglo-American interpretation of matrimonial cruelty.
His words offered Ellen little solace: "Mere austerity of temper, pet-
ulance of manners, rudeness of language, a want of civil attention,
and accommodation, even occasional sallies of passion, if they do
not threaten bodily harm, do not amount to legal cruelty; they are
high moral offenses in the marriage state undoubtedly, not innocent
surely in any state of life, but still they are not that cruelty against
which the law can relieve." Stowell decreed that behavior wounding
"not the natural feelings but the acquired feelings arising from rank
and station" could not be included as cruelty "for the court has no
scale of sensibilities by which it can gauge the quantum of injury
done and felt. . . ." Instead the cruelty warranting a separation or
divorce existed only if there was reasonable apprehension of danger
to life, limb, or health. Stowell's message could not be clearer. To
prevail in a divorce court a woman must prove actual or threatened
physical attacks. In yet another lesson in the law's commitment to
marital permanence, Stowell rationalized his definition of marital
cruelty with a testimonial to matrimonial sacrifice strikingly similar
to Gonzalve's sermons on marriage: "The general happiness of
married life is secured by its indissolubility. When people understand that they must live together, except for a very few reasons
known to the law, they learn to soften, by mutual accommodation,
that yoke which they know they cannot shake off. They become
good husbands, and good wives, from the necessity of remaining
husbands and wives; for necessity is a powerful master in teaching
the duties which it imposes."[24]

Though Stowell's ruling expanded the traditional English definition of marital cruelty to include threats not just actual violence,
the precedent offered Ellen little hope that judges would brand
Gonzalve's acts cruel. Despite her father's confident declaration to
Couvreu the year before, she learned that the Massachusetts courts
had adopted the English standard.[25] To impress on Ellen the tenu-

ousness of her claim and to suggest that even forum shopping might not help, her lawyers could have dredged up the words of an 1829 Kentucky court: Even though the death of a "sensitive female" might be hastened by neglect, coldness, indifference, or unmerited reproach, such behavior could not be labeled as cruelty sufficient to grant a divorce. "On the contrary," wrote Justice Joseph Underwood, "we conceive it must be some injury to the body, intended or inflicted, which will endanger life, to justify a divorce. We can not with sufficient certainty, ascertain the operation of particular acts, upon the mind, and then trace the influences of the mind upon the body, in producing disease and death."[26]

Learning law in 1839, Ellen came to understand that American statutes and common law defined cruelty as real or apprehended physical suffering, not unhappiness, misery, or the absence of affection. And yet in what would be a recurring theme of her legal education and a key tenet of her legal beliefs, she also began to understand why more and more wives rejected the law's received logic and forced their way into courtrooms to insist that marital cruelty could be mental as well as physical. Like Ellen, these women became convinced that the law turned a blind eye to the reality of their suffering. And like her, at the base of their complaints lay a conviction that marriage ought to be more of a companionate than a hierarchical relationship; it should be a union of hearts and minds. Charges of mental cruelty gave voice to the specific conviction held by Ellen and countless other women that they should receive respect from their mates. In doing so, they aligned marital cruelty with a larger humanitarian movement that labeled as cruel acts not previously considered moral infractions. Inspired by a newfound respect for the autonomy of the individual and the dignity of ordinary life, the very notion of cruelty was expanding during these years spurred by movements such as the campaigns against corporal punishment. In the nineteenth century, claims of psychological harm became the controversial outer limits of cruelty, and thereby turned the divorce ground of cruelty into a contested legal doctrine.[27]

Claims like Ellen's also revealed that in the law's shadows men and women often acted upon different notions of legitimate marital practices. Charges of mental cruelty were exclusively made by women. Such claims suggest that when drawn into the shadow of the law and forced to voice their legal beliefs, wives like Ellen expressed a separate, gendered legal consciousness. Not only did she and many other women refuse to accept marital behavior earlier generations had endured, they began to demand that the law recognize and legitimize their complaints. In doing so, wives became the most powerful agents of change in family law as they brought their gendered sense of justice into the law's arenas.[28]

Though she did not recognize it yet, Ellen was already well on her way to becoming one of those agents. Learning that judges might not accept her pleas of cruel treatment did not alter Ellen's conviction that Gonzalve had turned out to be a cruel and tyrannical husband. Even though she found yet another legal exit from her marriage blocked, Ellen rejected the obvious conclusion of her lawyer's instruction: return to Gonzalve or be declared a marital deserter. Instead lawyerly recitations of separation and divorce reinforced her growing sense of the gap between justice and law. Though she recognized that defiance of the law and Gonzalve made her a marital rebel in an age when even the decision to seek a divorce was a bold assertion of individual rights at odds with the submissive demeanor expected of wives, her dawning consciousness of the law forced her to search for other ways to justify her actions and other means to achieve her goals.

While Ellen digested another bitter legal lesson, Gonzalve once again found the law quite palatable. Judicial opposition to expansive definitions of marital cruelty echoed his own declarations that duty and obligation outweighed demands for personal happiness. Just as he had repeatedly expressed bewilderment at Ellen's charges, so he must have agreed that only actual threats of violence or physical injury – but not claims of misery or even bodily suffering arising from mental torment – could be considered cruel treatment. He refused to see himself as a spousal tormentor. Once again the law seemed to give him backing. Consequently, David's threat of legal action against him now seemed a very hollow attempt at intimidation. In fact, thus far Gonzalve's legal education did little to dissuade him from turning to law as a weapon to force Ellen into meeting his demands. On the contrary, it strengthened his resolve to protect his legal rights. Such stances by Gonzalve and other husbands made the defense of male family power an important check on radical changes in family law. Their determination to preserve and protect male authority over families became a cause as fervently championed as married women's rights. It meant that a transformation of family life would be neither quick nor complete.

Thanks to her law office education in desertion and divorce, Ellen understood her bargaining goal just as clearly as Gonzalve. She sought an informal separation with custody of Frederick. However, Ellen now also understood the weakness of her bargaining hand. The lawyers had made it clear that her story lacked legal adequacy. That is, it clashed with the reigning public narratives of the law because it differed "substantially in form and content from the accounts judges [were] accustomed to dealing with by training and experience."[29] Conversely, Gonzalve's story seemed to conform to judicial notion of legal adequacy and the public narratives of family law.

As she resumed bargaining, Ellen tried to overcome the weakness of her negotiating position by appealing to her husband's manly honor and asserting her maternal responsibilities. Like other wives trapped in failed marriages, she prayed that an often expressed husbandly concern about their wives' happiness could be used to weaken the power of paternal rights: "[H]appiness I shall never know again; and all my earthly prospects, which a few years since seemed so fair, are darkened, never to be bright again! You alone can restore me to tranquility, by ceasing to pursue my child; but be assured that in whatever situation I am placed, I shall never leave it. My only care is watching over it – my life is its happiness." Buried in her plea was a conviction so fundamental that Ellen need not even give it voice. She considered herself bound in marriage to Gonzalve for life even if she would not live with him. For her, as for many other nineteenth-century women and men, separation was not a way station in the inevitable journey to divorce it would become in the next century, but the permanent place they sought. Ellen had accepted her fate as a husbandless wife; now she feared being a childless mother.[30]

Angered by his wife's continued defiance, Gonzalve dismissed her pleas and once more flashed his legal sword. Yet he did so in words that indicated that for him, as for Ellen, at this stage of their bargaining religion still vied with law as a vocabulary and set of external standards through which he could explain his actions and judge those of his spouse. Consequently, the d'Hautevilles' bargaining disclosed that at the heart of their struggles lay uncertainties about the clash between assertions of individual will and acceptance of religious duties that troubled many other husbands and wives caught up in the marital changes of their times.[31]

Gonzalve accused his wife of breaking the most sacred human contract, marriage. Though he now knew that the law could not be used to force her return, Gonzalve could appeal for divine intervention: "I do not wish my wife, if she does not return with the feelings *of a* wife for her husband; but I take this last occasion to make you reflect upon the immense responsibility that you are taking, not only with regard to myself and your child; but before God, and what you call *society*, in voluntarily deserting your husband, and concealing a child from its father." Underscoring his warning, he asked Ellen if she was ready "to render an account to humanity and to your *final Judge,* for the violation of the most *inviolable obligation?*"

To induce such reflections, Gonzalve switched from invocations of God to assertions of manhood. Gender, along with religion and law, provided a third set of trans-Atlantic words and beliefs for these marital bargainers. Marriage and fatherhood had transformed him just as it had his wife. He had eagerly accepted the powers and duties of his new position as husband and father. They had become critical parts of his self-identity. Ellen had threatened the essence of Gonzalve's manhood by challenging his fundamental right to govern his family. Assuming the pose of a wronged but confident patriarch, the outraged Swiss husband declared himself "no longer disposed . . . to see the most sacred rights of nature thus violated with respect to me." With such words, he tried to counter Ellen's claims of maternal deprivation by voicing his own laments about paternal loss.

Nevertheless, after his legal lessons, neither religion nor gender seemed as potent a weapon as law to the spurned spouse. "As to my incontestable legal rights," he declared converting education into action, "in that respect I am assured by every one, and they are all freely acknowledged, as I am told, by your *friends.*" He emphatically rejected her request for an informal separation: "The idea of permanent flight, or of any arrangement be it what it may, are equally unreasonable, without counting the state of perpetual suffering that would be attached to it." Gonzalve warned Ellen against thinking she could simply remain in hiding until he tired of the chase and sailed home. "Neither days, nor weeks, nor months, nor constant efforts," he vowed, "would succeed in changing my *determination* with regard to it. It is so fixed, that, if to have the child, it would be necessary, again to ask for the mother, I would not hesitate."[32]

Despite these threats, Ellen continued to shun the role of submissive wife that Gonzalve demanded. But, she remained trapped by Gonzalve's decision to invoke the law. Searching for a way out of her legal predicament, Ellen also turned to gender and religion. Hoping to change Gonzalve's course of action by appealing to his sense of chivalry, she charged him with violating his manly responsibilities to protect her from his family and from his own treacherous acts. In her attempt to shame him into concessions, Ellen linked Gonzalve's violation of masculine duties with his legal threats against her. "Without even informing me you were here," she reproached him, "you first applied to a lawyer, and with him by your side, and having expressed a *determination to pursue me* to the extent of what *the law* could do, you called at my father's door and inquired for me; and with no promises for the future, no repeal of the hard terms laid down for me, in your letter to my father, endeavoured, by *epithets alone* of affection, to induce me to return with you." Adamant in her resistance to a marriage without love and mutual respect, Ellen also explained to Gonzalve how she had reconciled individual self-determination with religious obligation: "*The arrow has passed through my heart,* and I am so unfortunate as to have no longer, there, a feeling towards you which would induce me, according to my conscience, either before God or to the world, to live with you again as your wife." Through such an assertion she not only echoed the opposition to Calvinism so dominant among the Boston elite, but also voiced the outcome of her personal struggle between self and God. Yet Ellen's expression of faith in the "theology of Self-hood," which contrasted so sharply with Gonzalve's religious call to matrimonial duty, had not come easily.[33] Feeling the tensions between romantic love and divinely ordained duties, Ellen sought an equitable separation that would ease her anxieties about what she was doing. She pleaded that Gonzalve "not reject every amicable overture; think again of my youth and feeble health; think that you have forced me to fly, like a *hunted felon,* from my father's house, and in your own heart, if you ever had a feeling for me, let it intercede." In one last bargaining gambit, Ellen again distinguished between law and justice by invoking the power of divine judgment: "Remember, you are accountable to your final Judge for the sufferings you occasion. Arbitrary and artificial rights will not weigh in the balance against humanity and mercy, before Him."[34]

Gonzalve spurned Ellen's pleas for further negotiations. The law was simply too appealing to him. Its promise of victory without compromise overwhelmed Ellen's appeals to gender and religion. Gonzalve later defended his refusal to continue bargaining as a necessary defense of his rights. He had concluded that "negotiations, through third parties, on such a subject as my right to my wife and child, could lead to no other result than to weaken my claim to the protection of the laws, on which even as a stranger I confidently relied."[35] Ellen too felt the weight of the law. She would complain that Gonzalve had chosen "to stand, sternly, upon his *supposed legal rights.*" Legal hubris, she argued, led him to ignore pleas "written in the spirit of peace and compromise, and from a heart crushed under the weight of its own wretchedness," and instead to seek "the aid of the law to take away from its mother, [a] child of twenty months old!"[36]

The Bargaining Ends

Learning the law of separation and divorce led to the breakdown of the d'Hautevilles' negotiations. The impasse also narrowed the

remaining choices for both Ellen and Gonzalve. He could not force
her to return, but he could still seek his son; she could stay away
from him, but unless she was willing to remain in hiding indefinitely
she could not keep Frederick without either reaching an accommodation with her husband or going to court to challenge his legal
right to the boy. As a result, a second body of domestic relations
rules began to dominate the couple's dispute: the law of child
custody.

Custody involved the right of a parent or someone acting as a
parent to control a minor. It contained a volatile mix of parental
and filial interests, rights, and duties. Custody could be awarded as
part of a formal separation or divorce, but it could also be determined in habeas corpus hearings convened solely for that purpose.
In custody law as in all other American domestic relations, male
authority reigned supreme. Paternal rights formed the basic narrative of all custody discussions. However, doubts about the legitimacy
and efficacy of male family power combined with a growing belief
in the innate nurturing abilities of mothers to make custody a hotly
contested issue in America and Europe. As the d'Hautevilles' focused on their fight for Frederick, custody law framed the choices
they made in their final negotiations.[37]

Clashing maternal and paternal claims for Frederick had already
surfaced in the couple's negotiations. In one of his final bargaining
letters, Gonzalve made the extent of his determination to get Frederick very clear. He used declarations of his own paternal duties to
turn aside Ellen's plea to be left alone with her son: "I now come to
your last request – that I should leave you our child! My heart
bleeds at the idea of a separation, but *I am decided, and I wish to have
him!* There is a duty reposing on me as a father, as a Swiss, as a
member of society, that leaves me no alternative. I ought to do what
I can to watch over his education, whether it is for this life, *or for the
next.* He is the natural inheritor of my estate, he is destined therefore to enjoy a position in his country, that he can find no where
else, and only if he is brought up there: *I am surprised that you wish
to deprive him of it.*" Like his marital demands, Gonzalve's claim for
Frederick expressed his conviction that a man had a fundamental
duty to govern his family. His words expressed the confident conclusion that the law would support him.

Struggling to find a legal voice as a married woman trapped in a
regime of male dominance, Ellen had a more difficult task. In her
letters, she had tried to challenge to Gonzalve's paternal rights by
depicting herself as a responsible mother trying to fulfill her maternal obligations to the infant Frederick. However, Ellen had to bargain in the law's shadow. While a claim of maternal duty seemed a

compelling bargaining ploy in her dispute with Gonzalve, it also drove her to an oppositional view of the law. Like so many legal critics before and after her, Ellen attacked the existing distribution of legal power by distinguishing between law and justice and by appealing to commands higher than man-made rules: "The law may be on your side, for I know nothing of these matters, but ah, Gonzalve! there are *other laws* than the laws of man, and in the quiet stillness of your own chamber, *consult the laws of your God!* Would he counsel you to tear your child from the arms of its mother? Would he counsel you to persecute an unfortunate being, whom, in following the path of her duty, you pursue with unrelenting zeal – tell you to consign her, in the spring-time of her life, to rest in an early grave? No, Gonzalve! You never can do this before your Almighty Father! You would never know the semblance of happiness again."

Ellen's assertion of maternal caretaking as a social responsibility also clashed with her insistence on marital individualism as a personal right. Her contradictory claims of self and duty revealed the difficulties she and many other family combatants of the time experienced as they struggled to reconcile a desire for personal happiness with a determination to fulfill domestic duties. Like many others, she tried to resolve the contradictions by separating the roles and thus the duties of spouse and parent. At the same time, in voicing a newly conscious maternal version of herself Ellen found the language of collective duty much more congenial than that of individual rights. It expressed the almost religious zeal with which many women justified their devotion to child rearing, while at the same time countering confident declarations of paternal responsibilities like Gonzalve's. Forced by the intensity of her struggle to articulate a maternal legal consciousness, Ellen found herself trying to add a new dialect to the rights talk coming to dominate American law. Yet by doing so, she also raised the stakes of the bargaining for herself. Such a profound identification with mothering meant that the possibility of losing a child became a calamity to be avoided at all costs. Indeed, out of her anguished attempts to keep Frederick, Ellen would try to make the law recognize those feelings of maternal loss.[38]

The d'Hautevilles' clashing claims to Frederick expressed the conclusions they drew from a rapid study of custody law. Yet their words also suggested that this time their lessons had been a bit more ambiguous than had their instruction in separation and divorce. Both had been told that American custody law, as Gonzalve assumed and Ellen feared, granted fathers a presumptive right to their children. Mothers' custody claims had become a source of contention in the law; but, like Ellen's lay legal ideas of husbandly misconduct and mental cruelty, maternal custody existed as custom not law.[39] Even though mothers often received de facto custody, maternal custody stood in opposition to the public narrative of the law which decreed custody a paternal right. By their very nature, such customs were not legislated or mandated by judges, but existed as expressions of popular moral understanding and everyday legal practices. As such, they surfaced in legal discourse only in conflicts like this one that forced individuals to articulate the unwritten conventions of their times. Equally important, the authority of custom differed significantly from the power of formal legal rules. Though English law had long recognized custom as a legitimate source of legal claims, when in conflict legal rules generally prevailed over customary practices; however, custom could inspire resistance to existing interpretations of legal rules.[40] The d'Hauteville case illustrates this dynamic. In 1839 maternal custody remained an everyday legal practice conducted without formal legal sanction. But it was also a practice that encouraged growing resistance to custody law's paternalism.[41]

Challenges to paternal custody rights by English mothers provided a critical legal backdrop for the d'Hautevilles' dispute. The most significant rulings had been issued by the crusading English jurist Lord Mansfield late in the eighteenth century. Like theirs, the cases involved parental fights over children. The most influential was the 1763 ruling of *Rex v. Delaval*. A father seeking custody of his daughter faced criminal charges for fraudulently apprenticing the girl as a prostitute. Mansfield decided that upon issuing a writ of a habeas corpus, which demanded that person alleged to be illegally restrained be brought before a judge, courts could set an infant free from an improper restraint, but they were not bound to deliver the child to anybody in particular: "This must be left to their discretion, according to the circumstances that shall appear before them." The decision opened the door for challenges to paternal care through expanded judicial discretion. Mansfield widened the opening even more in 1774 when, for the first time, an English court granted custody to a mother rather than an unfit father. In *Blisset*'s case, he allowed a woman custody of her six year old because the father, a bankrupt, had mistreated mother and child. Mansfield argued that "the public right to superintend the education of its citizens necessitated doing what appeared best for the child, notwithstanding the father's natural right."[42]

Critically for Ellen and Gonzalve, in the years since Mansfield sat on the bench habeas corpus had become a common method of resolving the growing number of contested custody cases in America as in England. A parent could seek a writ demanding that his or

her spouse produce their child in a court. Most importantly for the
estranged couple, the procedure allowed for jurisdictional maneuvering. No residency requirements had to be met. Writs could be
issued in any jurisdiction where the child and parent could be
found, or *chose to be found*. After the infant was produced in court,
the judges – without a jury – would determine whether or not the
child was under "improper restraint." This procedure authorized
judicial evaluations of both parental claims rather than merely a
determination of fatherly fitness.[43]

Even so, Mansfield's innovations had proven to be quite compa-
tible with superior paternal custody rights. A series of dramatic decisions by the jurist's reactionary heirs had reinforced paternal rights.
The first decision went against Mrs. De Manneville. She had married a Frenchman, who lived in England. Charging him with cruelty, she fled with her infant shortly after their wedding. De Manneville reacted by breaking into her hiding place and carrying away
the child. Her counsel relied on Mansfield's decisions to argue that
the court had the discretion to consider the circumstances of a case,
and, if the father's conduct warranted it, remove the child from his
custody. Lord Ellenborough disagreed. He narrowed judicial power
by emphasizing that the father is the person "by law" to have custody. Mere impropriety, he decided, was insufficient to grant judges
discretionary power to alter or sustain custody. They should intervene to protect the child only upon evidence of parental "abuse" or
"sacrifice" of the child. Ellenborough ordered the child to remain
with her father, even though "she was an infant at the breast of
the mother."[44]

And but three years before the d'Hautevilles learned the law, an
English court had issued an even more dogmatic endorsement of
paternal custody rights. Adultery convinced the mother in the case
to leave her husband. The Court of King's Bench found her free of
any taint of impropriety as wife or mother, while the evidence revealed that he lived with his mistress in London. Despite these facts,
the judges ordered Mrs. Greenhill to deliver her three daughters,
all under five years of age, to their father. Chief Justice Denman
explained that "there is, in the first place, no doubt that, when a
father has the custody of his children, he is not to be deprived of it
except under particular circumstances." Justice Coleridge added:
"Where the person is too young to have a choice, we must refer to
legal principles to see who is entitled to the custody." Mrs. Greenhill
rejected the ruling and fled England with her daughters. As a result
of these decisions, only the most dissolute conduct by an English
father threatened his custody rights.[45]

American judges often cited these cases, and their message of

presumptive paternal custody rights was clear and welcomed to
Gonzalve. It echoed the law in Vaud. Just as he refused to be cast as
the tyrant in Ellen's tale of marital cruelty, so he rejected a place in
the roll-call of abusive or dissolute fathers who lost their children.
The English stories of lost children and broken-hearted mothers
made Ellen's hopes sag even more. Though she clearly endorsed
the customary practice of giving children to their mothers, she now
learned that the law could, and often did, act differently.[46]

Even so, the d'Hautevilles' English lessons had a mixed message.
Only two years before their instruction in Anglo-American custody
law, an English mother had refused to accept the law's paternalism.
Poet and novelist Caroline Norton's campaign for maternal custody
rights was a very public example of how a mother's determination
to keep her children could turn her into a family law reformer. Norton's marriage had crumbled over her claims of spousal violence
and her husband's failed charges of adultery. Spurred to political
action when she learned that he could still take her two sons and
even bar her from seeing them, Norton turned to Parliament for
relief. After a failed attempt in 1837, a bill drafted by Serjeant Talfourd passed two years later. As Gonzalve and Ellen bargained, Parliament granted mothers the right to petition equity courts for the
custody of children up to the age of seven, and periodic access to
children seven or older. Adultery, however, barred such claims as
did the lack of financial resources to enter courts that would soon
be pilloried by Charles Dickens in *Bleak House* for their excessive
costs and interminable delays. Norton's campaign against the arbitrary power of husbands over their wives and children dramatized
the appeal of maternal custody and the possibility of formally institutionalizing it. Her crusade also broadcast the possibility of legislative solutions to individual family problems.[47]

A final lesson in custody law reinforced the contradictory messages the d'Hautevilles received in their lawyers. Though American
custody repeated the paternalism of the English rules, it did so with
an increasingly distinct American dialect. The American Blackstone,
James Kent, cited Lord Mansfield and a number of American decisions to contend that paternal custody rights could be overruled
when, as he put it, "the nature of the case appears to warrant it."
He also gave the recent English cases far less emphasis. Similarly,
after Supreme Court Justice Joseph Story parroted the paternal biases of English rules, he too stressed the exceptions: "For although,
in general, parents are intrusted with the custody of the persons,
and the education, of their children; yet this is done upon the natural presumption, that the children will be properly taken care of,
and will be brought up with a due education in literature, and

morals, and religion; and that they will be treated with kindness and affection. But, whenever this presumption is removed; wherever (for example) it is found, that a father is guilty of gross ill treatment or cruelty towards his infant children; or that he is in constant habits of drunkenness and blasphemy, or low and gross debauchery; or that he professes atheistical or irreligious principles; or that his domestic associations are such, as tend to the corruption and contamination of his children; in every such case, the Court of Chancery will interfere, and deprive him of the custody of his children, and appoint a suitable person to act as guardian, and to take care of them, and to superintend their education."[48] And during the 1830s some American legislatures, like the British Parliament, had begun codifying custody law and granting mothers the right to apply for custody.

The American deviations from the firm paternalism of English custody law created uncertainty about precisely when fathers could lose their children. Mansfieldian inclinations on the part of American judges left paternal rights superior, but no longer beyond challenge. In courtrooms around the nation, as Mansfield had urged, more and more judges seized the discretionary authority to award custody. Their actions were making "the best interests of the child" a new judicial yardstick for measuring all parental custody claims. The meaning of the new doctrine, however, was far from certain. Instead of a clear guideline as absolute paternal custody rights had been, the best interest of the child doctrine introduced a set of intangibles into custody decisions. Its meaning at any particular time had to be determined by judges who blended their own understanding of children's needs and parental skills with their professional interpretation of legal rules. The legal uncertainty spawned by the doctrine encouraged further challenges, primarily by mothers who entered courtrooms in increasing numbers to fight for their children.[49]

As a result of the legal controversies over child custody, the d'Hautevilles' lawyers had a more difficult time advising the pair about custody law than the law of divorce and separation. Whether or not their situation might constitute an exception to the general paternal biases of custody law was more of an open question than the possibility of Ellen's success in a suit for a separation or divorce. And, given their circumstances, the attorneys had to point out one major doctrinal dent in the armor protecting paternal custody rights. Despite English rulings to the contrary, lawyers in states around the republic had argued with some success that young children ought to stay with their mothers. In a judicial policy that paralleled age demarcations in the recent Lord Talfourd's Act, American

*Tender years"
rule* (margin handwritten note)

judges had begun to decree that during what they called "tender years" remaining in the nurturing care of their mothers best served a child's interests. Joseph Story, for instance, advised judges to examine the fitness of each parent when selecting a custodian, but admitted his own inclination to place a girl of "very tender years" with her mother.[50]

What was coming to be called the "tender-years rule" dictated that infants, children below puberty, and youngsters afflicted with serious ailments be placed in a mother's care unless she was proven unworthy. Through it mothers could gain a presumptive claim to their young children for the first time in Anglo-American custody law. The doctrine translated into legal language two growing judicial commitments: a determination to make nurture the primary element in legal definitions of the best interest of a child; and a conception of women as more legally distinct individuals with a special capacity for moral and religious leadership and child rearing. As such, it illustrated the interaction between external and internal forces reshaping American family law. The new doctrine was a judicial contribution to the larger social construction projects making mothering a singular and noble calling and childhood primarily a time of nurture. It expressed in law an emerging conviction that a natural bond existed between mother and child that was uniquely different from – and superior to – the ties between the father and child. Indeed the tender-years rule became a judicial expression that echoed the defiant words of a contemporary advocate of omnipotent motherhood: "Compared with maternal influence, the combined authority of laws and armies and public sentiment are little things."[51] Constructed on assumptions of fundamental differences between men and women, judges used the doctrine to rearrange the gender balance in custody law while retaining male control by seizing for themselves the discretionary authority to determine the fate of individual children. Yet the tender-years doctrine, like the other contested family law rules, had triggered national debates over just how the law should respond to social change. Consequently, some mothers who relied on the tender-years doctrine had triumphed, others had failed.[52]

For Ellen, though, the nascent tender-years rule provided one of her few positive legal lessons. She understood and endorsed the logic of the new rule. It verbalized her often expressed conviction that Frederick belonged with her, and that Gonzalve was simply not as fit to rear their infant. The doctrine also reinforced her faith in the justness of her cause, and gave legal voice to her new sense of herself as a mother and to the importance of mothering. In fact, Ellen had crafted her own version of the tender-years rule in one of her spurned pleas to Gonzalve. The worried mother had suggested that she would "watch over the early youth of your child, and return it to you with as good, as moral, as religious feelings as you could instill into its mind in Switzerland. I will send it to you when it no longer requires a mother's care, and can profit by an European education."[53] The ploy failed, but the sentiment remained.

Though he had rebuffed his wife's offer, the tender-years rule forced Gonzalve to consider the gender elements of their fight. Like his wife, he began to understand that if they entered a courtroom the adversarial imperatives of American law would compel each of them to defend themselves and attack the other for their actions as husband and wife, mother and father. Yet Gonzalve rejected the tender-years rule as neither logical nor applicable to his situation. He embraced his paternal duties and longed to care for his child. Vitally concerned about being a good father, he considered rearing Frederick one of his major responsibilities. He refused to concede Ellen either a greater ability or duty to care for the boy. Even so, the contested tender-years rule was the first real legal threat he had faced.

Whatever hopes and fears the tender-years rule inspired among the d'Hautevilles, the lawyers had to tell them one last custody story: the 1834 *Briggs* case. The tale of Samuel and Mehitable Thatcher and her father Wales Briggs was doubly relevant to them. It had been decided in Massachusetts, which made it the key precedent in Ellen's home state. Equally important, it had been written by the state's chief justice, Lemuel Shaw, who in just ten years on the bench was becoming one of the most influential jurists in the republic.

The case began when Samuel secured a writ of habeas corpus against his wife and father-in-law demanding the return of his son. Mehitable had fled complaining that her husband's excessive drinking made life with him unbearable. In court, she charged that he was "intemperate, and in other respects an unfit person to take care of the child" or be a responsible husband. Mehitable had found shelter in her father's home, but she did not file for a formal separation.

Shaw supported Samuel. He used the case to denounce judicial encouragement of unauthorized marital separations. Judges did so when they granted custody to wives like Mehitable, who deserted their husbands "without any justifiable cause" and failed to obtain divorces or legal separations. Shaw insisted that courts "ought not to sanction the unauthorized separation" by ordering the child into the mother's possession. In doing so, he raised an issue that Gonzalve believed lay at the heart of his dispute with Ellen: her illegal departure from his home. Her flight challenged his power. Like Shaw, he did not want custody law to endorse domestic rebellion.

Shaw also supported the discretionary right of judges to use the "good of the child" as the "predominant consideration" in awarding custody of "a child of tender years." But the chief justice insisted that this judicial power should only be exercised when a man was proven unfit: "as where [the father] is a vagabond" or "wholly unable to provide for the safety and wants of the child." Only then could a mother claim custody. In most cases, he declared, "the father is by law clearly entitled to the custody of his child." Shaw cautioned that "a clear and strong case of unfitness" must be established against a father, because in the absence of such proof, the court "will feel bound to restore the custody, where the law had placed it, with the father." Samuel Jr. went back to his father.[54]

The *Briggs* case was precisely the legal lesson Gonzalve sought. It suggested that in his wife's very home state, the law stood squarely with him. It also spurred him into action. Gonzalve and his Boston lawyer Peleg Sprague decided to try and end the stalemate by serving a writ of habeas corpus on Ellen and her family so that she would be forced to produce the boy in a courtroom and justify withholding him from his father. They hoped to find her in Massachusetts so that they could invoke the *Briggs* decision. In an attempt to flush her out, Sprague had the Searses and their sons-in-law served on September 28, 1839. When room-to-room searches by the county sheriff failed to locate Ellen and Frederick, the petitions had been quashed and a hearing before Chief Justice Shaw canceled. But convinced that custody law supported his claims, Gonzalve remained ready to haul his wife into court whenever he could find her. Frustrated once again, he returned to New York City.[55]

Ellen responded to her custody lessons quite differently. After Gonzalve rejected her bargaining pleas and turned to the Massachusetts courts, Ellen stayed in hiding. She found refuge with relatives in New Hampshire. Ellen and her family were now convinced that the courtroom must be avoided. Her father explained just how fearful of a trial the Searses had become in a letter to Lewis Cass. Sprague had arranged for the American minister to France to give a deposition for a possible Massachusetts trial. David wanted to clarify his daughter's position in case Cass had to testify again. After a detailed defense of Ellen's actions, he shared his fear that Gonzalve would eventually force them all into a courtroom. Explaining that his Swiss son-in-law had spurned every attempt at compromise, David complained bitterly that "nothing would satisfy Monsieur d'Hauteville but law, and the notoriety of a public trial. The only question our Courts can decide, is, – to whom shall be given the custody of the child? He seems sure of success, and thinks that the seizure of the child will compel the mother to follow him." David also acknowledged that he too had learned some legal lessons. Reporting that Gonzalve's firm defense of his legal rights stemmed from a conviction that he was "all in the right, and us, all in the wrong," David admitted that his own legal threats had backfired and that his understanding of the law had been flawed. Now he and his daughter fought to avoid the courtroom.[56]

But the law and Gonzalve's tactics trapped Ellen. His vow never to give up the search haunted her. She could not stay in hiding forever nor could she seek refuge in her parent's home. Where was she to go? What was she to do?

When it became apparent that Gonzalve had broken off the negotiations, Ellen's frantic parents rushed to New York to resuscitate the talks. Their efforts went for naught. Hoping her presence would spur a settlement, they urged her to join them. However, since the stalled negotiations increased the chances of a courtroom fight, the Searses first hired local lawyers. David arranged for Boston lawyer William Howard Gardiner to coordinate his daughter's now farflung legal team. A graduate of Harvard College and former student at Harvard Law School, Gardiner selected John McKeon as Ellen's chief New York counsel. McKeon, a Columbia University graduate who had practiced law since 1828, had recently completed his second stint in the United States Congress after a term in the state assembly. Though a self-styled Jeffersonian Democrat, McKeon's lawyerly skills had impressed even the Whiggish Sears. McKeon added prominent attorney James Gerard to his team of lawyers.[57] In the meantime, Gonzalve continued to rely on Henry De Rham.

Ellen left her New Hampshire hiding place, and arrived in New York City with Frederick in October 1839. Having eluded Gonzalve's lawyers in Massachusetts, Ellen lived openly in Manhattan. She did so in part in a desperate attempt to restart the negotiations, but also because of the security she received from a case strikingly similar to hers that had erupted in the New York courts and spilled out into the newspapers.

Indeed the bitter battle between Eliza and John Barry became yet another legal lesson for both d'Hautevilles. They must have been startled by the similarities of the two conflicts. Both arose out of the ashes of crumbled marriages and centered on the right of a wife to live apart from her foreign-born husband and retain the custody of her child. And when forced into legal arenas, Eliza and John, like Ellen and Gonzalve, had experienced the troubling translation of their most heartfelt convictions into the phrases and rules of the law. These striking similarities would link the two at the time and over time. The two cases would ultimately influence each other and the law. In the fall of 1839, though, the Barry case became a telling demonstration for the d'Hautevilles of the vagaries of custody law.

John, an English immigrant resident in Nova Scotia and a widower with four children, had married Eliza, daughter of a prominent New York labor leader and insurance entrepreneur Thomas Mercein in 1835. Their courtship had been protracted because of Eliza's demand to live near the Merceins in New York. In an informal antenuptial agreement, John had agreed to move there within a year after their wedding. Later it turned out that he had assumed that once the pair spent some time with her family, he could move on and expect his wife to follow. Conversely, Eliza presumed that they had agreed to reside in New York permanently. In anguished prenuptial letters the couple tried to reach a compromise. John wanted to marry Eliza but also retain his patriarchal rights; Eliza wanted to marry John but retain her place in the Mercein household. Each believed that their goals had been achieved when they wed.

Very soon, however, the Barrys' marriage began to fracture much like the d'Hautevilles'. Fights broke out over John's dogmatic demands for wifely obedience and Eliza's equally insistent demands that her needs be accommodated. In May of 1836, the pair returned to New York. With capital from her father, John opened a business but the Panic of 1837 drove him into bankruptcy. Meanwhile Eliza had given birth to a son and a daughter. In the spring of 1838, while Ellen and Gonzalve battled in Paris, John took the four children from his previous marriage and returned to Nova Scotia to start a new business. He came back for Eliza and for more funds from her father. She refused to leave or endorse his plea for additional capital. On June 7, 1838, the Barrys and Thomas Mercein, signed a "separation agreement," which declared that neither wished a final separation but in the event one occurred John would relinquish his parental rights to their infant daughter Mary yet retain his rights to their four-year-old son Mercein. John returned to Nova Scotia hoping his wife would soon follow. When Eliza did not come, John returned to retrieve his son. He would later explain that he hoped to use the son as bait to force Eliza's return. Neither she nor her father challenged his actions. But, when this ploy failed, he came back to claim Mary. This time Eliza and Thomas Mercein resisted.

In the spring and summer of 1839, as Ellen and Gonzalve's negotiations reached an impasse and the pair began their legal educations, John turned to the courts. In May he obtained a writ of habeas corpus from the Recorder of the City of New York to recover custody of his daughter. Both Thomas and Eliza were served. They responded by hiring Gerard, now also Ellen's lawyer, as their counsel. Admired for being "[i]ndefatigable in the preparation of his cases, gifted with intuitive knowledge of human nature, and knowing when to stop in addressing a jury," Gerard had a reputation as a very effective trial lawyer.[58]

Following Gerard's advice, Thomas had replied to the writ by filing the voluntary separation agreement and Eliza with an affidavit charging John with being a man "of irascible temper, of domineering and vindictive spirit, [and] of intemperate habits" as well as having been "unfeeling, harsh, tyrannical, and cruel." The recorder ordered Mary into Eliza's custody. In July, John obtained another writ, this time from the chancery court. In it he sought Eliza as well as Mary. Thomas replied with a special return arguing that he did not hold his daughter against her will and that his granddaughter was of "delicate and sickly habit" requiring the special care of her mother. Though he dismissed the separation agreement as void, Chancellor Walworth found that "no good reason now exists for the taking of the said infant child from its said mother." And Walworth rejected the very idea that Eliza herself could be forced to return to John. Instead she was left "only responsible to her own conscience and to her God, for such a violation of her conjugal duties."

Even though Walworth concluded that Eliza had not established a legal right to a separation, he decided that enough "had occurred to justify the wife, both legally and morally, in refusing for the present to place herself under his entire control, in a land of strangers." In what the d'Hautevilles must have recognized as a telling example of the uncertainties of the judicial process and interpretive differences sanctioned by American federalism, the New York chancellor endorsed the very logic that Chief Justice Shaw had denounced in the *Briggs* case. Walworth condoned Eliza's flight and custody of Mary: "If [her husband's] misconduct toward the partner of his bed and his bosom has furnished her with good cause for seeking again the protection of the paternal roof, no law, either human or divine, required me to remove the infant from her arms, or from the same friendly shelter." Finding Eliza equitably justified in refusing to accompany John to Nova Scotia and thus not acting immorally or illegally, the chancellor wielded the tender-years rule to buttress his decision. He argued that the welfare of the child must govern cases like this one because they involved only the temporary issues of custody not permanent guardianship. A mother, he held, "all other things being equal, is the most proper person to be entrusted with such a charge in relation to an infant of this tender age. And where no sufficient reasons exist for depriving her of the care and nurture of her child, it would not be a proper exercise of discretion in any court to violate the law of nature in this respect."[59]

John learned his judicial lesson and henceforth only sought to recover his daughter. In October, just as Ellen and Frederick arrived in New York, he obtained a third writ but once again met defeat. Judge Inglis of the New York City Court of Common Pleas found no illegal restraint and dismissed the application. John then filed an appeal to the New York Supreme Court. Angered by Walworth's opinion, he seized his pen to begin writing what would ultimately be a sixty-five-page public defense of his character and his rights. His polemic defended patriarchal power by attacking the growing judicial authority over domestic relations. It found a ready market among men like Gonzalve, who were just as determined as John to protect the masculine dominance of the family.[60] After publishing his defiant treatise, John Barry continued to immerse himself in the law of child custody and champion paternal rights as his appeal wound its way through the courts. Soon the d'Hautevilles' fight would enter his field of study just as his had entered theirs. At the same time, Ellen and Gonzalve had to measure their conduct and their tactics against the Barrys'. The intricate and very public Barry case reinforced their sense of the law's hold on them. From it they learned a bit more of what it would mean to cease bargaining in the law's shadow and enter the bright light of the courtroom. It also changed their tactics.

While Eliza's victories helped make New York a safer place for Ellen, John's thus-far futile attempts to gain custody of Mary forced Gonzalve and his lawyers to abandon, at least temporarily, their strategy of serving Ellen with a writ of habeas corpus wherever they found her. Instead they postponed initiating a New York court contest until a final ruling on John's claims was handed down. But Gonzalve still refused to negotiate, though he did agree to an arrangement that allowed him to see Frederick for the first time.

As the impasse continued, the Barry case forced Ellen to change her legal strategy as well. Despite Eliza's courtroom successes, Ellen's legal lessons made her worry whether another judge would assess her reasons for fleeing and her maternal care of Frederick as favorably as Walworth had Eliza's. And John's ability to obtain repeated hearings for his claims, the uncertain outcome of his appeal, and his sheer persistence made Ellen and her counsel wonder just how long New York would be a maternal haven. Rather than pleading for further negotiations or waiting for a writ to be served, Ellen and her lawyers decided to tilt the legal balance of power in her favor by following Caroline Norton's lead and seeking legislative relief. David, who kept his vow to use all means at his disposal, bankrolled lobbyists to push a bill through the legislature giving mothers married to foreign nationals greater custody rights. His actions were hardly unusual. He relied upon the longstanding Anglo-American practice of private sponsorship of particularlistic legislation. Such bills constituted much of the business of state legislatures.[61] Gonzalve, however, attacked both the process and substance of David's bills. He would later charge that "[u]tterly distrustful of the laws of Massachusetts" and "under the pretext of patriotic solicitude for the public welfare," a bill was introduced that would have divested foreign fathers of their custody rights. He claimed that "without notice to him legislative interposition was clandestinely invoked . . . to divest his most sacred rights, and to meet a special case, for which existing laws were supposed to be inadequate."[62] Success came in March 1840 with the passage of "An Act for the Protection of Minors."

But it was only a momentary victory. Like so many others in the months ahead, Governor William Seward was drawn into the maelstrom of the d'Hauteville fight. He vetoed the bill. Forced to explain why, the Whig politician, again like the rest of the growing cast of characters in the dispute, tackled the intricate issues of law, family, and the state embedded in the case. In a detailed veto message to the state senate, Seward delivered an impassioned defense of existing custody laws and paternal control of the home. Each of his complaints against the bill echoed Gonzalve's charges against Ellen. The veto demonstrated anew the massive legal obstacles she faced and how controversial her claims would be if aired in public.

Like Gonzalve and John Barry, the governor considered fathers' rights to their children a necessary element of a universal patriarchy. Such power could only be forfeited by a father's "neglect or violation of his conjugal duties, or by conduct which renders him an incompetent person to support or educate his child." Only then could a mother claim and receive custody. However, he argued, the vetoed bill had exceeded the bounds of legal and social propriety by denying alien fathers the right to take their children to their homeland without maternal consent. Seward rejected the logic and the xenophobia of the bill. As Shaw had in the *Briggs* case, the governor also faulted the act for undermining marriage by rewarding fleeing women with their children. Even so, Seward recognized that the law could victimize women. As he well knew, New York was already a site for feminist activity and the legislature the chosen forum for reform. A married women's property rights bill had been introduced four years before, and Seward would shortly sign an act that allowed wives to own life insurance on their husbands and receive benefits free of creditors' claims.[63] However, he argued that the vetoed bill did not offer wives any legitimate protections. Instead it applied only to the special circumstance when a wife refused to follow her alien husband. Under it, he complained, "a wife may unreasonably or capriciously refuse to abide the fortunes of a faithful husband in the country to which he belongs, and where his interests and duty may require him to reside," and yet still receive custody of her child thanks to a chancery court.

Seward, already engaged in a protracted campaign to limit the power of chancellors, added this provision of the bill to his Dickensonian charges that delay, high costs, and unwieldy procedures bogged down American chancery courts just like those in England.[64] Like John Barry, he feared statutory language authorizing judicial action only when "the welfare of the child will be promoted" did not sufficiently protect "the father in his just and natural rights." Child welfare was simply too ambiguous a concept. Seward challenged the very legitimacy of such judicial interventions into families. "I cannot believe," he argued in defense of male family rights, "that the Chancellor would be a more competent judge of what would promote a child's welfare than its virtuous and unoffending parent, even though the parent be a foreigner." Seward extended his attack on the courts by asking rhetorically: "Who would not revolt at the idea that the Chancellor should have the power to enter the family circles of our citizens, and, without convicting the parent of neglect or omission of duty, overrule parental authority and separate helpless children from unoffending parents upon the arbitrary pretext of promoting the children's welfare?" The governor closed his veto message by expressing surprise that even though the bill passed both houses with large majorities, he had been unable to find "any report, petition, or other paper, which might show a necessity for the passage of the law, or explain the views of the Legislature on the subject."[65]

The silent legislative record indicates just how well Ellen's lawyers covered their tracks. Not surprisingly, the *New York Sun* even reported that the vetoed bill was "assumed to have arisen out of the celebrated Barry Case."[66] But Gonzalve would later claim that Seward could find no records because the Searses had used their influence to ram the act through both houses of the state legislature. Even so, Seward's veto was yet another welcomed message for the Swiss father about the power of paternalism. Though Gonzalve still shunned the New York courts, at least until he learned whether John Barry's custody rights would be vindicated, he took heart from Seward's dramatic public testament to male solidarity. Now determined to see his cause as the rightful defense of male domestic governance, he read the words of Seward and Barry as favorable omens of his own legal fate.

Ellen denied acting clandestinely and justified her actions as a necessary response to her legal education. After acquiring "a general knowledge . . . in consequence of the painful circumstances of this and other cases, which, besides occasioning the deepest domestic affliction, threatened the expatriation of native citizens of the United States, whose prospects and means of future usefulness to our country would be defeated by their exile," she had learned that "many persons were desirous that a public act of legislation should take place, for the ascertainment of the law, which on this subject was not definitively settled." Ellen clearly began to feel a kinship with other women waging individual challenges to male power and the organized efforts by other women who championed the collective rights of all wives. Despite Seward's veto and Gonzalve's charges, she defended her right to petition the legislature as the legitimate act of an American citizen. Voicing her growing legal consciousness, she lodged a "respectful protest against any attempt to abridge or interfere with the unrestrained liberty of any citizen of the United States, to promote such acts of legislation as may be conducive to the public interest of his fellow-citizens at large, or to the private interests of those who are nearest and dearest to him." Nor did the veto deter her from other attempts at legislative redress. But her agents failed in New Jersey and Pennsylvania; and McKeon and his associates could not convince Seward to accept a modified bill.[67]

Legislative failure reinforced the message of the *Barry* case for both d'Hautevilles: Ellen's challenge to paternal rights was not an isolated protest, nor was Gonzalve's defense. On the contrary, as they experienced the ongoing transformation of their problems from a domestic quarrel into a domestic relations case, the d'Hautevilles were being drawn into a trans-Atlantic debate over family governance. The Barry case and the failed legislation added yet another set of legal lessons for the d'Hauteville's to master as they bargained in the shadow of the law. Ellen and Gonzalve, of course, reacted quite differently to their growing legal knowledge. Not only did legal learning rearrange their bargaining positions, it forced each spouse to accept roles they would henceforth play throughout their legal contest. Gonzalve became a defender of domestic traditionalism; Ellen became an agitator for family change.

The d'Hautevilles' new roles also suggest a final lesson to be learned from their experiences bargaining in the shadow of the law. The pair experienced the law's hegemonic power to order their dispute in a way that focused on the meaning of particular rules and procedures rather than on the legitimacy of the law itself. Such legal experiences, though, did not produce uniform beliefs. On the contrary, like others drawn into the law's shadows, Ellen and Gonzalve developed their own legal convictions and conclusions. Gonzalve's faith in the dominant family beliefs of his age led him to defend legal traditionalism, while Ellen's contradictory consciousness led her to challenge that same orthodoxy. At the same time, the d'Hautevilles' bargaining experiences reveal a complementary point about the clashes produced by such conflicting legal ideologies. Ellen and Gonzalve reacted to their legal lessons by taking active steps to control their fate. As they did, they were influenced by the press of legal rules as well as by forces external to the law such as gender values and religious convictions. The mixture of legal ordering, individual agency, and social forces visible in the d'Hautevilles' bargaining provides a distinct example of the specific sources of legal conflict.[68]

In the end, bargaining in the law's shadow led the d'Hautevilles to the courtroom. The failed legislation had been Ellen's last desperate attempt to avoid a trial. Like her doomed attempts to use religion, masculine responsibility, and pleas for mercy to deter Gonzalve, legislative defeat demonstrated just how thoroughly the law now dominated her life. As she lamented in a letter to her sister Anna late in 1839, "There is, I fear, no hope of compromise, although it certainly appears strange that nothing of any sort has as yet taken place. Though my mind is fully decided, that as everything has been refused, the law must now decide between us, yet I cannot tell you the abhorrence I feel about such a course, – to be made the subject of court reports, and newspaper writers, makes my heart sick, but what can I do?"[69] From her legal lessons, she understood that Gonzalve's reliance on the law had left her but one choice: where to take her stand? Ellen's decision came in the spring of 1840. She and Frederick settled in Philadelphia.

3

Out of the Shadow

Nancy Shippen Livingston would have been shocked that Ellen decided to fight for Frederick in Philadelphia. In the 1780s she had waged an unsuccessful battle there for the custody of her daughter. Her fight too had followed a disastrous marriage. In 1781 the Philadelphia belle entered a loveless union with wealthy New Yorker Henry Beekman Livingston arranged by her socially conscious father. Quickly her husband revealed himself to be a scoundrel and she left him less than a year after their wedding but not before the birth of a daughter, Margaret. Seeking refuge with her parents in Philadelphia, Nancy like Ellen years later searched for a way to discard her husband but keep her child. And, again like Ellen, she discovered the law's paternal priorities. Lawyers advised her that Henry could claim the child by asserting his custody rights with a writ of habeas corpus. Even if she could somehow obtain a divorce, he would likely get Margaret.

The most hopeful assistance came from Nancy's uncle, Philadelphia lawyer Arthur Lee. He assured his niece that "nothing but the power of the Law should tear her from you, & that upon all circumstances being stated the Law will not destroy you." Barred from direct legal action, Lee urged Nancy to seek legal aid by lobbying the wives of the state supreme court justices: "Try to interest the Ladies . . . It is the cause of humanity – & in that cause the female voice is irresistible." Despite her uncle's confident declaration that "none but a Butcher of a Judge, who has never had, or wish'd to have a parent's feelings will venture to decide against humanity and you," all her efforts at backdoor legal redress came to naught. She had to work out a private arrangement granting her limited visitation rights with Margaret, who stayed with Livingston's family.[1]

Just fifty years later, Ellen decided to take her stand in the very city that had failed Nancy. Clearly something had changed in Philadelphia. Ellen and then Gonzalve learned what it was. As they did, the d'Hautevilles experienced yet another encounter with the law. This time, they discovered the tactical realities of American federalism.

67

The division of power between the states and the national government under the federal constitution stymied the growth of a uniform national law. Statutes and common law could vary from region to region, even state to state. In no subject was that more true than in domestic relations. Though core principles like coverture governed family laws throughout the republic, the states jealously guarded their authority over the family. Legislators and judges used their primary jurisdiction over American families to construct particular domestic relations policies. These ranged from the complete denial of family rights to slaves in the South to the adoption of relatively easy grounds for divorce in states like Indiana.[2] The resulting maze of common and contradictory rules frustrated advocates of legal uniformity, while it opened up tactical opportunities for individual litigants and their lawyers.

Ellen was quite willing to take advantage of the vagaries of American federalism. While she waited in New York fearing that any day Gonzalve would serve her with a writ of habeas corpus and haul her into court, her lawyers frantically surveyed state custody laws searching for a better place to wage her fight for Frederick. Their hunt led them to Pennsylvania. It also led the d'Hautevilles into a new legal dependency. The failure of their private bargaining meant that they now must rely even more on attorneys. Philadelphia lawyers and judges would take Ellen and Gonzalve out of the law's shadows and into the bright lights of its most important forum, the courtroom. The process through which the pair turned their case over to Philadelphia lawyers vividly illustrates the importance of the legal maneuvering that precedes a courtroom confrontation. Those same maneuvers also reveal critical components of the setting in which the most important legal event of the d'Hauteville story would take place.

Forum Shopping

The d'Hautevilles' journey to Philadelphia began when Ellen's lawyers searched for a maternal haven. As they studied American family laws, Boston lawyer William Gardiner and his colleagues were struck by what they found in Pennsylvania. As in Massachusetts and New York, divorce was simply not an inviting option for a wife in Ellen's situation there either. Her claims of mental cruelty would have been difficult to sustain under the state's divorce code.[3] But in a habeas corpus hearing over Frederick's custody, chances for a victory seemed more promising in Pennsylvania than in any other American jurisdiction. By the winter of 1840 when Ellen had to decide where to go, her lawyers had singled out Pennsylvania as the best place for her to stand and fight Gonzalve for Frederick.

Ellen's lawyers had done their work well. Amidst contests over married women's legal rights in courtrooms around the nation, Pennsylvania judges and litigants had built the most secure place for maternal claims within the dominant paternal custody regime. They had done so with the legal tools of maternalism, child welfare, and judicial discretion. Judges oversaw the construction project. They had used their interpretation of the "best interest of the child" doctrine to shift the terms of debate in custody law from paramount paternal rights to child welfare. Most critically for Ellen and Gonzalve, those same judges had taken the lead in developing and defining the "tender-years rule." The presumption that infants and other children in need required maternal care and thus custody remained the fugitive wife's best legal hope for keeping Frederick. Nevertheless, Ellen's lawyers could make no ironclad predictions about the outcome of a courtroom battle between the d'Hautevilles. The uncertainties of a trial remained too great. Any single verdict would depend on the collision of the particular circumstances of a case with the relevant general legal rules.

Pennsylvania's leading custody case offered a telling example of that legal reality. The tortuous tale of Pennsylvanians Joseph and Barbara Lee began in 1813 when Joseph petitioned for the custody of his children after obtaining a divorce from his adulterous wife. He argued that Barbara's misdeeds and subsequent marriage to her paramour Addicks in violation of a state ban on such unions disqualified her from rearing the couple's seven- and ten-year-old daughters. Chief Justice William Tilghman, citing Lord Mansfield's *Delaval* decision to legitimize his assumption of discretion in the case, expressed the court's "disapprobation of the mother's conduct." But, like Ellen and many others who experienced or evaluated troubled marriages, he also distinguished between the roles of wife and mother. Tilghman noted that Barbara's care of the two girls had been faultless. "[O]ur anxiety is principally directed to the children," he explained. "It appears to us, that considering their tender years, they stand in need of the kind of assistance which can be afforded by none so well as a mother." Consequently, "[i]t is on their account . . . that exercising the discretion with which the law has invested us, we think it best not to take them from her."[4]

The court monitored the situation, however, and three years later in a second petition for his daughters Joseph triumphed. Tilghman again relied on the court's determination of the girl's interests, but this time he was much less inclined to segregate Barbara's spousal conduct from her parental duties. He now ruled that the girls' maturity rendered them less dependent on maternal nurture. Once more invoking his power to place children, the judge decreed that two potential wives should no longer be reared by a mother who had so flagrantly flaunted her marital vows. "At present they may not reflect upon it," he sagely proclaimed, "but soon they will, and when they inquire why it was that they were separated from their mother, they will be taught, as far as our opinion can teach them, that in good fortune and bad, in sickness or health, in happiness or misery, the marriage contract, unless dissolved by the law of the country, is sacred and inviolable."[5]

The enigmatic *Addicks* cases had become the legal touchstone for all custody trials in Pennsylvania. Like other custody cases that relied on best interest of the child doctrine, it helped turn custody hearings into adversarial contests about the meaning of parental fitness and child welfare and the proper exercise of judicial discretion. Unlike decisions in most other jurisdictions, though, it did so in a manner particularly helpful to Ellen's cause. Unlike Massachusetts Chief Justice Lemuel Shaw in the *Briggs* decision, his Pennsylvania counterpart Tilghman refused to grant paternal custody its traditional deference. He accepted child welfare and a distinction between spousal and parental roles as legitimate curbs on male authority. He also regarded maternal care critical to the upbringing of the young and thus qualified the use of marital fault in awarding custody. In this way, Tilghman and his fellow Pennsylvania justices struck a different balance between maternal and paternal custody claims than had the Shaw court in Massachusetts.

The contrasting priorities of the *Briggs* and *Addicks* decisions not only had obvious implications for the d'Hautevilles' tactical choices, they spotlight the jurisdictional pluralism produced by American federalism. However, determining the sources of jurisdictional differences like these is a perplexing problem. It raises in a different context questions about the relationship between changes external to the legal system and changes occurring within the system that are critical to understanding the story of the d'Hauteville case.

Some sources of Pennsylvania's maternalist biases do seem apparent. For example, despite Nancy Shippen Livingston's experiences, Philadelphia with its heritage of Quaker egalitarianism had been a site for women's rights agitation since the Revolution. Tom Paine had condemned discrimination against women in the *Pennsylvania Magazine* of 1775 and in 1787. Dr. Benjamin Rush had been one of the nation's first advocates of equal education for women. And in the 1790s the city had given birth to the republic's first periodical devoted to women, *The Lady's Magazine and Repository of Entertaining Knowledge*. Local novelist and renegade lawyer Charles Brockton

Brown had written an enthusiastic review of one of the most important Anglo-American women's rights tracts, Mary Wollstonecraft's *Vindication of the Rights of Women,* for the journal and devoted his first book, *Alcuin* (1789), to the theme of women's rights. The tradition had continued into the d'Hautevilles' time with the recent founding of *Godey's Lady Book,* which had quickly become the nation's leading women's journal.

Pennsylvania women had also taken direct action. Most importantly for the d'Hauteville case, they had persistently sought greater legal rights. As a result, statutory and common law revisions had expanded the powers of married and single women to act in the market and in their families. After the Revolution divorce had been "restructured as part of the state's republican reforms and tied to new beliefs about marriage and the family, even while the law maintained its patriarchal standards."[6] Since the switch from legislative to judicial divorce, custom and practice made the courts increasingly receptive to wives' claims against their husbands. Significantly more women than men received judicial decrees terminating their unions. Not surprisingly, in 1785 Pennsylvania had been the first state in the nation to grant women the right to charge cruelty as a ground for divorce. And, as in New York and a few other states, campaigns were under way demanding sweeping changes in married women's property rights.

In other words, gender power was being renegotiated in Pennsylvania during these years. The postrevolutionary construction of ever more tightly compartmentalized gender spheres not only undergirded the changes in married women's property rights and divorce, it also had other legal consequences. Since independence, women's presence in the state's courtrooms had declined. The new belief in feminine modesty and innocence combined with revised notions of sexuality deemphasizing women's carnal instincts while accentuating men's to alter patterns of criminal law enforcement. Women were less and less likely than in colonial days to be charged with criminal conduct and hauled into criminal courts. Indictments for fornication, bigamy, and adultery declined most notably. But women did not disappear from the courtroom. Instead their presence was tied more clearly to the era's assumption of gender spheres. Going to court to divorce an adulterous or abusive husband or to fight for children conformed to the new gender prescriptions and thus secured social as well as legal validation. In short, the legal status of women had been changing in Pennsylvania for decades. Even though no single development had placed the state in the forefront of the growing women's rights movement, the new role of maternalism in child custody represented both a product of

and contribution to the ongoing creation of a new and more autonomous legal place for married women. However, similar developments had occurred in other states, most notably New York and
Massachusetts. Thus women's rights was a contributing but hardly
a singular source of Pennsylvania's jurisidictional distinctiveness.[7]

Pennsylvania's Quaker legacy of family egalitarianism, which had
encouraged a longstanding concern with child rearing in the state,
was a second basic source of the state's domestic relations rules.
Americanized advice books on child raising had been published in
Philadelphia since the 1780s. Rush had promoted universal school-
ing for the city's children as well as women's education. By the 1830s
schools were available for many students and other child saving institutions had been created, most notably the Philadelphia House of
Refuge founded to care for poor, delinquent, and orphaned young
people. Such attention to the young, and the new concepts of child
development that informed them, had compelled Philadelphians
like growing numbers of other Americans to consider children more
and more as distinctive individuals with their own particular needs
and interests. A new conception of child welfare naturally flowed
from such intellectual and social currents. It encouraged the replacement of a traditional definition of child welfare in terms of
property accumulation and protection with one that emphasized
proper nurture. Though increasingly such social convictions were
shared around the nation, Pennsylvania does seem to have been a
leader in developing new ideas about children's place in the republic.[8]

Nevertheless, determining how developments like changing gender relations and revised conceptions of children had been translated into jurisdictionally distinctive custody rules emphasizing
maternal nurture and child welfare remains a puzzle. Most explanations of American jurisdictional pluralism focus on regional
differences. Such legal variations in the republic could be explained
to a certain degree by noting geographic peculiarities like the New
England watershed and its impact on water law or cultural distinctions such as the South's continued embrace of slavery and its translation into apartheid rules.[9] But differences between adjoining
states like New York and Pennsylvania, or even reasonably close
ones like Pennsylvania and Massachusetts, have been subjected to
much less analysis. Beyond the unpredictable impact of particular
individuals such as Massachusetts Chief Justice Lemuel Shaw with
his uncommon ability to phrase solutions to common legal problems
in appealing ways, or specific events such as the constitutional con-
volutions over voting rights that led to the Dorr War in Rhode Is-

land, the sources of state-bound legal cultures are very difficult to discover.

A few attempts to understand Pennsylvania's distinctive legal culture are both revealing and enigmatic. They do, however, suggest something about the state where Ellen and Gonzalve decided to wage their custody battle. At the end of the nineteenth century, for instance, amateur historian Sydney George Fisher tried to explain what he considered Pennsylvania's particular commitment to egalitarianism. The descendant of a leading Quaker family, he stressed his ancestors' intense interest in education, which had led them to promote "the education of women, and also women's rights, which is the natural outgrowth of the liberty always allowed by them to women in preaching and in the conduct of church affairs." Fisher cited as well the pluralistic population of the state, its Quaker, Pennsylvania German, Moravian, Scotch-Irish, and Welsh immigrants, as a source of its uniqueness. Demographic pluralism, he argued, nurtured the "freedom from dogma" that bore fruit in a persistent liberalism in law and public policy. "It was not merely the fertility of the soil and the mildness of the climate," he asserted while citing the interest Pennsylvania had attracted among European intellectuals like Voltaire, "but the liberal laws and customs which, in their opinion, had attracted settlers and forced on development."[10] A more pointed attempt to explain the state's legal culture by E. Digby Baltzell is particularly relevant to the d'Hauteville case. In trying to account for basic differences between what he labeled "Puritan Boston" and "Quaker Philadelphia," Baltzell contrasted Boston's "*rights* tradition of egalitarian individualism" with Philadelphia's "*duties* tradition of hierarchical communalism." Though variations on a common American legal theme, his assertion of a greater concern with individual rights in Boston and an equally significant emphasis on duty in Philadelphia corresponds to a degree with the way decisions like *Briggs* and *Addicks* interpreted clashing paternal and maternal custody claims. Also relevant here, Baltzell used an intriguing cliche as part of his comparison: "Philadelphia is the city of *firsts*, Boston of *bests*, and New York of *latests*."[11] Finally, a similar though quite differently focused comparison had been published by Viennese immigrant Francis Grund in 1840: The "society of Philadelphia is, on the whole, better than that of Boston or New York. There is less vulgar aristocracy than in other Northern cities. Not that I mean to say that there are not people to be found in Boston and New York that could rival the Philadelphians in point of 'gentility;' but in the good 'city of brotherly love' there is, probably owing to a seasonal admixture of a large number of European, and especially French families, a higher tone, greater elegance, and, in every respect, more *agremens*. The New Englanders are an arguing people, and annoy you, even in society, with mathematical and political demonstrations. The Philadelphians have more taste, and have the best cooks in the United States."[12]

Taken together, these various strands of analysis combine to suggest a tentative explanation for Pennsylvania's distinctive domestic relations rules. The tendency to grant greater authority to mothers paralleled a pattern of support for relatively activist humanitarian policies, especially those involved with children. It was that very reputation for humanitarianism that brought Alexis de Tocqueville to Philadelphia on his American tour.[13] In addition, unlike Massachusetts and New York in particular, Democrats dominated Pennsylvania politics. Attacks on paternal custody rights echoed their challenges to other vested interests. At the same time, the Democrat-controlled state courts, especially the Supreme Court, were characterized by an "attitude of judicial self-abnegation" that tended to produce judicial deference to humanitarian initiatives sanctioned by the legislature.[14] Indeed an 1838 state constitutional convention abolished lifetime judicial appointments and instituted terms of office. Pennsylvania's most prominent antebellum jurist, John Bannister Gibson, even refuted Chief Justice John Marshall's seminal opinion in *Marbury v. Madison* legitimizing judicial review.[15]

One example of these converging forces is a particularly relevant instance of state support for an expansive conception of the public duty to children. In 1838 the state chartered Philadelphia House of Refuge faced its greatest judicial test. A father challenged the right of the state to commit his daughter to the asylum. In *Ex Parte Crouse*, the state supreme court responded with the era's most forceful endorsement of state authority over children. Upholding the right of public officials to take a child out of its home on grounds of parental failure, the justices declared: "May not the natural parents, when unequal to the task of education, or unworthy of it, be superseded by the *parens patriae,* or common guardian of the community?" Explaining the assertion, they added: "The right of parental control is a natural, but not an unalienable one. It is not excepted by the Declaration of Rights out of the subject of ordinary legislative power, which, if wantonly or inconveniently used, would soon be constitutionally restricted, but the competency of which the government is constituted, cannot be doubted."[16] Just such a mix of concern for child welfare and skepticism of vested interests like paternal authority seems to have produced Pennsylvania's distinctive legal culture and domestic relation decisions like the *Addicks* rulings. As a result, Pennsylvania was the most attractive state in the union for a mother forced to enter a courtroom and fight for her child.

Thanks to habeas corpus procedures all Ellen had to do was move into Pennsylvania to place her claim to Frederick under the jurisdiction of the state. Though her decision to fight for Frederick in Philadelphia represented a strategic choice that revealed the weakness of her custody rights, Ellen had little choice once she decided to risk the uncertainties of a trial rather than accept Gonzalve's demands. And, unlike Nancy Shippen Livingston, she could enter the courtroom through the front door. So Ellen moved to Philadelphia and waited for Gonzalve.

Ellen's legal tactics had frustrated and then defeated Gonzalve's bargaining strategy. His threats had failed to force Ellen's surrender, and now, as he too learned about Pennsylvania's custody law, he feared Ellen had taken away his tactical advantage as well. Angered by her flight to Philadelphia, Gonzalve would later turn Ellen's legal maneuver into a charge against her. He claimed that his wife's sole reason for coming to Philadelphia was that "after a careful scrutiny of statutes and decisions, she was advised and counselled to make Pennsylvania her asylum, not so much, as is now averred, for quiet and retirement, as for security from the enforcement of the right of an injured husband and father." Gonzalve and his lawyers dismissed as rhetorical camouflage Ellen's later claim that she had come to Philadelphia because doctors advised her that residence in the city would be beneficial for her health and that of Frederick. The real reason for her move was that "the laws of Pennsylvania were more favourable to maternal rights than those of Massachusetts, which were, in her own language, on the basis of the common law, or, in the language of another member of her family . . . because the government of Massachusetts was not so easy as that of the state whither she fled."[17] Despite such fulminations, Gonzalve had no choice but to follow Ellen to Philadelphia.

Philadelphia Lawyers

A new jurisdiction not only meant different laws, it also meant that the d'Hautevilles had to hire new lawyers. Facing the certainty of a trial, each spouse needed attorneys well versed in local law and well skilled in courtroom combat. The fate of their clashing causes would now be largely determined by how well these new lawyers translated the domestic dispute between Ellen and Gonzalve's into two sets of litigating claims and strategies. In many ways, the d'Hauteville case would henceforth be the lawyers' as much as it was the estranged couples'. The skills, interests, and even prejudices of the attorneys would be as important as those of the litigants themselves. The d'Hautevilles' choice of counsel thus also provides a glimpse of the working bar of antebellum America.

One of the leading legal communities in the republic, Philadelphia offered the couple a wide choice of lawyers. Indeed by 1840 "Philadelphia lawyer" had already become a stock American phrase. Since Andrew Hamilton's stirring and successful defense of Peter Zenger in the famous 1735 libel trial, "Philadelphia lawyer" had become synonymous with skillful legal advocacy. It had even been translated into a slang retort. Countless Americans dodged difficult problems by declaring, "that would puzzle a Philadelphia lawyer." The city's bar had retained its professional authority since Hamilton's day. In the early 1830s, British traveler Thomas Hamilton had pronounced, "I have never met a body of men more distinguished by acuteness and extensive professional information than the members of the Philadelphia bar."[18] And in a survey of the city's antebellum bar, Gary Nash tried to capture the importance of the city's legal community by simply declaring, "[i]n Philadelphia law was in the air."[19] At the top of the local professional hierarchy, stood a group of gentlemen lawyers most of whose families had dominated the bar since the Revolution. It was from this group of skilled advocates that the d'Hautevilles recruited their Philadelphia lawyers.[20]

Settled in the nearby village of Germantown, Ellen and her father picked John Cadwalader to head Ellen's legal team. The choice was easily explainable. John was the son of Sears family friend General Thomas Cadwalader. Episcopalians like the Searses, the Cadwaladers had long been a leading family of the city. A local saying involving the family of then infamous Philadelphia banker Nicholas Biddle even parodied a famous Boston quip: "It is said that the Biddles and Cadwaladers are to Philadelphia what the Cabots and Lowells are to Proper Boston: While 'the Cabots speak only to the Lowells and the Lowells only speak to God,' as the saying goes, 'when a Biddle gets drunk, he thinks he's a Cadwalader.'"[21] For the Whiggish Sears, Cadwalader's pedigree was tainted only by his recent conversion to Jacksonian Democracy.

John Cadwalader had been born in 1805 and easily assumed local professional leadership. After graduating from the University of Pennsylvania in 1821, he had apprenticed in the office of Philadelphia's most prominent lawyer, Horace Binney, and then married his mentor's daughter. Gaining admission to the bar in 1825, Cadwalader became an expert in real property law, but like all of his elite colleagues handled an array of legal problems from commerce to crime. In 1830, he had plucked a juicy professional plum by being named chief counsel for the Bank of the United States. He took the lead in litigation over its later failure. He also helped his father manage the Penn family's vast Pennsylvania properties. A year before the Searses approached him, Cadwalader had earned further professional notoriety by representing the federal revenue department in the notorious cloth cases, a widely publicized series of lawsuits involving fraudulent American importers and English exporters who tried to evade the heavy duties on woolens through a variety of complex subterfuges.[22] Thus after just a decade and a half of practice, Cadwalader had "acquired a prominent position through his thorough preparation and exhaustive study of his briefs, and this trait, combined with a forceful style and remarkably wide knowledge of law in general, gave him professional prestige second to none."[23]

Cadwalader's professional success rested in part on his approach to law. The recollections of one of his apprentices, John Samuel, captured Cadwalader's style. Samuel recalled that the "whole prescribed course [of study] shows that Mr. Cadwalader was a believer in the historical method." The fledgling lawyer had been led through Anglo-American legal classics from Glanville and Coke to Blackstone and Kent. Over the course of an apprenticeship in which he ran messages, transcribed legal documents, and helped prepare cases for trial, the young lawyer learned to appreciate his master: "It was not merely law that we were listening to, but the daily affairs of life, social, family, and business occurrences and how they were managed and solved. He made us understand that laws were not made to be fitted to people or communities, but grew out of the relation of individuals with each other." Samuel also took pride in the fact that Cadwalader's office was not a "legal junk shop" nor were his relations with clients or students tainted by "commercialism."[24]

The Searses and Cadwalader recruited two other leading lawyers for the fight with Gonzalve. Their first choice, William M. Meredith, was lauded as Philadelphia's leading courtroom advocate. He had entered the law in 1817. After a decade or so of meager success, his legal career had taken off in the late 1820s by mingling law and politics. Following in the footsteps of his father, who had served in local politics before assuming the presidency of the Schuykill Bank, Meredith took a seat in the state legislature from 1824 to 1828 and had been elected to the Select Council of Philadelphia each year since 1833, serving as Council President since 1834. These offices had made him a leading local political figure, and like most of the profession Meredith understood that political and legal careers could be mutually reinforcing. His conservative Whiggism born of

Federalist sympathies balanced Cadwalader's Democratic leanings, and had compelled him to take a leading role in the 1838 state constitution convention. On the convention floor, he waged unsuccessful battles against egalitarianism by fighting provisions extending manhood suffrage and subjecting judges to term appointments. He had also attacked the abolitionists led by Thadeus Stevens and fought the antimasonic sentiments that surged in the convention. In 1837 his political and legal careers had merged to great public acclaim when he won a case giving all Philadelphians the right to use the city's public squares. Meredith's civic activities had also included participation in Episcopal Church affairs and acting as one of the incorporators of the city's House of Refuge.[25]

According to the professional lore of the day, "no important cause was argued in the State in which [Meredith] was not retained on one side or the other."[26] His reputation rested on an ability to grasp facts and "in establishing them from the real points at issue. With all this, he would have been a dull advocate if had not been for a wonderful play of humor which he possessed and which was available as well in illustration of an abstruse theory as in assisting him to bridge over the weak points of his case."[27] Even so, another Philadelphia lawyer reported that Meredith had little appreciation for wit like that of the lion of Boston's salons, Oliver Wendell Holmes, Senior: "I do not think, in fact, that Mr. Meredith was ever much in sympathy with the New England mind or habit of thought. He was a Pennsylvanian of Pennsylvanians, and represented a different intellectual development and history."[28] No doubt the Searses recognized that such chauvinism, however it might offend their Boston sensibilities, could be very useful in a Philadelphia courtroom.

Besides his courtroom renown, Meredith brought to Ellen's cause an approach to law quite different from Cadwalader's academic style. His interest lay in the courtroom fight itself not intensive research. According to a fellow lawyer, Meredith had little use for extensive forays into English and American legal sources and theories. On the contrary, he "seemed to think that the old English decisions before the Revolution and our own Pennsylvania case supplemented by some of the reports of the decisions of great jurists in our sister states, and the federal tribunals, furnished sufficient sources from which to draw the legal principles he sought to enforce."[29] In an 1830 article on "The Uncertainty of Law," Meredith had explained his trial tactics by distinguishing between the clarity of legal rules and the capriciousness of legal combat. The "event of *LITIGATION* is indeed almost always uncertain," he instructed, "the *LAW* rarely so, nor could any plan be devised for destroying this quality of litigation. If the most minute, distinct, and intelligible rule were laid down for every variety of possible circumstances (which, by the by, never has been or can be done), there would remain sources of uncertainty almost as fruitful as those which now exist. For after all, what would be the rule of law proper to be applied in any case would depend entirely upon the *facts*, and those facts must be proved by human testimony, and to the satisfaction of a human tribunal. The testimony and the tribunal both being human, therefore both fallible; the former liable to incorrections or incompleteness occasioned by intentional falsehood, imperceptible bias, or defect of memory – the later (throwing out of view willful error of rare occurrence) equally liable to misdecision from prejudice, misapprehension, or defect of judgment."[30] Meredith relied on his lawyerly understanding of the uncertainties of the courtroom and the need it created for skilled advocates to mold himself into a successful courtroom gladiator.

The last and most prominent of Ellen's legal trio, Horace Binney, had all but abandoned the courtroom in 1840. Though he had recently teamed with Meredith in the city's biggest legal contest, the fight over banker Stephen Girard's will leaving vast sums to found a college that launched years of litigation over the meaning of charitable estates, Binney was in semiretirement after a long, illustrious career. It was that luster that Cadwalader hoped to add to Ellen's case by signing on his old law teacher.

Born in 1780, Binney had attended Harvard College. Returning to Philadelphia, he had been trained by the lawyer Nancy Shippen Livingston had consulted, Jared Ingersoll. Like other gentlemen lawyers, Binney had mixed politics and civic stewardship with legal practice. Admitted to the bar in 1800, he was serving in the state assembly by 1806. Later he won election to the city's common council, 1810–12, the Select Council from 1816 to 1819, and then served a term in the national Congress from 1833 to 1835 as a Jackson opponent. But unlike the other lawyers in the case, Binney developed little taste for politics. He won greater professional fame as the editor of Pennsylvania Supreme Court decisions. He had also taken an active role in the Episcopal Church, including service as a delegate to its 1826 and 1829 general conventions. Along with scores of other elite attorneys, Binney had added a cultural meaning to the phrase "Philadelphia lawyer" with his poetry, criticism, and essays. But practice had been his prime interest, so much so that he had refused all offers of judicial office, including appointment to the United States Supreme Court. Instead he had become one of the most prominent lawyers in the republic, hired to plead important cases in Washington as well as Philadelphia.[31]

As a seasoned trial lawyer, Binney brought his own view of the courtroom to the case. "Every question in the longest life at the bar comes within the range of one or two inquires," he once mused cynically. "Does the thing in controversy belong to A or B, or had C done something to D which he ought not have done? And after a lawyer has for thirty years employed himself in such inquires, he may write his life in a single sentence – He spent his time in investigating facts, which when known did not make him any wiser, or in investigating principles which were of little use but to enable him to investigate and apply the facts. At least, such ought to be the case to justify the sneer which is commonly directed against the mere lawyer. This, indeed, constitutes the greatest drawback from the profession of the law, not merely that the life of a lawyer has great sameness, but that the investigations which cost him the most time and labour do not in the slightest degree increase his stock of useful knowledge." The thoroughly jaundiced Binney even voiced the physician envy that would torment the American bar for years to come. He insisted that the "physician in the practice of his profession, and at the bedside of his patient, investigates facts which instruct him in medical treatment. He learns something for application in other cases, to soothe the pains of humanity, or to assist him in the investigation of some general truth not yet perfectly developed. His profession is also largely connected with investigations of profit in many departments of nature, – mineralogy, botany, zoology, and the like. But the lawyer's facts are unproductive of all benefits, except for the fortunate client. When the cause is tried, the facts are of no more importance to the lawyer himself than last year's price of calicoes, nor to the rest of mankind perhaps half so much. They are forgotten as soon as the verdict is given, and well for the lawyer it is that they can be forgotten."[32]

Whether Binney would dismiss the star-crossed tale of Ellen, Gonzalve, and Frederick so easily from his mind remained to be seen, but Cadwalader wanted him as a senior advisor. His advice was sure to be useful, and his name sure to impress the judges and public even though he confined himself "to office practice, mainly to giving opinions on legal questions."[33] Binney accepted a role in Ellen's case perhaps because of his knowledge of the Sears family and its wealth or because of his lifelong interest in habeas corpus, the legal issue at the heart of the dispute. Whatever the reason, he became the *éminence grise* of Ellen's three lawyer team.

While David and Ellen gathered their lawyers, Gonzalve and his advisors assembled their own corps of gentlemen attorneys. They picked William B. Reed to head their efforts to retrieve Frederick from Ellen's clutches. Like Binney, he combined a thriving practice and political service with a growing literary career as an essayist and critic. And like Meredith, Reed stood at the top of the trial lawyers in the city. The son of long-term Philadelphia Recorder Joseph Reed, after graduating from the University of Pennsylvania in 1822 at the precocious age of sixteen, he had studied for the bar with his uncle John Sargeant and entered the profession four years later. Before beginning practice, however, he initiated what would be a lifelong interest in diplomacy with a year's stint as secretary to the American mission to the Congress of Spanish-American Republics headquartered in Panama and led by his uncle. Reed launched his Philadelphia practice in 1827 and simultaneously began publishing essays and reviews in journals such as the *American Quarterly Review*. Perhaps because of his grandfather, revolutionary war general Joseph Reed, the American Revolution was his favorite theme and his work eventually earned him a spot on the University of Pennsylvania history faculty. His writing and travels also brought him into contact with other writers, most notably British novelist William Thackery. The rumor even circulated that Reed had been the model for the character Barnes Newcome in Thackery's *The Newcomes*. In the mid-1830s Reed entered politics by serving two terms in the state assembly. In 1838 he had been appointed the Attorney General of Pennsylvania and served for a year. Though wavering in party affiliation, Reed became a stalwart supporter of state Democratic party leader James Buchanan.[34]

With Reed on board as lead counsel, Gonzalve and his advisors filled out their legal staff with two other prominent Philadelphia lawyers. Ironically it had been the father of one of their choices to whom Nancy Shippen Livingston had turned in her desperate effort to gain custody of Margaret. Fifty years later, Joseph R. Ingersoll agreed to defend the very paternal rights Nancy had challenged. Known, at least locally, as the "Cicero of the American Bar," Ingersoll was a practiced and polished courtroom orator. His prominence in the Philadelphia bar capped a career begun when he graduated first in his class at Princeton in 1804. He then read law with his father, Jared, who had not only served as the state's attorney general but also joined the galaxy of American political demigods in 1787 when he signed the Constitution. The younger Ingersoll began practice in 1807 and, unlike the other lawyers in the case, resisted the lure of politics for almost twenty years until his anger over President Jackson's repeal of the charter of the Philadelphia-headquartered United States Bank led to a successful run for Congress in 1835 as a Whig. Before his single congressional term, he had held local offices on the common and select council, but without active partisanship. After his term, he remained a Whig stalwart and reaped several rewards. Ingersoll served as lead orator at the 1835 memorial service upon the death of Chief Justice John Marshall in Philadelphia, and president of the reception committee for touring presidential candidate Henry Clay in 1839. He also took an active interest in civic affairs, serving on the Board of Trustees of the University of Pennsylvania, the Historical Society of Pennsylvania, and the Academy of Fine Arts. According to fellow lawyer David Paul Brown, he was "thoroughly read in legal science, thoroughly skilled in its practice" and "possessed the power of a most personal eloquence, which was never surpassed, if ever equalled, at the American bar." Ingersoll was at the height of his fame as a courtroom lawyer when he took on Gonzalve's case.[35]

Gonzalve's final choice was the only lawyer in the case not born in Philadelphia, John Morin Scott. His Scottish ancestors had settled in New York in 1702, and his grandfather and namesake had been a lawyer and revolutionary war soldier. His father died in Scott's youth and his mother brought him to Philadelphia when he was eight. Also a precocious student, and like Gonzalve and Ingersoll a Presbyterian, Scott graduated second in his class at Princeton at the youthful age of fifteen. After a year of further study at Princeton, he apprenticed to lawyer William Rawle and soon entered the bar. At first he practiced only sporadically, but after he squandered the family fortune in an investment failure, he became a full-time practitioner and specialist in insurance and commercial law. And he too entered the political lists serving in the city militia, the state assembly, the 1837 state constitutional convention, and many terms on the city councils. A "conservative" of the "Whig school of politics," he declined the party's nomination for Congress in 1836. Like the other leading lawyers in the city, Scott was an accomplished courtroom performer. He was "a very inspiring and eloquent speaker" though his "voice was not of the best kind for an orator. His action was free, animated, and graceful; his language chaste and grammatical, not fragmentary or injectional." Early in his legal career, Scott had been known for briefs of "the most laborious description," but by the time he joined Reed and Ingersoll in Gonzalve's case "they had become less so, and he preferred to speak not with minutely prepared notes, but with a mind thoroughly imbued with his subject. His kindly feelings were apparent in his speeches at the Bar, as well as elsewhere. He never used invective; he was not satirical nor cutting; nor did he aim 'bar wit' at his adversary. Hightoned, he could be roused; and then became impassioned or indignant, but never cruel or unkind."[36]

All in all, the six lawyers in the case could have been exhibited as evidence for Alexis de Tocqueville's recent assertion that the bar had become America's natural aristocracy. Indeed, when the Philadelphia bar "assembled of a morning, the courtroom, thronged with elegantly dressed gentlemen of refined manners, more clearly resembled a drawing room."[37] As in Boston and most other eastern

American cities, these men mostly had been bred in families headed
by gentlemen lawyers and many of them had wed the daughters of
other elite attorneys. They belonged to the upper class of a Philadelphia legal community that corresponded to similar communities in
other cities of the republic. These legal enclaves shared their own
particular forms of hierarchy, training, craft consciousness, and organization that set lawyers apart as a distinctive community of professionals.[38] Even the physical reality of that professionalism was evident in the lawyers' living arrangements. All of the lawyers in the
case lived and worked near each other in row houses close to Independence Hall and the courts. And they had other ties besides geog-
raphy. Each participated in the Philadelphia Law Academy, the elite
local bar organization that tried to govern all the city's lawyers. Just
a few years before, Binney, Cadwalader, and Ingersoll had led a
successful campaign to block the University of Pennsylvania from
creating a law department. The lawyers wanted to retain the control
over entry into the profession they wielded as masters of legal apprentices. Though their power continued to be challenged, in 1840
these men dominated the Philadelphia legal community.

The lawyers' membership in the Philadelphia bar had consequences for clients like the d'Hautevilles. The attorneys knew each
other very well. They had all tried cases together and against each
other, and thus they had ongoing relationships that would continue
long after the fate of Ellen, Gonzalve, and Frederick had been decided. Consequently, as in all trials, the d'Hautevilles' lawyers not
only had their own sense of each other's skills and weaknesses, they
brought their own interests to the impending custody hearing.

Besides their elite status, the six lawyers hired by Ellen and Gonzalve had one more thing in common relevant to the d'Hauteville
case. They were all married and had fathered children. Each knew
from his own experience something of the roles of son, husband,
and father. Most of them knew something of loss as well, though
none so well as Joseph Ingersoll. His two sons died in infancy and
his daughter in childhood. He also had buried his first wife. The
fight for Frederick would force these Philadelphia lawyers, like
everyone else soon to be drawn into the vortex of the d'Hauteville
case, to see the connections between their family experiences and
their legal ones.

The Writ is Served

Though Ellen had decided where the trial would take place, Gonzalve and his lawyers determined when it began. They plotted
through the spring and into the summer.

Before seeking a writ, they decided to stage a preemptive public relations strike. Gonzalve published a public statement of his case against Ellen. As they approached the courtroom, Gonzalve and his lawyers worried about the impact of public opinion on his cause. They understood the popular appeal of a lone woman fighting for her child. To counter that appeal, they designed a remonstrance aimed at currying support for Gonzalve's defense of paternal rights. Besides reiterating in detail his charges against his wife and his claim for Frederick, the Swiss sojourner warned Pennsylvanians that Ellen was once again seeking legislation that would strip him of "his dearest and most sacred rights, and may, from what has been seen, if unopposed and unexplained, be passed and fettered on him for-ever." He cautioned legislators against passing any bills bearing the titles "for the Protection of the Natural Rights of Married Women", "for the protection of Minors," or "for the Protection of the Prop-erty of Married Women." Anticipating the publicity of a trial that would judge his acts as husband and father, he also included tes-taments to his character. The broadside concluded with a testimo-nial from eleven Swiss notables, whose statements and stature were verified by Albert Gallatin, President Thomas Jefferson's Secretary of the Treasury and the republic's most eminent Swiss-American.[39]

Finally on July 3, 1840, Gonzalve petitioned the Presiding Judge of the Court of General Sessions for the City and County of Phila-delphia for a writ of habeas corpus to be issued to Ellen, David, and Miriam. He described himself as a "citizen and resident of the Can-ton de Vaud in Switzerland," and recorded his August 1837, mar-riage to Ellen "in the presence of the parents of both parties, and with their full approbation." He also informed the judges that "by the laws of the Canton, where the marriage was solemnized, a wife is obliged to live with her husband wherever he thinks proper to reside, and the husband has the absolute and exclusive guardian-ship over any children born of said marriage." Then he lodged his charges. Telling the court that Ellen had returned to her Boston home with his consent for "a temporary visit," Gonzalve claimed that she has since "without any just cause know to your petitioner, refused to return to him, or been prevented from doing so." After informing the court of Frederick's birth, he then reported his "fruit-less attempt to recover his wife and child" since his arrival in the United Sates. He claimed that "David Sears and Miriam C. Sears his wife, and Ellen Sears Grand d'Hauteville have for a long time restrained his child of his liberty, and prevented your petitioner from regaining him, and have been engaged in various clandestine attempts to procure the authority of law, by means of special legisla-tion, to prevent the petitioner from having the guardianship and controul of his child to which by law he is entitled." Gonzalve accused his wife and parents-in-law of legal chicanery by contending that "to avoid the service of this process, and to defeat the measures, thus according to law resorted to by your petitioner, his wife and child were, as your petitioner verily believes, by the agency of David Sears and Miriam C. Sears, secreted and clandestinely removed from the city of Boston and State of Massachusetts, whereby your petitioner was deprived of the redress to which by the laws of Massachusetts he was entitled." Now the pair, he believed, resided in Philadelphia.

Gonzalve asked for a writ demanding that Ellen and her parents produce his son "now aged twenty-one months or there abouts." Conforming to the words of the state's 1785 habeas corpus statute, he alleged that the boy was being "unlawfully restrained of his liberty" and detained by the Searses and his wife against his "permission and consent." He wanted Frederick brought to court so the judge "may examine into the facts relating to the case, and into the cause of such confinement, restraint, or detention, and to do with and of the child what shall then and there be considered by your Honour, and unto justice shall appertain."

George Washington Barton, the presiding judge, issued the writ that very day. "We command you," the court ordered Ellen, David, and Miriam, "that the body of Frederick Sears Grand d'Hauteville, by you restrained, as it is said, of his liberty, and detained by whatsoever name Frederick Sears Grand d'Hauteville may be detained, together with the day and cause of his being detained, you have before the honourable Judges of our Court of General Sessions of the Peace." They were commanded to bring the boy to the chambers of Associate Judge Robert T. Conrad at nine o'clock, Monday, July 6th, and "then and there to do, submit to, and receive whatsoever our Judges shall then and there consider in that behalf."[40] Ellen and Miriam received the writ and immediately notified Cadwalader.

After a couple of postponements, on Monday, July 13th, Ellen, David, Miriam, and their lawyers faced the General Sessions bench alongside Gonzalve and his attorneys. They produced Frederick as commanded by the writ. The meeting took place in a historic site, General Sessions Courtroom No. 2. It occupied part of the second floor of venerable Congress Hall next door to Independence Hall. Celebrated Philadelphia lawyer Andrew Hamilton had championed the erection of a county courthouse on the site in 1736, but the building had not been authorized until 1762 and did not open until 1790. Immediately the hall performed a different service. It became the first home of the nation's Congress meeting in Philadelphia, then the republic's capital. The United States Senate sat on the first floor, the House of Representatives met on the second. With the completion of the District of Columbia and the move of Congress south, the building reverted to its original purpose as a county courthouse. However, by 1840 the courtroom's deficiencies had become apparent. Poor ventilation, small chambers, and large crowds of spectators and reporters often made trial physical as well as mental ordeals.[41]

Though the d'Hautevilles sat where Washington, Jefferson, Madison, and other American political heroes had waged political warfare, the court that heard their dispute was a mere infant tribunal. It had been created by the state legislature just four months before their trial. In a typical attempt to deal with bulging urban court dockets through bureaucratic reorganization, the legislators had established the court to replace the jurisdiction of the Court of Criminal Sessions, itself but two years old at its demise. According to the legislation, the new court would consist of three judges, "learned in the law," and assume responsibility for the criminal complaints formerly heard by the Court of Criminal Sessions as well as the civil jurisdiction previously held by the Mayor's Court and the Recorder's Court. It also took over the duties of Clerk of Oyer and Terminer. In effect, it occupied the lowest rung in Philadelphia judicial hierarchy. But its jurisdiction included petitions for writs of habeas corpus like Gonzalve's.[42]

Like their court, the three judges who heard the d'Hauteville case occupied a relatively low place in the city's legal community compared to the attorneys hired by the battling parents. As has often been true of the American trial bench, none were from the city's professional elite. Nevertheless, the judges became the second corps of critical lawyer actors in the case. Along with the attorneys, their actions would dictate whether Gonzalve or Ellen got custody of Frederick. Equally important, their stature and that of their court would have implications that would influence the reception of the d'Hauteville verdict among the bar and the public. And the judges, like the lawyers, brought their own commitments and concerns to the case.

Presiding Judge Barton, though distantly related to Philadelphia's powerful Rittenhouse family, had been born and raised in Lancaster, Pennsylvania. He began his career as an assistant editor on a Nashville, Tennessee newspaper. Plying his trade in Andrew Jackson's hometown, he soon fell under the spell of Old Hickory and returned to Lancaster to stump for him. Electioneering success brought him to the attention of local Democratic leader, James Buchanan. Barton gave up his newspaper career for the law and politics. After apprenticing in Buchanan's law office, he moved to Phila-

delphia and then up the patronage ladder. After service as an
Assistant District Attorney, he secured appointment as the head of
the new Court of General Sessions at the youthful age of thirty-
three.[43]

An equally youthful though far better known Robert T. Conrad
served as one of Barton's Associate Judges. His career was in some
ways the reverse of the Presiding Judge's. Born in Philadelphia in
1810 and the son of a local publisher, Conrad had studied law with
attorney Thomas Kittera but had then forsaken the bar for a literary
career. He served as editor of the *Daily Commercial Intelligencer,* which
he later merged with the *Philadelphia Gazette.* Conrad also edited the
North American and helped fellow lawyer George R. Graham publish
Graham's Magazine. In the course of his editorial career, he also
became one of the city's leading playwrights, poets, and literary
figures. His most important work, "Aylmere, or the Bondsman of
Kent," had been completed five years before and won him local and
some national acclaim. Soon the play became part of the repertoire
of the city's leading actor, Edwin Forrest, who played Jack Cade the
leader of a 1450 insurrection against English feudalism. However,
ill health forced Conrad to abandon his editorial career and return
to legal practice. Winning appointment as Recorder, he achieved
even wider notoriety in 1835 when he took the lead in condemning
abolitionists as incendiary agitators and their tracts as threats to the
nation's peace and harmony. Conrad led a delegation that dumped
a box of abolitionist pamphlets into the Delaware River. His act elicited favorable newspaper comment. The next year, Conrad won appointment as a judge of the Court of Criminal Sessions and on its
demise to its successor the Court of General Sessions. On the bench,
he earned a reputation as an excessively stern jurist. Ellen and Gonzalve's tangled tale of marital woe and parental conflict would have
appealed to his well-developed taste for melodrama.[44]

The final judge on the panel, Joseph Michael Doran, had the
most extensive ties to the eminent counsel prepared to argue the
d'Hauteville case. The oldest of the trio, he had been born in 1800.
Though his parents had been Irish Catholic immigrants to the city
in 1795, Doran had attended a Presbyterian school and studied at
the University of Pennsylvania. He then won a spot as an apprentice
in the office of Gonzalve's counsel, Joseph Ingersoll. Upon his admission to the bar in 1824, Doran practiced with his mentor achieving his greatest success in criminal cases. He was known as a "man
of rare humor, and his addresses to juries were enlivened not so
much by sarcasm as by unctour ridicule of description or comparison which was always enjoyable." Like Barton, Doran was also an
active Jacksonian Democrat. He had served as a delegate to the

1837 constitutional convention, where he tangled with many of the d'Hautevilles' attorneys. His appointment as the second Associate Judge filled the required panel of the Court of General Sessions.[45]

On Monday, July 13th, Barton, Conrad, and Doran conferred about the d'Hauteville case. Before any pleas could be entered, the presiding judge announced, "We think the circumstances of this case make it proper to postpone the hearing to another time." Explaining the peremptory act, the court reporter later noted, "[i]t was understood that the judges considered the case of such a peculiar and delicate nature, as to make a degree of privacy, not to be secured in the courtroom, desirable." As was often done in custody cases, Barton ordered that the hearing reconvened on out of public view in his chambers.[46]

Immediately after the hearing adjourned, Ellen performed a symbolic act. She had Cadwalader draft a document declaring that "as soon after the commencement of a suit or habeas corpus as is convenient" the d'Hauteville family jewels and diamonds would be returned to Gonzalve.[47] With the jewelry declaration and the hearing about to start, Ellen and Gonzalve's tumultuous dispute entered a new and very public phase. No longer merely a battle of bargaining wills between themselves, their fight had been reborn and christened with a brand-new legal name: *The Commonwealth of Pennsylvania, ex relatione Paul Daniel Gonzalve Grand d'Hauteville v. David Sears, Miriam C. Sears, and Ellen Sears Grand d'Hauteville.* Now outsiders would seek the resolution that had eluded Ellen and Gonzalve for almost two years. Their Philadelphia lawyers would henceforth dictate the course of events more than they would.

4

Into a Court of Law

3) He says / she says
4.) Lawyers he says/ she says
5.) Judges   "   "
6) Frederick's health is issue

As their trial date drew near, the d'Hautevilles faced their most critical and most public legal experience. They knew that the trial would determine which of them got custody of Frederick. What they did not know was that it would become a major legal event with uncertain consequences for clients and counsel as well as the issues over which they battled. Most custody hearings lasted a day or two, but postponements and courtroom maneuvers would stretch theirs late into the fall. During those weeks and months, Ellen and Gonzalve learned yet another legal lesson: A trial was not a simple process of dispute resolution, but a complicated social drama.

Tribunals like the Philadelphia Court of General Sessions have long been popular public theaters. A seventeenth-century English diarist eagerly anticipated an upcoming trip to London, when he would indulge in three of his favorite pleasures: "good food and drink, the society of pretty women, and entertaining mornings in the law courts, watching the cases there."[1] The courts were equally attractive to nineteenth-century Americans. Located in the center of every city and many towns, courthouses staged a constant repertoire of social dramas like the d'Hauteville case. And these performances ought to be understood in the anthropological meaning of social dramas: events that reveal latent conflicts in a society and thus illuminate its fundamental social structures.[2] Such events turned the courtroom into a public theater and trials into morality plays that forced the litigants and the public to confront some of their most cherished hopes and crippling fears. In the courtroom, everything from the proper duties of parents and the meaning of sanity to the social responsibilities of corporations and the legitimacy of slavery became the subjects of social drama.

like the OJ Simpson case

Trials are particularly attractive social dramas because they are predictable rituals. Each follows a recognized script cast with identifiable characters. They proceed from pleadings and opening statements to the presentation of evidence, closing statements, and verdicts. The judge, the defendant, the accuser, the defense counsel, and the prosecutor star as easily recognizable characters in these productions. The evocative and understandable clashes of the courtroom tell stories that audiences can watch as spectators, and, even more significantly, ones in which they can imagine themselves as participants and judges. Difficult problems from the sanctity of marriage to the protection of private property can be better understood when performed in the courtroom as divorce hearings or burglary trials.

Most importantly, trials have one feature that distinguishes them from other social dramas such as political rallies or religious services. Whether happy or not, courtroom dramas must have clear endings. Every trial must declare a winner and a loser. The adversarial imperative of the courtroom forces judges, jurors, and the public to render and defend such verdicts. A fundamental commitment to solving disputes through adversarial contests makes neutrality not only difficult but suspect for lawyers, judges, and the public.

Every trial contains these ritualistic elements. And most cases are heard and resolved with little fanfare or lasting legal impact. Trials like the d'Hautevilles' became important social dramas by gaining a notoriety that distinguished them from the countless other legal disputes being waged at any particular time. Such trials reverberate

through the society because they acquire *both* legal and rhetorical significance. Cases gain legal significance by influencing subsequent legal argument and legal judgment. They produce rules and tactics that guide lawyers' construction and presentation of their clients' cases as well as the structure and logic of verdicts rendered by judges, jurors, and the public. Such power is not exercised only by appellate courts through the precedents they issue. By gaining public and professional notoriety, disputes decided in trial courts can also gain legal significance. These trials become influential largely by acquiring rhetorical significance. That is, they become standard references for public arguments and private disputes about controversial issues. As Robert Hariman explains, "[i]ndividuals and groups form their opinions, which are their means of making sense of the world and acting effectively to advance their interests, by interpreting the trials and reaching verdicts about the action under trial, including the institutions of law and government. Trials function in this way as forums for debate, as symbols of larger constellations of belief and action, and as social dramas used to manage emotional responses to troubling situations."[3]

A convergence of particular circumstances heighten the legal and rhetorical importance of a trial and transform it into a major popular event. Timing, litigant characteristics, conducive settings, and countless other unpredictable variables combine in these rare cases as a combustible brew of law and rhetoric that explodes out into the society beyond the courtroom door. These cases become legal fables that lay people and lawyers use to comprehend clashes over the changes swirling about them. In short, for reasons intrinsic to each case *and* its moment in time, some trials produce arresting social dramas that increase their rhetorical significance and heighten their legal consequences.

The d'Hauteville trial became just such a social drama. It erupted during what American political historians would later label one of the most important presidential elections in the republic's history. The "Log Cabin" campaign between incumbent Democrat Martin Van Buren and Whig challenger William Henry Harrison captivated the nation. Newspapers around the country carried daily reports as the election heated up in the fall of 1840. Nevertheless, periodically that same fall stories about Ellen, Gonzalve, and their families pushed the election off the front pages. Rather than rehearse yet again the merits and demerits of each presidential contender, women and men gathered in taverns, kitchens, parlors, hotel lobbies, and public squares to argue about the d'Hauteville case and thus about what it took to be a good mother and a good husband.

The d'Hauteville case could now and then displace presidential politics because it raised concerns as critical to peoples' lives as the sub-treasury plan and other issues being fiercely debated by Van Buren and Harrison. Social dramas like the d'Hauteville trial become widely shared experiences because they occur during "periods of heightened activity when a society's presuppositions are most exposed, when core values are expressed, and when the symbolism is most apparent."[4] Instead of abstract discussions about the family changes upsetting their society, the d'Hauteville case offered spellbound spectators and rapt readers concrete characters in a real story. They could, and did, weigh the relative merits of Ellen, Gonzalve, and their families by borrowing the words and rules of the law to make their points and by acceding to its adversarial demands to declare a verdict.

Capturing the public mind in this way extended the law's hegemony over contested social relations and further institutionalized the tendency to turn to law as the proper arena for waging individual battles over change. It did so because of the interactive reality of the courtroom. In a trial external beliefs, interests, and other forces are translated into the language and forms of the law. These translations are then transmitted to the public through particular client stories, lawyers' arguments, witness testimony, and judges' verdicts. The transmissions in turn help construct popular images of social relations. In this interactive manner, trials become active shapers of a culture not merely its reflections. Like other critical social rituals, trials thus serve the "double function of transmitting and transforming the values of a society."[5]

In other words, Ellen and Gonzalve stood poised to enter one of the republic's most conspicuous public stages. And even in a juryless habeas corpus hearing like theirs, lawyers and clients performed for both a judicial audience and a public one. Indeed, as the d'Hautevilles' lawyers prepared for trial word about the case had already leaked out of the judge's chambers and spread around Philadelphia. On July 13, the first hearing date, the same story had appeared in the city's two major dailies, the *Inquirer* and the *Public Ledger*. Readers learned that a "Habeas Corpus of more than ordinary interest is now in progress in the city." After printing a few tantalizing bits of information, the papers whetted readers' appetites by promising complete coverage of the case.[6]

Newspapers like the *Inquirer* and *Public Ledger* had become a new force in the law. Earlier Philadelphia lawyers had not worried as much about press coverage. Most papers had been expensive and edited for wealthy readers or party zealots. But high prices and bitter partisanship had very recently given way to the enterprise of mass dailies. Aided by printing innovations over the last decade, publishers like Benjamin Day had created the penny press. In 1833 his *New York Sun* pioneered the cheap urban dailies that catered to a mass audience of middle- and working-class readers by offering greater coverage of local news, especially crime. As the penny press spread through urban America, lawyers quickly felt its impact. Each day, mass audiences read press columns describing lawsuits and reviewing the performances of judges and lawyers. Editors gave sensational trials prominent coverage because they attracted wide readership. Criminal trials were the main staple of court reporting, but on occasion arresting civil suits like the d'Hauteville case also received extensive coverage. As a result, newspapers had become the chief public critics of courtroom theatrics.[7]

Newspaper coverage of the law not only highlighted the theatricality of the courtroom, it also reinforced a new sense of legal pluralism and uncertainty that haunted every trial. Colonial accounts of trials had been written primarily by the clergy and designed to spread received religious truths. By the 1830s, as Daniel Cohen has argued, newspapers and other forms of popular legal literature displayed a world in which "truth was no longer certain, monolithic, and rigidly patterned, conforming to a few spiritual models; nor was it simple, linear, and naively empirical, corresponding to a single reliable narrative." Quite the contrary, popular accounts of

the law fed a view of legal truths as "complex, elusive, and frag-
mented, approximated only by balancing the conflicting testimony
of fallible witnesses and the competing arguments of partisan advocates; adversarial trial reports were natural vehicles for the expression of that new approach to reality."[8] By filling their pages with
renditions of the stock characters of legal dramas and by printing
lawyer's arguments, judges' verdicts, and their own trial stories,
newspapers turned cases into public events and at the same time
promoted higher levels of popular legal literacy.

Philadelphia attorneys and their clients had dealt with this new
legal literature since 1836, when William Swain launched the *Public
Ledger,* the city's first penny paper. The *Ledger*'s price and Swain's
creativity proved irresistible to Philadelphians. Unwilling to wait for
news to be delivered like most editors, he sent reporters out to find
it. And rather than depend on pooled information with other papers, he sought exclusives. More shocking to the citizenry, he created a corps of roving newsboys hawking the *Ledger* throughout the
city's narrow, gridwork streets.

When the d'Hauteville case opened, the *Ledger* had the largest
circulation in the city. Every issue carried stories about the local
courts, while occasional editorials critiqued the bench and bar. Innovations had continued as well. The previous winter, reporter
Charles Ritter began publishing a daily "City Gleanings" column. It
carried local news and earned its author immediate notoriety. The
d'Hauteville case, with its enticing blend of wealth, exotic locales,
bitter family conflict, and infant pawn, seemed a natural subject for
the column and Ritter began following the case. Consequently, lawyers for both sides had to worry about favorable coverage in the
Ledger. They knew that the case could well face dual judgments:
verdicts rendered in a court of law, and in the court of public
opinion.[9]

Extensive press coverage would make the d'Hauteville case a particular kind of experience for readers as well as spectators, litigants,
lawyers, and judges. The trial would become a shared but not a
uniform experience. Nor would the many participants in the trial
derive the same meaning from the case. Instead, the very nature of
the social dramas of a trial like this one meant that it provided "vary-
ing possibilities for the constitution and ordering of experience, as
well as for the reflection on and communication of experience."[10]

The press's enhanced role as trial commentators made the courtroom that the d'Hautevilles now had to enter an even more treacherous place. While under the public gaze they had to endure the
inevitable thrust and counterthrust of trial combat. Then they had
to confront the equally inevitable verdict that would make one of

them a winner, the other a loser. As their case lumbered toward the finality of its end, its lawyerly and press jousts produced revealing exchanges about the family and the law. Buried in the mounting details of the case's rapidly accumulating record, those critical interchanges provide telling commentaries on the major issues of the case and the trial experience itself.

Statutory rules and courtroom custom demanded that the d'Hauteville trial be a three-act drama. First David, Miriam, and Ellen had to respond to Gonzalve's writ by producing Frederick in court and explaining why they held him. These explanations must take the form of legal briefs called "returns" to be read in court by the lawyers, though expressed in the third person voice of the client. After the returns had been read, Gonzalve would then plead his case in a statement labeled his "suggestion," also cast in his voice but read by his counsel. Once these statements had been presented, the lawyers would perform the trial's second act with opening statements, introduction of evidence, examination of witnesses, and closing arguments. In the final act, Judges Barton, Conrad, and Doran would announce their verdict.

Act One: Client Stories

Conforming to the statutory directives, lead counsels John Cadwalader and William Reed drafted returns and suggestions that translated the d'Hauteville dispute into two client stories. These narratives justified each parent's claim for Frederick with renditions of the facts of the case and suggestions about their legal implications. They were, of course, very different tales. Troubled marriages taken to court produced two distinctly different client stories just as they had spawned two distinctly different spousal stories. Client stories were specialized tales in which lawyers tried to make sense of a case by translating the "real life" experiences of legal "outsiders" into the particular forms required by legal "insiders."[11] The lawyers rephrased the complex, multilayered d'Hauteville spousal conflict into a much more narrowly defined child custody case. Former law student David Sears understood this translation process. In a note accompanying a large packet of documents, he advised Cadwalader: "If any of the suggestions are of use to you – please put them into your own language and insert them."[12]

Trial procedures thus forced Reed and Cadwalader to engage in a "narrative competition." They had to write stories designed to convince the judges of the merits of their client's claims and the demerits of their opponents' contentions. The winning tale would control the story framework through which the judges read the case. And their tales would demonstrate that "arguments presented in trials are often important clues as to what stories count as good, true, or compelling stories within a particular culture."[13] They also revealed that at any particular time contests are waged over what is compelling if not true or even good.

The lawyers also had to write their stories within the constraints of the courtroom. The most pressing were client demands, evidentiary limitations, procedural rules, and doctrinal categories. Even though their private bargaining had failed and they had turned their problems over to lawyers, Ellen and Gonzalve were not passive recipients of legal largesse. They monitored their lawyers' work, injected their own opinions, and in doing so set boundaries on narrative construction. So did the evidence that they and their counsel could assemble and present. Each courtroom tale also had to balance client versions of the events with complementary interpretations of relevant doctrinal and evidentiary rules. As these constraints combined to shape the d'Hautevilles' courtroom stories, the Court of General Sessions became the site of a fierce struggle over the legal meaning of the keywords of marriage and parenthood at a time when they were being fought over throughout North America and Western Europe.

The narrative competition began on July 16th, when all the actors reassembled in Judge Barton's chambers. Cadwalader began the proceedings by reading David and Miriam's returns. Ellen's parents asked to be dropped from the suit because they neither had nor claimed custody of Frederick and did not control their daughter's movements. Through what Cadwalader called "simple disclaimers," he sought to make the contest strictly a battle between Frederick's parents.[14] It was in Ellen's return that Cadwalader staked a claim to Frederick. He did so by focusing directly on child custody and motherhood, and downplaying the d'Hautevilles' marital woes. The emphasis represented his tactical conclusion that Ellen had little to gain from judicial scrutiny of her marital conduct. It also represented the first way in which his retelling of his client's marriage gave voice to some of her experiences while silencing others.

Cast as "respondent" to Gonzalve's role as "relator," Ellen's story began with the admission that she indeed had the child. She produced Frederick in the court, and then through Cadwalader staked her claim to him in the third person vernacular of the courtroom: "That she is his guardian by nature, and for nurture, and that her care of him is indispensably necessary for his present and future welfare." After asserting her moral and financial ability to rear Frederick, Cadwalader had his client justify her custody claim by invoking the commitments to maternalism and tender years that he hoped lay at the heart of Pennsylvania child custody law: "The present age of her child does not admit of his separation from her, without the greatest danger to his health, which requires care, and even to his life, which had been more than once seriously threatened by attacks of illness. He needs, and for some years to come will need, a mother's nursing care, which no one else can supply."[15]

Cadwalader then told a severely truncated version of the d'Hautevilles' stormy marriage as he, echoing his client, tried to distinguish between the roles of wife and mother. Treading lightly on the union itself, he had Ellen express her growing sense of outrage at Gonzalve's conduct. Cadwalader relied on intimations of marital fraud and abuse to explain why his client must live permanently "separate and apart from him, under the protection of her parents." But he wanted the court to hurry through the minefield of marital fault and linger only on questions of child welfare and maternal care so he could cast Ellen as a victimized, but courageous mother. Accordingly, his client asserted that "she is not required by law, for the purposes of a hearing involving merely the present custody of her infant child, to enter upon the most painful task of detailing the particular causes which have led to this melancholy result of her marriage."[16]

Instead of marital failures, Cadwalader wanted the judges to think about the infant Frederick and compare Ellen and Gonzalve as parents. In a city already beginning to feel the heat of nativism, he tarred Gonzalve as a foreigner seeking to take an American-born child back to the old world. To block the unspecified horrors of expatriation, Cadwalader turned to the "best interests of the child" doctrine. Through his pen Ellen pleaded that "the interests of her child, in every respect in which an impartial person can regard them, will be prejudiced by such a removal at this time, or for some years to come; his personal expectations in this country, as well as the relations he bears to it by birth, securing to him advantages hereafter of the highest value, if his early years are permitted to pass here." And then Cadwalader specifically invoked the tender-years rule by having his client insist that "in consequences of the tender age of her child at this time, this last consideration may not require the special notice of the judges, as the laws and usages of this commonwealth would not, even if such future advantages were not in prospect, permit her child to be taken from her, until his age shall be much more advanced than it now is."[17]

After staking her claim to Frederick, the rules of courtroom competition demanded that Ellen answer the charges listed in Gonzalve's petition for the writ of habeas corpus. Cadwalader had her issue four defiant rebuttals. First, she denied any attempt to conceal

Frederick from his father explaining that fear of abduction drove her into hiding. Ellen also disputed the charge of avoiding the courtroom, and suggested that it was Gonzalve who had feared a New York trial because of the legal losses suffered by the now notorious John Barry. Second, Ellen challenged Gonzalve's assertions that she had violated Swiss family law by leaving him and keeping his child. She recalled assuming that no major differences existed between the laws of Vaud and those of "her own country and the general usages of the civilized world." While still believing that to be the case, she also argued, in yet another attempt to keep a debate over her marital conduct out of the courtroom, that "whether they are so or not is not material to the purpose of the present hearing." Third, Ellen rejected charges of sponsoring secret legislation aimed at divesting Gonzalve of his custody rights. She insisted that her father's efforts had been public not clandestine and once more claimed the right of a citizen to petition for legislative relief. Finally, Ellen dismissed out of hand Gonzalve's claim that she had been the witless pawn of her parents instead of the author of her own fate.

After refuting each of Gonzalve's charges, Cadwalader ended Ellen's story by having her assume the pose of a defenseless female supplicant seeking justice. He hoped that casting Ellen as a dutiful mother fighting to keep her child would appeal to the judges' paternalism and simultaneously undercut Reed's inevitable attempt to portray her as a Jezebel flaunting her marital vows. "The respondent concludes by throwing herself upon the judgment of the court," Ellen declared in a final attempt to have the court concentrate on motherhood not matrimony, "upon that part of the return which particularly adverts to the age and circumstances of her child."[18]

Reed then stood and began telling Gonzalve's story. Unlike Cadwalader, he did not have to silence any of his client's fundamental claims. On the contrary, he could retell them in the words and forms of the law. But his story had its own omissions. Reed passed over without comment Ellen's actual care of Frederick as he combined a detailed description of the d'Hauteville marriage with abstract assertions of paternal rights.

Prior to the hearing, Cadwalader had given Reed a copy of Ellen's return. Immediately and emphatically Reed had Gonzalve refute all his wife's assertions of fact and law. Most importantly, Reed used Gonzalve's story to reconnect the links between Ellen's roles as mother and wife that his opponents sought to sever. His story justified Gonzalve's claim to Frederick by relying on two of the major themes in the public narrative of American family law: marital fault and superior paternal custody rights. "By the laws of this and every christian land," he proclaimed in words that had reverberated through Gonzalve's letters and now found expression in the vernacular of the law, "the wife is bound to adhere to her husband, to remain with him, to make his home her home, and his country, her country; and if a wife, causelessly, (as your petitioner avers is the case here) abandons her husband and refuses to live with him, she forfeits all those privileges which the law so largely bestows on a faithful wife." Marital sins must be punished; the penalties should include the loss of custody. Reed linked spousal and parental roles by having Gonzalve invoke *Addicks*. Casting Ellen as the adulterous Barbara, Gonzalve as the virtuous Joseph, and Frederick in the role of the innocent Addicks girls, he insisted that the judges must use their discretion to reward virtue and punish sin. Arguing that a woman who violated her marital vows could never be a suitable teacher of religion and morals, he had Gonzalve claim that Ellen's marital faults prevented her from performing the most vital motherly duty: moral guidance. Ellen, and her parents, had "fallen into a fatal error, on at least one fundamental point of morals – the obligation of the marriage contract; which in good fortune or bad, in sickness or health, in happiness or misery, binds a wife to her husband, a mother to the father of her children. Such precepts and such example, your petitioner suggests, must exercise a pernicious influence on the child he now seeks to reclaim."[19]

Reed also countered the latent chauvinism of Cadwalader's return. Without denying Ellen's obvious financial ability to rear Frederick or directly challenging the benefits of American citizenship, he emphasized the value of the heritage awaiting the boy in Switzerland. Reed wanted the court to consider Frederick a Swiss, and not let a childhood spent in America turn him into a foreigner in his father's land. He had Gonzalve claim Switzerland not as a foreign state but the natural home of his son and the voluntary home of his wife.[20]

Not content with merely countering Ellen's return, Reed presented an elaborate retelling of the star-crossed d'Hauteville marriage with marital fault as its ordering theme and moral. Marital fault, he insisted, must be the standard for judicial determinations of clashing parental custody claims. He followed this declaration with the very act Ellen and her lawyers had done everything to avoid. To exonerate himself and indict his wife, Gonzalve told a detailed courtroom story of the doomed marriage.

The client tale Reed penned mixed generalizations designed to turn the law in Gonzalve's favor with full readings of numerous letters as evidentiary support. It began with the assertion that the union had been "one of sincere affection" and "sanctioned and approved by the parents on both sides." Gonzalve then denied that he had broken promises to his wife or tyrannized her. The marital violations had been Ellen's. He cataloged her sins: false charges about the seriousness of her father-in-law's sickness, fancied fears of abduction in Paris, duplicitous promises to return to her Swiss home, and double-dealing marital bargaining between her father and Vevey Syndic Frederic Couvreu. He insisted that her actions had legal consequences. For instance, Ellen's decision to ignore his explicit instructions about naming and baptizing their child was "a significant illustration of the necessity of granting the prayer of his petition, as well as an illustration of the unhappiness likely to result from a training for his child over which he can exercise no controul." Furthermore, Reed had Gonzalve inject, he was "advised, that, by the laws of Pennsylvania, and of all christian lands, the courts will, in the guardianship of children, have a faithful regard to the religious opinions of a father." Though "well knowing this," Ellen and her parents, "regardless of his wishes thus expressed, and in opposition to that universal sentiment, which leaves to the father the privilege of naming his first born son, gave to the infant a name utterly repugnant to his wishes, and indicating exclusively, its descent on the maternal side; and caused the baptism to be administered in a communion different from that of which your petitioner and his family are members."[21] Returning to his story, Gonzalve used more letters to call David's threat to sue him "one of the many artifices which have been resorted to, to deter your petitioner from an attempt to enforce his rights."[22]

As a final salvo, Gonzalve once more accused Ellen of trying to circumvent his rights through special legislation. Refuting his wife's claim that the failed acts would not have aided her because they applied only to older children, this time he warned the court about the legal plot Ellen had hatched: She would rely on the tender-years rule now, and special legislation later so that "should he be enabled at some future day to come to claim his child, when it shall have attained riper years, he may find his now undisputed rights divested by clandestine legislation; and he will, he fears, too surely find the mind of his child alienated from that one of his parents whose surname he bears, and who cannot reproach himself with having, by his conduct or example, done him an injury."[23]

Reed brought Gonzalve's story to an end by returning to his major story line of marital fault. He had Gonzalve insist yet again that to determine "the best interests of this his child" the judges must examine "the alleged causes of his wife's desertion." He confidently predicted the outcome of their inquiry, and in doing so also shared his strategy for gaining his child and perhaps even regaining his

wife: "Your Honours, in ascertaining that such desertion is unauthorized by the laws of God or man, and is justified by no act or
omission of your petitioner, will decree and adjudge to him his
child, leaving to his said wife to determine whether she will separate
herself from her child, or, by returning to her husband, whose duty
it will be to forgive and welcome her, discharge at once the sacred
obligations of a mother and a wife."[24] To help the court reach those
conclusions, Reed submitted five exhibits to his brief. Though
mostly more letters, specifically the full correspondence between
David Sears and Swiss Syndic Frederic Couvreu, the submission included New York Governor William Seward's lengthy veto message
striking down the 1840 Act for the Protection of Minors.[25]

Reed's story startled Ellen's lawyers and forced a new round of
narrative competition. Recognizing the failure of his attempt to
avoid a thorough discussion of the d'Hautevilles' marital troubles,
Cadwalader asked for additional time to rewrite Ellen's story. The
dimensions of his task became clear when, in response to a question
from the bench, Reed asserted: "We desire a full inquiry into the
merits of the separation."[26]

Determining a hearing site produced another critical exchange.
Judge Doran proposed reconvening in the chambers of the Guardians of the Poor. "If we sit there," worried Judge Conrad, "there will
no doubt be a crowd." Recommending a private hearing, Cadwalader worried that "[i]f we meet in any public room we are likely to
have a very inconvenient audience." Reed immediately countered,
"We know of no audience that would be inconvenient." As Reed
argued for a public hearing, Meredith and Cadwalader beat a strategic retreat. Though most custody hearings were held out of public
view, once the issue had been raised they did not want to appear
fearful of public scrutiny. Even so, Meredith provoked a clash that
would surface again and again in the hearing. He put the issue to
the judges in terms of their masculine responsibility to protect feminine sensibilities: "We merely made a suggestion in regard to privacy, addressing it to your Honours as men and gentlemen." Reed
quickly rephrased the judges' task as one of masculine solidarity not
paternalistic duty, "And it is to your Honours as men and gentlemen, that we suggest the opposite course."[27]

The lawyers' exchange underscored the gendered realities of the
antebellum courtroom. Only men could perform the central roles
in the courtroom: judge, lawyer, juror, and bailiff. Women could
not be official dispensers of justice. They entered the courts only as
plaintiffs, defendants, witnesses, and spectators. Despite its central
place in the lives of all citizens, the courtroom had been defined
ever more rigidly as a masculine space since the Revolution. The

era's separate sphere ideology not only removed many women from the courts, particularly the criminal courts, it demanded circumspect behavior by those who had to brave the terrors of a trial. Ellen's lawyers relied on that behavioral code when they appealed to judicial chivalry by presenting their client as an aggrieved mother seeking to avoid having intimate details of her marriage dragged through the adversarial mire. Conversely, Gonzalve's attorneys hoped to ally the judges with them with bonds of shared manhood. They wanted the court to respect Gonzalve's public defense of paternal authority.[28]

While forced to ponder the gender implications of the courtroom, the judges as lawyer politicians also felt the lure of open hearings. Once Gonzalve had secured a writ of habeas corpus, he activated the nebulous but potent force of public opinion. Not only was a deeply felt aversion to private justice embedded in popular legal beliefs, so was the reality that the populace liked a good trial. Indeed the case promised the kind of publicity, if their performances elicited favorable reviews, that could help the careers of the judges as well as the lawyers. Though, of course, the converse was true as well. Accustomed to private custody hearings, the unexpected exchange caught the judges off guard. They huddled and then Barton adjourned the hearing until Saturday, July 18th, promising a ruling then.[29]

As the judges deliberated, the *Public Ledger* ratcheted up the pressure on them by making the d'Hauteville trial a major story. Reporter Ritter published an extensive piece under the heading "Novel and Important Case." The "Ledger Man," as he was called, reported "a good deal of smothered feeling in this city, for some days past, in relation to a case understood to be pending before the Judges of the Court of General Sessions." Ritter explained that the case had been "heard privately at the chambers of one or another of the judges, and the mystery thus thrown around it has naturally tended to excite the public curiosity in relation to its details." Warning readers against believing the rumors that had quickly begun circulating about the case, he assured them that the *Ledger* had taken great pains to ascertain the "real character of the proceedings." Taking care to squash any incipient charges of penny-press pandering to base instincts, Ritter emphasized the importance of the trial: "Were it simply a matter of news or gossip, it would find a place in another department of this journal; but involving as it does principles of universal application, every parent has an interest in it, and we feel it our duty to treat it with correctness and deliberation."

Ritter then told his version of the d'Hauteville dispute. The first round of client stories, which told the "history of this ill-matched, ill-starred couple," received a rave review because the stories had been "drawn up not merely with professional skill, but with touching eloquence, and each of them embodies letters and narratives of the most romantic and passionate interest." He introduced the two main characters with descriptions laden with gender stereotypes and assumptions demonstrating that popular gender ideology would be just as critical in the court of public opinion as it was in the court of law. Ellen, "the daughter of Mr. David Seers [sic] of Boston, a gentleman who inherited a fortune of nearly a million dollars which has greatly increased by a well-directed and intelligent enterprise," he described as "almost unequalled, being considered one of the loveliest of her sex. Her manners are lively and agreeable, and her mind is said to be rigorous and accomplished. Such of her letters as were read are characterized, by those who heard them, as admirable in sentiment and style." And, he added, while her husband had demanded a public hearing, and "his wife shrinks with proper delicacy from the exposure, she does not oppose it." Those words of praise, however, were followed by others intended to alert readers to Ellen's privileged status: "We are informed that she is fond of society, gay, fashionable, and accustomed to the best circles of Parisian life, to which she is greatly attached." Such a description did not match the imagery of dutiful motherhood that Cadwalader was trying to sketch; indeed, Ritter's words might weaken Ellen's maternal claims because again and again public accusations that a woman on trial showed too much interest in fashion and frivolity undermined her legal rights. Both the public and the professionals wanted the female recipients of legal largesse to be virtuous.

The husband, Ritter reported, "is under the ordinary size, and has nothing in person or manner to distinguish him from the throng. His eyes and face are dull, and his manner heavy and phlegmatic." Far from the dashing European aristocrat of romantic fiction, Ritter made readers wonder why Ellen had married him in the first place. Even the tense court battle, they learned, seemed not to disturb his placid demeanor: "At each of the different hearings, husband, wife, and child met without emotion – Not a nerve or muscle betrayed the presence of the least sensibility. Mr. d'Hauteville appears to be of melancholic temperament; he is a high-toned Geneva Calvinist, and his letters to his wife, though affectionate, manifest more of religion than love." Yet that picture of stolidity served Gonzalve quite well by giving greater credence to his claim to Frederick. Even so, Ritter could not resist extending his gender judgments by remarking that "we cannot contemplate with respect the conduct of a husband, who dead to all the better sensibilities of our nature, makes the sacred secrets of his household a ribald jest in the mouths of the vulgar, and unbinding his wounds, like a highway mendicant, that the nauseous exhibition may excite the disgusted compassion of the passer-by."

Ritter then retold the story of the d'Hauteville marriage as he had gleaned it from the lawyer's stories. Just like every other person drawn to the case, he created his own version of the couple's struggles. It demonstrated the lure of courtroom storytelling. Creating a story that made sense of the case became a way trial watchers could voice their own concerns and render their own judgments about the trial's cast of characters and its central issues. Nor did they wait until the trial ended to do so. Continuous judgments were critical parts of the shared trial experience.

Ritter's d'Hauteville story asserted that Gonzalve's pedigree had warmed David and Miriam to the match. Suggesting that their ardor lessened only upon finding out that their prospective son-in-law "was not so rich as had been supposed," the reporter highlighted David's letter contending that his daughter married out of duty not love. He added the acerbic comment, "If this were so, it was, perhaps, a generous fault in the girl, but does it not also prove that the father hazarded the happiness of his child for the gratification of his pride?" After implying that the Searses had cultivated the match for the status not love, he classified yearly sojourns in Paris and frequent trips to Boston as "the rocks on which their domestic happiness was wrecked." Even so, Ritter accepted Gonzalve's assertions that Miriam had fanned the flames of marital unhappiness: "The lady pursued a course all too common with inconsiderate mothers-in-law. She soon excited heartbreaks and unhappiness in the before happy family of the d'Hautevilles, and succeeded in persuading her daughter, that her husband, though exemplary and affectionate, was not so attentive and indulgent as he should be. The poison soon began to work. The bride, passionately devoted to the pleasures of Paris, repaired to that giddy and dissipated capitol, the husband, whose tastes and principles are more serene than those of his wife, regarded residence in Paris as dangerous to their happiness, and required her to return to Geneva." Narrating the struggle that led Ellen to seek refuge with Ambassador Cass, he reduced the conflict to a choice Ellen faced between "her accustomed gaieties and enjoyments and her husband's love." She had chosen the former, Ritter disclosed in a devastating gender judgment, and then sailed home after promising to return to Gonzalve, who remained to care for his sick father.

Readers then followed the marriage's death throes. Ellen's affectionate leaving and initial letters had soon given way, "scarcely had she placed herself within the influence of her parents," to a change in "spirit. She wrote a cold, stern letter to her husband concerning her determination to separate from him. His reply was manly and affectionate." Ritter chronicled Gonzalve's voyage to America and failed attempts to retrieve his wife. The bargaining continued by letters "with tenderness on the part of the husband, and on her part every evidence of settled dislike." Ritter reported that Gonzalve even had to beg to see his child. "Mr. Seers meanwhile," he disclosed, "used every exertion to procure the passage of a law that would deprive the father of the custody of his child." After this detailed narrative, Ritter returned to the current trial by explaining that Gonzalve had sought the writ only after "exhausting every persuasive effort."

Ritter's version of the d'Hauteville story represented a significant tactical victory for Gonzalve and an equally telling defeat for Ellen. It threatened to become the popular "story line" of the case. Both sides recognized that Ritter's story would help construct not only the public image of the d'Hautevilles as spouses and parents, but also the public's understanding of the proper legal solution to their problems. The "Ledger Man" made those connections very clear by explaining that in "all civilized countries the father is entitled to the custody of his offspring, unless he forfeits the privilege by his immorality. In this State, the Supreme Court has decided that this universal right is suspended during infancy when maternal aid and tenderness are necessary for the child. The law, however, is but loosely settled, and this case will probably induce an entire revision of the principles which govern the case. Every parent has an interest in the question, and we trust it will be settled without sympathy for any individual, but upon universal and enduring principles." When the law stood in flux, storytelling had immense implications.[30]

Two days after the *Ledger* article hit the streets, the parties filed into Barton's chambers to hear him declare that the trial would be open to the public and held in Congress Hall's second-floor courtroom. Shortly to be seated where Washington, Adams, and Jefferson had debated national and international controversies, the d'Hauteville trial became the latest performance in the Philadelphia's premier courtroom.[31] Cadwalader, reeling from Reed's successes, received a week's continuance to finish Ellen's new story.[32]

During the intermission of the first act in the d'Hauteville hearing, the *Ledger's* version of the case found more and more readers. Following the practice of the day, newspapers used subscriptions to papers like the *Ledger* as a rudimentary wire service. They clipped and reprinted articles of interest. In this manner, the *Ledger* stories became the primary national source for information on the d'Hauteville case. Readers in Ellen's adopted suburban residence learned about her plight when the *Germantown Telegraph* published the *Ledger* story on Wednesday, July 22nd. On that same day, the *New York Sun* splashed the article on its front page along with stories about the case from the *Inquirer.* Three days later the *Boston Post,* that city's leading Democratic party paper, also reprinted the *Ledger* article as front-page news. A couple of days after that, the Whiggish *Boston Courier* also published it, but with the preface: "Some of the circumstances stated in the following article are well known in this community, but how many of them are fact, and how many the progeny of fancy, we are not able to say. The case has been for two or three years a topic of conversation in circles where one of the parties is known; and the account will be sought for with avidity."[33]

Ellen and her supporters feared the impact of this newspaper barrage on the trial. "I assume that Mr. d'Hauteville has attained control of some of the Philadelphia press," her New York lawyer John McKeon wrote David. Expressing the fear they all shared, he added, "from the terms of the remarks in the *Ledger* and the *Philadelphia Inquirer* it is apparent that the impression is to be made that your daughter is fond of fashionable, thoughtless Parisian society, while her husband is such a humble, retiring Christian that it would be unsafe to trust the custody of a young child to such a mother while a father of such noble qualities as Mr. d'Hauteville stands ready to take it to his care." McKeon worried about the connections between law and public opinion, "it is well for us to consider that Judges are but men and they like other men yield even unconsciously to the influence of the opinion of the hour." He urged that counter measures be taken so that they did not lose the case outside the courtroom by the opposition's attempts to "produce a false impression on the public mind."[34] David immediately forwarded the letter to Cadwalader.

Had they read Philadelphia merchant Samuel Breck's scathing July 23rd diary entry, the Searses' fears may well have increased even more. As a legal experience with growing numbers of participants, the d'Hauteville trial was fast becoming a fable told and retold in Philadelphia and around the nation. Each storyteller used the tale of spousal conflict to offer her or his own moral. Breck's rendition emphasized the debilitating impact of wealth: "After building himself a palace in Boston, and surrounding himself with every luxury, [David] and [Miriam] were seized with a malady that attacks all our very rich people, and millionaires elsewhere, who do not work, or engage in some occupation; and that malady I must call it by its French name; for we have no word in English to represent it. I mean *Ennui.* This Ennui, or *weariness,* generally drives our American Nabobs to Europe. And there, at Paris or Geneva, or Florence, & c. They sit down for a while, with their sons and daughters, alienate their regard for home, bring up their children in ways, language and *Notions,* foreign to those of their native land, and expose their daughters to the hazard of contracting marriage with outlandish Counts and Barons, which lead to unhappiness, separation, and if practical, Divorce." Though he got many of the facts wrong, Breck easily fit Ellen into his story of the decline and fall of American aristocrats. Accordingly, he concluded that the Searses had insisted that their daughter, "born of Republican parents, in sober New England, the land of steady habits, should, forsooth, spend her winters in the midst of the frivolities of Paris. A child was born about 20 months ago, and after a winter or two at Paris, the phlegmatic Swiss, began to admonish and scold, and insist on keeping his young wife at home at his chateau, or castle as every frenchman calls a country residence of half a dozen rooms." Surmising that Ellen rebelled at these orders, Breck recorded that she then fled first to Paris and then to Boston after refusing to live with Gonzalve anymore. "He does not ask her to do so," he wrote, "but demands his child. A suit on this issue has been brought in our courts in Philadelphia where a mother is permitted to retain her child during infancy. Many great lawyers are engaged, and the proceedings are going on."[35]

As such judgments were being reached, Ellen's lawyers regrouped and tried to craft a more convincing story. Ritter's insinuations made it clear that legal safety for her, like other female litigants, came with conformity to popular stereotypes. To do that, Ellen had to be portrayed more effectively as both a victim of Gonzalve's marital misconduct and a virtuous mother. Press clippings harping on her wealth, youth, beauty, and love of Parisian finery and society undermined such a portrayal. Fashionable ladies could not easily be cast as dutiful mothers in either the courtroom or the press.

Cadwalader drafted a lengthy tale to counter the adverse publicity and Reed's storytelling successes. Forced by the reality of courtroom combat to go over ground already covered, he had to deal with the same issues and events that Reed had so successfully narrated. By directly joining the issue, the two lawyers began a debate about matrimonial duties and rights that would dominate each act of the trial.

In his first story, Cadwalader had given voice only to Ellen's maternal claims. Now, forced by Reed to tell her version of the marital discord, he penned a tale that minutely explained and justified each of Ellen's acts. To tell this more elaborate tale, he cut out portions of Ellen's own narrative and pinned them to pieces of paper. In between the cutouts he added legal connectors that turned her lay words into legal claims while reconstituting her as both a suffering wife and deserving mother.[36]

After the parties gathered in the courtroom on July 29th, Cadwalader began two days of storytelling he hoped would reframe the case for the judges and the public. The Philadelphia lawyer first had his client reiterate the maternalist claims of her previous story. To bring gender stereotypes into the courtroom in his client's defense and as a challenge the paternalist assumption of the law's public narrative, he had Ellen declare, "No male person is competent to take the necessary care of so young an infant, and no female, but a mother, can be expected to bestow upon it the care and protection which are necessary for its health and welfare. Removed from the affectionate devotion which nature has implanted in a mother's bosom, her infant must be neglected and abandoned to chances, of which the result may be most melancholy." She connected that message of gender essentialism to the law by reminding the court that its discretion could be exercised only "with an exclusive view to the safety and benefit of the child." Cadwalader then began his assault on the links Reed made between marital fault and custody by having Ellen claim that in such custody decisions "her own merits or demerits are of no importance, otherwise than as they may influence the question of the child's welfare, and if considerations of this sort, do not bear upon the question of her capacity to perform towards it the present duties of a mother, her custody of it is, for the present recognized as its most appropriate custody." In short, Cadwalader hoped to triumph by using his new story to disentangle Ellen's roles as wife and mother in a more persuasive manner than he had in his first attempt.

Even so, Reed's narrative successes could not be overcome easily. Besides dismissing as both false and "insufficient and untenable in point of law" Gonzalve's charges on everything from Frederick's citizenship to his baptism, Cadwalader had Ellen hammer away at the connection between marital fault and parental fitness. She directly addressed the vexing issue of legitimate marital exits that troubled so many others caught in unhappy marriages. Ellen refused to accept that her separation from Gonzalve marked her as morally unfit to rear Frederick. Besides denying the relevancy of the charge to her ability to nurture her son, Ellen contended that, despite his allegations to the contrary, no actual difference existed between her understanding of marital obligations and that of her husband. "The point of difference," she asserted, "is whether his conduct has not been such to dissolve the force of this obligation; for however binding the marriage contract, in a general point of view, there can be no doubt that the conduct of either party to it, may be such as to absolve the other from the obligation of continuing in his society." She then leveled her own charges: "The causes of her separation from the relator were a series of acts of systematic ill-treatment and oppression, accompanied and aggravated by a total disregard, on his part, of the sympathies, and neglect of the attentions, without which there can be no happiness in the marriage state." While she might have submitted to "occasional acts of oppression and ill-treatment," Gonzalve's constant tyranny destroyed her health and forced her to flee. Cadwalader borrowed a phrase from one of David's letters to portray Ellen as a victim of mental cruelty, and thus imply a putative legal justification for abandoning her husband. Using her father's phrase, she labeled Gonzalve's acts a "moral tyranny, which strikes its blows upon the mind until it totters, as equivalent to all that the body can be brought to suffer." The impact of combined acts of commission and omission left her "crushed and blighted in the earliest prime of her ripening womanhood." Yet still more cruel blows came: "And now, the climax of the wrongs of which she has been the victim is attained, in an attempt to turn these wrongs as weapons against her, to tear her child from her bosom, and thus take from her the only remaining tie by which she can be bound to life, in a world which to her must, at least, be a world of sorrow."[37]

To corroborate Gonzalve's oppression, Cadwalader presented Ellen's version of the massive collection of d'Hauteville letters and documents. He wrote the script so that its chronological narrative of the doomed marriage mixed assertions undermining Gonzalve's claims of being a pious patriarch with inserts offering legal justifications for his client's acts. Consequently, in an attempt to suggest that Gonzalve pursued her despite only lukewarm encouragement, Ellen played to American stereotypes of money-grubbing European gigolos by contending that "before this renewal of their acquaintance, in the spring of 1837, the relator had made particular inquiries concerning the worldly means and circumstances of certain American ladies, of whom she was one, and that she was not the first of her countrywomen, of reputed wealth, to whom he paid his addresses." At this point, Cadwalader turned to one of his additions to her story. First he had Ellen repeat a passage from one of her letters to David: "Young, and imbued with the sentiments ordinarily entertained at that age, she was peculiarly sensitive upon the subject of her duty to keep her word in this respect, and until freely released, considered it nearly as binding as the marriage contract." In one of his pinned additions that sought to confer legality on her acts, Cadwalader had her add that only now did she realize that as a minor she was not as accountable for her legal agreements as an adult. Returning to the story, Ellen explained that during her courtship she had feared her reputation would be forever sullied if word circulated that she had cast Gonzalve aside for lack of wealth. So, to her bitter regret, she had let the courtship continue. As Cadwalader read her tale, his theme became very clear. Misunderstandings, a misplaced youthful sense of honor, and deception not love had propelled Ellen toward her doomed union with Gonzalve.

Similarly, to combat the damaging press characterizations of his client as a frivolous creature of fashion, Cadwalader had her explain the importance of Gonzalve's promises to spend winters in Paris or Italy and journey frequently to America. Declaring that Ellen had considered the vows "an indisputable condition of the marriage," her lawyer heightened their importance by turning them into symbolic acts of martial despotism. As she had in her bargaining letters, Ellen insisted that her attachment to Gonzalve lacked the passion that might overcome the loss of family, friends, and country. Exile for her could only be palatable with promises of periodic trips to places like Paris and Rome where touring Americans gathered or to her home in Boston. Cadwalader deepened the etching of Gonzalve as a failed mate by having Ellen use the broken promises to question her husband's manhood. Honing in on what she and her lawyers knew to be a fatal flaw for a man, she suggested that his "subserviency to his parents, however meritorious in other respects, was carried to an extent, which, in the case of persons who had passed the age of minority, was different from that which she had been accustomed to see in her own country." Thus when his parents made clear their opposition to any American visits, so did their son. Acknowledging that a wife should, "according to the true character of the relation of marriage," fulfil her duty and "reside with her husband, and consequently to reside at such place or places as he should deem it expedient to select," nevertheless, Ellen argued that had she known Gonzalve would break his promises she would not have married him. Her attack on his manhood reinforced the claim by using popular assumptions of manly independence to undermine both Gonzalve's actions and his appeal as a mate for life. In this way, Cadwalader intimated that marital fraud had been practiced on his client by an unmanly and thus unworthy beau.[38]

Broken promises, Ellen lamented, were but one example of Gonzalve's tyranny. Reasserting her customary claim of mental cruelty, no matter its legal bastardy, she insisted that "when to other matters, in themselves oppressive and tyrannical, this abuse of power and violation of good faith was superadded; when the power itself was used as a measure of tyrannical oppression, the case was very different; and what would not alone have been her justification in her separation, became, when thus accompanied, too oppressive to be borne."[39]

Turning to the rapid collapse of her marriage, Ellen recounted her husband's jealousy and abuse in the weeks after their marriage. Cadwalader read to the court the biblical passages she had been forced to study, and described how Miriam had suffered from the hostility of Gonzalve and his family. Blow after cruel blow ruined Ellen's health and sapped her confidence in her new mate. Cadwalader hoped to cement the image of marital tyranny in the judges' minds by vividly recounting Gonzalve's bungled attempt to spirit her out of Paris.[40]

Once more forcing a comparison of her husband with popular standards of masculinity, Ellen argued that the Paris confrontation revealed Gonzalve's "unmanly jealousy of her mother" as well as his tyranny and treachery. Cadwalader focused on the meaning of force to develop the charge of mental cruelty. The issue of force, he had Ellen argue, "is not so much a question of fact, as of the true definition of the term *force*." Cadwalader supplied one by having his client claim as her own the words of an unnamed family friend, who had heard about Gonzalve's claim that no force had been intended: "No force – what does he mean? What is force applied to a feeble and defenceless woman, and she too his wife, with nobody but women and children about her, and armed, himself, with the authority of a husband, against which no one could lawfully interpose." In a revealing analogy, the friend declared, "The criminal who is carried to jail, is seldom dragged through the streets by actual violence. The officer is perfectly civil, he taps his prisoner on the shoulder, and the affair is done; because he acts by an authority which the criminal knows it is in vain to resist. But is he not forced to his prison? So Monsieur d'Hauteville would have come, not with a troop of horses, or corps of police officers, but with his carriage, his servants, and his friend, (for it was admitted he had one.) He would not have dragged her by the hair, for it would have been needless. He would not have entered with the air of a ruffian, but, probably, with the polite smile of a most affectionate husband. He would simply have said, in the most gracious manner, 'my love, the carriage is at the door, the servants at hand to take your baggage, my friend waits.' He would have taken her by the arm, and she would have been upon the road to Switzerland, as much against her will, as the criminal to his dungeon, and by just the same species of force, the force of irresistible authority." Through such vivid words, Ellen's new story not only tried to link her with other victims of oppression, it became a brief for legal recognition of mental cruelty as a marital crime sufficient to warrant legal redress.[41]

Finally, Ellen told of events in America after her voyage home. She explained away the affectionate letter she wrote at the Astor upon her arrival as the product of the kindness Gonzalve had shown her during their final days and the sorrow he expressed for all that had happened. Even so, Ellen minimized the differences between her first letter and the next one she wrote from Boston refusing to return to Hauteville. Her intent, she informed the court, had been to make clear her desire for reconciliation and her refusal to return to Hauteville. More important, she argued, were the words Gonzalve wrote. His letters never contained the apology she expected. In their absence, she continued to fear her fate if forced to return to a husband who could not wean himself from his parents. Accepting a responsibility to live with him, she decided that she could not and would not live with them. Instead, she demanded a separate residence, and vowed not to return until he agreed. The point, Cadwalader had her maintain in an attempt to undermine Reed's attempt to cast her as a marital rebel, was that she did not want a separation from her husband but from his parents. Gonzalve had thus misconstrued the warmth of her first letter and the declaration of independence in the second. A break came, she argued, because of his words not hers.[42]

Ellen concluded her defense of the decision to abandon Gonzalve with pointed summary of her charges against him. As a result of his deceptions, broken promises, and marital tyranny, Ellen told the judges, "her return to his society could not take place without a renewal of the state of health of mind and body, under which she had sunk, when her return to the United States first became necessary; and that in the present state of her feelings and of her powers of future endurance, she could not perform to him the duties of a wife and therefore cannot return to him."[43]

Cadwalader closed Ellen's new story with his own appendix. In it he placed numerous letters between the various actors in the d'Hauteville drama. He also attached a memorandum on Frederick's health to document the child's sickliness and Ellen's maternal care. The memo described the boy's constant afflictions beginning shortly after his birth when bowel complaints forced the "application of hot baths and mustard poultices in succession, every fifteen minutes . . . and after a very *severe* illness of a fortnight's duration, during which time Mrs. d'Hauteville never left him to any other person's charge, he seemed partially recovered." Yet eruptions soon appeared all over his body and the infant suffered from constant distress. "Mrs. d'Hauteville's health and strength," the document recorded, were "failing under these untiring exertions, and from want of sleep, and anxiety of mind. She frequently passed the whole night in walking up and down the chamber with the child in her arms; and was often obliged, during these hours, to put it into a bath, assisted by her mother, in order to cut off the clothes that had adhered to its body." Ellen had nursed the six month old child constantly. After her doctor advised weaning, Frederick began to recover but remained in ill health. Finally Ellen had taken him to Nahant for his health when Gonzalve's appearance forced her flight and the child's bowels had suffered ever since. "The child has been," the memorandum concluded, "during the whole of his life, always under the care of a physician."[44]

Cadwalader's lengthy story reversed the momentum of the narrative competition. Now Reed rose to request time to pen a second story for Gonzalve. Meredith objected to a delay on the "ground of public convenience." Scott entered the fray for the first time by claiming the moral high ground for Gonzalve: "If weeks and months are given to the consideration of questions of mere property, why should not an equal time be devoted to this case of immeasurably greater importance? The relator, far from the comforts and friends of home, detained in a land of strangers, is really the only sufferer by delay: When he asks it no one should object. I do not think the courts of the country can be better employed than in the consideration of questions so interesting and important as this." Barton agreed and the hearing stood in recess until August 31st.[45]

As the lawyers retired for a second intermission in the d'Hauteville trial's first act, the press once again reviewed their performance. Editors and reporters offered preliminary verdicts on the messy d'Hauteville case. In a front page story, the *Ledger* detailed Cadwalader's narrative calling it "a splendid piece of composition."[46] Pointing out the "very voluminous" documents read in the case, the *Inquirer* also gave Cadwalader's performance a rave review. He had given "a very able and eloquent production, and opened to view the entire particulars of the marriage and subsequent disagreement." Explaining that the presentation had consisted of reading intimate letters, the reporter offered a much more flattering portrayal of Ellen than in his first stories: "Whatever opinion may be entertained of the lady's affections, there can be no doubt of the strength of her intellect. Some of her letters are very finished and elegant specimens of composition, and many of the passages are masterly in their eloquence and beauty." Sharing the pathos of the tale, he called Ellen's letter to David on the eve of his departure for America "equal to any production that we have ever met with – and so endearingly affecting and affectionate in its nature, that, although probably perused by him a hundred times, it still drew tears from his eyes when read in court." Even at this preliminary stage of the hearing, the reporter confidently offered a judgment on the failed d'Hauteville marriage: "The real cause of separation, to our view, is the utter want to congeniality of sentiments and feeling. This want no doubt at times induced the husband to consider the wife capricious; and the lady to think her husband cold, exacting, and domineering. Instead of yielding to each other's dissimilarities of opinion and character, they appear from the commencement to have battled for supremacy. The result must be obvious to any one." After a detailed description of those difficulties, the story added the ritual statement of regret that the battling couple had allowed their innermost family problems to be "spread open for public gaze. Pity it is that the penetration of the domestic altar should thus be invaded by the eye of vulgar curiosity, and all of its sacred mystery developed."[47]

Miriam Sears not only resented such invasions of her family privacy, she continued to fear the impact of newspaper clippings on her daughter's cause. In a letter to Cadwalader, she worried that "Mr. d'Hauteville has so much larger a proportion of your townspeople on his side – notwithstanding our return" and that "the articles in the *Ledger* which have been very widely circulated has done as much harm in public estimation, that I fear our contest must, after all our hopes, be sharply fought and hardly won." She thought that "some of the wounds will be deep and lasting." Two days later, she wrote again asking Cadwalader if he remained "sanguine that we shall be done justice by – I'm constantly worried that Judge Barton is not on our side."[48]

David also worried about the bad press. Like Miriam, he shared his fears with Cadwalader, writing on August 19th that "we are somewhat alarmed at the current which seems to be against us." The "Ledger Man," using Ritter's well-known nickname, "has done us incredible mischief. The large and false statements he made, is in the hands of every one, I really believe, in New England." Amazed that "a private matter" like Ellen's case could "cause so much interest," he urged the Philadelphia lawyer to think of countermeasures pleading, "[i]s there no way of getting at the fact of who furnished the materials? You do not seem, in Philadelphia, to be aware of the *deviltry of the press*."[49]

Family members were not the only ones who shared their concerns about Ellen's unfavorable press with Cadwalader. New Yorker Park Benjamin, editor of the *New World*, asked the Philadelphia lawyer for a copy of Ellen's new story. Explaining his request, Benjamin asserted, "When you consider that this affair has been made public in all the principal journals of the United States and that many garbled accounts have appeared, I think that you will not regard this application as impertinent and that you would appreciate my motives in making it." He assured Cadwalader that publication of the recent version of Ellen's story would "set the matter right before the public and correct any erroneous impression that thus may have been formed. It seems that, after all the publicity, which the affair has had – that your account, which could be received as authentic, should be laid before the community." To make his partisanship clear, Benjamin explained that he had already culled stories from the *Inquirer* to write an account of the case "with the object, I confess, of creating an impression unfavorable to the conduct and claims of Mr. d'Hauteville." Assuring Cadwalader of his paper's wide readership "in the principal cities of the nation," he awaited Cadwalader's reply.[50]

At least two other editors shared Benjamin's fears. On August 5th, the *Germantown Telegraph* prefaced a story on the d'Hauteville case with the disclaimer: "The following remarks relative to this case, we copy from the *New York Courier and Inquirer,* as a matter of justice to the respondent, who it would appear, has not had her connection with this case fairly stated." Complaining of the "partial" story that had been reprinted in various newspapers, apparently meaning the earlier *Ledger* article, the *Courier* worried that "the greatest injustice has been done to the unfortunate mother. It contains representations to the effect that she was of a gay and heartless disposition, carried away by the follies of fashionable life, and bent upon their indulgence to the sacrifice of maternal duties and of the relation of a wife to her husband." Following Cadwalader's lead, the reporter also tried to refurbish Ellen's public image by assuring its readers that the charges were not only "false and unfounded," but that a "purer, nobler, and more elevated disposition was never infused into the heart of woman, that which governs the life of the lady whom a series of unfortunate circumstances have involved in this lamentable controversy." The editors justified their defense of Ellen by citing the "industrious efforts" made by "the friends of Mr. d'Hauteville to circulate these false impressions. On the general merits of the case we gave nothing to say in its present stage; but it is not improper nor indelicate to disabuse the public mind of the prejudices which have been excited against a lady, who is eminently endowed with all the graces and accomplishments that adorn, and all the virtues that lend dignity and elevation, to the female character."[51]

Attention shifted from the press back to the courtroom when all the participants returned to hear Reed's final version of Gonzalve's courtroom story. Titled a "Further Suggestion," Reed's new tale dismissed Ellen's return as "novel in form and erroneous in content." Even so, Cadwalader's successful storytelling forced Reed to caution the judges about the omissions, partial statements, and inferences buried in Ellen's return. To guard against "unsustained assertions" and accompanying misstatements of facts, he had Gonzalve urge them to ignore Ellen's statements and instead consider the correspondence – which only he had produced in an unadulterated form – between the parties as the "best evidence" in the case. By putting this potent litigation phrase in the mouth of his client, Reed hoped to activate the rule that created an evidentiary hierarchy. Convinced that the d'Hauteville letters supported Gonzalve's claims, he wanted the judges to place them above Ellen's assertions in their pecking order of proof.[52]

Determined to regain the narrative edge, Reed had Gonzalve tackle Ellen's version of their marital problems with a point by point rebuttal that retold the saga of the d'Hauteville marriage yet another time. Once more his client story linked marital fault with custody rights, while passing silently over Ellen's care of Frederick.

Though mainly a more detailed version of his first story, Gonzalve did make one significant admission. The bitter courtroom narrative competition had finally convinced Gonzalve that his wife did not love him. "Slow and painful," he admitted, "has been the process by which he has been brought to suspect that his confidence was misplaced, and that the words of affection which she so often uttered and so often wrote were insincere and deceptive." Reed had him leave it to the judges to determine just how far his admission would "strengthen the respondent's claim to the custody of the child of his affection at least." Little, he hoped.

Generally, Reed's new story constantly challenged "the gloss" Cadwalader had put on Gonzalve's deeds and words. To undermine the insinuation that he had forced Ellen into marriage, he argued that every time the path to the altar had been blocked, Miriam, David, and Ellen had removed the obstacle.[53] Once more, he denied making or breaking promises about trips to Paris or America. Pointing out that no stipulation about them had been made in the couple's intricate antenuptial agreement, he argued that the real source of the controversy lay in Ellen and her parents' desperate need, "by some means, to justify the course they have been induced to pursue." Similarly, Gonzalve tackled the chauvinism that surfaced repeatedly in Ellen's story. He asked that his national ties be accorded the same respect he granted his wife's. Tactically, he tried to counter antiforeign sentiment and to undermine the image of the calculating European that Cadwalader had constructed and make

Switzerland more palatable to the American political palate by praising its republican institutions. To revive the image of Ellen as a
spoiled creature of fashion and counter the latent nativism in her
return, Gonzalve recalled his hope that "his American wife would
find its simplicity that which would most resemble, and make her
least regret the home of her birth and infancy."[54]

Gonzalve also tried to reclaim his manhood. Advancing an appealing comparison for mobile Americans, he suggested that in a
new nation like America, "the sentiment of filial respect and venera-
tion is necessarily weakened by the interruptions, to which a young
and enterprising community is liable. The son scarcely feels himself
a man, before he wanders forth on some distant enterprise to make
his own fortune, and often does not return till he is surrounded by
a family of his own, who necessarily and naturally divide affection
which before had but one object. In Europe, and especially in Switzerland, as may be well known to your Honours, a different state of
things exits. In a society so small, whose habits are somewhat primitive, and where children are rarely separated from their parents,
where marriage makes no division, the wife coming at once to the
home of her husband and his parents, it will at once be seen, that
the relations between parent and child, and the feelings which
spring from them, are to be judged by other standards than those
which are applied to other countries." Gonzalve offered this comparison "not by way of admission of the justice of the unkind sar-
casms which in the return are directed at him," but to refute the
charge of "blind subserviency to his parents" and yet express his
love for them. In like manner, Gonzalve defended his religious faith
as a national characteristic and rebuffed charges of being a callous,
calculating European gigolo.[55]

Following Reed's script, Gonzalve took the opportunity to contest
another of Ellen's claims by returning to his dominant argument,
marital fault. He argued that the Searses' blatant disregard of the
sanctity of the marital contract rendered them all morally unfit cus-
todians for Frederick. Refusing to accept the separation of spousal
and parental roles, he rejected the contention that "misconception
of duty on one point, supposing it to exist, will not prevent its due
performance on others." Through Gonzalve's statement, Reed
wanted to force the judges to consider the larger policy implications
of such a division. Such revisions, he suggested, would fundamentally revise the law's commitment to marital permanence. To make
the judges understand what was at stake, Gonzalve warned that they
must decide "vital questions of law and morality, affecting the well-
being of society, and the permanence of those domestic institutions
which make society what it is. The marriage contract, that which the

Marriage contract

Aristotelian

respondent and relator once formed, is a high and holy contract. Its inviolability is the strongest bond which binds a christian community together. From it spring all other relations of domestic life, and with it, when it is loosened and weakened by the indulgence of caprice, or by the influence of theories which justify separation for trivial causes, the sanctity of those relations falls. It is a contract which the laws enforce, and the solemnities of religion are made to ratify. It is a mutual vow to love and cherish, a solemn invocation of religious sanction on the union of two human beings for life, for better or worse, in sickness and health, in happiness and misery. It is something even more still: it is a solemn compact which recognizes no higher domestic duty than that which it imposes. The faith a wife or husband pledges is their best security for long companionship." After this soliloquy on matrimony, Gonzalve pointedly reminded the judges that the "laws of Switzerland, where the contract was solemnized, the laws of Pennsylvania which your Honours are to enforce, recognize its sanctity and paramount obligation. And your Honours have now to decide a question in relation to this obligation, the effect of which on all society it is impossible to appreciate."[56]

In the same vein, Gonzalve argued that the only just resolution of the case must be clear to the judges. Their ruling must be, "as he is confident it will be, in accordance with universal law, as settled by the wisest judges, that to the father belongs his child." Given his son, Gonzalve pledged to "see that its best interests and permanent welfare are promoted, in that community to which of right he belongs, and where he must ultimately reside." Even so, Gonzalve, had to acknowledge that the court might rule against him. To foreclose that possibility, he warned the judges about the implications of a decision that made the illegal desertion of a wife "a reason for depriving him of his child " and allowed a mother, thus causelessly deserting, to "raise the plea of tender age, when her duty admonishes to follow and protect her child." Under such a doctrine "his rights would be altogether divested" as would those of other innocent men.

Gonzalve hoped to stop an adverse judgment not only by questioning the logic that would reward an errant wife, but by challenging the maternalism of his wife's tale. He demanded that the court respect his right to govern his family as he saw fit. Like John Barry, Gonzalve saw his custody fight as a defense of male authority itself. He had a willing spokesman for that cause in Reed. Through his lawyer's narrative, Gonzalve explained to the judges that he had defended himself against Ellen's charges only out of respect for the court and the need to vindicate himself. But, he insisted, the judges must understand the real issues at stake in the hearing. Speaking man to man in the hope that the judges would accept the need for male solidarity, Gonzalve asserted his paternal rights as a check on the court's power to intervene in his family affairs. "The domestic hearth is protected and the domestic government is justly administered," he declared unequivocally, "by its domestic head. The code of laws which he enacts and applies, upon a responsibility not less solemn than that of civil or political legislation, is founded in affection and obeyed from impulses of gratitude and love. The jurisdiction, in its narrow but important sphere, is perfect and supreme as long as it is exercised within the limits which divine and human wisdom have prescribed." To make sure the judges understood him, Gonzalve asserted that "[n]o external power will venture to question, let alone invade it" until the "limits of domestic authority and subordination are transgressed." It was, he maintained, "equally tyrannical and absurd to interpose, directly or indirectly, the influence of the judicial magistracy" on a man's family without legitimate cause. When such violations occurred, "the laws and the tribunals of the community which surround the domestic altar, and protect its proper offerings, exercise immediate and effectual control. Even they are powerless in the large class of cases which can only be determined before the paternal forum." Ever more defiant, Gonzalve argued to the three judges that while he had met and repelled every charge against him, "he protests against the right to arraign him on these points of domestic government. His responsibility is not to this, however just and eminent, tribunal, in any shape." Then he made the challenge to the court even more direct: "By what standard could you Honours judge whether the contents of a letter were better communicated or withheld? whether a supposed excursion was expedient? or whether an individual in conversation on topics of interests should be seated or moving, empty-handed or lifting up a book? If your individual intelligences could find the standard, to what end would be the determination, except to exhibit a profitless pursuit of uncertain theories or immaterial circumstances, out of which no substantial hypothesis in morals, and certainly no inferences in law, could be formed."

Warming to the cause of paternal rights, Gonzalve tried to place the contest before the court in its proper context. Compelled "to turn aside for a moment into the by-ways of disputation, on unimportant topics," he now wanted to return to the real issues of the case: "Is the father to be deprived of his only child, because in questions of domestic economy the other parent or her friends differ from him in opinion? Shall the other parent be permitted, in abandoning her home, and violating her duty, in indulging her caprice,

or submitting to foreign influence, to carry with her his most pre-
cious possessions, to sacrifice his tenderest affections, to rob him
not of herself alone, but more cherished and more indissoluble
hopes?" Gonzalve demanded the Philadelphia bench respect his patriarchy.[57]

Reed had Gonzalve conclude his second story by reiterating that
the case before the court could not be clearer. Before the judges
stood a father and husband with an unblemished character who
asked only for his son and heir. His legitimate claim was resisted by
a woman, who remained his wife yet had abandoned him and her
adopted country for trivial and legally insignificant reasons. Her
plea, Gonzalve declared in a final flourish, "is as unsupported by
judicial precedent, as it is inconsistent with sound reason," and so
he hoped that "this court will not, by yielding to its alleged force,
sanction and reward the voluntary abandonment of that union, pronounced by the laws of God and man, the most holy and indissoluble on earth."[58]

Reed's story closed the first act of the d'Hauteville trial. "The paper read was a very able and eloquent production," the *Inquirer*
raved, "and only equalled by that which it is intended to answer."
After two months of courtroom stories, the trial had captured the
imagination of the city. According to the *Inquirer,* "no case ever
brought before our courts contained so much matter exceedingly
interesting in its character, and eloquent in the form of its presentation as this." Once more disdaining mere sensationalism, the paper
insisted that the d'Hauteville case attracted interest, "not because it
gratifies the mere vulgarity of those whose education and standing
in society should render them less liable to such disagreeable scenes,
but because it conveys a lesson – not to be mistaken – to all who
assume the sacred ties of marriage, how necessary it is to yield to
each other's failings, and to look with a lenient eye on human falli-
bility."[59]

Act Two: Lawyers' Stories

In the second act of the d'Hauteville trial, Cadwalader, Reed, and
their colleagues had to convince the judges that their clients' stories
had clear legal meanings. Courtroom procedure gave each side
three chances to do that: opening statements, presentation of evidence, and closing arguments. Through September and October,
the two teams of lawyers used these opportunities to convince the
judges that both fact and law supported their clients' case.

Intense public interest aroused by Gonzalve and Ellen's heart-
rending yet combative stories increased the importance and the

difficulties of the case for the lawyers. As one of Philadelphia's prime public theaters, each day the Congress Hall courtroom filled with potential critics. Clients, judges, colleagues, courtroom spectators, and newspaper reporters and readers constantly reviewed their performances. These reviews differed in telling ways from those of Gonzalve and Ellen. The d'Hautevilles had been, and would be, judged by standards drawn primarily from popular and legal ideals of dutiful mothers, frivolous wives, tyrannical husbands, caring fathers, and similar stock characters in courtroom melodramas. Their stories had been written and rewritten to conform to those stereotypes. Reed, Cadwalader, and their colleagues, however, would be rated as lawyers. Their fellow professionals and the public had as clear-cut ideas about how lawyers should perform in the courtroom as they did about clients. Once again stock courtroom characters brought these expectations to life: the flamboyant defense counsel, the steely eyed questioner, and the pedantic prosecutor. Flights of oratory, skill in questioning witnesses, success in rebutting opponent's tactics, and even courtroom demeanor and dress would be closely scrutinized.

As in all major trials, the reviews would affect not only the outcome of the case but also the lawyers' standing in the professional and public world of Philadelphia. Yet the consequences of these judgments would also differ. Popular evaluations would have an impact on the lawyers' public reputation and ability to attract clients. Professional judgments had a more complex meaning. They determined the place of each attorney in the community of Philadelphia lawyers. It was in that community that they spent their working lives. Fellow Philadelphia lawyer, and later judge and law teacher, George Sharwood made the implications of these differing judgments quite clear: "Nothing is more certain than that the practitioner will find in the long run, the good impression of his professional brethren of more importance than that of what is commonly called the public."[60]

The memoirs of David Paul Brown, a Philadelphia lawyer and popular orator, explained the professional standards used to judge the trial performances of Cadwalader, Reed, and the other d'Hauteville attorneys. "The trial of a cause," he wrote in 1856, "may be aptly compared to the progress of a painting. You first lay your ground-work; then sketch your various figures; and finally, by the power and coloring of argument, separate or group together, with all the advantages of light and shade." However, he warned, "if the groundwork be imperfect, or the delineations indistinct, your labor will frequently commence where it ought to conclude – and even after all, will prove unsatisfactory, if not contemptible; or perhaps it

△ in paternalism

may more justly be likened to a complicated piece of music, wherein a single false note may destroy the entire harmony of the performance." Brown wrote golden rules for avoiding such sour notes. Acknowledging the theatrical reality of the courtroom, he advised: "Speak to your witness clearly and distinctly, as if you were awake, and engaged in a matter of interest; and make him also speak distinctly and to your question. How can it be supposed that the court and jury will be inclined to listen, when the only struggle seems to be – whether the counsel or the witness shall first go to sleep."[61] In September, 1840, Brown and other Philadelphia lawyers waited to see how well the d'Hautevilles' lawyers performed the courtroom skills of their craft.

While they waited for the next act, the lawyers put the finishing touches on their presentations. During July and August, as they had read their clients' stories, the teams of lawyers also had been drafting opening statements, compiling lists of witnesses, taking depositions, and, most importantly, devising strategies to turn the law in their client's favor. In bulging files, Cadwalader left the most complete record of this arduous work. His files not only document the basic work of a trial lawyer, they demonstrate the impact of the law's relative autonomy on the construction of a legal argument. As his notes make clear, the Philadelphia lawyer recognized the novelty of his client's cause and understood that he must construct a legal argument that gave the judges compelling reasons for departing from custody law's dominant public narrative of paternalism. The law's relative autonomy allowed him to do that because he, like other lawyers and laypeople, understood that legal rules could never be totally independent of popular beliefs and social change. However complex the relationship between law and society, they believed that one existed. The d'Hautevilles' lawyers had to confront it primarily in terms of gender change. Their task was both clarified and complicated by the uncertainties of custody law. Social and legal change had made it a category at risk. Forced to explain and defend their interpretation of its contested rules, the lawyers struggled to understand and use the connections between custody rules wedded to the "best interest of the child" doctrine and popular attitudes about maternalism and paternalism.

Yet as Cadwalader tried to meld contemporary concerns into his argument, the second element of the law's relative autonomy constrained his freedom of action. Though linked to society, the legal system did have partial independence. Social change was never automatically mirrored in the law. On the contrary, a belief in transcendent legal rules inspired the faith in the rule of law that formed the basic tenet of American legalism. It meant that effective legal argument had to be constructed within the forms of law and the patterns of argument built up over time by members of the legal community. Consequently, like other lawyers Cadwalader had to deal with both established precedents and inherited methods of constructing legal arguments. The dual force of the law's relative autonomy framed the way Cadwalader crafted Ellen's case.[62]

Cadwalader began to meet these challenges by giving full play to his scholarly inclinations. He conducted an extensive review of English and American custody law. What he found both appalled and encouraged him. Most dramatically, his research provoked a conversion experience as it often does as to lawyers who become enmeshed in their client's causes.[63] Taking a doggedly adversarial approach to his research findings, Cadwalader sketched ways to overcome the obvious paternal biases of English law. After reading cases like *De Manneville*, he thought that precedents that worked against his client "might be explained away" through stratagems like focusing on Frederick's young age. But soon he decided on a bolder approach and attacked the very reasoning of the English cases. Storytelling and research led him to the decision. As he read Ellen's story in court and studied the law in his office, Cadwalader began to identify with his client. He became a zealous convert to legal maternalism. As a result of his conversion experience, Cadwalader began "to view the [English cases] in [the] real deformity of their most monstrous and uncivilized cruelty." Drafting possible courtroom statements, he wrote to himself: "What was this ultra absoluteness of paternal power? When governments were absolute, paternal power was said to be absolute also, and upon this an argument was founded in favor of the indivisibility as well as the absoluteness of both political and domestic power. It was viewed by monarchical writers as an argument in favor of prevailing forms of government and among them had its vogue accordingly in Filmer." Thanks to that arch defender of patriarchy and other English apologists, he concluded, rules had been created that were "worse than the law of brutes and incapable of being enforced by Christian men or by liberal gentlemen."

Fortunately, though, Cadwalader also decided that this brutal custody law had never been "transplanted from Europe" so it had never taken "root in an American soil." Instead he catalogued English custody law with other European barbarities banned in the humane and progressive new republic: "It may be classified with . . . the burning of Heretics and of witches, the boiling to death and the racking to death of the human creature, the drawing and quartering and disemboweling of the victims of legal punishment when already dead – the mutilation of members of the living – the rack,

the pillory – the stocks – public whipping – duelling swords – Wa-
ger of Battle . . . [and] the doctrines under which a man was permitted to let his debtor starve to death and was allowed to flog his wife
or let her die without food or clothing." He returned to his subject
by insisting that the "degradation and subjection of the gentler sex
in the early laws of England was a fruitful source of examples of this
sort." Yet he acknowledged that "statutory reform" and "in some
degree the liberality of judicial decisions" had moderated the horrors of English law. After reading the Parliamentary debates that
preceded the passage of Lord Talfourd's Act granting mothers limited custody rights, he noted with approval the assertion of maternal essentialism by a Member of Parliament: "Men had very little
notion of the intensity of a mother's affection for her child."[64]

More importantly, however, the Philadelphia lawyer began drafting an argument asserting that the antipaternalism of Pennsylvania
law sanctioned greater legal rights for mothers and thus a new public narrative for custody law. In his state, "has been found the principle of rejecting those parts of the common law which were repugnant to the law of reason and of nature or incompatible with the
feelings and state of society of the commonwealth." Unaccountable
paternal power ought to be made one of those rejected principles.
Slavishly following the logic of the English custody decision would
take Pennsylvania law "backwards." The better path, he decided,
would be to follow the "dictates of experience and social philosophy." By doing just that, Pennsylvania law had rejected the principle
of "decisions uncongenial to our feelings of humanity." In analyzing
the commonwealth's key custody rulings, Cadwalader decided that
only by granting mothers greater custodial rights could judicial decisions conform to natural justice and progressive change. As American lawyers have always done to add legitimacy to their arguments,
he gave his newfound legal maternalism a common law pedigree.
"[I]n reality," he asserted in a revision of legal history, "the common
law [is] on the side of Pennsylvania decisions" not the brutish English ones.

As he mapped out a frontal assault on paternal custody, Cadwalader's notes reveal just how deeply he imbibed the maternalism of
his era. For the Philadelphia lawyer it seemed equally axiomatic that
nature had created mothers as primary child rearers and that
law must regard them so as well. Blind to any notion that such beliefs could be cultural constructions of his own time, maternalism
seemed so inherently true to Cadwalader that it had not even
needed a direct advocate to sway him.[65] Forced by Ellen's case to
confront the paternalism of family law, his conversion experience
documents the power of forces like gender beliefs in the construction

of legal arguments. When combined with Ellen's woeful story, his
version of the gender convictions of his age made him rail against
legal rules that would deny mothers legal rights. His brief for Ellen
was fast becoming a medium for injecting his own newly articulated
maternalism into the courtroom.

Once Cadwalader determined where he must strike, maternalism
became his basic weapon. He used Pennsylvania custody cases, especially the ever-present *Addicks* decisions, to bind maternal custody
with equally potent, and equally unassailable, ideas about child nurture. In doing so, he acted on the assumption that any reworking
of the legal regulation of gender relations must proceed from a recognition of the fundamental differences between women and men,
not their common humanity. Women required new legal powers
like custody because an enlightened age finally recognized those differences, and thus understood that men could neither represent or
replace the other sex. Through such logic, Cadwalader became
what later would be labeled a domestic feminist, an advocate for
achieving greater gender equity by emphasizing fundamental differences between men and women. He would have rejected out of
hand egalitarian feminists of the day like Elizabeth Cady Stanton,
who argued that both sexes had the same human character and demanded equality for women on the basis of that gender sameness.
Quite the contrary, he shared Tocqueville's conclusion that in "no
country has such constant care been taken as in America to trace
two clearly distinct lines of action for the two sexes and to make
them keep pace one with the other, but in two pathways that are
always different." Law provided a vocabulary for Cadwalader, Stanton, Tocqueville, and many others to debate the renegotiation of
gender relations occurring in their era. In the irresistible tendency
to do so, legal commitments like the paternalistic assumptions of
custody law were undermined because "[c]ategories are put at risk
every time they are used to interpret the changing world."[66]

Cadwalader was never driven to the same rhetorical flights by
child welfare as by maternalism. Women's rights not children's
seemed the greater cause. But he considered child welfare and maternal rights inseparable and directly relevant to Ellen's fight. He
even trudged over to the National Academy of Natural Sciences to
consult scholarly studies of child development, and returned to his
office with notes on the *Report du Physique et du Moral de l'Homme* and
Swiss educational reformer Johann Pestalozzi's *Manual for Mother.*
Both, he wrote to himself, "prove that the welfare and education [of
a child] requires the care of the mother. She understands and she is
understood . . . by the child. She observes and has more tact and
opportunities for care of the child in the moments of the day."

The connections Cadwalader made between maternalism, child welfare, and law emerged as he drafted his courtroom argument. Returning to the issue of separate spousal and parental roles that had dominated the d'Hauteville case since Ellen and Gonzalve first began their bargaining, he decided that "to regain custody of a child is a question independent of causes of separation or of faults of merits of respective parents except only so far as these considerations may bear upon the question of the fitness of either parent for the purposes of custody." Barbara Addicks's fate, he argued to himself, could be read only in that way. Any other conclusion would be a "fallacy through out – not *her* greater or lesser guilt – but welfare of the child."

Cadwalader's tactical deliberations were revealed in stark form when he sketched out two ways of handling the potentially explosive question of Frederick's citizenship. First, he drafted a blatantly chauvinistic argument: "But whatever may be the law in ordinary cases of removal of families, can it be [that] the *side of a foreigner* for purposes of expatriation of a citizen can outweigh maternal authority when [it is] to be exercised for purpose of permanent exile." After pushing that line of thinking as far as it would go, he decided that nationalism was simply less tactically potent than gender. So, he rewrote the sentence by scratching out "side of a foreigner" and penciling in "paternal power." In this way, Cadwalader devised a courtroom strategy that strained every major issue in the case, from nationality and judicial discretion to spousal cruelty and marital fault, through a sieve made up of maternalism and child welfare.[67]

During July and August as he constructed Ellen's case, Cadwalader also had the benefit of a widening group of legal advisors. Besides his fellow attorneys in the case, he received helpful advice from lawyers hired by David in Boston and New York. Bostonian William H. Gardiner served as Cadwalader's major assistant. He wrote frequent letters offering legal advice and information about depositions Reed conducted in Boston. McKeon performed similar duties in New York. He also paid special attention to the Barry case still winding its way through the New York courts.[68]

The most useful legal advice came from James W. Gerard, Eliza Barry's attorney who had also counseled Ellen during her Manhattan stay. Struck by the parallels between the cases, Gerard listed the key precedents that he had examined and that Cadwalader and his opponents must also address. After noting cases like *Addicks* as the "vein of American authority on which you will rely," he outlined the legal arguments Gonzalve's lawyers would probably use. Gerard identified a recent New York decision, *People v. Nickerson,* as the "great case" they would cite to argue that a mother who deserts cannot gain custody of her child. But, he suggested, Cadwalader could follow his lead and argue that the case merely supported judicial discretion in child custody disputes. At the same time, Gerard urged the Philadelphia lawyer to assert that the "authorities establish that the father has no iron, unyielding rights to his child, but that a habeas corpus does its duty by liberating the child from restraint if any – that the parental restraint of the mother, is no restraint in the eyes of the Law, and that the court will not interfere to take the child from her and deliver it to the father except in their *discretion* acting for the interest and benefit of the *Infant* alone [when] they think it proper to do so." Such an argument, he advised Cadwalader, "is the spirit of the whole decisions. They will go for the inflexible rights of the Father as it has been laid down in *some* of the English cases. They will cite against you *De Manneville*." But like Cadwalader, he thought the "whole current of American authority" opposed the dastardly English policy, and that the cases mostly dealt with fathers who had custody of their children not men who tried to wrest them from their mothers. Gerard not only shared lawyerly tactics but also the faith of a recent convert. As had happened to his Philadelphia comrade, trying a bitter spousal custody case had been a conversion experience for the New York lawyer who now also championed maternalism: "You will of course put the mother's claim on the great *Law of Nature*, which make her from *affection and duty* the proper guardian for nurture until years of infancy have passed."[69]

Cadwalader even received unsolicited advice. Philadelphia lawyer R. M. Lee wrote in early September with information about a custody case he had lost the previous June. *Commonwealth v. Kichline* seemed a reincarnation of *Addicks*. It pitted the parents of four children, a two-year-old boy and three girls, aged twelve, nine, and seven, against each other. Lee had represented the father, whom he proved to be a fit parent and good husband. He also provided evidence that the mother permitted men in her husband's employ "to take improper liberties with her and altogether conducting herself in the most exceptional manner. It is however fair to add that she never conducted herself improperly before her children but kept them with much care and prudence." Citing *Addicks*, Philadelphia common pleas judge William Randall let the children stay with their mother even though the father received a divorce because of her adultery. Lee hoped the information about the *Kichline* case would help Cadwalader prepare for the d'Hauteville trial. Even Judge Randall himself sent a note with a useful citation.[70]

In addition to advice from a growing network of lawyers, onetime law student David Sears also peppered Cadwalader with sug-

gestions. Like his daughter, who had reviewed each of her lawyer's
stories, he took a very active interest in the construction of the case.
David thought, for instance, that Cadwalader could make a stronger
case than he had done in Ellen's stories that Frederick's best interests would be served by staying in America. He suggested that the *status*
boy's citizenship rights be emphasized, and that the child be allowed
to stay in America "at least until he reached the age of election, and
would himself decide upon his future destiny."[71] David also in-   *Webster*
formed Cadwalader that he had added the eminent constitutional   *?*
lawyer and United States Senator Daniel Webster to Ellen's legal   *. worth*
team. A decade later, Webster, a fellow Whig and frequent benefi-
ciary of Sears's largesse, would utter the nineteenth century's most
celebrated paean to motherhood: "All that I am I owe my angel
mother."[72] In 1840 he dutifully accepted the assignment of protecting Ellen's motherly rights: "I am at your service and ready to
travel to Philadelphia on the shortest notice."[73] Satisfied with Cadwalader's handling of the case, David told Webster that he would
not be needed for the trial, but asked him to stand ready for the
expected appellate battle.

Reed and Gonzalve's other lawyers had also been busy putting
their case together. While Cadwalader had become a maternal
rights convert and a bitter critic of English family law rules, Reed
struggled to defend the paternal authority inherited from the
mother country. Though he left no record of his deliberations, the
d'Hauteville case seems to have also forced him to take a clear stand
in his era's gender wars. As it had for Cadwalader, the lengthy and
bitter custody battle became a crusade for him, not just another
case. Like his commitment to another cause a couple of decades
later, the Confederacy, Reed's fervent faith in paternal authority invested his arguments with added intensity.

In preparing for Gonzalve's trial, as he did in most of his cases,
Reed sought solace and authority in the basic primer of Anglo-
American law, *Blackstone's Commentaries*. "It is perfectly marvelous,"
he once wrote, "how, in these four volumes of elementary law, com-
prising at most some 1800 pages, less than the product of one session of a State legislature, so much variety of practical learning has
been compressed. There is hardly a judicial question of contemporary occurrence on which some light is not thrown, or some reference given to a source from which knowledge may be gained. Hence
is it, for this universal applicability, that these *Commentaries*, even
for practical purposes, are always useful." As he knew it would, the
Commentaries provided the bedrock legal principle Reed sought.
Blackstone's definition of marriage had become the common law
axiom that would be a cornerstone of the case Reed hurriedly

constructed: The husband and wife are one, and that one is the husband.[74]

In addition to working out his legal defense of paternal power, Reed had also taken advantage of the long August adjournment to interview witnesses and take depositions in Boston and New York. He too sought advisors, including Swiss-American attorney Albert Gallatin, who had publicly supported Gonzalve's cause just months before.[75] Cocounsel Scott had even packed his family off to a cooler vacation home while he stayed at his desk in Philadelphia to work on the case. In a letter to his daughter Maria, he complained: "It is ferociously hot – and I am hard at work – just now in a quite romantic case – love – separation – broken hearts – disputed claims for only child – the d'Hauteville case."[76]

The weeks of hard work had been largely completed when the trial resumed on Thursday, September 3rd. After a procedural skirmish in which Judge Barton upheld the jurisdiction of his court over the case, the second act of the d'Hauteville trial opened.[77]

"It is unnecessary to speak of the importance of this case," Reed declared in his opening statement, "in your Honours' wide jurisdiction you could hardly meet with one more worthy of your time and careful attention. It is a cause on which momentous results depend; the influence of which on society no one can appreciate." With those words, Reed began to lay out the perceptual framework into which he wanted the judges to fit the evidence and conclusions he would shortly present them. Rather than simply telling yet another version of Gonzalve's story, Reed now had to cement in the judges' minds a framework that tilted facts and rules toward his client by offering them a clear and compelling theory of the case. Through their clashing theories, the lawyers would continue the narrative competition in the trial's second act.[78]

Reed's theory emerged when he urged the judges to focus their attention on the case's momentous issues not on the "deep interest the parties feel." To help them think of policy not persons, Gonzalve's lawyer offered a comparison he would use repeatedly to undercut the emotional appeal of a mother fighting for her child. The the concerns of Ellen, Gonzalve, and Frederick were of "comparatively little moment. Bereavements more hopeless and agonizing than any which can occur here, take place every day, but leave no mark, except upon the recollection of relatives and friends." Reed then unfurled his basic theory of the case: "This question involves the whole law of parental controul and conjugal relations; your Honours are to decide what the law is – to decide whether a wife and mother may, without any cause known to the laws of God or man – none such is pretended here – desert her husband, and deprive him of his only child."

Reed heightened the importance of the case and the legitimacy of his theory by labeling Ellen's claim for Frederick unprecedented. In every other case in which a mother received custody of her child, he contended, "there has been some insuperable obstacle to her living with the father; either a divorce, or legal grounds for it. Such is not the present case. Mrs. d'Hauteville has never sought a divorce, and certainly could not obtain one." Against this legal reality, he posed the law's overriding commitment to paternal authority. Judges had on occasion, he admitted, postponed paternal custody during a child's tender years, but "never where no reason existed to prevent the parents from nurturing it together."

Melding his three points, Reed explained that "whether you look at the deep interest of the parties, the important social principles involved, or the novelty of the case, it is especially commended to your Honour's attentive consideration." Only they could resolve it; and only through the wise use of their discretionary authority. Returning to the issue of emotion versus law, Reed tried to make the judges feel how the force of relatively autonomous legal rules preempted a ruling from the heart not the head. He emphasized the constraints of custody law: "[I]t is no loose discretion, nor caprice or whim; not a discretion to be warped from sympathy with either parent; but a high, judicial discretion, fixed and limited by well settled principles. It is to be exercised with regard to the child's best interests: not fleeting, transient interests, but permanent ones; its interests as a Swiss citizen and resident, which it must hereafter be; its interests as an accountable being, in this world and the world to come." He pledged to prove that the child's best interests could be promoted only by giving Gonzalve custody. By doing that the judges could be sure that the boy secured his Swiss birthright and the moral influence of "one who has to reproach himself with no violation of the marriage vow." Proof of his claims would come through the submission of what Reed called "the best guide" to the case, the massive d'Hauteville correspondence.[79]

After introducing his theory of the case and framework of analysis, Reed devoted most of the opening statement to his version of the rise and fall of the d'Hauteville marriage. Its "history of his wrongs, his sufferings, and his hitherto fruitless efforts to obtain redress" repeated the story he had crafted for Gonzalve. Unwarranted challenges to pride and power, not callous masculine insensitivity drove his client into court. Like his client, he pinned the blame for the destruction of the d'Hauteville marriage on Miriam not Ellen.[80]

Reed closed his opening statement with a caution. He warned Barton, Conrad, and Doran against developing "an exaggerated sympathy" with Ellen and reminded them of the depths of fatherly love: "No one can pretend to say, however, with whose affections a child is most closely entwined, and whether the manly fibres of a father's heart endure more or less agony in his bereavement, than do the tender cords which bind an infant to a mother's breast." Disavowing any intent "to derogate from the intensity of a mother's love," Reed however offered his own psychological spin on maternalism by arguing that a mother's love was "a feeling not easy to analyze, but still less easy it is to believe in the theory here advanced, that a mother can so abhor a father, and so love that father's child. It is an idle, it is a wicked doctrine; it is an insult to a mother's love. The main ingredient of this and every mother's affection, is the lingering recollection of the lover of her youth, of him who sought and won her, of him, who, in the little church in Switzerland, led her a bride to the altar. She never looks in that child's face without a thought of that child's father; and every look of inquiry and solicitude which beams from that child's eyes; every time it stretches out its little hands toward her, she must think, and think with sadness, of the husband who, for one long year, has sought her in kindness, and, till hope was wearied out, has begged her to return to him." He urged the judges to steel themselves against claims "that it is hard to take the child from the mother *now:* leave it, you are told, for a season, and the agony will be less." On the contrary, he contended, the pain would merely be postponed and the agony increased as the day of departure drew near. Real judicial kindness would spare Ellen inevitable sorrow. "It is not for the 'best interest' of any to perpetuate such feelings and such suffering as these," Reed proclaimed in a final reiteration of his basic theory of the case steeped in the language of custody law. "Give this child to its father, and you pronounce the most just and gentle judgment your Honours ever gave."[81]

The press gave Reed rave reviews. "The courtroom was crowded," reported the *Ledger*, "and not intending to flatter Mr. Reed, we may safely assert that his address delivered yesterday morning was the most able we have heard." The *Pennsylvanian* agreed and labeled Reed's opening statement "a beautiful specimen of forensic eloquence."[82] Cadwalader, however, reacted far less charitably. Taking notes as Reed spoke, he dismissed the "gloss" Gonzalve's lawyer put on the events of the d'Hauteville marriage, but noted with glee Reed's decision to hold Miriam not Ellen accountable for the couple's miseries. "He thus concedes the whole case," Cadwalader wrote triumphantly, "if he fails as to Mrs. Sears."[83]

Reed's opening statement infuriated Ellen. Rather than just a process to determine Frederick's custody, the trial was becoming an agonizing legal experience for her. In a letter to her sister Anna,

Ellen attacked Gonzalve's lawyer: "Mr. Reed read *100* pages, filled with the vilest & most wicked accusations of Mother. . . ." Intimidated by the crowd, nonetheless Ellen reported, "I thought I could see, however, even in the rough & coarse face of some of the idlers around me, an expression of sympathy & good will, although Mr. Reed again held forth on the enormities we had committed, the charges are principally against Mother & I thought at one time I should be forced to shake my fist in his face & say he lied." She could not detect the reaction of the judges, though. They had "listened quietly & composedly to all he had to say, but I could not discover, by word or sign, to which side they leaned." Ellen reserved her wrath for Reed and his client. The lawyer had begun "at 10 & did not finish until 2 1/2 this afternoon, & helloed & screamed & shook his fist with agitation until I thought he would fairly lose his breath. Gonzalve sat directly opposite me, with no one between us & separated only by a small table; he did not raise his eyes once, and his face seemed made up with the expression of a *suffering saint*."

Reed's biting attack seared itself on Ellen's legal consciousness. Like many of her previous legal lessons it made her cynical about the law, but his words also made her fearful for her mother's fate on the witness stand and bitter about her own impotence. Under Pennsylvania's trial rules, a litigant could not testify on her or his own behalf. "For Mother," she confided to Anna, "it is a bitter trial, rendered harder still by the *justice*, as they call it of the law, as we must all hear her slandered & abused in the most dreadful way, but cannot raise a voice to help her, or refute the charges which if I were allowed to, I could throw the lie in their teeth, but they say I must hold my tongue & hear it in silence, as my word cannot avail *by law*." Though, Ellen added, "Our *Counsel is sanguine* still, but you, who are not in the fight, can hardly imagine the anxieties, & the *struggles* we go through."[84]

Reed continued to anger the Searses by introducing still more letters into the trial record as he shifted from opening statement to the presentation of evidence. The first, an April 26, 1837, note from Miriam to her future son-in-law accepting his offer of concert tickets, launched a week-long attempt by Gonzalve's lawyers to substantiate their client's claims. As he had done while telling Gonzalve's story, Reed read letter after letter to the judges and into the record. Many of these had already been used as part of each side's stories. Reed returned to them as the best evidence he could locate. Supplemented by witnesses and depositions, the correspondence became the evidentiary foundation of his case.[85]

Cadwalader recognized the importance of the letters and challenged their legitimacy. After listening to Reed use the first batch to chronicle the d'Hautevilles' antenuptial bargaining, he objected to Reed's attempt to introduce a translated version of David's letter to Miriam urging that the nuptial negotiations resume. Maneuvering for tactical advantage, Cadwalader charged Reed with selective use of the letters. Insisting that Ellen's parents were no longer parties to the suit, he argued that the letter could not be used as evidence against his client because she had not written it. Reed responded that David and Miriam were still parties and that the letters constituted "evidence of the *res gestae*," or evidence of things done that could be exempted from the rules against hearsay. Encouraged by the court to argue the point, the lawyers began a debate that perhaps tedious to courtroom spectators had significant implications for the trial. Unlike the lay audience watching them, the lawyers had to think of the evidence in the case simultaneously in legal as well as contextual terms. Rules could be used to break apart critical building blocks in their respective theories of the case. David's letter posed just such a tactical test. It raised the critical question of David and Miriam's status as litigants. If they were no longer parties to Gonzalve's suit, then they could testify on Ellen's behalf. Similarly, the letters themselves constituted critical evidence for Gonzalve's lawyers. Barring their use would be a major setback. Enmeshed in the tactical realities of courtroom combat, the procedural debate underscored David Paul Brown's warning to his fellow trial lawyers, "Like a skillful chess-player, in every move fix your mind upon the combinations and relations of the game – partial and temporary success may otherwise end in total and remediless defeat."[86]

After elaborate presentations by both sides, the judges gave Reed a critical victory. Though they postponed deciding whether Miriam and David would be considered parties in the hearing and thus if they could give testimony, the judges admitted the letter as evidence independent of the Searses' status in the suit. "If the question as to the causes of separation, raised by the pleadings, be of any relevancy, (about which we now say nothing)," he explained, "it must be, undoubtedly, no unimportant inquiry, whether the marriage was one of affection, constraint, or convenience; and, the lady being a minor, whether her parents consented." Acknowledging that Ellen had denied knowing of the letter's existence, contents, or use, the trio decided that had "it not been so shown [to the d'Hautevilles], it might not, perhaps, be received; but it cannot be regarded, since such disposition was made of it, as less than a leading, or perhaps, a closing feature of the negotiations. Mrs. d'Hauteville's want of privity weighs not against its admissibility, but its effect."[87]

Permitted wide latitude, Reed spent the next two days reading letters to the judges. He arranged the massive d'Hauteville correspondence chronologically so that the words of the participants followed the star-crossed couple as they stumbled toward the altar, experienced the unraveling of their marriage, and then engaged in futile bargaining. He interspersed relevant collateral documents such as the d'Hautevilles' antenuptial agreement and marriage certificate into his presentation of the letters. The cumulative impact of all these words, Reed hoped, would make the judges accept his primary factual claims: Ellen, after freely agreeing to marry Gonzalve, had been seduced into abandoning her wifely duties and persuaded to punish her innocent husband by keeping his child.[88]

Reed supplemented the letters with depositions taken in Boston during the hearing's long recess. Eliza Farrar of Cambridge was his star witness. He wanted the long-time Sears family friend to support his charges against Miriam. Farrar had visited Hauteville during October, 1837. After recalling "the paternal kindness of Mr. d'Hauteville, senior's, manner toward Madame Ellen, and the lover-like devotion of Mr. Gonzalve to his pretty bride," she described Miriam's low spirits. Farrar remembered a conversation during an after-dinner walk in which Miriam expressed regret at letting Ellen marry a foreigner. She had declared "Ellen can never be weaned from me." When Farrar suggested that the new bride might have an easier time without her mother around, Miriam had disagreed. Equally damaging to Ellen's cause, Farrar added, "I did not, at any time during my visit at Hauteville, observe any thing on the part of the relator, his parents, or family, calculated to wound the feelings, or to account for the depression of Mrs. Sears." On the contrary, immediately after her visit, Farrar had written Miriam and urged her leave Hauteville and let the newlyweds alone.

Aware of how harmful these comments might be, William Gardiner, the Boston lawyer who represented Ellen at the depositions, had tried to undermine Farrar's testimony by quickly inserting Miriam's reply into the deposition. Thanking Farrar for her advice, Miriam had assured her friend that only she and her husband knew the full circumstances and thus the best strategy for dealing with Ellen's marriage. Cross-examination failed to make Farrar recant her story. Instead, she recalled thinking that Miriam's low spirits sprang as much from being separated from the rest of her family as from Ellen's plight. After reiterating that she "considered the unhappiness of the daughter to proceed from the difficulty of being weaned" from her mother, Farrar admitted that she had no idea that the marriage had been consummated out of duty not love, that promised trips to America and winters in Paris had been recanted, or that Miriam's presence had been agreed to in advance of the wedding. But Farrar refused to speculate as to whether such information might have affected her advice to Miriam. When challenged about the veracity of her memory, Farrar bristled, "I am perfectly sure of what passed between us, and of Mrs. Sears' words, as quoted – that I am as sure of, as that I live. What fixed those words in my mind was repeating them to my husband that night."

In reexamination, Reed followed up Gardiner's failures by having Farrar embellish her benign portrait of Gonzalve. She testified once more that Miriam had not uttered a single complaint about Ellen's husband. "There appeared to be," she concluded, "in Mr. Gonzalve's deportment to his wife, at Hauteville, every thing to justify the attachment, because of which I supposed she married him. What I heard of Mr. Gonzalve's having paid attention to another American lady did not make any impression on my mind: but I regarded it as the common gossip of which young people are often the subject, without knowing, or pretending to know, if it was true or false. I never heard of this gossip about Mr. Gonzalve, till after the unfortunate difficulty."[89]

On Friday morning, September 11th, Reed's successful maneuvers came to a screeching halt when he tried to present an affidavit from a d'Hauteville family friend taken in Paris the previous February. Cadwalader immediately objected. He protested that the statement had been obtained without a chance for cross-examination and before any legal action had even been filed. Reed vigorously defended the use of the affidavit and others gathered to document Gonzalve's story of events in Europe. He relied on the best evidence rule, which allowed a party to introduce the best available proof of his or her claims, and argued that there had been no time to gather depositions. Cadwalader seized upon the evidentiary issue as a chance to deal a deadly blow to his opponent's case. He contended that there had been time enough since February to gather evidence in the proper manner and argued statements like this one could be admitted only by mutual agreement.

Ellen's lawyers won the critical joust. Speaking for the trio, Barton ruled that "the admission of such testimony would be a dangerous precedent." Stymied and threatened with the loss of critical evidence, Ingersoll immediately asked for a postponement to arrange European depositions. Trying to make the most of his victory, Cadwalader protested once more. He labeled the request "as altogether out of time, and unreasonable." Ellen had been in Pennsylvania since the spring, and Cadwalader argued that Gonzalve could have filed his suit sooner and asked for the right to conduct European depositions. Too much time had passed to make the request now. He invoked the ancient equitable bar to delay, the rule of *laches*, to demand that the hearing be conducted at the proper time or be forfeited. "After trying an experiment with affidavits," Cadwalader declared rubbing salt into Reed's wound, "he cannot now claim any indulgence. It is not alleged that the relator has been taken by surprise. When a cause has once commenced, you will not arrest it because a party finds a lame point in his case." Meredith then played one of his side's trumps by appealing to the judges' paternalism: "Month after month has this delicate female, already by her sufferings brought to the verge of the grave, been pursued like, to use her own words, *a hunted felon;* and now you are asked to leave her for months longer, writhing in agonies. We ask for justice without denial or delay."

Scott tried to save the critical evidence with yet another attempt to cast Gonzalve as the real victim in the case, and by intimating that an incorrect ruling against a foreigner would forever taint the judges' verdict. He proclaimed his side not "guilty of any laches." The affidavits had been presumed admissible because New York rules accepted them and the statements had been gathered in preparation for a trial there. Once more insisting that the statements constituted critical evidence, Scott pleaded, "Delay will no doubt occasion distress to the parties, but, in the meantime, our client stands in the more unenviable position." Gonzalve's counsel promised that the testimony would be relevant to the hearing and could be compiled and returned "within a reasonable time."[90]

The judges split over the critical request. Barton and Conrad rejected it, though they admitted being troubled by the refusal. The presiding judge expressed doubts about the need for the testimony and, picking up the line of argument developed by Cadwalader and Meredith, argued that Gonzalve's counsel had had ample opportunity to gather the evidence in the proper manner and that their collection of depositions in Boston suggested that they had harbored some doubts about the inadmissibility of the affidavits. He chided Gonzalve for his lawyers' tactics: "Having trusted to mere hope and conjecture, he must bear the consequences." Barton also justified the ruling as being in both Ellen and Gonzalve's best interests for a speedy resolution of their case. He repulsed Scott's plea that the court consider Gonzalve's foreign status a crippling liability. "The circumstances of the relator's being a foreigner cannot weigh on either side," he ruled judiciously, "while it ought not to abridge his rights, it is certainly no reason for granting him extraordinary privileges."

Doran disagreed. The associate judge concluded that the "counsel for the relator have been guilty of no laches." He accepted Scott's assertion that Gonzalve's lawyers had assumed the statements would be admitted. Refusing to decide whether the proposed evidence was material or not, Doran also took to heart the plea that Gonzalve be considered a stranger in Pennsylvania: "Mr. d'Hauteville is a foreigner, and it is desirable that he should have ample opportunity to maintain his rights, and go home satisfied, as to that point at least. I therefore think further time should be allowed."[91]

Blocked by Barton and Conrad, Reed ended his presentation of evidence by reading sections of the *Civil Code of the Canton de Vaud* that granted fathers primary custody rights and husbands the right to choose his family's domicile and to exercise parental authority over children "during the marriage." After reading the Swiss statutes to invoke conflict of laws rules that demanded deference to the policies of the place where a marriage had been consummated, Reed rested his case.[92]

As he stood to address the court with his opening statement on Monday, September 14th, Cadwalader faced the same challenges Reed had confronted the week before. He also had to present a compelling theory of the case to the judges and give them a perceptual framework within which they could fit his soon to be presented evidence. He joined the issue by directly pitting maternalism against Reed's invocation of paternalism.

Cadwalader began his case by immediately shifting the spotlight from Ellen and Gonzalve to Frederick. "The unusual extent of the pleadings will not have made the court forget," he pleaded, "that this is the case of an infant, not yet two years old, from its birth in the custody of its mother, who is not denied to have taken proper care of it." Admitting that "unfortunate differences" had separated his parents, nevertheless Cadwalader insisted that the judges must not dwell on those but that "the single inquiry for you to make, regards the infant's present welfare."

Having refocused the courtroom spotlight, Cadwalader presented his legal theory. Where Reed had used marital fault to construct his theory, Cadwalader built a three-tiered theory on a base of parenthood. Carrying out his decision to mount a frontal assault on paternal custody rules, he echoed John Locke by declaring unequivocally that the "term *paternal power* is improper: instead of it should be used *parental power*. It is a power conferred merely to facilitate the performance of a duty. The father's power is given, not for his own sake, but for the public good – the good of the child." Cadwalader then elaborated a trustee idea of parental authority by using his second major theme, maternalism, to challenge the lingering idea of custody as a vested paternal right. Unlike contests between a father and a stranger, in a fight "between father and mother, higher considerations are involved. The latter is the child's appropriate nurse, to whom the health and safety of its early years are committed. During those years her custody is by law preferred." Then he asserted his final theme with a burst of Pennsylvania legal chauvinism meant to undermine the authority of English custody law as well as the rules of American states like Massachusetts that had slavishly followed the British. Cadwalader lectured the judges that it was "immaterial what the rule of other countries may be. We have been told of infants, but a few months old, being torn from their mother's breast, to be given to unfeeling fathers. I do not believe these accounts. I am very happy that in Pennsylvania, at least, no such case has ever been known." On the contrary, he argued, depriving a mother of her child "would be an abuse of paternal authority, and in accordance with this feeling is the rule of law in Pennsylvania."[93]

Cadwalader wanted to make sure that Ellen's case did not reverse that pattern, and so he returned to his primary theme of maternalism. Drawing on his studies at the National Academy of Natural Sciences, he lectured that while the age at which "an infant no longer needs a mother's nursing care is not settled: suffice to say, that age is much more advanced than the age of this child." He leveled a maternalist barrage against Gonzalve's paternal redoubt by linking faith in mothers to popular fears about fathers: "Every one knows, that a father is unfit to take care of an infant – physically unfit, and unfit by reason of his avocations. A mother will do for her babe what, not only no male, but no other female will do. She has watched it, and knows all the peculiarities of its constitution – all its symptoms. There is a perception in the eye of maternal affection, to which nothing can approach – a perception, distinct from experience, implanted in none but the mother." No one, not a father, grandmother, aunt, or nurse, could take a mother's place.

Cadwalader, however, had to do more than present his theory of the case. His opening statement must also undermine the framework of analysis Reed had urged on the court. Ellen's lawyer tried to expose the weakness of his opponent's case by following New York lawyer Gerard's advice and arguing that Reed had misrepresented the law. Habeas corpus rules demanded that judges intervene only if they find the restraint illegal. They were not to settle questions of "mere guardianship" as Reed would have them do. On the contrary, Cadwalader argued that a parent's custody could never be considered illegal and that therefore to activate judicial discretion a suitor like Gonzalve must show "something positively detrimental to the child – not in time, or for the future, but for the present." Reed had simply failed to meet that test. Conceding Gonzalve was not only "highly respectable" but also worthy of "our hospitality, and to all the sympathy asked for him," nevertheless neither he nor his lawyers had questioned his client's care of Frederick. Highlighting Reed's decision not to attack Ellen as a parent, Cadwalader once more distinguished between her roles as wife and as mother. He insisted that his client's "character properly comes into consideration, only as affecting the present welfare of this child; and she is blameless. It is said that she deserted her husband without cause, and, therefore, is to be punished, while he should be rewarded; but this is not a suit either for divorce, or restitution of marital rights. You certainly will not, to punish the mother, overlook the child's interests."

Forced yet again to counter Reed's detailed narratives of the troubled marriage, Cadwalader turned necessity into opportunity by highlighting the shortcomings in his opponents' argument. He vindicated his client by insisting that even according to the evidence presented by Gonzalve's lawyers "there can be no doubt that good cause for separation did exist." Then he rebuffed Reed's conspiracy theory by promising evidence that would prove that neither of Ellen's parents, and particularly not Miriam, had conspired to destroy their daughter's marriage. Gonzalve's actions, not parental intrigues, had undermined the marriage and endangered his client's health. Cadwalader then launched into his own lengthy retelling of the doomed d'Hauteville marriage that reiterated the points in the second courtroom story he had penned for his client.[94] Turning his trial notes into a plea, Ellen's lawyer finished his tale by zeroing in on the tactical error he thought Reed had made: "If the theory of conspiracy is not supported by the proof, the relator's case must fail." He brought his opening statement to an end by shoring up his own weak flank. Once more distinguishing between the roles of wife and mother so that the causes of the d'Hautevilles' separation could be dismissed as irrelevant, Cadwalader urged: "Whatever those causes may have been, it is clear, that they in no way affect the moral character of the respondent, or her parents, so as to render her an unfit nurse for her child."[95]

Cadwalader began his presentation of witnesses by calling doctors that he had been coaching for the last month. He wanted expert testimony that would raise his client's case out of the mire of courtroom combat by uniting maternalism and medicine to give Ellen's claims scientific legitimation. The Philadelphia lawyer saw no contradiction in covering his case with the aura of dispassionate science through a blatantly adversarial presentation. His conversion to maternalism had sprung in part from the happy discovery that medical science supported Ellen's charges of mental cruelty as well as her insistence that Frederick needed care only a mother could provide.

Hoping for a similar conversion among the judges, he counted on the expert testimony to give the court a seemingly neutral standard for evaluating the d'Hautevilles' competing claims. He had found three physicians quite willing to make the diagnoses he sought.

Cadwalader began with Dr. Warren. The eminent Boston physician and Sears in-law had come to Philadelphia late in July hoping to testify. Marooned by the lengthening court stories, he finally submitted to a deposition on July 30th. After explaining that he had been Ellen's physician since her birth, Warren testified that until her marriage there had been nothing "defective in her constitution, bodily or mental." He also reported on his examinations of the new bride in the early winter of 1837, and then again in Paris the following spring when her condition had greatly deteriorated. The doctor diagnosed Ellen's problems as mental not physical. They sprang from "anxiety; namely, from a strong wish to revisit her own country, and from an apprehension that she should not be allowed to do so. She had, as I have stated, no bodily disease. Her mind was in a morbid state. She appeared to me like a person approaching a state of mental alienation." Warren recalled reporting his diagnosis to Gonzalve and being so puzzled by his reaction that he arranged a separate meeting between the two of them. As they conferred, he had handed Gonzalve a letter detailing his findings and labeling Ellen's malady as the mental disease "nostalgia." He explained the problem in detail and urged Gonzalve to grant his wife's desire to sail home. Failure to do so, he had warned, would result in "mental alienation." A few weeks later, after another examination, he had reiterated his diagnosis and pleas to Gonzalve. Once more he warned of the "danger of insanity" if Ellen's path home remained blocked.[96]

Having used the prestige and expertise of a founder of Massachusetts General Hospital to legitimate Ellen's claims of mental trauma, Cadwalader tried the same tactic to justify her demand for Frederick. Warren described the boy's sickly history and Ellen's diligent care, which he considered "a degree of affection and devotion, on the part of the mother, which I have not seen exceeded." The Boston doctor concluded his testimony with precisely the prognosis Cadwalader sought: "The child is decidedly not of an age to be separated from its mother. Since the birth of the child, Mrs. d'Hauteville has been exclusively devoted to it. She has not gone into society at all; not in a single instance, so far as I know. From my knowledge of the mental and physical constitution of Mrs. d'Hauteville, it would probably produce an alienation of mind, gradual decay and death, if she were compelled, against her will, to live with her husband in Switzerland."[97]

Reed then pursued a wide-ranging cross-examination hoping to modify the doctor's support of Ellen's cause. However, he had contradictory goals. He wanted to cast doubt on Warren's conclusions about Ellen and Frederick, and yet also compel the doctor to use his expertise in Gonzalve's cause. Reed did get Warren to admit that Ellen had come to Philadelphia for legal not medical reasons. Prodded by the attorney, Warren also admitted uncertainty about the effect on Ellen of knowing that after a few years her son would be sent to Gonzalve. Reed continued his foray over Warren's testimony by asking the question Cadwalader had long anticipated. Could, Gonzalve's lawyer wondered, an infant of Frederick's age be safely entrusted in the care of "an experienced, affectionate, and intelligent female," instead of its mother? Warren responded warily, "Although the attentions of the mother are most important during the two first years of life, yet the knowledge of the child's constitution, acquired during that period, would contribute essentially to the preservation of the child, during the whole period of infancy." Not satisfied, Reed pressed his attack by reminding the doctor that "large classes of robust children" in Europe were brought up "without the personal superintendence of their mothers." Warren agreed with that assertion as well as Reed's contention that a well-qualified and healthy female nurse would be a better child rearer than a mother suffering poor health. Honing in on the issue, Reed challenged Warren's assertion that Frederick remained too young to be separated from his mother. "I believe that the mother, having known the constitution of the child, physical and moral, from its birth, and through the trying period of the first dentition," Warren retorted, "and having been acquainted with the diseases to which the child is constitutionally liable, and which must vary in different individuals, would acquire a knowledge, highly important to conducting the child, with comparative security, through the various diseases of its infancy." But Warren had to admit that however desirable, such maternal care could not be considered "absolutely indispensable."

Determined to protect an essential element of his case, Cadwalader quickly rose to ask on reexamination if maternal care could be deemed "highly important." Warren readily agreed and also asserted that mothers had unique relationships with their children. When asked, "Is there not a perception in the eye of affection of a mother, important in regard to the diseases and health of a child?" the doctor replied: "Yes, certainly, from her experience, and, no doubt, from *moral* causes likewise." He expanded on the point by lecturing the judges that infancy extended to a child's eighth or ninth year. More importantly for Ellen, he declared, "I think the chances of life, with the mother, would be greater than with any stranger."[98]

Cadwalader then called two Philadelphia physicians to the stand. He wanted Charles E. Meigs and Nathaniel Chapman to corroborate Warren and place their professional stamp of approval on Ellen's claim for Frederick. The opinions of both doctors carried great weight in Philadelphia. Not only prominent practitioners and professors of medicine, the city had awarded each man a silver pitcher for devoted duty during the terrifying cholera epidemic of 1832.[99]

brilliant! (handwritten margin note)

Meigs, a specialist in obstetrics and women's diseases at Jefferson Medical School, clothed his testimony with a claim of disinterested expertise: "I have no interest in the case but that of humanity." Then he declared, "I think the chance of raising the child would be diminished, by separating it from its mother." He classified Frederick as a child at medical risk because of kidney stones and asthma. Cadwalader then used Meigs to blunt Reed's argument about the competency of a well chosen nurse. The doctor advised the court, "I can't say, whether if removed, and put in the care of a good, virtuous, and intelligent female, it will live, but I must say, that, in doing so, you diminish its chance of growing to a man's estate. So I believe, because there is no love like that of a mother. You can't, for money, obtain services equally conscientious."

Cadwalader also had Meigs open a new assault on Gonzalve's claim. The Philadelphia doctor stamped Switzerland as unhealthy for Frederick because its mountainous terrain, variable temperatures, and high elevation made it unsuitable for asthmatics. To reinforce his message, Meigs noted that the Swiss must drink a lot of snow water and explained in no uncertain terms that "cretinism and goitre notoriously result from that." Luckily, however, Philadelphia's low altitude and river water made it an ideal place for those afflicted with both asthma and kidney stones.[100]

Since he could not challenge the authority of the witness, Reed had no choice but to undermine Meigs's testimony by questioning its sources. He forced the doctor to admit his lack of knowledge of the water or other medical conditions in Switzerland, that he had examined Frederick but once, and that a child would be better off with a good nurse than an "abandoned mother." But Meigs refused to back away from his favorable judgment of Philadelphia as a residence for asthmatics.

Chapman took the stand next. Like Warren, he combined a fashionable practice with teaching and journal editing. Soon to be rewarded for his professional labors by election as the first president of the American Medical Association, Chapman had made a speciality of children's diseases. Ellen had consulted him about Frederick shortly after moving to Philadelphia. His testimony became a testament to American motherhood. "Most undoubtedly the mother is the best calculated to take charge of her infant, as well in regard to the preservation of its health, as the care of it when labouring under positive disease;" he preached, "because no individual can equal her in all those tender anxieties and watchfulness with which a parent acts." Asked to comment specifically on Frederick's needs, Chapman testified that he had witnessed the boy's asthma attacks. And he joined Meigs in extolling Philadelphia as a haven for asthmatics and its water, particularly from the Schuylkill, as a deterrent to kidney stones. Chapman also praised his city's medical establishment and declared that if forced to undergo surgery, Frederick would get as good treatment in Philadelphia as anywhere in the world. Except for a few caveats admitting little specific knowledge of Switzerland, Reed could not get Chapman to modify any of his assertions.[101]

Cadwalader had turned to the expert witnesses in the hope that the authority of medical science could become a legitimate means of judging the d'Hautevilles' competing claims and stories. Through the testimony of Warren, Meigs, and Chapman science became another external force in the trial. Like maternalism and paternalism, the power of such nonagentive forces to influence the ideas and actions of individuals caught up in events like the d'Hauteville trial was one way external social ideology had an impact on the law and on the broadcasts sent out by trials. Indeed Cadwalader hoped to harness that power to tilt the rules of law toward his client by putting maternalism on a scientific base.[102]

Cadwalader began the second of his three-phased presentation of witnesses by reading the deposition of the Searses' servant Martha A. Greene. Now that the doctors had given their scientific endorsement of his client's actions, Greene's testimony would be used to corroborate Ellen's story of her doomed marriage. The trusted family retainer had been with the Sears for twenty-five years, and had known and cared for Ellen since her birth. Retired and spending her last years living with the Searses as a family ward, Greene had accompanied the family on the ill-fated European tour and witnessed each act of the d'Hauteville marital saga.

Under careful questioning by Gardiner, Greene performed her role on the witness stand just as competently as she had her other duties for the Searses. Freely admitting her great affection for Ellen, she recalled scenes and conversations "in our family" that parroted chapter and verse of her mistresses' story. Greene made her story convincing by adding caveats about the limits of her knowledge and by sprinkling her testimony with asides that filled in the details of the portrait of Gonzalve that Cadwalader was sketching for the judges. She recalled, for instance, a conversation with Gonzalve during her stay at Hauteville in which he had plaintively asked her, "Do you think Ellen will ever get over it? do you think she will be happy, or be herself again?" After leading Greene through her story, Gardiner then elicited precisely the judgment Ellen's counsel wanted: "According to my best belief, Madame Ellen was not happy in her marriage. I know of nothing of her husband's conduct towards her. I know of no fact tending to show any other cause for her unhappiness, than his conduct towards her." Greene also successfully eluded Reed's attempts to blunt her story during cross-examination.[103]

Cadwalader finished the second phase of his case by introducing three other depositions. Testimony by family friend Sophia Ritchie and family coachman George Lee documented Ellen's panic when she learned Gonzalve was in Boston trying to find her.[104] The third witness, lawyer Francis C. Gray, was an intimate of the Searses and a Boston social reformer, orator, and scholar. In the midst of a European trip, repeatedly he had been caught in the tangled web of the d'Hauteville marriage. He had visited the married couple at Hauteville, chaperoned a distraught Ellen to Governor Cass's apartments, tried to persuade Gonzalve to accompany his wife to Boston, joined Miriam and Ellen on their voyage home, and become one of Gonzalve's few American correspondents. Both Gardiner and Reed found useful bits of information in Gray's testimony. He recalled, for example, agreeing with Miriam that Ellen should be taken to Cass's because she feared being abducted by her husband. Nevertheless, Reed got Gray to admit that while in Europe neither Ellen nor Miriam had ever complained to him about Gonzalve's cruelty. They had only criticized his effort to separate Ellen from her mother and sister.[105]

Cadwalader ended this second evidentiary phase by reading into the record Massachusetts statutes requiring the immediate registration of births and barring divorces filed by couples who had never lived together within its jurisdiction or for any actions that occurred outside its boundaries. The evidence was intended to demonstrate that Massachusetts law had forced Ellen's hand. Statutes demanded that she register Frederick's birth and that barred her from seeking a divorce on procedural grounds no matter how justified her claim. Neither vindictiveness nor duplicity, but law had dictated her decisions.[106]

Not unexpectedly, the final witnesses Cadwalader wanted to put on the stand provoked the most controversy. When he called David as a witness, Scott immediately objected. He argued that David should be barred from the witness stand because his client had been "deprived of the benefit of analogous testimony" and, as a participant in the dispute, Ellen's father lacked credibility. Gonzalve's lawyers, however, suffered another tactical defeat. The judges ruled that the Searses did not have custody of Frederick and therefore could testify.[107]

Like the other witnesses, Cadwalader wanted David to reinforce and supplement Ellen's story by shoring up its weak points. He peppered David with questions about specific incidents in Ellen's doomed marriage. In each instance, from assertions that his daughter married out of duty not love to declarations that the d'Hautevilles' bargaining had failed because of Gonzalve's obstinacy, David supported Ellen's courtroom story. Despite detailed crossexamination, his story remained fixed in substance and message. As Cadwalader had hoped, David's testimony left the court with the impression that Ellen had made the critical decisions in her fight with Gonzalve.[108]

Miriam, however, was Cadwalader's star witness. His questioning of Ellen's mother had one clear objective. As he had written to himself during Reed's opening statement, Cadwalader believed that Gonzalve's case rose or fell on his lawyers' success in making Miriam a villain who had schemed and plotted to destroy her daughter's marriage. Cadwalader hoped Miriam's testimony would absolve her of the charges, and by doing so win the case for his client.

Ellen's mother tried to give the performance Cadwalader had scripted for her. Speaking in measured tones, Miriam vindicated her daughter and herself by spelling out exactly what she done and, more importantly, what she had not done. In lengthy responses that chronicled the rise and fall of Ellen's marriage, Miriam presented herself as a reasonable parent who had offered counsel only when it was sought and who had tried her best to keep the d'Hautevilles together. Though occasionally indicating confusion about his words and deeds, she had only kind comments about her estranged son-in-law. Miriam intimated, though, that the elder d'Hautevilles had undermined the marriage. And she defended herself: "I am perfectly sure that, after the marriage, I never said to my daughter or any one, at any time, anything in disparagement of Mr. d'Hauteville, his country, its customs, his family, or his residence." She interspersed detailed descriptions of Ellen's troubles and defenses of her daughter's actions with similar declarations of her own restraint. She insisted, for example, that Ellen "went to the chateau with the best intention to do every thing to please her husband, and that, if a proper course had been taken – if there had been a due regard to her natural feelings, she would soon have been devoted to Mr.

d'Hauteville and his interests. Unhappily, a different course was taken." Similarly, she testified that her daughter arrived in America with every intention of returning to Switzerland. Ellen's determination had been altered by Gonzalve's letters not by parental intrigues.[109]

During two days of cross-examination, Miriam fended off repeated attempts by Gonzalve's lawyers to cast doubt on her story. As they led her through the sad events of the d'Hauteville marriage, she resisted being cast as an evil puppeteer pulling Ellen's strings. She also would not qualify her defense of Ellen's conduct. Instead she consistently rebuffed charges that Ellen's letters to Gonzalve had been dictated by her and David. Her only significant contributions had been an occasional phrase and willing eyes to look over finished letters before they were posted. Even then she had counseled compromise and reconciliation. When confronted by Reed with a copy of a letter in which he contended she had excised a paragraph, Meredith came to her aid by protesting that witnesses could not be compelled to comment on the contents of a paper without producing the original. Barton agreed and dismissed the question. When pressed on other contested points, her memory failed her. She could not recall particular carriage rides at Hauteville or exactly how many letters she received from her family back in Boston. Miriam simply could not be provoked into deviating from her story.[110]

Ellen exulted in her parents' performances. "Father was *tried* first & occupied one afternoon & part of another," she wrote to her sister Anna, "& gave his testimony as he does everything else, in a quiet, gentlemanly style so that every word he uttered fully impressed the judges, with a high sense that no false thought or dishonourable intention ever lurked in his heart." Like everyone else, though, Ellen devoted most of her attention to Miriam. Forced, ironically, to stay home with her sick son, Ellen recalled that her "throat was choked" as she bid her mother goodbye, but then proclaimed triumphantly, "From all I have heard since she succeeded even beyond the fairest hopes of the lawyers. Gonzalve sat next to Mr. Reed (who cross questioned her) during the entire time, and I should think his heart must have smitten him at our course toward him, she described her feelings for him at the onset in moving terms, & her regret that he had so misinterpreted his hopes of happiness as to pursue his present course. She pitied rather than reproached him, & and during the thousands of questions that were poured in upon her from all quarters, for her examination lasted 10 hours & 1/4, they could not bring her to utter one harsh word against him." Ellen told her sister that Cadwalader and Meredith had been so delighted with their mother's testimony that they had "often tried to

excite her eloquence to a still higher pitch by whispering 'Capital',
'Capital' as she set forth in glowing colours the merits of the case, &
endeavoured to exonerate me from the charges set forth with so
much art by Mr. Reed; of herself or her own feelings she said nothing, but her manner & looks alone were sufficient."

The effect had been clear to all present. "The lawyers on the
other side seem *struck dumb*," Ellen had been told, "she upset them
by her gentleness, so different from their expectations, for they
seemed to have imagined her some devil incarnate. Mr. Scott looked
grave & spoke not a word, & Mr. Reed shaded his face with his
hand & appeared lost in thought, when his turn came to question
her, he did it in a gentlemanly way, but his eyes lost the fire that he
had in the opening when he seemed to wish to *blast* us all." In fact,
Dr. Chapman had told her that Reed had been "very much astonished at Mother's testimony, & quite unprepared & that even Mr.
d'Hauteville himself had acknowledged he had wronged her."[111]

The day before Ellen wrote Anna, the *Ledger* had reported that
the "evidence in [the d'Hauteville] case was concluded on Thursday
evening, and the case was adjourned until Monday, when the arguments of counsel will begin."[112]

"The court is entrusted with the decision of a great question of
morals, as well as of law," Scott declared in the first of four closing
statements that would bring the curtain down on the second act of
the d'Hauteville trial. Having each proposed a theory of the case
and guided the judges through its factual logic, Scott and Ingersoll
as well as Cadwalader and Meredith, who would be sandwiched in
between Gonzalve's two attorneys, now had to pull theory and fact
together in a legally convincing summary.

Scott picked up the paternal refrain that had run through all of
Gonzalve's legal appeals. "To whom belongs the custody of this
child?" he asked rhetorically. "The answer is in the human heart,
and in the practice of all nations and times. The father, responsible
for its maintenance and education, for its moral standing – his title
is indisputable. The legal authorities on this subject are conclusive."
In support of this reading of the law, Scott listed a string of Anglo-
American precedents and authorities from Blackstone to Kent. He
marshaled similar lists to counter the claims of Ellen's lawyers that
she could be granted custody as guardian by nature or for nurture.
On the contrary, he insisted with yet another list of cases from both
sides of the Atlantic denying special legal status for mothers, the
"right of the father against the mother is the same as against all the
world beside."

String citations of cases, however, could not level the major legal obstacle in the path of his argument. He had to mould the law

and facts of the *Addicks* decisions to fit the contours of his client's case. As Gerard had predicted, Scott contended that *Addicks* simply meant that "a court, in such cases, has a discretion. You have a discretion, but a discretion to be guided by rules of law. The father must have the custody, unless incapacitated by bad morals or want of means." Determined to make paternalism outweigh maternalism, Scott insisted that a father must be considered "as competent to take care of the health of a child of two years old as the mother." Fearing the force of the medical testimony, he also rejected illness as a legitimate constraint on paternal rights. "Are you to establish the principle," he warned the judges with yet another indictment of Ellen as a marital sinner, "that a wife, leaving her husband without cause, may carry all his children with her, for the sake of their health?" Neither Frederick's health nor the law authorized such a radical departure from accepted practice. But, Scott continued, *Addicks* posed neither a legal nor a factual obstacle to Gonzalve's victory. The decision, though "so monstrous, that the court should not hesitate to override it, if it stood in the way," in fact "does not so stand, however." The situations simply could not be compared. Unlike Joseph Lee, Gonzalve could not have access to his child unless granted custody. Equally important, Scott urged in an appeal of masculine solidarity to the three-man court, the Addicks children had been girls and had been reared in their native country, while Gonzalve demanded his son and heir and that the boy be raised in his Swiss homeland. Unless granted custody, Scott declared, the "evidence shows that this child's heart will be alienated from its father." Combining law and fact, he ended his assault on *Addicks* by reminding the court that Barbara Addicks's remarriage forever blocked reconciliation with the children's father, while in the d'Hauteville case, reiterating a basic theme of Gonzalve's attorneys' legal theory of the case, nothing prevented "the re-union of these parties – there is no cause of final separation. The Court is bound to do all in its power to preserve the sanctity of the marriage tie."

On more comfortable terrain, Scott offered his own gloss on the evidence presented over the last month. He insisted that at least on his client's part the marriage had been one of love, and he heaped scorn on the attempt to prove Gonzalve guilty of "great barbarity." Trying to make up for the lack of depositions by Gonzalve's family and friends, Scott argued that the judges could not properly assess charges of incivility leveled against his client because they lacked reliable evidence. Even more importantly, the alleged acts themselves "are not sufficient cause for divorce." Nothing had occurred at Hauteville, Geneva, or Paris to "justify the allegation of barbarous treatment." Similarly, he contended, even though Ellen's letter from

the Astor House on her arrival in New York "shows there was no
good cause for separation" and her next letter revealed "a resolution to desert him," nothing in Gonzalve's subsequent conduct or in
his letters "authorize desertion or divorce."

Scott concluded the first of what would be two summary arguments for Gonzalve by repeating his major themes. "There is no
obstacle to re-union," he told the judges one last time, "and the
court will not make a decree that will perpetuate separation – a
decree so contrary to morality and religion." Returning to the
language of custody law, which constrained and channeled all
the lawyers' arguments, Scott raised the frightening specter of unrestrained maternalism if judges undermined necessary paternal
rights: "The best interests of the child demand a re-union of its parents – its health, its wealth – all of its prospects for the future. It is
due, too, to the laws and to the peace of society, to establish the
broach principle of the father's right; otherwise all the power is in
the hands of the wife."[113]

Ellen's counsel could not immediately respond to Scott. A delay
caused by a death in Judge Conrad's family gave Cadwalader a few
more days to compose his closing statement. Scott's words had given
him fresh ammunition. After the opposing counsel had tried to min-
imize Frederick's sickliness by declaring, "Every man in this room
has passed through the ordeal of perils of infancy," Cadwalader
penned a reply in his notebook: "Every man in this room almost
has had a mother to take care of him." When Scott later attacked
Ellen by asking the court, "[a]re love for her native country & disgust for Geneva causes to justify separation?" Cadwalader immediate rallied to her defense by declaring in his notes, "[t]hey may be
the subjects of cruelty and of torture and so may filial love of a
daughter for a mother." Nevertheless, Cadwalader found himself
agreeing with his opponent's defense of Gonzalve's character. "Had
he been an adulterer, a man of the world, he might have managed
these outward courtesies better," Scott had argued in support of the
hope that reconciliation remained possible for the d'Hautevilles. He
had even added that his client's missteps had been the "mistakes of
a man who has been too pure – honorable to his heart if not his
head." Yet Cadwalader could not accept Scott's indictment of Ellen
as a spoiled child suffering from a "[d]efect in her character" caused
by never having "had reproof from parent." He noted immediately,
"because she had never deserved" such punishment. Finally, Cadwalader penciled a defiant "No!" to Scott declaration, "you can't
consult the interests of the child in opposition to the law. This must
be considered *before* the interests of the child."[114]

Energized by Scott's arguments, Cadwalader spent two days in his final defense of Ellen. The *Ledger* captured the militarism of the courtroom combat when it reported that the "counsel again resumed their arguments with renewed vigor yesterday afternoon after two days relaxation. Mr. Cadwalader's battery was directed, the entire afternoon, against the relator."[115] Like his opponents, he used his closing statement to align his client's story with the law. He reiterated once more his primal themes of maternalism and child welfare by explaining their meaning for custody law. Trying to link law and popular opinion, he declared, "[w]hile addressing the legal reason of the court, I shall contend, that the rules of law must be founded on the laws of nature and humanity. The age of infancy has been distinguished from that of boyhood, by philosophers, theologians, physicians, and lawyers of all time. This age – the age of nurture – need not be exactly marked out. For some purposes it extends to seven years – for others later. Suffice to say, this child is within it – it is a nursechild – an appellation recognized by the law, never applied to a child over fourteen, and never denied to one under seven." After placing Frederick in his proper legal slot, Cadwalader made the consequences of categorization clear: "During this age, considerations connected with its nurture are paramount to all others." Seeking a pedigree for his declaration, he listed a string of English cases as precedent.

To convert the judges to a maternalist reading of child nurture, Cadwalader pulled together the threads of his attack on paternal rights. He began with an unproblematic reading of the pivotal *Addicks* cases: "[d]uring the age of nurture, the mother's is the appropriate custody, and is not considered incompatible with paternal authority." Once more mixing legal logic with what he considered axiomatic gender realities, he lectured the court that a "man cannot nurse a child: a woman is born a nurse. And no other woman can supply a mother's place: a child's chance of life is diminished by removal from its mother." Even the backward British had learned this lesson. They had finally overturned inhumane judicial decisions through a recent Parliamentary act granting mothers custody and thus "putting it on the same footing on which it rests in this state." To these contentions, he added in a revisionist reading of English law: No "case countenancing an opposition doctrine is to be found in the English books, prior to our revolution." Beginning in 1804 with the *De Manneville* decision, he lamented, English judges had ignored nature and humanity and thus the "statute of 2 & 3 Victoria was rendered necessary by the monstrous cruelty of that and the subsequent decisions." Even Switzerland, he argued citing Rousseau's *Emile*, rejected the paternalism of the aberrant English decisions. As for their own country, the "common law of United

States," he declared unequivocally, "is in favour of the mother's custody" and cited the *Barry* case from New York as his prime example.

Determined to make the judges distinguish between paternal and parental power, Cadwalader thundered that the "father's legal authority does not empower him to tear a nursling from its mother's arms, unless she cannot take proper care of it, or is likely to prejudice its morals. That authority is given only to facilitate the performance of paternal duties, which do not concern the nurture of the child." After citing a long list of Anglo-American cases in support of his argument, Cadwalader then made the point of his legal lesson clear with an unambiguous reading of Pennsylvania custody law: "[H]ere the rule is that the father has no right: the court exercises its discretion."

Cadwalader then directed his argument toward that discretionary power. Seeking to blunt appeals to the conflict of laws and the law of nations, he argued that the standard could not be "the law of Switzerland, though there is no evidence of its differing from ours." Instead, the "law of the forum of Pennsylvania must govern." Hoping to coat the weakest link in Ellen's case with a protective covering, he contended once more that state law dictates that the "causes of separation cannot influence your discretion, unless they bear on the fitness or unfitness of either party to have custody of the child." Turning yet again to *Addicks*, he insisted that the "burden of proving unfitness rests, here, on the other side. It is presumed that a mother of even bad character will take proper care of her infant." Nailing down the point, he challenged the judges with the always alluring promise of legal certainty and predictability: "There must be some certain rule, to prevent litigation about such matters." Will you, he asked incredulously, "take the English rule, which it has been found necessary to change by statute?" Instead he offered the rule of *Addicks*: "[T]here even desertion and crime were not good reasons for depriving the child of its mother: here there is desertion alone." Yet again he argued that the "question of the causes of separation, however, has nothing to do with the question before the court. You cannot decide whether there is ground for divorce, which depends on the law of Switzerland."

Having staked out his legal turf, Cadwalader tried to make the "peculiar circumstances in this case" match his rendition of the law. First, he declared that the "health of the child is such as to require a mother's care." Then he claimed American citizenship for Frederick and argued to the judges that the "child cannot throw off his allegiance, and you cannot disregard it. He can lose no Swiss privileges by remaining here: he may lose privileges here, if sent away – as eligibility to the presidentship of the United States, which requires fourteen years' residence. If he does, he will acquire an accent foreign to us: you must look at both sides: in fact he has a double birth-right, and should preserve it. An American court will not undervalue American privileges." Finally, Cadwalader attacked the very idea of urging the judges to use their discretionary power to force Ellen back to Gonzalve.

After addressing these preliminary issues, Cadwalader struck at the heart of his opponent's case. As he had written to himself during Reed's opening argument, Cadwalader now told the court that Gonzalve "stakes his case on the issue as to an improper maternal influence." But his lawyers had failed him. Instead of proof they had offered inconsistent and contradictory evidence. First they represented Ellen as "all softness and pliancy, completely subservient to her mother; then as all decision." The contradictions sprang from Gonzalve's "delusions" not the facts. Even so, his client had suffered greatly at her husband's hand. Using the popular definition of mental cruelty Ellen and her father had voiced, Cadwalader told the judges that she had been "stricken to death without bodily hurt" and reminded them that of Dr. Warren's testimony that "she laboured under a moral disease, and that a return of that disease, and insanity might be the consequences of forcing her back to Switzerland." Appealing to the judiciary's paternalistic concern for dependents like married women, Cadwalader reminded the court that Gonzalve had admitted tormenting his wife "in what he calls little things: those little things concerned the strongest feelings of a woman – her filial affection and maternal love. Her life was made insupportable by acts, small in detail, but, in the aggregate, overwhelming."[116]

While Meredith prepared to take up the argument, Cadwalader learned that in his zeal to defend maternal custody rights he had stepped on a legal land mine – the Barry case. Eager to give legitimacy to what he knew to be an uncertain legal position, he had read a letter from New York Judge Inglis to McKeon in which the judge explained why he had decided in Eliza Barry's favor. Tipped off to the possibility, John Barry had hurried to Philadelphia to attend the d'Hauteville hearing. "I had been in the Court scarcely an hour," he wrote in a letter printed on the front page of New York's *Evening Signal*, "when I found my anticipations fully realized. *My* name was used, *my* case, was spoken of and referred to, and the newspaper doctrines and opinions" of New York judges who had decided against him were "brought forward with some apparent triumph, by one of the Counsel of Madame D'Hauteville, as *proof* of the law of the case in *this* State." He had been taken by surprise, however, when Cadwalader had also read the letter from Inglis because the verdict was still under appeal and a decision had not yet been handed down. Complaining that the judge had refused his request to explain the ruling, Barry was outraged that Inglis's views were used "to aid in defeating the rights, *natural* and *legal* claims of Mons. d'Hauteville." As he explained in a subsequent letter to McKeon, Barry considered Gonzalve's plight "almost entirely similar to my own" and he hoped to append Inglis' letter to his appeal to "remove all doubt" that "Mr. Inglis and yourself differ so essentially" on the meaning of custody law from most "members of the profession."[117]

With the Barry controversy about to erupt, Meredith began the final defense of Ellen's claim to Frederick. After a brief restatement of the facts that waved aside the issue of marital fault as "immaterial," he posed the central question confronting the court: "Will you deprive the mother of the custody of this child?" *Addicks* compelled the court to say no. "So it was decided thirteen years ago, not by one, alone, but all the judges of the Supreme Court; and that decision has since been uniformly followed by the inferior tribunals of the State." Like his fellow counsel, he found sanction for maternal custody in the pre-*De Manneville* common law as well. Not only did a federal circuit decision of New England Justice Joseph Story support the *Addicks* decision, despite other rulings in Massachusetts, "[n]either the Roman law, or any other, ever allowed the barbarity of tearing a child from its mother's breast." The law of forum must govern, he declared echoing Cadwalader, and the court must protect Frederick's American citizenship rights. He also dismissed Scott's attempts to distinguish between the *Addicks* and *d'Hauteville* cases. The mere fact that the *Addicks* dispute involved girls not a boy, and that as a foreigner Gonzalve, unlike Lee, would not have access to the child if denied custody did not alter the basic rules of custody law. "Give the child that parent whose company and care are the most important to it," declared Meredith confident that maternalism provided the only compelling standard for making such a judgment.

Even though the causes of the d'Hauteville's marital separation "can have no influence on your judgment," Meredith felt compelled to underline the "obstacles to re-union." He launched into a final narrative of the doomed marriage that exonerated his client and her mother, and concluded on Monday, October 5th, with a peroration: "She arrived in this country broken-hearted, yet tried still to be affectionate; but his letter of the 24th of July compelled her to resolve on separation; in this, but obeying the first impulse of human nature, for the preservation of his own life. No law, human or divine, can prescribe a return to that condition of mental torture, which soon must end in death or madness. After he comes to this country, she proposes a compromise; his answer is a search warrant sent to her father's house in Boston."

Meredith brought Ellen's case to an end with a final declaration. "We entreat," he pleaded, "that your Honours should not only decide upon the law which governs this case, but also vindicate the characters of Mr. Sears, and the different members of his persecuted family. He asks you to leave the temple of justice, and look upon the broken fragments of his household gods, the dying embers of his domestic hearth."[118]

The d'Hauteville case remained one of the biggest theatrical draws in the city and the chance to see the lawyers give their summations drew a large audience. Sidney George Fisher, a gentleman farmer and part-time lawyer, joined the throng to hear Meredith. Sharing the experience of the trial forced Fisher to ponder its meaning. Like others who watched the trial or read about in the newspapers, the adversarial realities of courtroom dramas like this one also forced Fisher not only to identify with the people caught up in the trial but to choose sides. Finally, once more like the others, he did so by telling his own version of the case and giving it his own moral.

As he recorded in his diary, Fisher's musing began after Meredith finished his closing argument and the trial adjourned for supper. He decided to ride into the countryside and see the changing autumn foliage. The contrast between the breathtaking autumnal scenes and the morning courtroom performance led him to compare nature with humanity. He recalled the comparison in his diary: "External nature is wonderful, beautiful, but the soul of man, how much more awful its mystery, how much more exciting its development. We cannot however regard these merely as a spectator, we are an actor or a sufferer, we are pained, annoyed, disgusted, grieved, injured, outraged often, by society and individuals, and the sensitive and proud mind shrinks from the contact, and flies to nature who never wearies, but is always beautiful and great and impressive, the source of poetic feelings and elevated thought. Such were my musings in my ride. I had just left the court, and was in the country. In the one, were groups of men under the influence of different and conflicting passions; and one in the midst of the proud display of one of man's greatest gifts, eloquence. He was telling in strong and fiery language a tale of sorrow, vindicating a beautiful and injured woman, claiming for her and her infant the protection of law against a persecuting and tyrannical husband. The deepest feelings, the most interesting scenes and circumstances of life were his theme, the best sympathies of the heart were appealed to. He himself was a fine object: a strong man using his strength, a powerful intellect in action, a mind addressing other minds in the rich music of eloquent words, making them think its thoughts, kindling them with its passions, acting upon them, governing them. It was an interesting scene. I enjoyed it, I was interested and excited."[119]

Fisher voiced sentiments shared by many others but rarely phrased so clearly or powerfully. His diary entry brought to the surface the connections between romanticism and maternalism that had bubbled below the surface of the trial. Like the popular sentimental fiction of the era, responses to the case like Fisher's demonstrated the appeal of courtroom stories that stirred the heart not the head and that elicited empathy for the misfortune of others.[120]

While Fisher rode off into the Pennsylvania countryside, the d'Hauteville case resumed. Ingersoll presented the final argument in the case. He declared that the "counsel for the relator are the advocates of peace: we desire to reconcile, not to separate. It is a fundamental principle of law, that a father has a right to the custody of his child." Ellen's efforts to secure special legislation in three states, he insisted, demonstrated that she knew that "existing laws were against her." Repelling assaults on Gonzalve's masculinity, Ingersoll declared that "[c]onsiderations of gallantry, or accusations of barbarity, not in evidence, but merely in argument, are not to work a deprivation of a father's right."

Forced to confront the appeal of maternalism, Ingersoll at once proclaimed the "*general rule* of law establishes the right of the father" and then immediately admitted that "there are indeed, *exceptions* to that rule: the court exercises a discretionary power to control the father's right: on the other side, an effort is made to turn the *exception* into the *rule*." To prevent that doctrinal transformation, Gonzalve's lawyer countered each argument of Ellen's attorneys. First, he contended that the "age of the child is no reason for making an exception." Returning to the theme of reconciliation, he argued that in this case the "mother's care is not incompatible with the father's custody: we desire re-union. If law perpetuates this separation, it perpetuates crime." He entered the fray over *Addicks*. Insisting that the case stood as the only major legal obstacle to his client and "the ground of the respondent's determination to come to Pennsylvania," Ingersoll argued that anything detrimental to his cause in the first *Addicks* decision stressing the age of the children had been overruled in the second. Like Scott, though, he argued that differences between the cases outweighed similarities. "The point of law decided in the *Addicks* case," he told the court, "is merely that the court have a discretion – that the father cannot demand his child *ex debito justitiae*." It did not, however, stand for the rule that mothers may retain their children until they reach seven years old. Dismissing as irrelevant other precedents cited by his opponents, including the *Barry* case and the recent Parliamentary acts, Ingersoll insisted that the court recognize the primacy of paternal custody rights.

Ingersoll also insisted on the primacy of Frederick's Swiss citizenship. Contending that a child could not be a citizen of two countries, Ingersoll argued that the boy's home must be Hauteville. And he used that declaration to laud the character of his client and the virtues of his Swiss home. Ingersoll heaped scorn on Ellen's plea that a misguided foreign marriage had been her undoing. "I hope it may be a lesson against, not only foreign marriages," he declared in a thinly veiled attack on the Searses' wealth, "but also foreign tours." He tried to undermine her story further by insisting that she had wed out of affection and that her subsequent problems had not been caused by his client, whom even Miriam had given "the highest applause. She was affected by home-sickness – her disease was not the result of cruelty." Nor would he accept the doctors' contention that Frederick would be "more likely to live, if it remain with its mother. So is an old man. The physicians say Philadelphia is the healthiest place in the world: many persons would join issue with them on that point."

All in all, Ingersoll concluded, "there is nothing in the condition of the wife to make this case an exception." Once more emphasizing that Ellen had no legal cause for divorce and that her problems sprang from her disease, he exonerated Gonzalve from blame for his wife's illness and for causing the separation. "The right decision in this case demands great courage and nerve," Ingersoll told the judges as he entered his final plea: "Give the father his child, and you set an example of practical morality. I hope that the counsels of discord will not prevail."[121]

With Ingersoll's plea ringing in their ears, the judges adjourned the hearing late in the afternoon of October 6th and brought the curtain down on the second act of the d'Hauteville trial.

Act Three: The Judges' Story

On Saturday morning, November 14th, Presiding Judge George Washington Barton gaveled the d'Hauteville hearing to order for its final act. He read a unanimous opinion to the packed courtroom. His words announced the winner of the narrative competition that had been the d'Hauteville trial. The verdict also became a revealing example of how judges could use the facts of a particular case to redraw the boundaries of legal rights.

JUDGES

Forced to decide the bitter dispute, the Philadelphia judges
shouldered their manly duty to dispense justice by assuming the
role of judicial patriarchs, one of many parts scripted for an American bench granted the power to settle disputes over everything
from murder to bridge licenses. In criminal cases judges like Barton, Conrad, and Doran performed the role of wise policemen;
while in commercial disputes they played the role of public-spirited
entrepreneurs. The necessity of executing various roles when dealing with different types of disputes enabled judges like these three
to particularize their power and individualize justice. In family conflicts like the d'Hauteville case, they assumed the throne of Solomon
to act as responsible patriarchs sagely resolving the problems of
women and lesser men in troubled families.[122] As judges performed
these roles, they tried to "keep governmental action in line with
fundamental community expectations and values." When those expectations and values were ambiguous, as in the d'Hauteville case,
Lief H. Carter asserts that "judges imagined themselves both ca-
pable of and empowered to resolve the ambiguity not through
deeper research and analysis but by opting for that choice which
better fit their vision of community values and experiences."[123]

Like the lawyers and clients, the judges performed their role primarily by telling stories. But they did so in a much more authoritative way than other courtroom performers. Judges acted as both
critic and author. As they tried to make sense of clashing theories
and facts of a case, judges first critiqued each of the stories presented to them and then constructed one of their own. As an author,
Bernard S. Jackson argues, a judge "is, at one and the same time,
addressing a variety of different audiences: doctrinal audiences,
who will indeed view his decision in terms of its 'fit' with a pre-
existing body of doctrine, judicial audiences (fellow-judges, whose
criteria of a good decision may be somewhat different), and most
particularly the audience of that particular decision, and to whom
the nature of that decision is far more important than the legal
grounds on which it is given."[124] In other words, Barton and his
colleagues not only had to pick between competing stories, they also
had to craft one of their own and it must persuade their diverse
audience of litigants, laypeople, and lawyers.

Thinking of trial verdicts as stories underscores the reality that
judicial authority ultimately rests on the persuasive power of words
and the faith in legalism they can inspire. And it demonstrates that
language "is a strategic weapon in the framing and presentation of
disputes, and the way in which it is controlled may affect the attitudes of the participants toward the dispute resolution process" as
well as the attitudes of those who watch it.[125] Even so, like the law-

yers, the judges too had to write a tale within the doctrinal, procedural, and customary constraints of the legal arena. Verdicts, however, had to fulfill another distinctive demand; they must bring a
trial to the kind of symbolic closure that laypeople and lawyers demanded from the courts.

The always difficult challenge of crafting a verdict had been immeasurably magnified by the notoriety and length of the d'Hauteville trial. Publicity had already made the case an important trial
and given it rhetorical significance. Now it was up to the judges to
give it legal significance as well. The influence of the d'Hauteville
case on future custody trials would depend in part on the choices
the judges made about what stories they believed and what version
of the law they accepted. In making these choices, judges demonstrated the subjectivity of adjudication. As soon as a judge begins to
write, "he colors the event with his own subjective approach to it.
His articulation of the facts generates a perspective on the law that
can never be identical to any earlier perspective."[126]

As Barton began to read the verdict, his words quickly revealed
just how much the lawyers' narrative battle had guided the judges'
storytelling choices. Like everyone else drawn into the d'Hautevilles' struggles, the judges could not discuss the legal issues of the
case without passing judgment on the fateful events at Hauteville
and Paris. Their reluctance to craft their own version of those events
was overcome, Barton chivalrously claimed in the first of many critical choices, by recalling "the many unfounded rumours painful to
the feelings and injurious to the reputation" of Miriam Sears. The
judges came to her defense in Barton's first narrative judgment:
"We are bound to say that [Gonzalve] has utterly failed to establish
the truth of what he has thus alleged or intimated, and that all the
testimony has led to conclusions of the most widely opposite character."[127] The judges acquitted Miriam of destroying the d'Hautevilles'
marriage, and then convicted Gonzalve. Accepting Ellen's story of
being a reluctant bride and victimized wife, Barton lamented that
her ills had been caused by her husband's "singularly mistaken
course of policy." He condemned Gonzalve for producing "a total
estrangement of affection."

While Barton and his brethren eagerly accepted the role of judi-
cious public patriarchs honor bound to defend womanly virtue,
they carefully sidestepped the pitfalls of marital fault by cordoning
off the issue as legally irrelevant. Nevertheless, the d'Hautevilles'
protracted battle over the meaning of spousal tyranny forced them
to make it part of their story. Barton challenged Gonzalve's lawyers'
assertion that "nothing can justify a wife in taking the step of final
separation, but such misconduct on the part of the husband as

would furnish good legal grounds for divorce." On the contrary, Ellen's story led him to take a tentative step toward a new set of rules that included her claim of mental cruelty. He suggested that a husband's conduct could "stop short of the misconduct contemplated by the Act of Assembly, and yet might offer such indignities to his wife 'as to render her condition intolerable and life burdensome.'" Barton advanced a new standard of spousal conduct by appropriating other phrases from Ellen's courtroom story to speculate that a husband's "'moral tyranny . . . which strikes its blows upon the mind till it totters,' may rule with despotic sway, until the iron shall as effectually have entered the soul, as if the hand of unmanly violence had outraged the person of the wife."[128] Though dicta or offhand judicial comments without direct legal significance for her case, such public pronouncements conferred legitimacy not only on Ellen's story but on claims of verbal victimization voiced by her and other women. When broadcast outside the courtroom, they could contribute to a redefinition of marital cruelty based on "changing attitudes about husbands' marital misdeeds and women's claims to a new standard of husbandly behavior" as part of a larger "cultural redefinition of manhood and patriarchy."[129] More important for the case itself, though, Barton's absolution of Miriam and rejection of Gonzalve's brief for marital permanence were significant tactical triumphs for Cadwalader and Meredith. The judges had accepted the two central narrative themes of the lawyers' stories: the division of spousal and parental roles, and the consequent separation of the legal issues of marital fault and parental fitness.

If these initial judicial choices buoyed Ellen while filling Gonzalve with foreboding, an even bigger disappointment awaited him with Barton's next declaration. The judge emphatically denied the centerpiece of the Swiss father's courtroom stories by refusing to recognize the absolute legal superiority of paternal power that remained the public narrative of custody law. Barton rejected the proposition that "custody of the child is the vested and absolute right of the father" to be forfeited only if he was proven legally unfit. "After an investigation of the authorities, and the most careful reflection which we have had it in our power to give this deeply interesting and important subject," the presiding judge reported, "we have been unable to convince ourselves of the justice of what is thus contended for, or to become possessed of any decision, English or American, by which it is supported." In defense of what he knew would be a controversial reading of custody law, Barton led his audience through a lengthy review of the cases that had dictated the d'Hautevilles' courtroom stories and guided the judges in critiquing those tales and drafting their own. His detailed analysis demonstrated just how concerned he and the other judges were about lay and professional reactions to their verdict. They had taken to heart the repeated warnings by Reed, Ingersoll, and Scott against succumbing to the emotional pleas of a mother for her baby. Barton wanted to make it clear that the law, not sympathy for a distraught woman, had led the court to its verdict. Yet in pleading his case, Barton raised anew questions about the relationship between legal change and social change that repeatedly surfaced in the case.

As the d'Hautevilles' clashing courtroom stories had amply demonstrated, the rules of custody law were simply too uncertain and contested to offer clear legal direction. Critical choices had to be made. As a legal category at risk, the meaning of custody law would be determined in cases like this one. The notoriety of the case ensured that the Philadelphia judges' resolution of the issues would be broadcast widely. Giving meaning to the core rules of custody law required judges to negotiate the uncertain terrain between social belief and legal ideology. Like every judge forced to make a custody decision since King Solomon, the Philadelphia jurists relied on the behavior of the claimants to apply the rules. Behavioral judgments forced to the surface troubling issues about the autonomy of legal processes and rules by making visible the external social standards by which judges evaluated litigants like Gonzalve and Ellen. And yet, judges had to defend the legitimacy of their actions by asserting that internal legal rules not external passions had dictated their verdicts. As a result, the autonomy of the judicial process became a critical part of this and every trial.

Barton used his review of the cases to construct a legal foundation for his evaluation of the d'Hautevilles' behavior. He began by leveling Chief Justice Lemuel Shaw's decision in *Commonwealth v. Briggs,* which had placed paternal custody rights on a seemingly unassailable pedestal. Despite Shaw's dogmatic assertion that a father's superior custody rights could only be forfeited due to "a clear and strong case of unfitness on his part to have such custody," the Pennsylvania judge deconstructed *Briggs* by noting that "notwithstanding this seemingly unqualified assertion of the paternal right, a preceding portion of the same decision subscribes to the doctrine so generally received, that in deciding the case of 'a child of tender years, the good of the child is to be regarded as the predominant consideration' – a consideration in which, surely, are not necessarily involved the misconduct or unfitness of the father. . . ." Such logic led Barton to insist that in "every case cited by either side . . . it is expressly laid down, that such custody is always within the discretion of the court – a discretion to be exercised by the particular circumstances over every case."[130] His message was clear. Legal rules and the discretion they authorized, rather than irrelevant judicial empathy for a beleaguered mother, had determined how the Philadelphia judges resolved the d'Hauteville case.

In making that point, Barton expressed the central theme of the verdict. Judicial authority over troubled families would be his refrain. Barton thus seized the very power that Gonzalve had so vehemently protested. Instead of deferring to male heads of households, the Philadelphia jurist claimed for judges the broad discretionary power to rule over families who brought their problems to law.

Barton reiterated his critical theme by declaring that "[a]ll the American cases, without a single exception, which have been cited for the relator, recognize, to its fullest extent, the principles upon which, in the case of *Commonwealth v. Addicks and Wife* . . . Chief Justice Tilghman refused to take the children from the mother, and remove them to the custody of the father, viz. the discretion of the court, to be exercised according to the particular circumstances of every case." Even in New York, where decisions seemed most contradictory and where judges had taken children from their mothers and given them to their fathers, Barton insisted that in "no case has any court or judge strained the mark so far as to lay down the bald, broad *dictum* that the father's right of custody is absolute and inalienable; but all agree that while, in general, he has such right, circumstances may arise by which he may be deprived of it." Admitting that some judges had argued that paternal rights could be overruled only when a man's misconduct constituted grounds for a divorce, the Pennsylvania jurist insisted that the "bulk of the cases embrace broader grounds, and an examination of even those which at first blush seem to support this doctrine, manifests that they furnish no foundation upon which to really rest the structure of argument attempted to be based upon them."[131]

Barton nailed down his defense of judicial power over troubled families with a case-by-case critique of the precedents Reed and his colleagues had hoped would sustain Gonzalve's patriarchy. What the lawyers had considered props for paternal power, the Philadelphia judges recast as endorsements of judicial discretion. The presiding judge reserved his most detailed comments for the two cases that had haunted the d'Hauteville trial from the outset of lawyers' narrative battles: *Barry v. Mercein* and *Addicks*.

John Barry's numerous attempts at legal redress proved particularly troubling for the Philadelphia judges. As Barton and his colleagues had labored to write their verdict, Barry had finally triumphed. "[I]n these unhappy controversies between husband and wife," Justice Bronson declared as the New York Supreme Court overturned the decision of Judge Inglis and transferred Mary's custody from Eliza to John, "the former, if he chooses to assert his right, has the better title to the custody of their minor children." Bronson agreed that judges had the discretionary power to leave children with their mothers, but argued that it was not "an arbitrary discretion or a license to do what we please in relation to the custody." Pressing the point, he contended that a father's claim "cannot be set aside upon light grounds, or upon mere conjecture that the interests of the children require it." Instead, there must be evidence of "grossly immoral conduct."[132] Bronson's words voiced a reading of the law quite at odds with Barton's.

Yet if Gonzalve had hoped that Barry's victory would aid his own cause, he suffered yet another disappointment. After noting with approval each of Barry's earlier defeats and even reciting the ex cathedra pronouncements by Judge Inglis that had so enraged the New York father, Barton acknowledged that the "perseverance or affection of Mr. Barry" had finally prevailed. Nevertheless, he belittled the significance of Bronson's opinion by lumping it with "every other to which reference has been made," because it "admits the better title of the father, denies his absolute right, and refers the disposition of the infant's custody to the discretion of the court, to be exercised by a proper regard for its welfare."[133] By making these distinctions, Barton also ensured that the Barry and d'Hauteville cases would present the public and the bar clashing interpretations of custody law.

On surer ground, Barton even more decisively rebuffed Reed's demand that the Philadelphia court label *Addicks* bad law and "ride over it and ride it down." Instead, he defended Chief Justice Tilghman by arguing that the central principles in the case had not been illegitimate judicial creations, as Reed had argued, but rather "followed in the tracks which both foreign and American judges had imprinted; and the safety and wisdom of the path have been recognized by all judges who have followed them." Admitting that Tilghman and his brethren may not have used their discretion wisely nor in the Addicks children's best interests by placing the two girls in the custody of a mother "living in a state of semi-legalized prostitution," Barton nonetheless declared that the initial ruling and the subsequent decision to give the children to their father made the legal message perfectly clear: "Chief Justice Tilghman declares it to be the *settled law* of Pennsylvania, that the custody of the child is always to be regulated by judicial discretion, exercised in accordance with what may seem for its best interests."[134]

"Having thus arrived at the conclusion that the right of the father is not absolute, and that the custody of the infant is exclusively referable to sound judicial discretion," Barton declared in summarizing the judgments of his lengthy review of precedents, "I proceed to inquire in what manner the circumstances of this case and the interests of the child demand that discretion shall be exercised."[135] With those words, the judge outlined his legal framework for resolving the d'Hauteville case. Frederick's fate now rested on how Barton, Conrad, and Doran had judged the conflicting versions of fact in the courtroom stories they had listened to for so long. Turning from legal interpretation to behavioral analysis also revealed just how the judges gave meaning to the contested doctrines that they had used to construct their legal framework.

Gonzalve's spirits may have lifted a bit as the judge proclaimed that "not the shadow of stain can be found upon his moral reputation." Yet he must have soon realized that Barton carefully balanced praise with censure. "Apart from his somewhat Asiatic notions of a husband's rights and a wife's duties, and his conjugal misunderstandings and unprovoked treatment of Mrs. Sears," the judge explained in words knowingly drenched with chauvinist assumptions of superior American gender practices, "no evidence has been adduced or attempted which affixes the slightest reproach to his conduct or character as a good citizen; on the contrary, he has been shown to be habitually observant of all the proprieties of life, temperate and domestic in his habits, and apparently attached to the requirements of religion." After damning Gonzalve with praise, Barton once more blamed the Swiss husband for driving away his wife while refusing to pass judgment on the legality of Ellen's flight. He did take pains to emphasize that "nothing of that kind of 'misconduct' of which the law speaks," could be found "which would justly serve to deprive him of the custody of his son; nor do I question either his ability or inclination to rear it with a proper regard to its intellect and morals." Now whatever slender hopes for victory Gonzalve may have still clung to slipped from his grasp as Barton made the consequences of his carefully balanced character judgment quite clear: "It must be on other grounds that an adverse decision can be framed."

Barton, Conrad, and Doran had accepted Gonzalve's portrayal of himself as an upright, moralistic Swiss patriarch. If Frederick's custody depended merely on evidence of paternal propriety, then "there has been nothing developed in the present case which could properly interpose to take away from him that right." But their interpretation of custody law dictated another conclusion, as Barton explained: "I cannot believe that the exceptions to such a right are circumscribed within so limited a circle – a belief which would be in the face of nearly every decision cited as well as for the relator as by the other side. The reputation of a father may be stainless as crystal;

he may not be afflicted with the slightest mental, moral, or physical disqualification from superintending the general welfare of the infant; the mother may have separated from him without the shadow of a pretense of justification; and yet the interests of the child may imperatively demand the denial of the father's right, and its continuance with the mother."[136]

Having constructed as solid a legal foundation as they could, the judges finally rendered the verdict that had been awaited with so much eagerness and apprehension. "The pecuniary means of the respondent to properly attend to the education and interests of the child, are beyond all doubt," Barton declared unequivocally, "her maternal affection is intensely strong; her moral reputation is wholly unblemished; and, under these admitted or established facts, the circumstances of this case render her custody the only one consistent with the present welfare of her son."[137]

Barton did not stop with those words of victory for Ellen. He went on to justify the verdict not only as a correct legal analysis but as the only narrative judgment possible on the d'Hautevilles' stories. The judge's choices of what facts to emphasize revealed the limited degree to which legal interpretation could be insulated from popular attitudes. Barton repeated the maternalistic dogmas that had been the refrain of Ellen's courtroom tale, while dismissing Gonzalve's claims of fatherly love and duty. "The tender age and precarious state of [Frederick's] health, make the vigilance of the mother indispensable to its proper care," he proclaimed in what quickly became a judicial homage to motherhood and an maternalist alternative to the paternalist narrative of custody law; "for not doubting that paternal anxiety would seek for and obtain the best *substitute* which could be procured, every instinct of humanity unerringly proclaims that *no* substitute can supply the place of HER, whose watchfulness over the sleeping cradle or waking moments of her offspring, is prompted by deeper and holier feelings than the most liberal allowance of nurse's wages could possibly stimulate."

These statements seemed so clearly true to the Philadelphia judges that they need not even be defended. On the contrary, they declared that the best interests of the child rule must recognize the reality of mother love. The judges mingled biology and social ideology with the assumption of fundamental gender differences and allied belief that mothers were more nurturing and sensitive to children than fathers and that the welfare of children depended on maternal care. Like Cadwalader's various courtroom stories, the judges' verdict transformed differences between mothers and fathers into naturally proscribed family roles without ever considering such roles might be social constructions of their era. Instead they relied on seemingly clear commands of nature to allocate legal rights and duties. The result was to give judicial sanction to the classification of mothers as primary parents and fathers as secondary parents. In this way, the judges became mediums through which that social ideology of gender roles was imposed on the law.

Yet they did so in a particularly revealing manner. They tried to accept the logic of Ellen's opposition to her husband's demands without completely undoing paternal authority or granting married women autonomous legal rights. The Philadelphia jurists met the challenge by using their opinion simultaneously to empower and circumscribe mothers like Ellen so that the balance of gender power in domestic relations would be rearranged but not completely upset. By focusing on child welfare and judicial discretion, Barton and his colleagues found a way to reject Gonzalve's claim for universal paternal custody rights, while retaining in male judicial hands the power to choose the best custodian for children like Frederick. As their legal instrument for doing so, the judges seized the slowly coalescing legal fiction of the responsible mother that they had uncovered in the cases. It superbly expressed their ideal of a legally fit parent, while giving judges a legal tool for controlling maternal custody rights. They placed this family law character among the law's regular troupe of fictional actors. Like the ever-reliable "reasonable man," the new bit player could be put on the courtroom stage as an appealing artificial standard against which judges could measure the particular stories of men and women like Gonzalve and Ellen.[138] Similarly, doctrines like the tender-years rule seemed to them an obvious and appealing means of rearranging power in the home through the combination of judicial discretion and maternalism. The Philadelphia judges used these interpretations to negotiate the difficult terrain between law and society and to stake out new boundaries between them.

At the same time, true to their patriarchal role, the three judges took to heart the plea by Gonzalve's lawyers Joseph Ingersoll that they not place too much power in women's hands. Theirs had not been a simple translation of popular attitudes into legal rules. On the contrary, by making their verdict contingent on future conduct and dependent on compliance with judicially proscribed maternal standards, they found a way to grant Ellen a legal privilege dependent upon judicial discretion without giving her a legal right assertable as a legal trump. And they made their verdict a double-edged sword. They rewarded Ellen's resistance by allowing her to keep Frederick, but they also used her victory to advocate a new mix of gender power and subordination in the law. Through their verdict, the judges sent a message to other mothers and fathers that they too could triumph in the courtroom, but only by telling stories that conformed to the recast gender and legal assumptions of the law. Through these arguments, the judges essentialized gender differences and naturalized gender inequality.

Barton's homage to motherhood not only vindicated Cadwalader's decision to make motherhood a central theme of his stories, his defense of Ellen's custody claim also made it clear how successful her lawyers had been in crafting their courtroom strategy. The judge singled out the testimony given by "physicians of the most distinguished skill and reputation." Evidence about Frederick's chronically ill health and Ellen's vigilant maternal care as well as the fears raised about the adverse effects of the climate of Switzerland on the child had been very convincing. The doctors had provided an appealing scientific rationale for the judges' behavioral judgments. Their testimony helped make maternal custody seem natural and necessary, while simultaneously undermining Gonzalve's story of the necessity of paternal authority over children. "It is not possible to imagine, for a single moment, even did the relator intend to make Philadelphia permanently his abode," Barton declared, "that he could succeed in procuring a sufficient substitute for the maternal care, which the frail constitution and feeble health of his son must incessantly require." Yet, further damning the Swiss father's cause, the judge reminded his listeners that Gonzalve planned to take the boy back to the questionable climate of Hauteville. Like Ellen's lawyers, the judges used medical expertise to give their verdict added legitimacy.[139]

Finally, just as they had knowingly circumvented the legal quagmire of marital fault, the judges deployed their discretion to dodge deciding Frederick's citizenship. In evading the troublesome question, though, the Philadelphia jurists revealed the breadth of their conception of legitimate judicial authority over troubled families like the d'Hautevilles. Their decision gave Frederick to Ellen, but it did not endorse the unrestrained maternal power Gonzalve's lawyers had feared would result from an adverse ruling. Instead, judicial discretion not maternal rights remained the main theme of the judges' story. At present, Barton explained, Frederick's citizenship did not need to be determined. But in the future either party could raise the issue "here or elsewhere." The implications of his words became clear when he stressed that the court's verdict could "properly refer only to *the present custody* of the child."

By claiming the power of continuous judicial surveillance, Barton underscored the contingent nature of Ellen's victory. Her custody of Frederick could be challenged by Gonzalve at any time. All he had to do was seek another writ of habeas corpus and another trial.

And, if she left Philadelphia, he could give chase and choose the jurisdiction just as she had. Barton's words brooked no uncertainty; until Frederick became an adult he and his parents would always be subject to judicial monitoring. The General Sessions' ruling thus resolved the immediate contest but, like the Addicks and the Barrys, kept the d'Hautevilles standing in the law's shadow.[140]

Flushed with victory, Ellen may not have sensed how she had been recreated in the courtroom. She had been transformed into the law's conception of a good mother in the complicated process by which popular attitudes influenced the law. Ellen may have understood that the words and imagery of her performance had encouraged the judges to identify her as the ideal nurturing, self-sacrificing woman that she, like so many others inside and outside of the courtroom, regarded as a woman's natural and singular role. Only later, would she realize the consequences of her role playing. Her contingent victory, with its veiled threat of perpetual judicial surveillance, meant that for the rest of Frederick's childhood she must perform her newly scripted role or risk losing him.

However unsettling years of legal darkness might have seemed to Ellen, her anxieties paled in comparison to her husband's agony as Barton concluded the opinion by identifying the meager remains of Gonzalve's patriarchy. Should the Swiss father remain in America or visit again in the future, "we cannot doubt that every reasonable facility of access to his child will, at proper times, be afforded to him" by Ellen. The judges also suggested that it "would seem to be his right – one which possibly he could not enforce by legal proceedings, but of which we cannot apprehend the slightest disposition to deprive him – to exercise, through the medium of some proper agent, a share of tutelage and superintendence of the education of the child; an agent who could see the child from time to time, and communicate with him in regard to its health and discipline." But they did not demand that Ellen surrender Frederick to his father at some time in the future.[141]

For two years Gonzalve had fought to keep his marriage and family together, now he faced utter defeat. Not only had he lost his son, the judges had directly and pointedly dismissed his demand to be treated as an independent patriarch able to govern his household as he saw fit. Their attacks on his marital conduct and their rejection of his paternal rights struck at his very manhood. None of his stories had solicited the deference to paternal authority he devoutly believed it deserved. Neither his pleas nor his lawyers' arguments had been able to convince the judges that they must think about child welfare in paternal terms. Instead his opponents had successfully used ambiguous legal rules to bring popular doubts about the parenting abilities of fathers and the legitimacy of absolute paternal power into the courtroom. Skillful lawyers and powerful social beliefs had defeated him. As such, his defeat represented not just the loss of Frederick but also an ideological reversal of fortune being orchestrated in American courtrooms by judges like Barton, Conrad, and Doran. The maternalism his wife and her lawyers had so successfully seized to defy him was gaining strength, while the power of the paternalism he championed was declining. Ellen's lawyers and the judges had made this momentous shift seem natural and inevitable and thus ordinary. No doubt, as he left the courtroom in defeat, Gonzalve would have taken little solace from the knowledge that had he just become one of the first, but far from the last, fathers to lose their children under American custody rules dominated by an emerging trinity of judicial discretion, maternalism, and child nurture.[142]

Five months after it began, the d'Hauteville trial closed with Barton's empathic declaration that the "infant be remanded and restored to his mother, Ellen Sears Grand d'Hauteville."[143]

5

Into the Court of Public Opinion

Though the most momentous of the d'Hautevilles' legal experiences, the four-month trial did not end their encounters with the
law. Far from it; their case had become too notorious and the questions it raised about the family and the law too explosive to be
settled by a single verdict. Instead the Philadelphia Court of General Sessions' emphatic vindication of Ellen ensured that the
d'Hauteville case remained an important social drama with growing
rhetorical and legal significance. It did so because the judges' acceptance of Ellen's story of spousal victimization and maternal care
challenged the dominate legal narrative of parental conflicts over
children. Rather than repeating the standard story line – invocations of the primacy of paternal authority – the verdict championed
maternal preference in custody law and even suggested granting
wives greater legal autonomy with marriage. As such, Barton's
words used the d'Hautevilles' tangled problems to propose a new
way of telling the tales of warring parents. Then and now, as Edward M. Bruner argues, "[i]t is the perceived discrepancy between
the previously accepted story and the new situation that leads us to
discard or question the old narrative; and it is the perceived relevance of the new story to our own life situation that leads us to its
acceptance."[1] The d'Hauteville verdict and Ellen's story on which it
was based threatened to be just such a new narrative. As a result, it
ignited a fierce public debate pitting the orthodox legal story of paternal authority in the home against the new narrative of maternal
duty.

The ensuing narrative conflicts meant that, like other popular
trials, the d'Hauteville case became a two-staged public event; after
the trial in a court of law concluded, a second trial in the court of
public opinion commenced. Much more than a cliche, the court
of public opinion was, and remains, a critical component of the legal process and the legal experiences of litigants, lawyers, and trial
watchers. Law and legal judgments do not stop at the courthouse
door. On the contrary, it is in the court of public opinion that a trial
gains much of its rhetorical and even legal significance.

168

Equally important, verdicts rendered by the public had different meanings for litigants and trial audiences. For those facing judgment, public judgments had immediate consequences. They influenced both individual reputations and post-trial strategy. For laypeople who evaluated litigants and their causes, judging a case had less precise but equally critical implications. Such judgments became the means by which countless women and men combined the stories they heard about a case like the d'Hautevilles' with the experiences of their own lives to decide the meaning of the contested issues in a trial. In this way, reaching a verdict created social knowledge about critical issues like the legal regulation of gender rights and roles. At the same time, clashing public verdicts fueled conflict over contested social changes such as those occurring within early nineteenth-century Western European and North American families. And, significantly, public verdicts reveal not only a range of views on controversial questions, they also expose rifts between popular legal beliefs and dominant formal rules of the law. Finally, verdicts in the court of public opinion influence how lawyers and judges address similar cases in the future. In difficult-to-document but important ways, popular views about legal issues and rules create part of the larger context for professional decisions of all sorts from litigation strategies to the framing of judicial opinions. As a result of these multiple effects, the court of public opinion is a second major legal arena vying with courts of law for the power to give meaning to a legal experience like the d'Hauteville case.

Most public verdicts, of course, remain private. They are sequestered in letters, diaries, and unreported conversations. But public forums exist for expressing and shaping popular judgments. The most important forums in the court of public opinion at the time of the d'Hauteville trial were the press and the bar. Newspaper editors and lawyer writers were critical legal commentators in a newly created American public sphere. As Jürgen Habermas has contended, by the early nineteenth century in Europe and North America the bourgeoisie had invaded the traditional public sphere, which had been restricted to a small elite. As "private people come together as a public," they developed their own institutions such as coffeehouses, theaters, and journals of opinions that established a practice of rational-critical discourse on political issues. The reformulated public sphere existed between the realms of public and private activity. It functioned as a "sphere of nongovernmental opinion making" both powerful and distinct from either private judgments or state rule making, while influencing both. In it, public opinion came to be considered informed judgments that ought to influence both public and private relations.[2] Equally important, as critics of Habermas have made clear, the institutions of the public sphere were not monolithic. There were distinct clusters within the public sphere. As featured actors in this powerful new sphere of nongovernmental opinion making, American newspaper editors and lawyer writers occupied two of those clusters. In legal matters, they both helped inform and shape lay and professional legal beliefs by making trials like the d'Hautevilles' widely shared legal experiences and thus provoking public verdicts. And like the courtroom itself, the court of public opinion within the antebellum American public sphere was a fundamentally gendered realm. Newspapers and law journals were male domains. Women, like other unrepresented groups, had to depend on virtual not direct literary representations in these debates as male editors and lawyers disputed the legal issues of the day.[3]

Of course, reporters, editors, lawyers, and a vast corps of other self-appointed "judges" had played crucial roles in the d'Hauteville case all along. Ellen, Gonzalve, and their lawyers had recognized their power over the courtroom, and tried to devise strategies that would curry support from each group. But now as the case passed out of their hands and entered the public sphere, these popular critics replaced the warring spouses as the main actors in the d'Hauteville drama. Consequently, Ellen and Gonzalve's trial was no longer merely a device to solve their particular marital and parental problems, but rather it became the focal point of intense public debates about marital responsibilities, parental rights, child welfare, and the other contested issues that had so bedeviled the Philadelphia judges and everyone else forced to confront Ellen and Gonzalve's troubles. And yet the pair could not ignore these debates. Judgments rendered in the court of public opinion would not only influence the verdicts of countless other men and women and affect the personal and professional reputations of the d'Hautevilles and their lawyers and judges, they would have an impact on any future legal battles between the couple. As the debate swirled about them, Gonzalve had to decide whether to appeal Barton's verdict, and Ellen had to decide whether she could leave Philadelphia and whether to seek remedial legislation once again. And so just as they had followed press reports and professional commentaries during the trial, the d'Hautevilles and their lawyers closely monitored the flood of public verdicts released after Barton gaveled the hearing to a close.

Press Verdicts

Newspapers became the principal public judges of the d'Hauteville case. Papers in Philadelphia and around the country announced

Ellen's victory and reprinted Barton's verdict. And just as quickly the press rushed to its own judgments.[4]

Though never able to equal the drama and legitimacy of the courtroom, the press's prominent place in the public sphere made it a critical arena for disputing social issues. The new penny mass dailies eagerly grabbed the role that in the past had been performed by published sermons and pamphleteering.[5] The press grasped an opportunity not merely to chronicle public events, but also "staked a preemptive claim to the exercise of reason in the public sphere; it was the success of this claim that allowed it to boast of its function as the *vox populi*."[6] Mastheads like those of the *New York Sun*, "It Shines for All," and the *Philadelphia Public Ledger*, "Virtue Liberty Independence," announced the press's new role as self-proclaimed independent public commentators on critical issues. Surging sales testified to the success editors achieved by mixing news and views on controversies like the d'Hauteville case.

Equally important to the litigants, lawyers, and judges who fell under its editorial gaze, the press quickly acquired the power to give "rhetorical significance" to some cases. That is, newspaper stories could make cases "a standard reference in public argument" about contentious issues.[7] By giving cases like the d'Hautevilles' such rhetorical significance newspaper editors magnified their importance. For a brief but intense historical moment, they made the d'Hauteville case a fuse that ignited a national debate about the law and balance of power between the state and husbands and wives, mothers and fathers.

Commentaries about the deeds and misdeeds of the d'Hautevilles, Searses, and their lawyers and judges supplied the scripts for those debates. And like the General Sessions' judges, the editors and their readers confronted the volatile mix of class, gender, and law raised by the fight for Frederick. In doing so, however, the press also had to confront Barton's verdict and the lawyers' stories. The judges' version of the d'Hauteville case, even more than the courtroom stories drafted for Gonzalve and Ellen, framed the public debate by supplying its primary terms and issues. The judicial verdict would be the starting point for every public judgment about the case.

However, while Barton's words framed the newspaper stories, they did not dictate press judgments. On the contrary, the range of legal arguments provoked by the d'Hautevilles' struggles inside the courtroom allowed editors outside wide but not unlimited opportunity to construct their own stories. Equally important, the adversarial demands of legal conflict compelled the editors, like the lawyers, to take sides and press their views just as vigorously and as persuasively as they could. Unlike Barton, Conrad, and Doran, however, the press did not render a unanimous judgment. Instead the single d'Hauteville courtroom clash produced multiple newspaper stories and verdicts. Press commentaries also revealed a newspaper variant of the legal regionalism that afflicted the bench and bar. While editors in Philadelphia vigorously defended and promoted Barton's verdict, newspapers in New York City and Boston denounced the decision. Gender power and state chauvinism became the major themes of the press war over the d'Hauteville case.

Newspapers began rendering their verdicts just four days after Ellen's victory. The gentlemanly *Philadelphia Gazette* ended a self-imposed silence on the case to offer its "humble but unqualified approval" of the verdict. The decision, the paper attested, "is fortified by legal precedent, the principles of our common humanity, and bears the impress of impartiality and righteousness."[8] Ominously, however, just two weeks later, the *Public Ledger* complained to its Philadelphia readers that some "newspapers are endeavoring to execute a clamor against the Court of General Sessions, of its decision in this case, and, in these attempts, they display as much ignorance of the laws of the land as they do of the laws of nature." The penny daily lashed out at an unnamed paper that had the temerity to declare: "Every independent press is beginning to see the gross, unnatural, absolute folly, and egregious ignorance of the decision of the court. Speak out." Speak the *Ledger* would on that day and many more to become the chief champion not only of Barton's verdict but of a maternal preference in custody law. Its editorial endorsement helped make the public debate over the case a contest between maternal preference and paternal rights.

The *Ledger* warmly defended Barton, Conrad, and Doran by declaring Ellen's victory as "right according to the laws of the land; and had it been different, it would have violated the laws of nature." Readers learned why in a story steeped in the language and forms of the law as the *Ledger* continued its self-created role of popular legal educator. It was as well a story that accepted Barton's unorthodox maternalist themes as the proper narrative framework for parental conflicts over their children.

The *Ledger* told Philadelphians that English common law granted custody to fathers, upon a parental separation, unless proven to be "physically or morally incompetent" or the child required "the care of the mother." After detailing the range of paternal afflictions that could lead to the loss of custody, the *Ledger* introduced the basic theme of its d'Hauteville story: The law demanded that judges protect the welfare of children, not the rights of fathers. The paper also endorsed the discretionary power of judges to evaluate the evidence and to place children with the most appropriate parent. The facts of the d'Hauteville case, as the *Ledger* reconstructed them in its final version of the story – Frederick's infancy and delicate health, Ellen's vigilant maternal care, and Gonzalve's ill-conceived plans to spirit the boy to unhealthy Switzerland – had made the court's choice clear. "Here, then, are the very exceptions to the father's right of custody which the law contemplates," readers were instructed, "and the decision of the court is according to these circumstances. They decide that, under these circumstances, the father is not entitled to the custody of this child; and where is its inconsistency with law? But the evidence shows that the mother is both physically and morally competent to the custody of this child and is therefore able and willing to bestow the very care without which it cannot dispense. Accordingly, the court decides, not only the father cannot retain the child, but that the mother can. Where is the illegality of this decision? We cannot perceive any."

Not content merely to defend the particular application of law to fact in the d'Hauteville case, the *Ledger* attacked the paternal assumptions of the verdict's critics and launched a campaign for a maternal preference in custody law that carried the narrative conflict of the courtroom into the public sphere. The paper dismissed out of hand editorial demands that fathers be recognized as the natural guardians of children. Such "an assertion proves nothing but their ignorance if they mean that he is so in preference to the mother, or to her exclusion," the Philadelphia editors declared as they expressed their belief in naturally determined sex roles. "The case is exactly the reverse of this, for nature, who speaks loudly and distinctly upon this subject, has given to the mother alone the sole care and subsistence of the child during the whole period of infancy," the *Ledger* argued in a sociobiological defense of maternal custody that demonstrated how new gender beliefs were used to attack legal orthodoxies like paternal custody. "Therefore, the mother is more emphatically the natural guardian than the father. If the father perish, the infant can be nourished and reared by its mother. If the mother perish, the father must procure a *female* substitute for the mother, to furnish the care and subsistence for which the father is physically incompetent. The whole animal creation furnishes analogies in support of this and thus the decision of *nature* is plain in favor of the mother. Again, after the period of infancy, and during the whole period of childhood and beginning of youth, the child is mostly confined to the society of the mother. This is the fact in all states of society, savage, barbarian or civilized; and its universality proves it to be an ordinance of nature. The father is employed in procuring subsistence for the family, and the mother is employed in regulating the household or family while he is thus occupied. In

Separate Spheres

no state of society does the reverse of this exist, and human society could not exist on any other foundation. Whether the fathers hunt as a savage, attend flocks as a barbarian, or attend to the thousand occupations of civilized life, the tender age of the child incapacitates *them* from participating in his labors, and prevents *him* from bestowing upon them requisite care. Hence they must be entirely neglected, or rely upon the mother. Nature proclaims the necessity of this and acts upon this necessity in every modification of society. If, then, the father be the natural guardian of the child, so far as concerns the procurement of subsistence, and defense against occasional dangers, the mother is their natural guardian, in furnishing them with *necessary* subsistence for a certain period, and general superintendence afterwards. Again, while the father can toil for their subsistence, and defend against dangers, the mother can do the same *if he* be removed. But while the mother can nourish them in infancy, and bestow necessary care upon them afterwards, the father cannot do the same if she be removed. Hence they can dispense with the care of the father, but cannot with that of the mother; and consequently *she* is more emphatically their natural guardian than *he*."

Relying on a maternalist reading of their era's gender beliefs, the editors also asserted the innate role of mothers as moral teachers that lay at the heart of the period's separate gender spheres ideology. To sway any remaining skeptics, they enlisted science in their cause. "Now phrenology proves," the *Ledger* lectured, "that the moral instincts of women are stronger than those of men, and consequently shows that she is best qualified for their moral teacher." Nature and science revealed the "most perfect harmony" between need and ability and thus decreed that the "mother is more emphatically the *natural* guardian of the child than the father."

The *Ledger* concluded its ringing endorsement of the d'Hauteville decision with a direct attempt to promote legal change. It demanded that the law recognize nature's preference for maternal custody and thus make tales like Ellen's the dominant narratives in parental custody conflicts. "All this being proved," readers were told in no uncertain terms, "we insist that the general rule of the common law is *wrong*, which in case of a separation between the parents, gives the custody of the child to the father, in preference to the mother, where no disability attaches to him. The rule ought to be the reverse. The custody should be given to the mother, in all cases where she be physically and morally competent, and to the father *only as an exception*. The custody of the mother should be the rule, that of the father the exception."[9]

Philadelphia editors found the *Ledger*'s broadside convincing.

The *Philadelphia Monthly Album, and Literary Companion* quickly reprinted the article with its heartfelt approval: "The following beautiful and talented remarks by the Editor of the *Public Ledger,* are so
superior to what usually emanates from the hurried pen of a daily
paper, that we cannot refrain from giving them the place in our
columns which they so richly deserve. The subject, too, is one which
cannot fail to interest every class of our readers."[10]

However, publishing plans afoot in the city quickly transformed
the growing public controversy over the d'Hauteville case. While
the trial had lumbered on, Samuel Miller, Jr., a lawyer and namesake of a leading Presbyterian theologian, had gathered briefs, testimony, and other materials from the case. Miller made a specialty of
publishing important and controversial trial transcripts. He hoped
to take advantage of a rapidly growing market for trial reports, and
to expand the genre by adding accounts of religious and moral
hearings to the countless crime stories hawked to the public. The
d'Hauteville trial was just his kind of case. And Gonzalve's status
as a fellow parishioner and the religious themes of the trial surely
enhanced its appeal to him.

Working assiduously during the month-long wait for a verdict,
Miller managed to publish his *Report of the d'Hauteville Case* just a
week or so after the trial ended. Released in an expensive leather-
bound edition to distinguish it from the cheap chapbook editions of
criminal trials that overflowed the bookstalls of Philadelphia and
other cities, the *Report* advertised itself to be "as full as the nature of
the case, and the probable demands of the public seemed to warrant." Miller reprinted most of the d'Hautevilles' correspondence,
and pledged impartiality: "[f]or the selection made, as well as for
the accuracy and impartiality of the whole work, the reporter alone
is responsible: neither of the parties litigant, nor their counsel, have
had anything to do with the preparation of it; excepting that to the
counsel for [Gonzalve], the reporter is indebted for the free use of
all the papers and materials in their possession, for which he asked.
The interlocutory opinions of the court, on points of evidence, &c.,
and the arguments of counsel, are given in a closely condensed
form, embracing, however, enough for the professional and too
much for the ordinary reader. The final opinion appears in full."
He peddled his book by sending copies to newspapers up and down
the coast. Even the widely read *North American Review* listed it as a
new publication. The *Report* soon became the primary source for
public verdicts on the d'Hauteville case. And its timing could not
have been more critical. Coming out just as the debate was heating
up, the *Report* became a seemingly neutral yet fulsome source for all
judgments on the case.[11]

Miller's *Report* produced a whole new spate of verdicts. Editor Willis G. Clark of the *Philadelphia Gazette,* for instance, found little in it to question his initial endorsement of the verdict, but used it to defend his state's domestic relations law deviancy. Like the editors at the penny *Ledger,* the editor of the genteel daily vented his anger at out-of-state press criticism of Ellen's victory. He reprinted a favorable judgment by the *New York Times* to challenge New York critics who had begun comparing the d'Hauteville verdict unfavorably to the New York Supreme Court's decision upholding John Barry's custody rights. "The decision in [New York] was based on the strict technicalities of the law, where the father – the legal guardian – obtains possession of the child;" the *Times* had explained, "whereas in Pennsylvania, the decision was rightly based upon the principles of humanity – upon the justice as well as the necessity of the case and which consigns an infant to the tender care of the mother – nothing appearing in her conduct or character against her exercising her maternal duties. And so we think the decision should have been made in the Barry case. The law should have been stripped bare of its technicalities, of its harsh construction, of its rigid philosophy, if indeed there is any positive law on the subject, and made to yield to the dictates of common sense and common humanity." Clark endorsed the *Times*'s legal logic, and added the coda that there existed other views on "this matter, in the Pennsylvania case, in which it can be established that there is a plenitude of law on the side of the mother – enough to produce a similar decision in any court in Christendom having the least pretension to philanthropy or justice."[12]

As the defensive tone of the Philadelphia press suggested, Barton's verdict had not played so well on the road. His endorsement of Ellen's cause provoked bitter protests as a radical departure from accepted family law rules and a dangerous invasion of male power. Papers in New York and Boston led the attack in stories that invoked the orthodox narrative of paternal power and focused attention on issues of marital fault not child nurture. In a front page story, the *New York Herald* used the publication of Miller's *Report* to editorialize that the "maxims of law, which governed the Court of General Sessions in Philadelphia, in depriving M. d'Hauteville of the charge and custody of his own child, do not accord with the feelings or sense of justice entertained by enlightened persons in any part of the country." Printing several of the d'Hautevilles' letters as evidence, the *Herald* offered its own legal lesson: "Nothing can be more unjust, more monstrous, than the principles laid down in the opinion of the court. Strip the decision of the paltry sophistry with which the Judge had invested it, and what does it amount to?

To this, and this only – a mother, who chooses, from whim or caprice, to abandon her husband, upon whom no moral impunities
of any sort rests, can maintain possession of the offspring of their
union, and preclude the father from that guardianship and control
which is his natural, and under such circumstances, his inalienable
right." Nor did its condemnation stop there. The *Herald* repri-
manded Philadelphia's journalists as well as its judges: "We regard
this decision as a violation of all the principles of christianity, all
sound morality, and all well established legal precedents; and neither the belstering of the corrupt press of Philadelphia, nor any
other press, can vindicate it in the estimation of an intelligent and
right judging public."

Warming to the subject, the *Herald* invoked its own version of
gender stereotypes to convince its readers of Pennsylvania's folly.
Like all others drawn to the case, the paper revealed the range of
judgments possible even within shared beliefs. Editors assumed that
they and their readers shared a common set of standards of proper
manly and womanly conduct and would see the case as a story of
gender extremes. Yet they differed about which parent occupied
that extreme and the implications of his or her actions. The *Herald*'s
editors did not disagree with their Philadelphia counterparts' expression of gender rights and duties, only with how those commonly held convictions should be applied to Ellen and Gonzalve.
For the New Yorkers too, idealized visions of womanly women and
manly men formed a cultural template used to judge litigants like
these.[13] Pointing to the letters reprinted on its front page as character references, the paper applauded the Swiss father for writing "in
a frank, manly spirit, and his admonitions are the suggestions of
prudence and wisdom," and dismissed the Boston mother's letters
as a "mere tissue of vague generalities. There is no specific or tan-
gible charge against her husband – no direct allegation of severity
or unkindness – nothing but the captious and querulous complaints
of a spoiled child, abridged of that unlimited indulgence to which
she had been accustomed from infancy." Reporting that Gonzalve's
harshness had consisted of his refusal to allow Ellen to spend her
winters in Paris, the *Herald* relied on a different set of gender stereotypes than those used in the verdicts issued by the Philadelphia
press. In its version of the story, the "facts of the case may be stated
in a few words. The lady was reared in the best society of Boston,
in the lap of luxury, by parents whose tenderness and devotion
knew no limits, while d'Hauteville was bred among the mountains
of Switzerland, in a primitive state of society, and where the habits
of the people are comparatively plain and simple. There was no
sympathy, no compatibility between them. His demeanor, which to

another would have been deemed cordial, courteous, and kind, was by her thought neglectful, unfeeling, and harsh. But she pledged herself to him for life, and the laws of God and man required her to abide the fate she had chosen."

Returning to its main theme, however, the *Herald* blasted its neighbors to the south once more. It offered New York readers a comforting comparison by first praising their governor, William Seward, for vetoing the custody bill Ellen's champions had ushered through the legislature the year before, and then lamenting that "a pliant court of Philadelphia, where morals, and law, and indecency are all on a par, required no statutory enactment to warrant the violation of a known and long established principle in morals and law."[14]

A few weeks later, the *Boston Post* joined Barton's critics. Citing the "great surprise" the decision had occasioned among "the soundest counsellors" and the widespread discussion it had stirred, the paper offered its own chauvinistic comparison. Instead of the Barry decision and Governor Seward, the *Post* touted homegrown examples of proper family law judgments by telling the story of Bostonian Henry Brokston's efforts to reclaim his infant children from his wife, who had taken them and run off to live with her mother. Like Ellen, Mrs. Brokston adamantly refused to return. Ruefully, however, the *Post* admitted that Ellen's defiant defense of maternal custody was already influencing the legal experiences of other women and men. The "new importance given to this question by the case in Philadelphia," the paper explained, had led Massachusetts Justice Samuel S. Wilde to schedule a full hearing on the matter. But, the paper reported triumphantly, "the difference between the husband and the wife, which had grown out of family jars and a hasty complaint on the part of the wife for alleged violence, was in the meantime reconciled by the good offices of friends, and especially by the influence of the full conviction the wife had, from all the sources she could consult, that if she resisted the habeas corpus, the children would be delivered to the father."

Just such a threat of judicial disapproval, the *Post* explained, "might have produced a similar result" in the d'Hauteville case. The paper also held up Chief Justice Lemuel Shaw's *Briggs* opinion endorsing paternal rights as the only proper solution to parental custody conflicts. It had decreed that in Massachusetts children could not be taken from their father unless he was proven unfit or a legal ground existed for a separation or divorce. "This is the only sound or safe principle it seems to us," the editors lectured the public, "and in departing from it, the Philadelphia judges have allowed their sympathies to get the better of their judgment. The fatal error in the decision in the d'Hauteville case, is in the court entertaining the question of separation in fact, as if it were separation in law, and [in] the doing thus, they have shaken the *moral*, as well as the legal foundation of the marriage contract." In support of the accusation that Barton, Conrad, and Doran had succumbed to emotion and failed to uphold the law, the paper invoked the orthodox Blackstonian ideal of marital unity: "The husband and wife are *one*, until severed by some legal cause. While one, the custody of the children cannot be severed from either. It is joint and mutual, and a separate custody is never to be entertained, as a legal question, but in connexion with *legal* causes of separation between the parents."

The *Post*'s editors then tried their hand at lawyerly logic to make their verdict on the case even more convincing. They created a hypothetical situation, an argumentative tactic so loved by the bar: "Suppose a wife, while living in her husband's house, should insist upon the right to keep her infant in the nursery, and the husband claim to have it in the parlor – would a court sit upon a question between them, and decide which location was best for the child? And yet it is the d'Hauteville case right over, only substituting Philadelphia for the nursery and Switzerland for the parlor." In the Searses' hometown, though, even the editors of Democratic *Post* felt compelled to add the caveat that they spoke "only of the moral and legal bearing of the case; for the respectable parties connected with it, we entertain none but good wishes." Even so, they poked one last jab at the decision: "We cannot altogether set aside the impression, that in this matter a foreigner has found less of strict justice in the Pennsylvania courts, than would a citizen."[15]

The national press, however, did not speak with a single voice of condemnation. *Niles's National Register,* one of the country's most widely read journals, reprinted the *New York Evening Signal*'s review of the *Report.* The *Signal* had used Miller's transcript to endorse Barton's maternalist challenge. Recounting Gonzalve's treatment of his new bride at Hauteville, the paper fumed that "Mr. d'Hauteville's ideas of the necessity of female subjection to the more powerful sex are worthy of Blue Beard himself, and such as not one but a tyrant and a fool would attempt to enforce in this enlightened age, when woman has been elevated to the equality of a reasonable companion to man." Like the *Herald,* the *Signal* reprinted Ellen's letter to her departing father. But this New York newspaper found in her words not vanity and selfishness but "a most exalted idea of her character, her intelligence, and her superior worth." And, driven to the same extremes of gender judgments as other journalists, the *Signal*'s editors closed their commentary with a patronizing attack on Gonzalve's manhood: "Our parting advice to Mr. d'Hauteville is, to hurry back to his anxious mamma with all possible expedition, and never to stray out of reach of her apron strings again until she gives him permission to put off his swaddling clothes."[16]

Despite such support, the *Public Ledger* responded to the New York and Boston editorial assault on the d'Hauteville verdict in words that suggested the tart pen of editor Russell Jarvis, whom a contemporary editor considered "a writer of vast ability, a little too personal and trenchant, but possessing a style of rare force and fascination." Undeterred by occasional libel suits, Jarvis "grappled with every question" and made sure the paper did not "hesitate to criticize courts and juries, and to expose oppression" at a time when the *Ledger* wielded "enormous influence."[17]

In the final *Ledger* of 1840, Jarvis tried to refocus the now bitter and muddled d'Hauteville debate on "The Rights of Mothers." Significantly, he did so in two commentaries that tried to legitimate the replacement of the orthodox paternal story line of custody cases with the new narrative of maternal preference without ever directly mentioning Ellen and Gonzalve. In the process, Jarvis penned a thorough analysis of American family law and the gender assumptions upon which it rested. His companion commentaries revealed not only the depth of division in the era's gender wars, but also the seriousness with which editors took their role as public legal educators.

Jarvis began his brief for maternal preference by identifying the enemy. "The independent penny press are distinguished from the partisan sixpenny papers by their views concerning the rights and dignity of women," he charged. "The latter rarely allude to the subject in connection with any principle, and, whenever they do, almost invariably contend for the prevalent errors about the superior authority of man and the due subordination of women." Nor did the *Ledger* shrink from explaining why. The sixpenny papers avoided this and other principled issues for fear of lost circulation. They knew that their columns attracted a mostly male readership dominated by "that class of men, merchants and traders, who are, of all classes, least accustomed to philosophical reasoning, they very justly suppose that a free discussion of principles would alarm the prejudices and wound the self-sufficiency of these limited thinkers, and induce them to cry 'Stop my paper.'" Penny papers like the *Ledger,* however, which circulated among all classes had no such monetary fears and no such constraints. Only they could "discuss principles, and do discuss them with a freedom which spurns all trammels, and with a desire of discovering and proclaiming truth which wins general confidence. Hence we find them expatiating upon that ground which their larger contemporaries seem afraid to tread; and reaching conclusions upon it, in favor of women, and against the vulgar prejudices of men, which, as we conceived, no intelligent mind could avoid after careful examination."[18]

However, Jarvis faced constraints of his own. He wanted to challenge orthodoxy but not be dismissed as a radical. So he took pains to denounce the era's symbolic leader of sexual liberation, the notorious Fanny Wright. By 1840, the Scottish-born activist who championed women's rights, sexual frankness, utopian experiments, and many other radical causes had become the public symbol of sexual immorality because of her advocacy of "free love" or greater sexual freedom for women and men. Reformers like Jarvis invoked Wright's name to legitimate their calls by claiming a middle ground for themselves between her and their opponents.[19] The penny press, he insisted, "repudiate all her abominations about the laxity of the marriage tie, and her vagaries about the political rights and actions of women. While they admit that nature has prescribed different duties to the two sexes, they contend for women's entire equality with men as a rational, accountable and immortal being, and consequently for her entire equality with him in social rights, as the only means of duty answering the great end of her creation." To make it clear that he proposed only to aid women in performing the sacred duties of their special sphere, Jarvis declared unequivocally: "The penny papers are the only portion of the press which philosophically expound and strenuously defend the *rights and dignity* of woman."

Jarvis justified his defense of the mass dailies by critiquing a story on "The Rights of Fathers" in the *New York American*. In yet another example of how widespread parental conflicts over children had become and how much the press relied on individual stories to discuss the issue, the *American* commentator had favorably described the outcome of a South Carolina custody case. The father, a Virginian simply called Doctor Nelson, had wed a South Carolina woman and the couple had lived for a time with her family. After the birth of a son and two daughters, Nelson decided to return to Virginia and asked his wife to accompany him. She refused. He took his son with him and later the two girls as well. But a raiding party led by his wife and her brothers retrieved the toddlers. Nelson then turned to the South Carolina courts and obtained a writ of habeas corpus for his daughters. His wife defended her actions by claiming that a verbal antenuptial agreement had stipulated that she would not be separated from her mother. Nelson denied such a pledge and admitted only a vague promise to stay in Charleston if circumstances allowed. Though his wife also claimed he acted violently when aroused about the subject of moving to Virginia, no evidence

had been presented showing him to be an unfit father. Consequently, the court, relying on the endorsement of paternal custody
rights by New York Chancellor James Kent, had granted his writ
and given him the girls. "The ground of its decision," the *American*
had reported, "is that the father's right is not only coeval with the
common law, but *almost* with the foundation of society and the institution of marriage; a right universally authorized and mentioned
by all legal writers as absolute and perfect!!" The South Carolina
judges had asked, "as if in a tone of *manly* indignation, if the father
shall not have a writ of habeas corpus to obtain possession of his
children, when the wife *invades his province,* refuses to form part of
his household, separates from him, and, in her character of mother,
withhold from him their mutual offspring, to whom he is equally
attached, for whom he is equally bound to afford maintenance and
protection!" And demonstrating yet again that the d'Hauteville case
had become the public yardstick for measuring custody decisions,
the *American* had declared that the South Carolina ruling "contrasts
favorably with the rose colored romance, so inconsistent with judicial dignity and the gravity of a solemn law proceeding, recently
pronounced by Judge Barton in a case remarkably analogous."

Jarvis would have none of it. Every state seemed to have its own
d'Hauteville case and he wanted them decided properly. Like Cadwalader had done in writing his stories, the editor placed both the
southern judge and the New York editorialist among "that narrow-
minded, hard-hearted school, who derive all their maxims of human conduct from a barbarous age, when force was regarded as the
only instrument of authority, and when women were reckoned with
the personal property of men." Jarvis then aligned the *Ledger* with
the forces of progress: "We cordially detest all these doctrines, and
rejoice in perceiving that they are rapidly disappearing before a
more enlarged view of human rights." He rejected the South Carolina court's attempt to make paternal custody rights "coeval with the
foundation of society and the institution of marriage." Instead the
Philadelphia editor championed maternal preference by arguing
that marriage must be considered the "foundation of society, and
that, under this natural institution, the mother has a natural right
to the custody of her children, in preference to the father, until they
are able to take care of themselves." As in previous commentaries,
he asserted that nature herself had ordained maternal custody by
making children physically dependent on their mothers for suste-
nance during infancy and by making fathers incompetent to render
such care. The editor insisted that legal rights must flow from the
commands of nature: "Nature gives no *rights* that would defeat her
own purposes. Therefore 'common sense and equity,' quoted by the

New York American in its own favor with such supercilious self-complancy, are against it." Elaborating his argument, Jarvis used his version of common sense to contend that nature also has "given larger moral instincts to women than to men. If, then, the father separates children from their mother, and especially daughters, he must superintend their education, for which he is less qualified than she by both instinct and pursuit, or he must provide a substitute. And this would promote morals, Mr. American?"[20]

On the first day of 1841 Jarvis took aim at a much larger target than the *New York American*. Titling the second installment "Chancellor Kent and the Rights of Mothers," he attacked the most prestigious law writer in the republic. As his words made clear, Jarvis took the responsibility of the press to educate the citizenry about the law very seriously. "In dissenting from any legal opinion of this justly distinguished jurist," the editor acknowledged, "we shall probably induce the charge of temerity from every member of the bar." Nevertheless, like many others in the public sphere, the Philadelphia editor considered himself competent enough not only to reach his own verdict about cases like the d'Hautevilles' but even to judge the legitimacy and logic of legal rules themselves. Jarvis declared that the chancellor's "opinion about the right of a father to his children may be correct, so far is it *is* the law; but we deny the sufficiency of his reason for this opinion, and insist that if the weight of *argument* is to prevail in deciding a legal question, his opinion should have been the reverse of what he has given."

Jarvis then picked apart the sentences from Kent's *Commentaries* used by the South Carolina court to sustain Dr. Nelson's paternal rights. He zeroed in on Kent's assertion that a father's duty to maintain and educate infants entitled him to claim their custody and services. Kent's rules, he argued, "means that *such is the law, because such is the reason.* The chancellor will admit that the Anglo-Saxon common law has two foundations, *reason* and precedent. A maxim of this code is that *itself it is the perfection of human reason;* and consequently, in the absence of precedent, that is the law for which the best reason can be given." As for precedent, the newspaper editor noted that it was not always binding and that "where courts find the whole current of decisions in favor of a particular doctrine and yet find that doctrine inconsistent with the public good, they claim the right of reversing such decision, and upon the ground their being *against* the law. And so the only *immutable* foundation of the common law is reason, and precedent is binding or not, according to its consistency or inconsistency." Like countless other legal critics, Jarvis followed the logic of his analysis to its inevitable conclusion about the political character of judging by contending that the sway of reason over legal interpretation "converts common law courts into legislative bodies, with powers to repeal or enact law, according to the requirements of reason, or in other words, the necessities of the community. The chancellor will surely admit all this, for no enlightened judge can conscientiously deny it; and admission of it grants us all that we might require for proving that his opinion is against the law; for we can give a better reason for this right in the mother than he gives for it in the father." After this analysis of judicial logic, it would hardly have surprised the editor to learn that Kent himself had once frankly described his instrumental method of judging equity cases by admitting, "My practice was, first, to make myself perfectly and accurately master of the facts. I saw where justice lay, and the moral sense decided the court half the time; and then I sat down to search the authorities until I had examined my books. I might once in a while be embarrassed by a technical rule, but I almost always found principles suited to my view of the case."[21]

Having exposed judging as an act of subjective individual reasoning not blind precedent worship, Jarvis returned to Kent's argument for paternal custody rights and subjected it to his own natural law logic. Nature, as he had explained the previous day, made infants dependent upon their mothers not their fathers, and thus if custody followed the obligation of maintenance it must go to the mother. The common law, he deduced, "which is *the perfection* of human reason, according to the lawyers, never abolishes the rights or obligations of nature; and that, consequently, whatever contradicts them cannot be law." The editor not only attacked the link between custody and maintenance but also challenged Kent's contention that fathers' obligations of maintenance gave them the right to the services or labor of their children. On the contrary, he argued with words that revealed his complete conversion to a nurturing view of child welfare as well as to maternalism, children could "render no service" during most of the period Kent had marked off as the years of paternal custody.

Following the logic of the rigidly separated gender spheres that lay at the base of his belief in sexual distinctions, Jarvis also argued that nature imposed the obligation to educate children on mothers, "a task for which the father is disqualified by the performance of the very obligation to provide maintenance." Combining these contentions, he concluded that since "both experience and science prove that the moral instincts, and consequently the capacity for imparting moral instruction to children, are greater in women than in men, and in addition to this, the period of life under fourteen, is the very age when the moral instincts of a child most require direction." And then, following Kent's own logic, Jarvis insisted that if custody rights flowed from obligations then they ran to mothers not fathers and "we must deduct from his right all that period of childhood during which moral instruction is most needed." He even argued that if children's services could be claimed by parents, they ought to go to mothers to help them fulfill their natural obligations of maintenance and education.

Jarvis continued his assault on Kent by turning his sights on errant husbands. He hoped to undermine paternal custody by invoking the fault principle so deeply embedded in American legal consciousness. Claiming without fear of contradiction that in "the great majority of separations, the husband is in fault," Jarvis maintained that most marriages fell apart because of male infidelity, cruelty, intemperance, and gaming. "In the first of these," Jarvis reported in his own statistical analysis of marital breakdown, "the proportion of the guilty is ten husbands to one wife; and in either of the other three the proportion is one hundred to one." And he used those numbers to reiterate his legal message: "Here is a fearful balance against husbands; and we doubt not that it would be greatly diminished and domestic tranquility greatly promoted, if, in all cases of separation, the children should be awarded to the mother, where no disqualification existed in her for their maintenance and education."

Jarvis ended his two-part endorsement of a maternal preference with one last blast at Kent. He condemned the New York jurist's views on paternal custody for being "against the law, because, as every principle of the unwritten common law depends upon its consistency with reason, or, in other words, with public good, the reason he gives for his opinion is not so forcible as those that can be given for the opposite opinion. The weight of argument is on the other side, and consequently, he is authorized to say, after the custom of common law courts, that the cases which can be cited for his opinion are *not law, and should be overruled.*"[22]

As Jarvis's words proclaimed, neither he nor many others in the press and public conceded a monopoly on legal interpretation to the bench and bar. Law was simply too important to be left to the lawyers. And its cases were too inviting mediums for broadcasting the editors' views on critical social issues like marriage and child welfare to be ignored. And yet they did recognize that the legal system operated in ways that somehow separated it from other realms of life in the republic. They granted it, in other words, a degree of autonomy from the rest of society. In its own sphere set a bit apart from the rest of society, particular forms of reasoning and particular practices had to be followed. Yet the separation from society was always relative, never complete as is evident in Jarvis's demand that lawyers and judges accept the seemingly natural sense of maternal custody. In acknowledging the power and relative autonomy of law while objecting to specific applications of legal rules and legal analysis, Jarvis and others on both sides of the war of words over the d'Hauteville case expressed their faith in legalism. The words of the *Ledger*'s editor revealed just how much the language and forms of the law framed and constrained even its external critics. They also demonstrated how the law served as a popular vocabulary that could be used by laypeople to debate the critical issues of the day.

Professional Judgments

Newspapers editors had spoken first, but in January of 1841 the lawyers began to render their verdicts on the d'Hauteville case. They did so in journals issued from the bar's own cluster in the American public sphere. Separate from the public press, lawyer periodicals monitored legal events for professional readers. And they subjected those events to the bar's increasingly distinctive analysis. The journals tied together the various communities of lawyers scattered among the republic's cities, towns, and villages with information on critical cases, uplifting biographies, commentaries on law reform, and professional gossip.[23]

The d'Hauteville case was as compelling a subject for the professional journals as it was for popular ones. And lawyer editors were just as eager as their newspaper counterparts to render a verdict on the couple and their judges. Unlike the cacophony of the press, however, the bar spoke with a more consistent voice.

The Searses' hometown produced the most vociferous and influential commentator on the case. Peleg Whitman Chandler, a Boston attorney with a thriving commercial practice and Whiggish political tendencies, responded to the verdict on the pages of his journal, the *Law Reporter*.[24] Like entrepreneurial lawyer-editors around the country, he had launched the monthly legal periodical to keep fellow practitioners apprised of the most important developments amidst the bewildering outpouring of American law. Federalism and manifest destiny had combined to make American common law an ever denser thicket of opinions and thus made knowing the law in an English sense of the phrase ever more difficult. Yet American lawyers, like their counterparts in the centralized British legal system, retained enough faith in a unitary common law that they valiantly tried to promote national legal principles. Treatises like Kent's *Commentaries* and journals like the *Law Reporter* led the effort at constructing an American common law. Their editors hoped to bring order out of common law chaos by sifting through the multitude of decisions handed down each day and reprinting and commenting on the most important of them. In his first issue, Chandler had promised to serve the needs of "practicing lawyers" by educating them in professional standards, which would help dispel "the prejudices so rife in the community at large in regard to law." He also pledged to defend the "dignity and consistency of the law."[25] Though it would turn out to be short-lived like so many others, Chandler's journal was at the height of its influence when Barton issued the d'Hauteville verdict.

Chandler's editorial gaze fell on the d'Hauteville case in November. He reprinted Barton's verdict in the December issue of the *Law Reporter,* thus making it available to lawyers around the country. In that way, he ensured that the case would have the kind of professional audience usually reserved for appellate opinions not unreported trials. But Chandler had broadcast the opinion only to damn it. In January he published a blistering forty page attack on the verdict and its judicial authors, and then reprinted it as a separate pamphlet.[26]

Like other critics, Chandler proclaimed his impartiality and offered his own story of the tragic d'Hauteville marriage. Relying on Miller's *Report,* he sketched a damning picture of Ellen as a spoiled girl who refused to accept the responsibilities of marriage and motherhood. Chandler explained that however much Gonzalve's wealth may have been misrepresented, his "property was not vastly out of proportion with that of his intended wife." And he insisted that Gonzalve had committed "no overt acts" that caused his wife to spurn him. Instead, like the beleaguered Swiss husband and his lawyers had done in their courtroom stories, the Boston legal critic credited Miriam as the author of the d'Hautevilles' marital woes: "The relator does not hesitate to charge upon the mother of his wife the chief agency in sowing the seeds of this dissension. This was a question of no importance any farther than it addressed itself to the discretion of the court in relation to the custody of the child; for if the averment of the relator is true, he might reasonably object to having his child in a situation where this lady would have a great influence upon its character, education, and moral character." Suggesting that Miriam hoped to compel the newlyweds to live in Boston, Chandler lamented, perhaps in pity, that Gonzalve's great mistake had been "to marry at the same time, a mother and her daughter."[27]

Using ample selections from the d'Hauteville correspondence, the lawyer chronicled the incidents that led to Ellen's husbandless voyage to America, her defiant refusal to return to Switzerland, and the couple's failed negotiations. By the summer of 1838, with Ellen safely ensconced in the Searses' Beacon Street mansion, Chandler asserted that "any means seems to have been taken to prevent the relator from obtaining his just and legal rights; and to convince him that he was to have no influence over the guardianship of his child." After explaining that Gonzalve had refused to be deterred by these threats and that Ellen had fled into hiding upon his arrival in America only to surface in Philadelphia because of its maternalist prejudices, the editor's voice began shifting from storyteller to legal commentator.

Chandler summarized the rise and fall of the d'Hauteville marriage with a terse professional judgment: "nothing, which, in a legal point of view, can excuse the wife." Even so, before presenting his direct legal analysis of the case, Chandler felt compelled to acknowledge the faults in Gonzalve's character. The facts of the case and the courtroom forum forced everyone who experienced it to make such character judgments. Even a lawyer intent on enunciating clear rules like Chandler could not resist the impulse. The evidence had convinced him that Gonzalve lacked a worldliness and seemed "to a considerable degree destitute of that liberality of sentiment and feelings, which would have been of more use to him in his domestic troubles" than all the useful advice he received from family and friends. Chandler also accused him of making too much of minor points and lacking "that nice and delicate sense of propriety which characterizes the true gentleman." At the end of his character analysis, however, the Boston lawyer brought his professional readers back to their duty: "But all this proves nothing more than that Mr. d'Hauteville partook of the infirmities that belong to our race; and a fact should be mentioned here, which is not referred to in the opinion of the Court, namely, that all of the evidence that Mr. d'Hauteville had caused to be taken in Europe was rejected by the court upon a technical point of law, and a continuance which was asked in order that he might have it taken over again, was denied."[28]

As that pointed comment on Gonzalve's major tactical defeat suggested, Chandler reserved his most poisonous professional venom for Barton, Conrad, and Doran. He attacked their court by expressing "a deep regret" that the "very eminent legal advisors of Mr. d'Hauteville thought proper to select the Court of General Sessions for the hearing of a case of this magnitude." Quickly adding a disclaimer that his words would soon belie, Chandler suggested that "[w]ithout intending any disrespect of that court, of whom, as individuals we have no knowledge, we do not hesitate to say that neither their judicial station, nor their customary and appropriate duties peculiarly fitted them to determine a question of the grave importance here presented." Chandler deepened the attack by raising the significance of the d'Hautevilles' dispute for the law, while lowering the Philadelphia court to the bowels of the legal system: "A case of more importance seldom arises. The parties occupied an exalted station in society; and the public mind was deeply excited, most eminent counsel were retained, and yet a tribunal was selected of whose existence a larger proportion of the legal world were ignorant, and which has emerged from its insignificance by making one of the most extraordinary decisions of the age; which is calculated to exert a greater influence for good or evil, than any decision ever made in that great state." A "right decision" demanded "great courage and reserve," Chandler asserted in an unvarnished expression of professional autonomy and elitism, "and inferior tribunals do not feel that responsibility to the profession which is expected in superior tribunals, whose decisions are reported, and involve the personal reputation of the judges. Such tribunals have too much at stake to permit a suspicion of having acted from improper motives in their determinations; and we never expect to hear them set up with flippant confidence their 'discretion,' in cases and under circumstances, where the most learned judges that ever lived shrink from interposing their wishes or views against the plain dictates of the law."[29] Chandler, however, seized his position as editor of the *Law Reporter* to police the presumptuous Philadelphia judges.

The Boston legal editor dissecting the opinion by commenting on its "tone." "It was evidently prepared for popular effect," he complained in leveling the most damning accusation a lawyer could lodge against the bench. Barton and his brethren had violated professional codes of conduct, he charged, by refusing to protect the autonomy of judging from the play of popular passions and thus had compromised judicial independence. Chandler reported finding "throughout the opinion a disposition to color the facts, which is so evident, that many will not hesitate to style it judicial quackery. There appears to be an overstrained attempt to compliment one of the parties in the case, which is not merely in bad taste; it shows how far a judicial tribunal must descend to pay its humble respects to one of the parties' litigant, and such extraordinary efforts would, in other times, be extremely apt to give rise to a suspicion that the court were determined to shape their law to their personal desires." He singled out Barton's exoneration of Miriam and condemnation of Gonzalve's moral tyranny as proof. Even more damning, Chandler accused the court of furnishing its verdict "to the public prints as soon as delivered" and derided the opinion itself for not rendering an "impartial statement of the facts" or even admitting that Gonzalve's case had been purposely weakened through the exclusion of key evidence. "These considerations may not be considered of any importance," Chandler loftily declared, "further than they show the character of the tribunal which decided the case." He urged a close reading of Miller's *Report* by those lawyers who wanted to make their own judgments about Ellen and Gonzalve.[30]

Speaking as the self-appointed but confident voice of legal consensus, Chandler expressed amazement that Barton and his colleagues had even suggested that Ellen's flight might have some sort of legitimacy. Determined to stifle support Barton's asides might give the growing demands that mental cruelty be recognized as a male marital offense, he called "a most extraordinary intimation" the judges' assertion that a wife "may be justified" in separating from her husband "for such conduct on his part as will not furnish good legal grounds for divorce." Aghast at this judicial assertion of companionate marital ideals yet fearful that the circulation of such comments might encourage popular support for such sentiments, he fumed: "We are at a loss to know whether they mean it as an expression of their individual opinions or whether it is a judicial dictum." Assuming it to be the latter, Chandler considered the judges' aside on mental cruelty to be "as unfounded in law as it is pernicious in morals. This is the first instance that we are aware of, in which a court of justice has undertaken to justify those who live in open violation of the marriage vow, or to weaken the bond which binds husband and wife."[31]

Chandler saw great evil in the Philadelphia judges' contentions. Determined to rebuke them, he defended the existing marriage rules as moral necessities and offered his own professional rationale for protecting them. "We should be glad to know what this court thinks of the religious obligation of the marriage covenant," the legal editor bellowed as mixed his professional and private beliefs, "or how they would expound the doctrines laid down by the great Law Giver himself upon this subject." He demanded to know "where this legal intermediate state between marriage and divorce is. Upon what moral map is it laid down; and what are its boundaries? Where does it begin and where end? What degree of domestic discord will justify a wife escaping to this debatable land? Or is this to be left to the 'discretion of the court under the circumstances of each particular case?'" Dismissing such a doctrine as not "merely false in point of law" but "the very opposite of truth," he turned to Kent as authority for the assertion that the "law knows nothing of difficulties between husband and wife which do not amount to a cause for legal separation." Most importantly, he rejected what he considered to be judicial support for consensual uncoupling in the d'Hauteville opinion; marital obligations remained until death or divorce. Echoing Gonzalve and his lawyers, he entered the raging popular and professional debate over martial failure by endorsing the trade-off Anglo-American law had long sanctioned in "its usual wisdom and humanity, with that true wisdom, and that real humanity, that re- ·gards the general interests of mankind": "For though in particular cases, the repugnance of the law to dissolve the obligation of matri- monial cohabitation, may operate with great severity upon individ- uals; yet it must be carefully remembered, that the general happi- ness of the married life is secured by its indissolubility. When people understand that they *must* live together, except for a very few rea- sons known to the law, they learn to soften by mutual accommoda- tion that yoke which they know they cannot shake off; they become good husbands, and good wives, from the necessity of remaining husbands and wives; for necessity is a powerful master in teaching the duties which it imposes. If it were once understood, that upon mutual disgust married persons might be legally separated, many couples, who now pass through the world with mutual comfort, with attention to their common offspring, and to the moral order of soci- ety, might have been at this moment living in a state of mutual unkindness – in a state of estrangement from their common off- spring – and in a state of the most licentious and unreserved im- morality. In this instance, as in many others, the happiness of some individuals must be sacrificed to the greater and more general good."[32]

After this spirited defense of the law's commitment to marital per- manence and its long-lived but now teetering balance between indi- vidual desire and common good, Chandler found little problem in determining the proper legal solution to the d'Hauteville case de- spite the extraordinary number of "collateral issues" in Barton's opinion. All the "adjudicated cases" made it clear that Gonzalve's claim "is completely made out." The Philadelphia judges had erred grievously in making a false distinction between Ellen's interests and those of her husband. As a necessary corrective, Chandler like the press critics of the decision reiterated the Blackstonian ideal of mari- tal unity. A husband and wife, he reminded his lawyerly subscribers just as the *Post* had its lay readers, "have no rights as contradistin- guished from each other. They are one. The rights of the wife have not been lost, they are merged in those of the husband." He went on to offer the standard legal depiction of marriage as a trade-off in which a wife forfeited her legal rights and independence in ex- change for her husband's responsibility to care for her and protect her. Emphasizing how jealously the law protected this marital ex- change, Chandler also voiced the orthodox Anglo-American legal conviction that the bargain favored the weaker sex: "The common law, with a true delicacy, entirely consistent with its stern morality, recognizes the wife in her place, and seeks to protect her in her station. She cannot be forced out of it. She is seen in no other view. The sanctity of private life is for her sake made legal. She is not only not obliged in law to appear before the world, but her doing so is entirely discouraged." Conversely, the Boston lawyer explained in words that echoed many of Gonzalve's, the husband must be "looked upon as the head of the family, and represents the family. He is also invested with an authority commensurate with his duties, and his jurisdiction in its narrow but important sphere, is perfect and supreme as long as it is exercised within the limits which divine and human wisdom have prescribed."[33]

Having repeated the standard legal line on marriage, Chandler could turn to the question of child custody and endorse the ortho-dox public narrative of the law. Once more insisting that wives had no independent legal existence, he explained that a deserting mother must surrender her child to its father. The logic of paternal rights seemed so irrefutable that it was not "necessary to vindicate the policy of the law. It is sufficient that the rule is well established; but those who are dissatisfied with it will do well to consider, that no other rule can be adopted with any propriety until the whole order of marital rights is changed." To make the point clear, Chandler offered a Sadie Hawkins description of the only change possible within a regime of marital unity: "When the husband takes the name of the wife – when he goes to her home – when his domi-cile follows her, then, and only then, will it do to change the present rule." The obvious absurdity of such a world turned upside down allowed the lawyer to declare once more than only fathers could claim a legal right to custody. Ridicule also allowed him to ignore the growing authority of maternalism in interpretations of custody and other family laws and to avoid addressing the sociobiological arguments of those championing maternal preference.

Chandler well knew, however, that his assertions would only con-vince other lawyers when backed by the expected rendition of cases. He had to conform to the practices of his profession's mediums of persuasion just as the newspaper editors had followed the dictates of their craft. Chandler proceeded to summarize the leading En-glish and American decisions upholding paternal custody rights. After nutshell explanations of *De Manneville, Briggs, Mercein,* and the other leading precedents, he apologized for details that ran the "risk of being tedious to our legal readers, to whom they are doubt-less familiar." But he wanted to proclaim the uniform voice of the law before admitting an exception: "When the father wants either capacity, or the means of the proper training of his child, or is in

any way disqualified, his right may be controlled or absolutely denied." In this backhanded way, Chandler introduced the thorny issue of judicial discretion at the heart of his era's debates about custody law.[34]

Forced to admit that custody law authorized the use of judicial
discretion, the lawyer wanted it bounded by sturdy definitions that
kept surging popular passions at bay. Chandler insisted that those
linemarkers had already been staked out by the bench and bar:
"Clearly it is not a mere license to the court to do what they please.
The common law knows no such discretion in anything. It is a judicial discretion governed by strict legal rules, within which it must
be exercised." Those rules, he maintained in voicing a common
lawyerly concern about protecting the power of professional self-
policing, must limit the power of judges like those on the Philadelphia Court of General Sessions. If not, he asserted in lawyerly pique
of reductio ad absurdum, then "courts of law might interfere with
the custody of every child in the state. They could even determine
in cases brought before them, whether it would not be best to deprive father and mother both of the custody of their child." Instead
of sanctioning the unchecked judicial power feared by lay people as
a threat to democracy and by the bar as a threat to professional
autonomy, Chandler contended that discretion only "exists when
there is some disqualification on the part of the father for the custody of his child. This is the fact which must first appear. This is the
foundation on which the discretion of the court rests."

Once more Chandler used an exegesis of cases to argue his point.
This time he even addressed the *Addicks* decisions and asserted that
neither the Pennsylvania rulings nor any other cases supported the
unlimited judicial discretion wielded by Barton, Conrad, and Doran. On the contrary, Chandler derided the first *Addicks* decision
giving Barbara custody of her daughters as "completely erroneous"
since fatherly incompetence had not been proven. Law circumscribed discretion, he said in repeating the professional mantra over
and over again, and thus judges could not act as they "may happen
to desire, or think expedient." Instead they must accept and support the superior rights of fathers as all the leading legal authorities demanded.[35]

Chandler expressed astonishment as much at the Philadelphia
judges' assumption that Frederick had an interest separate from his
father's as he did at their assertion that Ellen had a separate legal
identity. He rejected outright their anti-patriarchal interpretation
of the best interests of the child doctrine and its assumption of the
family as a collection of distinct legal individuals not a corporate
unit headed by a patriarch. "They speak of the interests of the child

as being the paramount consideration," he exclaimed in wonderment before lapsing into his own version of natural law, "and they seem to forget that the rights and interests of others are to be taken in account at all. But the interests of the child and of the parents are so identical, that they are not to be separated. The law – religion – nature herself, declare the presumption to be that it is best for the child to be in the custody of the authors of its being. It is not for courts of justice to decide that this great law of nature, sanctioned and enforced by the law of society, is to be controlled upon slight grounds. Let the child remain with the natural guardian which God has provided for it, unless it clearly appear that he is unfit for that guardianship."

Not only did Chandler endorse paternal rights, he championed Gonzalve's cause. A bare-bones statement of the case without the distracting embellishments of Ellen's attorneys, he insisted, revealed the wisdom of the common law "doctrine that the rights and interests of the father and his child are the same; and that the mother shall not be permitted, with unnatural violence, to attempt to sever them." But Barton, Conrad, and Doran had failed because of their sympathetic response to Ellen's stories. They had committed the cardinal professional sin of the day: thinking with their hearts not their heads. As a result, Chandler charged, the judges had not used their power to protect the sanctity of matrimony and thus had become a court "so lost to its own dignity and duty" that it sanctioned unacceptable behavior and even took "especial pains to justify conduct, which must be considered as illegal as it is immoral." The frightful result was that the judges had ignored the "future – the general – the eternal interests of this boy."[36]

The Boston lawyer also disparaged the Philadelphia judges' excessive reliance on the tender-years rule and testimony about Frederick's feeble health. He ridiculed the very idea that Philadelphia could be considered the "only place where its health can be preserved! Philadelphia water is indispensable! Of all grounds ever assumed by a court of justice for the determination of a question of law, this is the most futile and shallow." He simply could not believe that a court would use such flimsy reasons to invade the "domestic forum" and decide "questions which are exclusively within the province of him, who is by law constituted the head of his family."

The sweep of the d'Hauteville verdict aroused Chandler's fear that it might ignite the tinderbox of popular antilegalism. Assuring his professional readers that he was not one who entertained "fears of judicial encroachments on private rights," nevertheless he expressed dismay at the Philadelphia court's brazen invasion of Gonzalve's patriarchal rights despite the losing father's valiant defense of his patriarchy. "This is certainly a most singular interference with domestic rights," he exclaimed before once more spelling out the most frightening possible implications of the courts' logic much as New York Governor Seward had in his veto message the year before. "If a court may upon the process of habeas corpus, sued out by a wife, control the wishes of a father on account of the health and age of his child, what is to prevent their interference as against both parents? Why may they not regulate the whole domestic economy of families?" Through such rhetorical questions he hoped to convince his fellow lawyers not only that child welfare must be given a limited definition but that they had a professional interest censoring wanton acts of judicial indiscretion. "A court of justice," he lectured, "has no more right to tread upon the appropriate duties of a father, than he has to assume the functions of a judge." Gonzalve, not the Philadelphia judges, should have decided where and how Frederick would be reared because a court "has no right to assume that in all things appertaining to his proper duties, a father will not act for the best interests of his child."[37]

Adamantly rejecting the maternalism that had infused the verdict, Chandler argued that the real consequence of the verdict was "to encourage separations between husbands and wives." The court's verdict approved and broadcast courtroom tactics that allowed mothers to get their children "however much in fault they may be. They have only to procure medical evidence that their infants of a tender age ought not to be separated from their mothers; that they are somewhat feeble, and that it may endanger their lives to remove them out of Philadelphia, and the Court of General Sessions will, in its discretion, order the children to remain in the custody of their mothers for the present." By endorsing Ellen's illegal resistance to her husband's legitimate demands, the judges encouraged maternal challenges which might well destroy paternal rights and thus the home itself. A decision, Chandler fumed, "which leads to results like this needs condemnation when it is understood."

Having tried his best to make his professional colleagues aware of the horrendous implications of the d'Hauteville verdict, Chandler did not hesitate to issue just such a condemnation. The decision, he thundered, "is one of the most extraordinary ever made in this country. It is altogether anomalous in point of law; it is immoral in its tendency. It has no parallel in the English or American reports. It is in direct violation of a principle as old as our law, and which is recognized in the jurisprudence of all civilized nations." Chandler brought his drawn-out assault on the verdict to a close by assuring his readers that real protection for married women came not with judicially sanctioned legal independence, but when wives relied

on the "strong arm of the law" for protection. As long as married
women performed their "appropriate duties" in their appropriate
sphere, they could rely on the law. However, he warned, if a wife "is
tempted to depart from her duty, let her know and feel, that the
domestic hearth will be protected; that her husband and her children may still gather around it, and if she attempts to disturb them
in their rights, the whole force of the law may be moved in their defense."[38]

While Chandler became the principal professional critic of the
d'Hauteville verdict, he was not the only lawyer to denounce it in
print. *The American Jurist and Law Magazine* issued a more concise
but equally scathing denunciation of the Philadelphia court shortly
after Chandler's. In its "Critical Notices" section, the national law
journal reported that the d'Hauteville case, "which has created so
strong an interest among all classes of people, has now been decided; and to the astonishment of the profession, generally, at the
result, viewed as a judicial decision, is not less than the disappointment which it has occasioned to those who consider it only in its
bearing upon the morals of social and domestic life." Speaking
to its lawyerly constituency, the journal offered its story of the case
and stressed that Ellen had offered no legally legitimate reason for
living apart from Gonzalve nor had she proved him an unfit father.
Nevertheless, the Philadelphia court had awarded her custody.
"The absurdity of this decision is so glaring, that if had not proceeded from a court of the state of Pennsylvania, where there is the
semblance of a precedent in its favor, we should be inclined to consider it as entirely incompatible with that good faith, for which our
courts are not undistinguished, and which has hitherto remained
unsullied."

The *Jurist*'s editors found Barton's verdict so appalling that they
tried to banish it to legal oblivion by neglect. The opinion, they explained, though "a novel one, we shall not insert in our pages: it
can never become a precedent, inasmuch as it is not well reasoned,
and the authorities commented upon in it are nearly all of them
perverted or misrepresented." The inherent contradiction of the
decision demonstrated its absurdity. The law, as the editors' assumed their readers well knew, gave a husband custody of his wife,
even one living in a state of illegal separation. Yet the court gave
her custody of his child. As a result, the journal explained, "to make
her conduct coincide with the law of the court, Mrs. d'Hauteville
must disregard those legal duties of the marital relation, which are
as old and as well established as the common law itself. In other
words, she is protected by the decision of this court, in her disobedi-
ence of the law."

The *Jurist* took one last swipe at "the judicial anomaly of the d'Hauteville case" with ridicule. If the Philadelphia judges accepted the responsibility of regulating child nurture in such cases, the editors suggested, then "we hope that no husbands and wives in that good city will ever hereafter take upon themselves the responsibility of deciding upon the propriety and expediency of putting their children out to nurse, or of consigning them to the custody of their grandmothers, but will at once apply to the sound judicial discretion of that honorable court." Like Chandler, the journal considered the verdict a product "not of a failure of evidence to support a charge, but a rejection on technical grounds of all the proofs in its favor." The editors ended their attack on the decision with a final professional judgment intended to add one last damning charge to their indictment of Barton, Conrad, and Doran. They praised "the admirable manner" in which Reed and his two colleagues had conducted Gonzalve's case and the "able and eloquent" documents they had drafted but the court had ignored.[39]

Despite the bitter contests over child custody being waged in courtrooms across the country, the Chandler and the *Jurist* editors had few doubts that they expressed the verdict of a united legal profession. Like many members of the legal elite, they defended existing rules such as paternal custody rights as the just expressions of a uniform legal order. They used their professional journals to stamp out jurisdictional anomalies like the maternal biased Pennsylvania custody decisions that might hint at conflict or division within the bar over the proper meaning of legal rules. They hoped professional condemnation would stifle doctrinal deviancy and protect the bench and bar's independence. Yet the very stridency of their attack on the d'Hauteville verdict suggested the depth of their fear that legal pluralism simply could not be contained. Lay critics like Jarvis, determined litigants like Ellen, and renegade rules, lawyers, and jurisdictions constantly resisted their efforts at legal uniformity.

Perhaps as Chandler and his colleagues worked out their fury at the potentially divisive d'Hauteville verdict, the lawyers recalled a similarly derisive dismissal of the Quaker state bench then current among attorneys. "All of the judges of the United States follow the Pennsylvania decisions as a beacon," one lawyer had apparently declared. "It is no wonder, then," a wag supposedly responded, "that they are so often wrecked, or run ashore."[40] The *Law Reporter* and the *American Jurist* hoped their dogmatic denunciations would ensure that the same fate befell Barton's opinion. Those hopes were fed by the Whiggish political allegiences of lawyers like Chandler. They found expression not only in attacks on the Democrat-dominated Pennsylvania bench but also in condemnations of the

Jacksonian United States Supreme Court headed by Chief Justice
Roger Taney. The uproar over decisions against vested interests as
in the 1837 *Charles River Bridge* case, where the chief justice ruled
against the proprietors of a Boston toll bridge and in favor of entrepreneurial competition, became a constitutional example of the
same professional divide provoked by the d'Hauteville verdict.[41]
Though differences over judicial standards and legal rules did not
occur consistently along political party lines, they did tend to group
American lawyers into different ideological camps. As a result, while
lawyers like Chandler could not contain the rhetorical significance
of words like Barton's, they tied mightily to stymie their legal significance. He and his like-minded brethren must have been immensely gratified when no major legal journal defended the verdict.
Nevertheless, federalism allowed the verdict to stand unless it was
appealed and overturned in Pennsylvania.

Though compartmentalized in different clusters of the American public sphere, legal journals and newspapers were not self-
contained mediums of public discourse. The d'Hauteville case
forced a merger of the two. Boston newspaper editors tried to limit
the rhetorical significance of the case by relaying the lawyers' professional condemnations. They hoped that the lawyers' words
would convince readers that the verdict was bad law as well as bad
policy. By turning to the bar, the newspapermen acknowledged not
only the dominating influence of lawyers in the case but also the
growing role of lawyers as moral critics. In New England, as in the
rest of the country, lawyers were displacing ministers as cultural
leaders, trial reports replacing published sermons as moral guides.
Just a decade before, New England's own United States Supreme
Court Justice, Joseph Story, had noted and approved the change:
"Eloquence for the bar is far more various and difficult than that
which is required for the pulpit – it addresses the very souls of men
in the most touching and pathetic admonitions."[42]

The newspaper editors hoped the lawyers would save a few more
souls by guiding the populace out of the wilderness that was the
d'Hauteville verdict. On Thursday, January 9th, the front page of
the *Boston Post* introduced excerpts from Chandler's attack by declaring, "The *Law Reporter* contains a very elaborate, a very able,
and, in our opinion, a just review of the celebrated case." An entire
reprint of the *Jurist* condemnation accompanied the excerpts.[43] The
Whiggish *Boston Courier* had reprinted the *Jurist* piece a couple of
days before and on the 11th the paper praised Chandler's analysis
of the case. "We have read with a satisfaction approaching to enthu-
siasm, in the *Law Reporter* . . . a review of the d'Hauteville case," the

paper proclaimed. "The writer is to be commended for a spirit of independence which is seldom seen in a review of a dispute between two parties, of which one is poor and the other rolling in wealth that might excite the envy of a modern Croesus. He speaks boldly of the injustice of the decree of the Pennsylvania Court, before which the case was tried, and exhibits the illegality of that decree by reference to a long line of judicial decisions."[44]

Despite the apparent convergence of press and professional opinion in Boston, the d'Hauteville case split both the bar and the press outside of Philadelphia. Even some Boston lawyers supported Barton's verdict. On January 27th, the *Post* offered its front page to a "legal gentleman," whose "Common Sense" defended the verdict. After noting the commentators who had treated Barton's opinion with "contempt and disapprobation," the lawyer dismissed them with equal venom: "The ignorance of the reviewers of the true ground upon which the decision was made, and of the principles which are applicable to the subject of inquiry properly before the court, is very apparent." He hoped to set straight both professional and law critics of the verdict and thus protect both its rhetorical and legal significance.

The only proper issue, the lawyer explained in a thumbnail rendition of habeas corpus procedures, was whether the infant had been illegally and improperly restrained and must be liberated by the court. "All other allegations in the petition were irrelevant and immaterial." Most importantly, he told readers, the only legitimate question before the court had been "a controversy between the father and mother as to their relative legal right to the custody of the child." The appropriate legal principles, the lawyer contended, "are simple and plain." Fathers had a primary right to custody of their wives and children, but that right "is subject to many limitations, as all other rights known to a civilized community are." Turning to the best interests of the child rule, "Common Sense" asserted that the welfare of the child had to guide the court.

The verdict's defender also challenged critics who considered Ellen's victory a threat to the nation's morals. Acknowledging the desirability of amity between husbands and wives, nevertheless he launched an indirect attack on marital unity by maintaining that "no court ever undertook to enforce, by its decrees, such kindness. Many cases undoubtedly exist in which a wife is morally authorized to leave her husband, although no overt act exists, or is susceptible of proof, of which the law takes cognizance." Consequently, the decision cannot be considered "immoral in its tendency" or a "legal sanction to a state of separation between husband and wife altogether unauthorized. It is neither. The decision does not sanction the separation in any respect – it remains as before the decision was pronounced – neither more nor less legal."

Returning to the habeas corpus rules of child custody, the lawyer declared that the Philadelphia court's primary responsibility had been to determine if Frederick had been illegally detained and "not what are the rights of the father." The judges also had to select the best custodian for the boy by weighing "a variety of circumstances." These included the superior legal rights of fathers, but the "interest of the child must be considered; this is in all cases paramount to the right of the father and mother." Judges determined those interests by considering the child's age, sex, and health while all along keeping the "well being of the infant" paramount. Following this logic, the "learned gentleman" could conclude magnanimously: "Whether the court at Philadelphia decided as to the matter of fact upon the principles here suggested, of which I have no doubt, is not material in a review of the law assumed by the court. That part of the decision which remanded the child into the custody of the mother, is simply saying that the court does not feel called upon to interpose its authority in favor of the petitioner, because, in the judgment of the court, the child was not illegally restrained of its personal liberty. The rights of the father have not been abridged. They remain as before. The court has regarded the well being of the child, and have given evidence of much learning and sound judgment, which is in no wise diminished by the fact, that the existence of this court has not heretofore been known to the learned reviewers of this city."[45]

Whether they changed any minds or not, the measured words of the "legal gentleman" disclosed for all to see that the verdict of the Philadelphia Court of General Sessions had provoked clashing views about some of the most fundamental problems of its time. By being tried and retried in newspaper offices, lawyers' chambers, and family parlors across the land, the case's importance had continued to grow. No longer merely a dispute between two parents, the d'Hauteville case assumed the dubious stature of a popular trial. As such, it gained rhetorical as well as legal significance by becoming a parable for the gender conflicts that raged throughout the republic. Men and women wrangled over marriage, divorce, domestic cruelty, and parenting by judging the acts of Ellen and Gonzalve and the needs of their son. The d'Hauteville case had become a widely shared legal experience.

6

Back into the Shadow

The torrent of public verdicts that cascaded over the d'Hautevilles made it clear just how momentous had been Gonzalve's decision to fight for Frederick by going to law. Not only had their problems been retold so many times that Gonzalve and Ellen became stock players in countless family law morality plays, but the trial had been a transformative legal event for both of them. It had been, using Wilhelm Dilthey's critical distinction, not mere "experience" but "*an* experience." Unlike commonplace, unstructured events that are accepted and endured without major alterations in a person's life, the trial stood apart as a distinct and formative event for both Ellen and Gonzalve.[1] Like their marriage and Frederick's birth, it had transformed their lives. Unlike those events, however, the trial had primarily been a legal experience. As such, it became the d'Hautevilles' most important lesson in law.

Struggling to comes to terms with their trial experience, Ellen and Gonzalve had to confront the reality that the verdict of the Philadelphia Court of General Sessions had not ended their encounters with the law. On the contrary, recourse to the courtroom condemned them to remain in its shadow until Frederick became an adult. Instead of a single experience in a Philadelphia courtroom, the law had become a permanent reality of their lives. Cast into this legal purgatory, each parent had to continue playing the part scripted for them in their courtroom stories. Their courtroom stories too had become part of their lives. Now they had to face the consequences of their narrative decisions as they fought one final round of legal battles.

Post-trial Maneuvers

Ellen and Gonzalve both had to respond to Barton's verdict and the public clamor it generated. Each had tactical and personal decisions to make. Their lives dominated by law even outside of the courtroom, they had to assess the meaning of their past legal experiences and predict the consequences of future ones. Their initial decisions demonstrate that they reached a common understanding of the meaning of Barton's verdict for their fight over Frederick. And yet, where Gonzalve's choices had orchestrated their courtroom experiences, Ellen's would direct their next legal contests.

Indeed Ellen acted first. By January of 1841, she and her parents began to worry about their bad notices in the press. The trial had taught them to respect and even fear the subtle but meaningful connections between public opinion and legal decision making. Though Gonzalve remained silent, the ferocious attacks on the judges and on Ellen in newspapers and law journals angered and dismayed the Searses. Fearing the legal implications of hostile publicity, they did not want to win in a court of law only to lose in the court of public opinion. Such a loss would not only be a personal humiliation, it might encourage Gonzalve to haul Ellen back into another courtroom to face another trial.

At first, Ellen and her family kept silent. They were a respected family and no doubt assumed that the complaints would die out quickly, particularly in Boston. In December Miriam optimistically reported to daughter Anna the judgment of a family friend, who had become convinced that "the trial has had the effect of entirely changing the morals of all those who thought on the other side, and of confirming those who have already been our supporters." Even so, she toyed with the idea of publishing Ellen's own version of the dispute before reiterating her conviction that the Searses must "remain on the defensive, and not be the accusers. It would never suit *my notions*, whatever, might be the effect, to pursue a different course."[2] But as 1841 dawned it became clear that the attacks would continue and the Searses decided that they must break their silence and mount a public defense of Ellen's victory.

David took on the task of trying to sway public opinion in his daughter's favor. The steady stream of attacks angered him, particularly what seemed to be a collusive campaign against the verdict in the *Law Reporter,* the *American Jurist,* and several Boston newspapers. The decision of the *Daily Advertizer,* for whom Chandler served as law correspondent, to reprint the *Jurist* diatribe, was the last straw. To do nothing violated David's personal code of honor. He must have been particularly upset at the *Advertizer* attack because the Whiggish paper, which back in 1813 had been Boston's first daily, was no penny press rag but an influential commercial newspaper that had a large circulation among his fellow businessmen. Unlike the dispassionate "legal gentleman," who had defended Ellen's victory in the *Post* with "common sense," David demanded space in the *Advertizer* for a spirited attack on his daughter's critics.[3]

The Boston Brahmin charged conspiracy. He considered it

"somewhat remarkable" that the *Advertiser*'s decision to reprint the *Jurist* polemic had so closely followed the pamphlet publication of Chandler's polemic, and that "several commendatory paragraphs and quotations, should have appeared in this city almost simultaneously – within the last few days – all tending to produce an impression highly disadvantageous to myself and family" as well as "wholly uncalled for by any new event" since the November 14th verdict. David explained that until the latest flurry of articles appeared, he had avoided comment on the "painful subject" and had expected "to find diversity of sentiment, on the merit of such a controversy" and even "mistakes and misrepresentations." His silence had ended because of the "appearance of a deliberate and systematic attack, from some unknown quarter, through the public press in my native city, not on myself only, but also, and chiefly, on the ladies of my family dependent upon me for their protection." Reluctantly he turned to the pages of the public press "for the sole purpose of defending myself and them, as well as I may by such means as the law will allow."

David fully admitted that some lawyers might well disagree with Barton's verdict. Unlike Chandler's dogmatic declaration of a professional consensus on the law of child custody, he acknowledged "differences of opinion, among professional men, on some of the legal questions involved. I have no means of judging which opinion, or set of opinions, is the most prevalent. They are important questions, of public interest, and I admit them to be fair topics of discussion, among those who are competent to discuss them professionally." Nor did he feel the need to defend Barton, Conrad, and Doran "from charges which seem to me nevertheless somewhat gross – charges of perverting and misrepresenting authorities, and pronouncing a verdict so 'glaringly absurd'" as the *Jurist* had complained.

A recent event strengthened David's argument. In the seesaw New York custody fight between the Barrys, Eliza had just won the latest round.[4] David tweaked Chandler and the *Jurist* by noting that their harangues against the Philadelphia decision ignored Eliza's victory on quite similar grounds. "Why is it," the onetime law student wondered, "that the contemporaneous Boston reviewers find themselves so much roused of a sudden against a single Pennsylvania decision in the d'Hauteville case, while in the Barry case, *four* New York decisions, of like import, some of them from Courts and Judges of the highest grade, have passed without any perception of their dangerous tendencies to law and morals?"

Not only did David acknowledge custody law as a fit topic of public discussion, he also accepted that his daughter's story would become fodder for that debate. He had no "quarrel with any fair statement of the facts proved at the trial, however painful to myself and family such publication may be, so far as they are proper, or useful, for a right understanding of the legal decision under examination." But Chandler's attack, he warned the *Advertizer*'s readers, "is a work of a very different stamp." It contained neither evidence from the trial nor Barton's opinion, but rather "referring to and commenting upon them, it presents a mere argument for Mr. d'Hauteville, appealing in his behalf from the judgment of the Court to the bar of public opinion." David claimed that he would have even accepted this in silence had Chandler been fair. But the "argument states inferences and matters not in evidence *as facts*, and *misstates* material facts which were in evidence, and makes comments and animadversions founded upon its own errors and gratuitous assumptions, grievously wounding to the feelings, and deeply affecting the character of individuals, in matters with which the public have no concern. Under the guise of reviewing a judicial question, discussing the law, and determining its proper application to a particular case, the writer goes wholly out of his way to commit a most wanton, unprovoked, cruel, and unmanly assault upon the private characters, conduct, and motives of respectable ladies, (to say nothing of myself,) to whom he imputes base acts and criminal designs, without a shadow of *evidence,* to support the imputation, and directly *against* the opinion of the Court who heard the parties, and examined their respective proofs. He is not content with setting himself up as a reviser of judicial law in a distant State, but he also assumes the responsibilities of a public censor of morals, and in that capacity stoops to the unworthy office of holding up these individuals, as far as his ability will permit, as fit objects of public indignation and contempt." All of this had simply been too much for David. He rejected Chandler's claims of professional objectivity and refused to defer to his legal judgments. Instead, he contended that from "whatever unknown enemy it may directly or indirectly come, whether written for hire, or for the sake of notoriety, or for profitable sale, or whatever hidden motive may have prompted its author, it is sufficiently obvious that there is some cause at work beyond mere calm professional regard for justice and a sound interpretation of the laws."

Performing what he believed to be his manly duty to issue a public rejoinder, the Boston Brahmin shared with the *Advertizer*'s readers what he had learned about Massachusetts divorce law. As he did, once more a newspaper page became a legal lectern. David refuted the charge that he had purposely issued a meaningless warning to Gonzalve in the hope that the threat of a lawsuit might frighten the young father into remaining in Switzerland. "The truth is," David explained, "that at the time of writing that letter, I was ignorant of the fact to which I would now call attention, namely, the Courts of Massachusetts are expressly prohibited by statute from inquiring into any cause of divorce which had occurred in a foreign country, when the parties have not lived together in the married state within this Commonwealth." Had the law been otherwise, he would have carried out his threat and sued to expose Gonzalve's tyrannical treatment of his daughter even though it had been "unaccompanied by any act of that mere brutal and physical violence which is the common case presented to a Court, and constitutes the ordinary 'cruelty' of the law." And so, once more, the d'Hauteville case prompted a public brief in support of mental cruelty as a legitimate ground for divorce and a public assault on male marital mores.

David even became an advocate of family law reform. He reduced Chandler's and the *Jurist*'s interpretation of Massachusetts law to three basic and, in his mind, quite dubious assertions: Under all circumstances a husband had complete custody of his wife and no person could lawfully harbor and protect her from him; a mother living separate from her husband, "without justifiable cause," could never be permitted to keep her child, "even at the most tender age," against her husband's will if he was a fit parent; and there could be no justifiable cause of separation, unless by mutual agreement, that was not a legal ground for divorce. The consequences of these interpretations, David argued in his own form of lawyerly reductio ad absurdum, "seems to be that if a Massachusetts woman, marrying out of her own state, should be actually beaten by a brutal husband, and personally abused even to the danger of her life, if she should fly from him in terror, and return for protection to her father's roof, she would find herself, in her native state, literally *an outlaw*." Unable to sue for divorce and being in a state of unjustifiable separation, he continued, she could not even keep her child, and her parents, "according to all law and *morality*, in the opinion of some," must drive her from their door and deliver her into the hands of her brutal husband. Though he deferred to the lawyers to settle the exact meaning of Massachusetts rules, David rejoiced that Pennsylvania and New York interpreted their law quite differently. "If it be otherwise here," he mused, "it must at least be admitted, that under our law *may* arise cases of hardship beyond all human endurance and yet wholly without remedy."

Driven by his own legal experiences in Ellen's struggle, the Boston patriarch assumed the contradictory role of championing challenges to the very paternal power he felt compelled to assert. Only by increasing the legal autonomy of wives and daughters could women gain the rights he now advocated. So caught up in his daughter's cause, David simply failed to realize that the marital independence he championed could only come at the expense of fathers and husbands like himself.

Chauvinism too remained a constant in the d'Hauteville struggle. Having first tarred Chandler as a defender of domestic brutality, David next cast him as an aristocratic Anglophile. He challenged the *Law Reporter*'s attempt to give Massachusetts law an English pedigree. Not only did David question whether the patriarchalism of English custody rules had ever been grafted upon American law, he reported that "several decisions of English judges on this subject since the revolution were such gross outrages on the law of nature and of common sense, that they roused the indignation of the whole British public," and led Parliament to pass Lord Talfourd's Act giving mothers of children under seven greater custody rights. Even some of the offending judges had voted for the bill.

After rebutting Chandler's dogmatic declarations of legal unanimity by revealing the controversies and uncertainties that bedeviled American custody law, David told his version of Ellen's story. As he had done since his first letters to the Swiss Syndic Frederic Couvreu, he defended his daughter as the faultless victim of a tyrannical husband whose mental cruelties had driven her to death's door. Over and over again, he declared himself satisfied with the evidence of Gonzalve's tyranny and reported that eminent physicians had been convinced as well. And he defended his own actions as unavoidable paternal responsibilities: "She clings to me, as her father and natural guardian, and implies protection against him. Would any man, with the feelings of a father, or *more* than the feelings of a brute, refuse it to such a child under such circumstances? Others may arrive at a different conclusion upon the facts, so far as they known them – or may disbelieve the facts upon such evidence as they see – but it is impossible for me, with the information I possess, while I am a free agent, to act otherwise than according to my own personal convictions of the truth of the case, and sense of what is right in this matter." Whatever legal remedies Gonzalve sought, David publicly pledged to support and protect Ellen and save her from certain death in Switzerland.

Returning to Ellen's story, David contended that he and his family had resisted Gonzalve's persecution not the law. Nor had they tried to arouse public sympathy for her plight. Instead, they had waited quietly first in New York and then in Philadelphia for Gonzalve to act. David insisted that Ellen's husband and his counsel had selected the forum and demanded a public hearing. He also charged Gonzalve with constantly raising irrelevant issues about the failed marriage and unfairly attacking Miriam Sears. But all had been for naught, the judges rebuffed all his claims and ruled, according "to the long settled law and practice of Pennsylvania, [that] the child could not at a tender age be taken from its mother."

David then dropped his own bombshell. He reported that, unlike Chandler and his minions, "Mr. d'Hauteville, for the present at least, appears to acquiesce in that decision, and has left the country instead of carrying his cause before some higher tribunal of the same State, as he might had he so chosen, and probably would, if his Counsel had advised him there was any chance of success." The message was clear: There would be no appeal, at least for now; Ellen would keep Frederick, at least for now; and, Gonzalve had finally learned the proper legal lesson, also at least for now. Despite the lawyers' laments, Barton's verdict would continue to guide Pennsylvania custody fights.

Finally, David appealed for public support. "I beg leave to ask of all candid persons," he pleaded, "whatever their ideas may be on any other questions of law or morals presented to them, whether there is any thing in these circumstances, which can justly render unobtrusive persons, who in all other matters have passed blameless lives, so far at least as the public is concerned, liable to be dragged from their privacy, not only to have their characters and conduct and secret motives made a moot question for discussion in the common prints, but to be held up as malefactors, meriting the scorn of the whole community – violating the common decencies of life – and *guilty* of an *indictable conspiracy* to effect an *unlawful purpose by unlawful means?* And all for what? No better *ostensible* reason, than because in the opinion of the Law Reporter, of Boston, whoever he may be, a certain Court in Pennsylvania did not rightly understand the evidence before them as to the conduct of certain parties collaterally inquired into, nor the law of their own State, respecting the custody of an infant." If such charges be "admissible," David concluded, "I have yet something new to learn of the law of Massachusetts."[5]

David's measured yet outraged editorial reply to the Boston verdicts on Ellen's case only partially vented his anger. He let loose his full rage in a January 13th letter to one of his daughter's Philadelphia lawyers. David assumed that William Meredith had seen the "libel" written by Chandler. Dropping the public pretense that he did not know who edited the *Law Reporter,* he dismissed Chandler as "a vulgar person, a lawyer from Maine, recently come among us, and neither known, nor noticed by gentlemen." Yet the powerful Boston Brahmin conceded, "He cannot be touched in any way."

But David wanted to exert all the pressure he could to end the editorial conspiracy. He told Meredith that "[n]o one here credits the assertion of Chandler, who really is a pitiful fellow beneath notice, that he is the *sole* author. Every body thinks that some one is behind the curtain, and moves the wires." He wanted Meredith to investigate the rumor that Gonzalve's Philadelphia counsel, William Reed, had been the puppet master. Gossip had it that Reed had suggested the attack would be more effective if it came "from a Boston pen." David asked Meredith to confront Reed, demand an explanation, and insist that the attacks cease. If private suasion failed, then threats might succeed. Taking his manly duty to the battlefield of personal honor, he suggested that Meredith hint that David would publicize Reed's clandestine role as well as the widely circulated charges that Reed's "father was a knave, and his grandfather a traitor, and repeat the words already addressed to his face, that 'he is a scoundrel, without a drop of gentlemanly blood in his veins.'"[6]

Frustrated by his inability to provide the protection he thought his family deserved, David took every opportunity to aid Ellen's cause. In March he even agreed to bankroll the *Philadelphia Gazette*. The paper's editor, Willis Clarke, had written asking for financial help. He claimed credit for galvanizing public support for Ellen, but disclosed that Reed had vowed vengeance as had Samuel Miller because the *Gazette* had denounced his *Report of the d'Hauteville Case*. The pair had conspired to buy up outstanding notes from his paper's creditors and threatened to shut it down. David loaned him the funds he needed.[7]

Ellen's sentence to legal purgatory had driven David to such actions. The contingencies of custody law made the public verdicts critical to her future legal success and the continuing controversy ever more frightening. Besides the anger and frustration he and his family felt as objects of public attack, they knew that at any time Gonzalve could sail back to America and serve Ellen with another writ of habeas corpus. The whole nightmare would then begin again. And thanks to Chandler's emphatic defense of Massachusetts' paternal custody rules, they feared Ellen could never return to her Boston home while Frederick remained a child. Federalism had been her salvation; now it threatened to become her prison.

In an April letter to the European agents handling Ellen's financial affairs, David confessed, "We are ignorant of Mr. d'Hauteville's intentions, nor do we know in what part of the world he at present is; but we are anxious, in any way to procure a dissolution of this unhappy marriage. Unfortunately my daughter finds that our Courts in Massachusetts cannot take cognizance of her case, in consequence of the marriage having been made abroad, and the cruel treatment inflicted beyond their jurisdiction, – the parties never having lived together, as man and wife, within the State."[8]

As the Searses searched for a way out of Ellen's legal predicament, across the Atlantic Gonzalve acted. Finally convinced that Ellen would never return yet still determined to get custody of Frederick, he continued to rely on the law. But Gonzalve chose a very different forum from the Philadelphia courts. Counseled that appealing Barton's verdict would be fruitless, he sailed home and filed for a Swiss divorce. He charged his wife with desertion and requested custody of Frederick. Ellen received notice of the suit in early May. A Vevey tribunal ordered her to appear at a June hearing.

The Searses responded to the suit by directing their European agents, Hottinguer & Co. of Paris, to have a Swiss lawyer monitor the trial and obtain copies of all relevant documents. But they did not want him to represent her at the hearing. The divorce would be uncontested. Fearing that Gonzalve, armed with the Swiss decree, would renew the fight for Frederick, David also asked that the lawyer let them know immediately if he should "hear of any intention of Mon. Gonzalve d'Hauteville again to the visit the United States. I should be happy to receive such information from any quarter, in order to prevent a surprise, as on his late visit he came very unexpectedly, and suddenly, to the great terror of his wife, and landed privately, and under an *assumed* name."[9]

While they awaited the outcome of the Swiss divorce, the Searses searched for a way to free Ellen from her Philadelphia refuge. David's threats had borne some fruit. In a June letter to Ellen's Philadelphia physician Nathaniel Chapman, he expressed pleasure at hearing that Reed had offered to intercede on Ellen's behalf with Gonzalve's New York lawyer, Henry C. De Rham. Though pleased that the public campaign against his daughter might end, he doubted that Reed or anyone else could dissuade Gonzalve from hounding her. David told Chapman that the vanquished father had instituted "a public process against [Ellen] in Switzerland, with the avowed object of tearing away from her, her child, under a new form of law, and without giving her a fair opportunity of showing that his own misconduct is the cause of their separation." He feared Gonzalve would never end his persecution. The Swiss father, David charged, "was not ignorant that she was miserable, and wasting daily, and that one word from him would mitigate her suffering, and yet that word he would not speak, and his last declaration to her was 'that neither days nor weeks nor months nor years, nor constant efforts would succeed in altering my determination.'" Those words haunted Ellen and her family like an evil spell.[10]

Creating Safe Havens

Gonzalve's bitter pledge cast a pall on all the Searses' maneuvers to find a safe legal haven for Ellen. Despite the victory in Philadelphia and Eliza Berry's triumph in the New York, they still feared the uncertainties of the courtroom. Their legal lessons had produced as much, if not more, distrust than faith. Contested custody rules, unpredictable judicial temperaments, and the vagaries of litigation simply created far more uncertainty than they wanted to chance. Yet Ellen wanted a refuge as near the Searses' hearth as possible. After discussing their options, David, Ellen, and their advisors revived an earlier strategy. Once more they decided to create a safe haven through legislation. Their lessons had convinced them that greater legal safety came from clear statutory directives than from uncertain judicial discretion.

During its June session, the General Assembly of Rhode Island passed "An Act to secure the fulfillment of certain contracts, and for the relief of Married Women in certain cases." The statute granted married women who entered the state without their husbands the right to establish a legal residence, transact business, acquire or dispose of property, and enjoy "the exclusive care, custody, and guardianship of her minor children, if any, living with her, in like manner and in all respects as if she were unmarried." In addition, the new act conferred on married women whose husbands had secured a divorce against them in other states or countries the right to retain their property and custody of their children unless a husband petitioned the Supreme Judicial Court and proved that his ex-wife was "not a person of good moral character, suitable to have charge of her children, or unless the Court shall thereupon in its discretion, having due regard to the well being of the infant, order its custody to be changed." The act significantly increased the custodial rights of mothers who left their spouses. It not only offered present protection, but also provided for future aid once a child grew out of infancy and thus beyond the reach of the tender-years rule.

On June 29, 1841, Ellen wrote Gonzalve's counsel, De Rham, that "in conformity with the advice of her Physician for the restoration of her own health and for the benefit of that of her son, she intends, in the course of the week, to remove from Philadelphia, and make her residence in Rhode Island."[12] She arrived in Newport on Independence Day, and began staying at a boarding house.

Despite his daughter's move, David complained to one of his lobbyists, Providence attorney John Whipple, that the Rhode Island statute had been "ill drawn and defective." Nevertheless, "such as it is, it is of importance to retain it, and the objective of my letter is to

express the wish that in consequence of the above consideration
[David had sent along a note for $250 for Whipple and his partner
George Rivers] you would keep your eye upon the moving parties,
and in case of need use your best efforts to prevent any adverse
action – a reference to the vote will show who are friends of the
measure."[13]

David's fear that the act might be attacked soon came true. On
September 28th, De Rham notified Ellen that he would petition the
General Assembly at its October session to exempt Gonzalve from
the just passed married women's rights act. In his subsequent peti-
tion, the New York lawyer offered legislators a truncated version of
his client's tale. It stressed the Searses' consent to his marriage and
Ellen's desertion. De Rham also told them of the Court of General
Sessions' verdict that "on account of the tender years of [Frederick]
he should for the present remain in the custody of his Mother" and
Gonzalve's decision to seek a Swiss divorce. To intimate collusion,
De Rham charged that Ellen had moved to Rhode Island shortly
after the act's passage and immediately retained local counsel. If the
act were applied to his client, he argued, it would threaten Gonzalve's "Marital and Parental Rights." To explain why, the lawyer
shared what he and his client had learned about the logic of the
tender-years rule: "The infancy of the Child may operate to preclude Mr. d'Hauteville from instituting proceedings now, to protect
and preserve his rights, till said act will by its provisions have taken
effect as regards him, thereby either uttering debarring or greatly
impeding him in recovering them in the future." He explained
to the lawmakers that Gonzalve continued to believe that as a father he had the "vested right to the care and custody" of Frederick
and the duty to "exercise that right and to superintend the moral
and religious and intellectual upbringing of his offspring." Consequently, De Rham pleaded that the legislators exempt Gonzalve
from the act. The petition thus continued Gonzalve's defense of paternal authority and brought the fight for Frederick into a new legal
arena and a new jurisdiction.[14]

Gonzalve's petition galvanized the Searses into action once again.
David wrote Rhode Island legislator Richard Randolph on October
4th to condemn De Rham's request as a breach of international customs: "It is unheard of that a Foreigner, and an Alien, should petition an Independent State to exempt him from the operation of a
general law, and make his wishes the rule for public legislation." As
in New York, Pennsylvania, and New Jersey, he also denied that the
measure had been designed specifically for Ellen, who, he assured
Randolph, felt perfectly safe under existing Rhode Island law. Instead, David derided the petition as yet another act of persecution:

"I am sorry to say that [Gonzalve] has shown himself both malignant and mercenary, – He has broken the heart of my child, and her days hereafter must be days of sorrow. – Her fortune he has possession of, and is now using against her, perhaps with the hope that a still larger sum may be given him to keep him quiet." David added that when final, Gonzalve's Swiss divorce would grant him custody of Frederick and possession of Ellen's dowry. He apologized for being so candid, but explained that the "sorrows of my child press heavily."[15]

Apparently Randolph had heard of the Searses' attempts to create a safe haven for Ellen through legislation because two days later David wrote a second letter defending his actions in New York. He admitted that the rumors had some truth to them, though he insisted that Ellen's "sorrows have excited both zeal, and sympathy, and many persons have volunteered their services in her behalf." The New York bill, he contended, had been vetoed by Governor Seward because of pressure from De Rham. Yet David denied directly lobbying for the failed act, and claimed it had been a general statute not a bill designed merely to fit his daughter's case. He also disclosed that similar acts had been passed, again without his direct intervention, in Maine, New Hampshire, Maryland, and Missouri, and thus suggested that Gonzalve would have to seek exemptions in all of those states as well as Rhode Island. He then entered a plea: "And what is Mr. d'Hauteville's object? Is it not to tear a child only three years old, and of feeble health, from the arms of its mother, and transport it to a foreign country, where the mother can never hope to see it any more? And what are his means if they are not his wife's property which he now has in possession, and can use against her? Under such circumstances, my dear Sir, I feel justified in taking every proper measure to soften the hard fate of my unfortunate child, and if a representation of her sad case, combines with others, perhaps equally distressing, to produce an effect among men of feeling, it surely cannot be required of me to be silent." David buttressed his case by asserting that American law would never allow the expatriation of a citizen before the age when he or she could make their own choice. "Chancellor Kent," he argued invoking the hallowed name of America's most eminent law writer despite *Ledger* editor Jarvis's recent denunciation of the jurist's paternal biases, "has given me his written opinion that no court in the United States would suffer an American child to be deported out of the country against the consent of its American parent. He declares it to be against all precedent, and unconstitutional." David urged the legislator to support the June act.[16]

While David lobbied, Ellen and her lawyers compiled a lengthy response to Gonzalve's petition. Once more, she and her lawyers drafted a version of her story. This time, she sought to counter not only her husband's petition but also what she considered the misrepresentations broadcast by Miller's widely read *Report*. Her *Remonstrance* called Gonzalve's petition "a renewed public assault . . . upon her peace, happiness, and honor, which she is bound to repel." She ridiculed his request by rephrasing it as a demand that "Mr. d'Hauteville only, of the whole human race, if he shall choose to step upon your soil, may not be *bound* by a general law of the land. In substance, he asks, that the Respondent, alone among women, if *she* shall venture to breathe the air of Rhode Island, *may be out of the pale of its common protection.*" Instead Ellen asked only to be treated like all other citizens and urged the legislators to deny Gonzalve's petition.

As in the d'Hautevilles' private bargaining and their trial, however, Ellen had to defend her tactics and her marital conduct. She denied that the June act had been specifically designed for her benefit. To defend herself from Gonzalve's charges, though, Ellen explained with frustration why she had to tell her story in some detail and challenge other versions of the d'Hauteville case: "It is among her misfortunes, that the merits of her case cannot be stated, intelligibly, *in few words.* If a husbands *beats* his wife, and *menaces her body with violence dangerous to life,* and she therefore *quits* him; that story is soon told. If, on the other hand, a wife *deserts* a kind and affectionate husband, *without any just cause,* and *refuses to return to him,* and *withhold from him his only child;* that story, too, is soon told; and this is Mr. d'Hauteville's story, at least, that which he always first tells. It is *substantially* the story of the present petition. But if a wife has been *driven* from her husband, by *his own willful and cruel conduct,* reducing her to a state *verging upon the grave,* and that conduct does not consist of *open acts of bodily violence,* but depends, for its effects, upon numerous *circumstances hanging* together and *all conducing to the result,* her story requires both time and patience to hear."

Ellen's latest tale continued the public legal education that had become so much a part of the d'Hauteville case. She told the legislators, and through them other audiences, a slightly revised version of her Philadelphia courtroom stories. She added to it a sworn deposition by Sears family physician John C. Warren that documented the life-threatening impact of Gonzalve's mental abuse and the loving maternal care she had lavished on sickly Frederick. Only with the addition of these two documents, she argued, could Miller's *Report* be relied upon.

The narrative, the deposition, and the *Report* revealed conduct, Ellen argued in phrases honed from months of legal combat, that

could be described "in *two words* of the English language, stronger
that she would wish to use, if they were not, as she is advised, the
appropriate terms of the law to represent a case of marital misconduct, such as she esteems his to have been, which would have been
the proper subject for a divorce, at the wife's suit, if the courts of
her own State could have entertained jurisdiction of a cause in a
foreign country: they are *fraud* and *cruelty*." Deceived by false promises and drive to near death by marital tyranny, Ellen declared:
"This is the *cause* of separation; – of which *she for herself must necessarily judge*, and submit to all the painful consequences of her honest
judgement. Others may discuss the question of *what* circumstances,
or whether *any* circumstances, can in law, or morals, or in the sight
of Heaven, justify a wife in refusing to live with her husband, where-
soever he chooses to live, and under whatever conditions he may
choose to prescribe, and they must decide them according to the
light of their own consciences, and their own powers of reason. She
decided according to hers. And, without undertaking to say *where
precisely*, the line shall be drawn, distinguishing the state of facts under which a woman *may*, and under which a woman *may not*, be justified in such separation, the Respondent simply maintains, that
there is at least *one state of facts* which clearly falls *within* the line. It
is *where reason and life are jeopardized*. Whether this is, or is not, her
case, with others may be matter of opinion; with her, it is that deep
and irresistible conviction, which is *practically* knowledge." With
those words, Ellen continued her campaign for the recognition
of mental cruelty as a form of male marital tyranny and for independent legal rights for wives as a necessary defense against victimization.

Ellen then used the *Remonstrance* to bring her story up the present
and to attack the logic and legitimacy of Gonzalve's petition. Once
again, Ellen told how Gonzalve had chased her down the east coast
from Boston to New York and finally to Philadelphia. Once more,
she accused him of rebuffing all attempts at compromise in a ruth-
less determination to vindicate his paternal rights. Yet again she
charged him with forcing her to face the humiliation of a public
trial. But now Ellen claimed that since the Philadelphia verdict neither Gonzalve nor his counsel De Rham had replied to her letters
about Frederick. Their only communications had been legal summons. She accused her husband of filing for divorce in Switzerland
knowing she could not defend herself. Consequently, Ellen argued
without a nod to Gonzalve's predicament the year before, that for
"all *practical purposes*, a notice to a party *here*, of suit brought in *Switzerland* in *such* a case, whatever may be its legal effect there, is little
better than a suit *without* notice." Gonzalve would have his way with

Swiss law and their marriage would be dissolved on his terms. Then, she feared, he would once again sail to America but this time "*armed with his decree of a Swiss court, obtained in her absence, as evidence of his right,* to inflict the *last* injury he *can* inflict, and *to take from her, if the laws of her own country will permit it, her only child,* born *here, after* the separation, *nurtured and supported hitherto, wholly by her,* without a particle of aid from its father; and yet, in the first years of *tender infancy,* with a constitution peculiarly subject to disease, *relying upon a mother's care."*

Turning from storyteller to legislative supplicant, Ellen recited her hardwon legal lessons to urge that Rhode Island lawmakers not succumb to Gonzalve's demands. She "has found by Experience, they will not in *Pennsylvania.* She has seen by recent decisions, that they will not *in New York.* She has learned, that even in *England,* where modern judgments had stretched the rigorous notions of the common law, to an extent, quite unknown in that country, *before* the American Revolution, and *never* known or practiced here, (taking even the *new born infant* from its mother's *breast* to deliver it to the father, *however worthless,*) a recent statute abolished that barbarity. And in her own country she has heard of modern statutes in *various* states from Maine to Michigan and from New Hampshire to Georgia, enlarging the privileges of married women, and regulating the custody of infants, in some manner, *not utterly adverse to the laws of nature."* This liberal legal trend steeled her determination not to "consent to any legislative act of Rhode Island, which shall have the smallest tendency to impair her liberty of action, on this vital subject." She demanded the full rights of citizenship and, in purposely chauvinist phrases, challenged the right of a foreigner to seek special legal privileges. For herself, Ellen "sought no *special privileges"* and claimed "no exemption from *common* liabilities."

Finally, Ellen defended herself against De Rham's insinuation that she had procured the bill and then hired counsel to invoke its protections. Denying any direct involvement with the act, she admitted retaining lawyers but pleaded that Gonzalve's oppression had trapped her in the law's shadow: "Such has been her unfortunate position, and such the relentless persecution with which she is pursued by that man, whose *willful determination to press to the utmost,* at *all* hazards *not his own, whatever right the law may give him* – '*Neither days, nor weeks, nor months, nor years, nor constant efforts,'* as his own language avows, can change, or turn him one hairs breadth from his unalterable course; that she had been compelled to retain counsel, to inform her of her rights, and defend against him, *wherever she has been,* and *wherever she has thought of going."* [In that shadowland, she had been forced to determine the legal consequences of her every move. And so, her hopes to bring Frederick to Rhode Island for his health had to be weighed against the chances of yet another lawsuit. She had consulted lawyers "for the purpose of ascertaining, whether she should be safe there, and whether her *child* would be safe; whether the law of *this* state would protect them, as well as the laws of the *state where she then was;* or whether they would permit a *foreigner,* no longer *connected with her,* she believes and trusts, by the laws of God or Man, *to take her child from her,* and *carry it out of the country,* at the *imminent hazard of its own life.*" Assured that Rhode Island would protect her and her child, she remained ready to put that advice to the test if hauled into another courtroom: "She is contented to abide by the unfettered discretion of any intelligent and impartial judges, not bound by positive statute or technicalities of law, to judge her case and decide upon her rights." Unlike Gonzalve, all she wanted was to be treated like any other Rhode Islander. Ellen ended her *Remonstrance* with the plea that "she may not, at their foreign suit, be deprived of the benefit of [the act's] equitable provisions, so far as they cover her case."

Gonzalve's *Petition* and Ellen's *Remonstrance* greeted Rhode Island legislators when they met on Thursday evening, October 28th. Representative J. H. Clarke provoked a contentious debate by challenging the legitimacy of the June act. He claimed that no one could tell him who had authored the bill or how it had passed. Bribery, he intimated, must be its true source. Though Clarke avoided names, he recited the details of the d'Hauteville case, including Seward's veto of a similar New York bill, to charge that provisions of the act specifically fit the situation of the "daughter of a wealthy citizen of Massachusetts." Calling it special legislation enacted at the behest of a monied out-of-stater, he declared that the act "affected deeply the honor and dignity of the state and the independence of its legislation." It conferred no benefits on Rhode Island citizens, and instead threatened to turn the state into an "asylum for all runaway wives." Clarke demanded that it be repealed.

Representative Atwell rallied the act's defenders. He argued that it conferred no new rights on married woman. It only evened the rules of custody contests by compelling fathers to demonstrate why they should have custody instead of forcing mothers to prove why their spouses should not. Pointedly, he declared that the act had been passed after a full discussion, and defended its legitimacy as a general law not a piece of special legislation. Atwell claimed it would benefit hundreds of women not just Ellen d'Hauteville. In fact, he argued that Ellen's personal misery could be redeemed by legislative cures for other women. In his version of how progressive legal change occurred, the representative argued that her story had prompted legislators to enact needed reforms because "laws derive their origins from particular cases; we get to the knowledge of general evils from particular grievances." In a textbook example of the legislative impact of debates in the public spheres, Atwell contended that thanks to the intense publicity generated by Ellen's fight for Frederick, Rhode Island legislators had been able to remedy "an evil which exists among poorer classes of society" not just among the wealthy. "Where there is one Madame d'Hauteville," he declared, "there are hundreds of married women in this state who deserve this protection." In reality Ellen did not need the act because judges would protect her in Rhode Island just as they had in Pennsylvania. Not the rich daughter of a Boston Brahmin, but the wives of factory workers dragooned into supporting "dissolute and degraded husbands" would benefit from translating the lessons of the d'Hauteville case into legislation. Most importantly, the act would allow courts to make child nurture the central issue of a custody fight. In this way Rhode Island would be once more the asylum for the oppressed it had been since the days of Roger Williams.

Presented these clashing stories about the act, the Representatives heatedly debated the repeal motion. Clarke reiterated his opposition to the act and insisted that employers not the courts should police malingering husbands. Several others agreed, and supported his repeated charge that the act was special legislation. Randolph rose to defend David Sears. Ellen's Rhode Island counsel declared that he had voted against the measure in June and had witnessed no money being lavished on legislators, though he admitted conferring with David about the act. He turned personal experience into legislative argument by asking his fellow male lawmakers whether as fathers they too would not have done everything they could do to help their daughters. Other legislators argued that the measure would assist countless women faced with the horrifying prospect of losing their children. And Representative Cranston defended the act by declaring that it conformed to the gender realities of American family life: "In nineteen out of twenty cases where divorces have been obtained, it is safe to leave young children in the custody of their mothers."

When the representatives tired of hurling charges at each other, the House voted forty-one to twenty-four against repeal.[17] The next morning, after the legislators summarily refused to accept the request for an exemption, De Rham withdrew Gonzalve's petition.[18]

On Saturday, October 30th, the *Providence Journal* gave its readers a blow-by-blow account of the repeal battle.[19] The editors followed up the story with a Monday morning editorial. After reprising the key issues, they expressed regret that the d'Hauteville case had so dominated the debate. "We know nothing of the merits of the d'Hauteville case, although sympathy is naturally excited for a mother, struggling to retain her child," the editors explained. "Whatever may be the abstract merits of the case, still, had the law been passed by any improper means, its repeal would have been demanded by every principle of justice and honor, even if it was a good law and was re-enacted the next day; but the General Assembly, by their vote, decided that such was by no means the case."[20] An enterprising Providence publisher made sure that others would learn the virtues of the legislation by quickly getting into print a chapbook with the d'Hautevilles' petitions, the legislative debate, and the disputed statutes. It became part of the case's bulging public record.

Like their other legal skirmishes, the Rhode Island controversy taught Ellen and Gonzalve yet another hard-won lesson about law. It reinforced Ellen's faith in legislation, while further eroding Gonzalve's belief in American justice. As the Searses pursued their renewed strategy of creating statutory havens, they immediately put this latest legal knowledge to use in New Hampshire.

Still a legal exile from Massachusetts, Ellen hoped she would not have to return to faraway Philadelphia for the winter of 1841. After summering in Rhode Island, she wanted to remain as near as possible to her Boston home by setting up residence in the Granite State. As in Rhode Island, her way had been cleared by June legislation. The act granted a woman married either to an alien or the citizen of another state the right to apply for a divorce after residing in New Hampshire for two years if during that time her husband had not come into the state and claimed his marital rights to her and her property. During her separate residence, such a woman would be granted the exclusive custody and guardianship of any minor children born in the United States and living with her.[21] As the Providence *Gospel Messenger* noted, "This law fits the d'Hauteville case in every essential point."[22]

Ellen and Frederick left their Newport boarding house at the end of the summer season, and took up residence in Nashua, New Hampshire, just across the border from Massachusetts.

Not only had David secured a more effectively drafted statute, he had learned from his experience in Rhode Island and immediately engaged in public advocacy as well as private lobbying. Early in October he wrote Nashua lawyer David Abbot to stifle rising complaints about the June act. As in Rhode Island, he denied charges that the legislature had acted merely on his daughter's behalf: "This is not true. Mrs. d'Hauteville is already divorced legally, and wholly divorced, and therefore has no occasion of a law for the purpose."

Before leaving Philadelphia, she had known that "a few months would set her free from her thraldom, and she felt that if she could preserve her child, she might still be happy. This is her last and only hope."

David went on to complain to Abbot about the bind in which Ellen found herself thanks to the notoriety of the d'Hauteville case. "Whenever a law is framed to extend 'protection to females,'" he lamented, "it is ascribed to the influence of Mrs. d'Hauteville's friends, who I assure you have neither the presumption, nor the vanity to suppose that it is enacted in her behalf alone." David acknowledged only that the barrage of stories about his daughter's plight "may have turned many minds to the general subject." And he admitted that her fate had forced him to act: "It is true that I have taken legal advice on the existing law, and legal precedents in several states before my daughter has entered them, – for from her own state she is excluded by the revised statutes from all remedy. On every fit occasion I have pointed out the hardships of the case but I have never obtruded her misfortunes on anyone." Assuming once more the pose of a family law reformer, he declared that if "the broad circulation of her story in private circles has at last caught the attention of gentlemen in office, and turned their thoughts to the subject I am glad of it, for in regard of protection to females, but in their persons and property, our laws are very defective. If a representation of my daughter's sad fate combines itself with that of others, perhaps even more unfortunate, to produce an effect among men of feeling I surely shall not withhold it."

Finally, David claimed that the provisions of the New Hampshire act had been unknown to Ellen and her supporters until they read about them in the press. He dismissed the relevance of most of its provisions to her, except "so far as it protects her child. To that part of it her attention has been called, and upon the faith of it she now rests in security." Once more he defended Ellen by depicting her as a marital martyr: "To her persecution I fear there is to be no end." Again accusing Gonzalve of destroying his daughter's health and relentlessly pursuing her, he bemoaned the fact Ellen "to this day is in great fear of what his malice may effect against her. His fierce determination seems to be, to make the mother childless, and if he cannot succeed in that, to make the child motherless by bringing her to the grave. He cares not which." David hoped that Abbot would rally to her cause and prevent any attempt to repeal the June legislation.[23]

By now, however, experience in the public sphere had taught Ellen and her family that private lobbying was simply not enough. David tried to preempt yet another challenge by Gonzalve and De

Rham with a public appeal in the *New Hampshire Patriot*. The newspaper wars over the d'Hauteville case had also taught him something about popular legal passions. Tactics that brought success in a court of law did not necessarily ensure victory in the very different court of public opinion. David and his advisors reversed the strategy Philadelphia lawyer John Cadwalader had devised the year before. They replaced Cadwalader's compassionate pleas for maternal rights with xenophobic tirades against a foreign father. Chauvinism seemed to elicit greater support than did calls for gender justice. As a result of this tactical choice, a shrill nativist message for the *Patriot* muffled David's usual call for family law reform.

Readers of New Hampshire's largest daily learned that "Mr. d'Hauteville, or his hired agent intends again to obtrude his private affairs upon the Public and in an offensive manner." David then gave them a nativist version of Ellen's story. After enlightened legislation had made it possible for her to follow medical advice and take her son to Rhode Island, her husband's minions had once more tracked her down and this time sought a special exemption for him. The unsigned appeal labeled De Rham's petition unconstitutional, but warned that the crafty and unprincipled Gonzalve might well launch "a crusade" in every legislative hall where compassionate Americans had enlarged the rights of women. He might even come to their state: "Are the doors of the New Hampshire Legislature to be besieged by his agents praying to exempt him from their laws also? And is he to dictate to that respectable body, what they may retain, and what they must repeal of their enactments? We want no such legislation."

The appeal curried support by presenting *Patriot* readers with a sinister picture of the Swiss intruder. The merciless man, who had forced an invalid twenty-year-old mother "to stand in her own defense in a public bar, and in a crowded court, where the vilest criminals are tried for the vilest crimes, has now obtained an ex parte divorce in Switzerland." His poor wife did not even know the grounds, and had not been able to defend herself due to distance and maternal duties. Playing on one of the most deep-seated American stereotypes of degenerate European aristocrats, the appeal portrayed Gonzalve as a money-grubbing gigolo who had pocketed Ellen's property through a patently unfair legal process. Yet, thankful to be rid of the tyrant, the virtuous American woman would not regret "the loss of her fortune." But in greedily using the Swiss divorce to take her estate, the appeal proclaimed in words drenched in xenophobia, Gonzalve had shown his true colors. He had "given up the child. All pretense of a right to an American Boy, born in America, and of an American woman, is merged and gone, when an

Alien and a foreigner of his own will and pleasure throws off all claim to that boy's mother. The tie is severed forever, – the parties are distinct and separate. The American Boy has independent and vested rights in the country of his birth. Its institutions and its privileges are his own, and neither father nor mother can deprive him of them. No decree of a Swiss court to take that child from its mother will be of any authority to her. No French Swiss, no Alien, no foreigner can even hope, or will probably ever attempt by any process of law to force an American child, born of an American mother, from that mother's arms for the purposes of expatriation." Predictably, Gonzalve "appears to have made his election, and to prefer the enjoyment of twenty thousand dollars of his wife's property, which an ex parte divorce will give him, to the cries and feverishness of a sickly infant."

Yet, the appeal lamented, Gonzalve's persecution would probably continue. He would petition for legislative exemptions, obtain search warrants to harass his ex-wife's family, and through "writs of habeas corpus bring Mrs. d'Hauteville a second time, and all her connections, into courts of Justice, but he can never wrest from her, her child. That child is beyond his reach. Tho' but three years old, he is as firm upon American soil as if he were twenty one, nor can any Foreigner, be he who he may, nor any foreign power tear him from it." Repeating yet again Gonzalve's bitter vow that neither days, weeks, months, nor years would stop his relentless pursuit of Ellen, David and his co-authors made one final appeal to New Hampshire readers by playing to the popular sense of feminine fragility and dependency: "Unfortunate lady, her fate is a sad one, and we come to the conclusion with regret, that her prospect of repose in this life is small, – of happiness none. – She is a bright and beautiful flower cut down by the hand of man, and now lies low and withering. Separated from her parental stem, and exposed to a wintery storm, none but a brute would trample on her drooping head."[24]

David's tactics finally succeeded. Gonzalve ended his legislative challenges. The New Hampshire statute would stand. Now Ellen had two safe havens flanking her Boston home.

The Legal Battles End

The skirmish over the Rhode Island legislation and the Swiss divorce were the d'Hautevilles' last legal battles. No more would they seek legal resolutions for their problems. Their legal experiences complete, Ellen and Gonzalve drew their own conclusions from their multiple legal lessons.

The intricate wording of the Rhode Island and New Hampshire

acts suggested that Ellen had changed more than her tactics in the year since the Philadelphia trial. She had set new legal goals. She was no longer content to abide by the logic of the tender-years rule that had brought her judicial victory and had been inscribed in the recently passed legislation. Ellen knew that custody law doctrine dictated that infants ought to remain with their mothers, but that older children, especially boys, should be returned to their fathers. In every one of her failed attempts to reach a negotiated settlement, she had promised to follow those gendered legal assumptions of child development and parental training. But Gonzalve had re-buffed her overtures and gambled that the law would give him im-mediate custody of Frederick. He had lost, and now Ellen decided to challenge the gender assumptions of custody law and seek per-manent custody of Frederick. She did so because the legal struggles that had consumed the last two years had forced her to live out the role Cadwalader had so meticulously scripted for her in the Court of General Sessions. Now she was, above all else, a mother. It would be the performance of her life.

Ellen made her determination to keep Frederick quite clear in a final letter to De Rham. She wrote on October 5, 1841, to say that "her child is well." More significantly, though, she relied on the combination of legislatively created maternal havens and Gonzalve's Swiss divorce to declare herself completely independent from her former husband, and excuse herself from having to report on Fred-erick's well-being and consult Gonzalve about his welfare and edu-cation: "Her position in regard to Mr. d'Hauteville now being en-tirely changed, she holds herself absolved from any requisition on his part, or on that of his representative." Ellen would, of course, happily respond to "any proper inquiries when made by gentlemen so circumstanced." Letters could be addressed care of her father's Beacon Street mansion.[25]

Yet simply declaring independence from Gonzalve did not free Ellen from the law's grasp. Despite legislative success, she remained trapped in its shadow. Every day she faced the prospect of a new summons and a habeas corpus hearing. Though she could never escape completely as long as Frederick remained a minor, one more legal triumph could greatly ease the pain of her ordeal: ending her forced exile from Boston. It became her final legal challenge.

Five days before Christmas of 1841, David wrote an anguished letter to fellow Brahmin Thomas Perkins explaining his daughter's legal dilemma. He turned Perkins's kindly inquiry about Ellen into a treatise on gender inequities in Massachusetts law: "It has been repeatedly asked, why my daughter does not reside with me in Bos-ton, under the protection of the laws of Mass[achusetts]? Why I do not consider her child safe here? Are the courts of my native State as just and equitable to the rights of females, as the courts of any State in the Union?" Clearly more comfortable as a legal reformer than a xenophobic polemicist, David answered his own rhetorical questions with a detailed legal analysis drawn from his own painful legal experiences. Like so many others, he converted the d'Hauteville case in a body of social knowledge about family law.

Citing chapter and verse from the Massachusetts revised statutes, he told Perkins that "great injustice may be done to Mrs. d'Hauteville, and to all persons in the commonwealth under similar circumstances, for which the law as it now stands, affords no remedy." No matter what the marital oppression, to obtain a divorce in the Bay State the law demanded couples had to lived together within the jurisdiction and the spousal misconduct must have occurred during their lives together in the state. Most egregiously, the statutes granted legally competent fathers full custody rights. Like a former law student, David offered a horrifying list of hypothetical examples of female victimization produced by the archaic Massachusetts rules. Each tale of brutalized wives denied legal redress touched one element of Ellen's story from mental cruelty and ex parte divorce to maternal distress and pilfered property. But his daughter's fight for Frederick led him to end his stories by railing against the state's narrow custody law. Under it "no cognizance can be taken of the marriage, or of the cruelties practiced under it. The case cannot be examined. The parties are divorced, their rights are separate. The female, though the mother, is without rights. The male, because the father, takes the child. And where are the rights of the child? A trial may have been had in another state, under a writ of Habeas Corpus for its custody, and it may have been decreed to the mother. Yet this is of no avail. The father may be weak or vicious, ignorant or criminal, and the mother the exact reverse, – but it is all the same – the child is his property, and he must have it, so says the law."

David even accepted the possibility that his rendition of legalized marital injustice could be wrong. But he feared advising Ellen to take a chance when "the matter is doubtful and the law obscure, and uncertain." The costs of losing a fight over the meaning of the law were simply too great. And so, he bemoaned, his poor daughter "is now alone, living in retirement, shut out from her home, her parents, and her domestic circle, and confined to that spot where the law protects her – In New York and Pennsylvania she was safe, and the Courts of the latter state gave her the legal custody of her child. In Rhode Island and New Hampshire she has ample protection, and in other states for all I know, but in her native Massachusetts *she has none*." Though Ellen pined for home, restrictive laws and a vengeful husband kept her away in her safe haven. His daughter's case, he lamented, was stalemated. Each parent, armed with a custody decree, waited and wondered what to do next.[26]

By the spring of 1842 both Ellen and Gonzalve had devised plans to break their legal logjam. Not surprisingly, their strategies not only diverged widely from each other, they compelled the battling couple to continue performing the roles for which they auditioned in Philadelphia before Judges Barton, Conrad, and Doran.

Ellen's lawyers found a way to end her legal wanderings. It required one last burst of publicity. On March 31st and again on April 4th and 11th, Bostonians opened the *Daily Advertizer* and read a petition by Ellen to the Supreme Judicial Court asking that a commission be appointed to authenticate the Swiss judgment dissolving her marriage.[27] As the divorced mother was a Massachusetts citizen, the court could then accept her custody of Frederick in any challenge by Gonzalve. But to protect her rights, Ellen had to retain residency in New Hampshire.

In a letter to his daughter's Swiss lawyer asking him to give a copy of the notice to Gonzalve, David expressed regret at the publicity but explained that there was "no alternative, and we are compelled to it, to enable us to secure important rights to the parties here."[28] By June, the court had authorized the commission, and David wrote again with specific instructions for the lawyer on how the divorce could be documented. He also requested that an accounting be obtained from Syndic Frederic Couveru, the curator of Ellen's marital property. Now that the end of his daughter's legal ordeal seemed in sight, David wanted to recover as much of Ellen's dowry as he could. He also used the letter to defend his actions by urging the lawyer to explain to any interested parties that "the measures we are now pursuing are rendered necessary in self defense, and are forced upon us by the *very extraordinary* conduct of Mr. d'Hauteville while in this country." But David also softened his condemnation by suggesting that Gonzalve had been the victim of poor counsel: "Had this unfortunate young man fallen into other hands, or had he been governed by wise or more disinterested heads, much misery might have been spared on both sides, and the sufferings of her whom he had always declared to be good and amiable, might have been softened by some deference, at least, to the civilities of refined life, all of which were outraged by Mr. d'Hauteville, according to our notions here, when, *absolutely refusing to listen* to any compromise, he summoned respectable ladies to appear and defend themselves in a public, and criminal, and crowded court." As the struggle drew to an end, David could only lament that the young man's "blindness to his true interests – His ignorance of our laws and usages, and his

subjection to the views of ill disposed persons have been his mortification, and our misfortune. – But we forgive him – Hereafter his
own conscience will be a severe though silent reprove, and we are
willing to spare him an additional reproach."[29]

As Ellen's petition moved its way through the Massachusetts judicial process, Gonzalve set about on a much different course of action. Yet he too stuck to his long-standing role. He would be a patriarch and in command of his domain no matter the severe setbacks
of the last few years. Over and over again, American judges and
legislators had denied his claims of vested paternal and marital
rights. He would challenge them no more. Ellen's petition went uncontested. Instead of continuing the now seemingly hopeless battle
with her, he decided to create a new patriarchal preserve. By late
spring of 1842 he had asked a young German woman to be his second bride. They would marry in November, when his divorce from
Ellen became final. Gonzalve could then start a new family at Hauteville and recreate the role he had so fervently defended. There
would not be a second voyage to America. Only by such an abdica-
tion of his cause could Gonzalve release himself from the law's grip
and leave its shadow.

As 1843 dawned, the d'Hauteville case had almost come to an
end. In the fall, curator Couvreu had sent David an accounting of
Ellen's marital property. He added a stinging rebuke accusing the
Bostonian of unchristian and ungentlemanly behavior in the sad
affair. The Swiss official chastised David for trying to drive a wedge
between Gonzalve and Frederick. David offered a spirited reply. He
not only questioned Couvreu's handling of Ellen's property, he denied ever trying to sever Gonzalve's filial bonds with Frederick. On
the contrary, he insisted, the Swiss father had "every facility offered
to him in Philadelphia, and to his friends since, for intercourse with
his son; – and that same has been again intimated to his friend and
advisor – Mr. Charles G. Loring – who has been invited to see the
child whenever he is disposed to do so." Like his daughter he
pledged to respect any wishes Gonzalve may make about Frederick's
education. Trying to ease the tensions, he offered a bulletin on the
boy: "My grandson is well, and growing stronger in constitution.
He is still subject to severe disease, and at times suffers from
asthma – but at the present moment he is in good health."[30]

As their marriage dissolved, Ellen and Gonzalve remained intran-
sigent. Gonzalve refused to accept delivery of the d'Hauteville
jewels from his former bride. He let them gather dust in a Paris
warehouse. Ellen ordered her Swiss lawyer to receive three boxes
of her personal effects sent from Hauteville, but instructed him to
sell them at auction and use the proceeds to set up a fund for the

local poor. Both of them wanted to obliterate all memories of their ill-fated union.[31]

After the Massachusetts Supreme Judicial Court authenticated Ellen's divorce and accepted her custody of Frederick, the d'Hauteville case slipped out of the public sphere. Ellen now had sole charge of her son and freedom to end her exile. At the first opportunity, she moved back to Boston and had a house built in Longwood, a suburban Boston township being developed by her father. She refused to consider remarriage and clung to her role as mother. She also remained trapped in the law's shadow. Haunted by the thought that Gonzalve might send agents to spirit Frederick off to Switzerland, Ellen lived with a constant fear of losing her child. She worried about another trial. And as Frederick grew, she spoke little to him of his father and he asked few questions. For his part, Gonzalve sired a new family and made no attempt to play a part in the life of his first son. Hauteville remained the center of his world, just as Boston remained the heart of Ellen's. It was almost as if they had never met.[32]

Afterward

"The memoirs of that family are a romance of the nineteenth century," Representative Randolph declared in the 1841 Rhode Island legislative battle over married women's rights, "and the story of Mrs. d'Hauteville, is sufficiently remarkable to attract uncommon interest and sympathy."[1] So had been Gonzalve's. And both had aroused intense outrage and opposition as well. Together their stories made the d'Hauteville case an avidly watched and vigorously debated legal event in 1840 and 1841. Slowly, however, the case faded from the pages of the press and the memory of most Americans.

Despite its inevitable journey to the sack-heap of forgotten cases, the d'Hauteville case left a particular kind of mark on American law and society. Unlike the d'Hautevilles' multiple encounters with the law, though, the case's imprint cannot be found in the words and deeds of the participants. Their passionate involvement produced the vivid expressions and charged events I have used to recount the case as a series of legal experiences. But that same timebound passion prevents them from being its final commentators. The case had outcomes and consequences unknown and unknowable to Ellen, Gonzalve, and the rest of the cast of the long-running d'Hauteville drama.

Every version of the d'Hauteville case not only told a story, it had a moral. My version of the tale has one as well. The lesson I want to draw from the case, however, is not a Solomonic judgment about which parent should have gotten Frederick. Instead, I think the ultimate meaning of the case as a legal experience lies in explaining how and why it forced so many people to ascend to Solomon's throne and render such a verdict. Doing so suggests how a narrative of a case like this one can be used to probe the legal dynamics of social change.

Just like other headline-grabbing trials in the American past and present, the moral of the d'Hauteville case can be found in its transformation into *a precedent* not of legal rules but of *legal experience*. Unlike precedents of legal rules and more meaningful than the la-

question class What does he mean by?

bel "popular trial," the phrase "precedent of legal experience" is intended to suggest the multidimensional impact of cases like this one. Such cases enter the collective memory as common references for *both* laypeople and lawyers to construct legal claims, conceive legal relationships, and constitute legal identities. Though difficult to measure in precise and verifiable terms, precedents of legal experience not only affect the people caught up in legal events themselves, but their influence continues long after the particulars of a case are forgotten. These cases become embedded in the very fabric of a legal culture as ways to translate individual and collective problems into legal disputes. My story of Ellen and Gonzalve's fight for Frederick has chronicled how such a precedent is created. Now I want to suggest what the creation of such exceptional cases can tell us about the critical but complex relationship between American law and society.

Like other extraordinary cases that periodically burst out of the dockets of American trial courts to become popular events, a unique combination of rhetoric and law made the d'Hauteville case a meaningful legal moment. The rhetorical power of Ellen and Gonzalve's riveting stories of love, hate, and law, especially its seminal event – their trial – transformed it into a widely shared legal experience. For its brief season, the d'Hauteville case became a fable of family conflict gone awry – a domestic melodrama in Representative Randolph's apt words – that captured the hearts and minds of countless Americans. It did so because like other precedents of legal experience, the case contained an alluring mix of the exceptional and the commonplace. The case attracted attention because it offered spectators and readers a voyeuristic excursion into the lives of the rich and famous. By following the trial, the public vicariously experienced a life of Paris balls, Swiss chateaus, and Beacon Hill mansions. At the same time, all the trial watchers could identify with the dogged determination of a mother to fight for her child or a husband to preserve his family. Family problems like those transcended class, region, and even nationality to strike a common chord of understanding.

Details divulged in the Philadelphia courtroom enhanced the case's appeal. Testimony about Gonzalve's attempt to spirit Ellen away from her mother in Paris, letters revealing Gonzalve's lonely vigil waiting for news of the birth of his son, descriptions of Ellen's frantic search up and down the East Coast for a maternal haven, repeated accusations by Gonzalve that David had bribed legislators, and numerous other bits and pieces of the pair's stories increased public fascination with the case and thus deepened its rhetorical significance. The tangled tale of Ellen, Gonzalve, and Frederick was

Gender anxieties

a drama that simply could not be ignored; and that allure helped make it a precedent of legal experience.

But the d'Hauteville case became an arresting legal event as well because of the moment in which it was staged. Gender anxieties of the era provided the temporal connection to the intense controversies of the time that made it come alive. The case is a telling example of why every precedent of legal experience must have such a tie to the fundamental controversies of its time.

As the clashing public verdicts made clear, Ellen and Gonzalve's personal traumas exposed the raw nerves of a society deeply divided over gender roles, rights, and duties. The relationship between the appeal of the d'Hautevilles' stories and this setting was critical to the case's notoriety.[2] Their case was transformed into an event, in part, because a moment of discontinuity opened space for new gender beliefs and practices. Ellen and Gonzalve's bargaining, trial, and legislative battles replayed in dramatic form the struggles over marriage, child rearing, paternal power, and female independence engulfing countless other men and women. Their stories violated motherhood and defied patriarchy-voiced questions bedeviling everyone: What is a good mother? What is a good father? What kind of parent does a child need? When can a wife leave her mate? What rights should such a departing woman retain? What power should men have over the women and children in their families? All those who experienced the d'Hauteville case had to answer such questions to reach a verdict. And everyone who experienced the d'Hauteville case had to render a verdict.

By becoming a popular family fable, the d'Hauteville case dramatized and personalized conflicts breaking out across antebellum America. The power to do so is the hallmark of a precedent of legal experience and the source of its hold on popular and professional consciousness. Thinking about popular cases as events that reorder an audience's ways of dealing with the world gives new meaning to Tocqueville's observation that in America "all parties are obliged to borrow the ideas, and even the language usual in judicial proceedings, in their daily controversies" and thereby turn the language of the law into "in some measure, a vulgar tongue."[3] It also explains why an 1840 contest over the custody of a two-year-old boy could at times even outduel presidential candidates for space on newspaper front pages. Historians would look back and label the hard-fought "Log Cabin" election battle between Martin Van Buren and William Henry Harrison an electoral turning point. But few voters at the time understood the election in those terms. Similarly, historians have labeled the years in which Ellen and Gonzalve fought for Frederick an era of gender realignment, yet few women and men at

the time would have explained their experiences with those words. Instead of abstract discussions they dealt with the gender anxieties of their time by telling their own stories of the d'Hauteville case and reaching their own verdicts. Through the familiar setting and format of the courtroom, they could, and did, weigh the relative merits and demerits of Ellen, Gonzalve, Miriam, David, and the elder d'Hautevilles. They borrowed the words and rules of the law to make their points and, by acceding to its adversarial demands, to declare a verdict. The known courtroom ritual furnished antebellum Americans, as it repeatedly would their descendants, "a stable format, and so a way of interpreting events in a world temporarily become ambiguous."[4]

An 1846 collective biography of monied Bostonians, *Our First Men*, told Ellen's story as just such a fable of its time. In his profile of David Sears, social sleuth Richard Hildreth repeated what had become the basic public narrative of the family's famous tragedy: "The case of Madame d'Hauteville . . . has brought into discussion a great question of domestic law. Her marriage, though it seemed to ally the family with European nobility, proved unhappy. The young wife could not live in the gloom of an old tumble-down Swiss castle with an austere Calvinist of a husband; and taking advantage of a clause in her marriage contract, she came home to visit her parents. A child was born here: after which she declined to return to her husband. He came over, claiming wife and child, and invoking the aid of the law. The law said that the child was his; but all the women said, and all human hearts said, the child was the mother's. The child and mother were found by the husband in Philadelphia; and though by decision of the court there, which our lawyers greatly growled at, they escaped for the time, it was judged best to retire to New Hampshire. A special statute was enacted by the Legislature of that democratic State, that so hates gold and rich men, no doubt by an incorruptible Legislature, out of pure chivalrous sympathy for female distresses. By that statute the husband is incapacitated from claiming his child, on the ground that he is an alien."[5]

Capturing the public mind in this way gave a precedent of legal experience authority. Like many such cases, however, the d'Hauteville case did not follow the standard route to legal influence. Gonzalve's decision not to appeal Judge George Washington Barton's verdict meant that Ellen's victory could never become a conventional legal precedent like *Marbury v. Madison* or *Dred Scott v. Sanford*. Only authoritative opinions handed down by state supreme courts and federal appeals courts gained the unquestioned power to dictate the resolution of subsequent cases. The lowly origins of the d'Hauteville case in a municipal criminal court prevented it from

ever becoming such a vaunted precedent. But the case was so potent a legal drama, its rhetorical significance so profound, that it became influential anyway.

Blocked from inclusion in the reports of appellate cases that lawyers and judges read to find leading cases, the d'Hauteville case was transmitted through the alternative outlets that had sprung up in antebellum America as mediums for legal debate and education. Men and women found it in Samuel Miller's *Report of the d'Hauteville Case,* Peleg Chandler's articles in the *Law Reporter,* countless stories in newspapers and magazines, and published versions of the Rhode Island debate over married women's custody rights. Manuscript copies even circulated by hand among the bench and bar. And, of course, people spread news of the d'Hauteville case by word of mouth. Through these varied channels the case reached an audience that could never be counted.

The backdoor route to legal prominence even won the case a place in what was fast becoming the primary source of legal knowledge for American lawyers, the legal treatise. Law writers crafted these specialized guides to the law by collecting and organizing leading cases on everything from railroads to watercourses. In 1858 John C. Hurd included the d'Hauteville case in his authoritative *A Treatise on the Right of Personal Liberty and on the Writ of Habeas Corpus.* He cited it as an example of how and why judges should take the superior nurturing care of mothers into account when they decided child custody cases.[6] Hurd's treatise ensured that Barton's verdict would be read by lawyers across the country just like the appellate decisions that filled most of the pages in his book.

Timing played a critical role in giving the d'Hauteville case legal authority just as it did in making it a significant rhetorical event. The case occurred during a moment of doctrinal discontinuity as well as of fundamental gender uncertainty. Confusion and conflict about the proper governance of the home constituted one flank of the era's gender wars. Old rules were being challenged, new ones had yet to be firmly established. In the midst of this legal chaos, Ellen and Gonzalve's struggle not only acted out on the public stage of the courtroom the hopes and fears of many other spouses and parents, but their Philadelphia judges took such a clear stand on the ongoing contests over governing the family that their words too became a template for debate because they addressed the two most fundamental elements of family life and family law: marriage and parenthood.

The judges' unequivocal, widely read vindication of Ellen's custody rights added support to maternal preference, the tender-years rule, and the best interests of the child doctrine as governing rules

of American custody law. Soon all of these would be firmly embedded in the law as would fathers' secondary parental status. Just forty
years after Barton's verdict, the Philadelphia Court of Quarter Sessions would proclaim: "We do not look upon the wife and the children as mere servants to the husband and father, and, as therefore
held, subject to his will so long as he does not transcend the power
of an absolute master. We do not hold that though a husband drive
his wife from his house by his crimes or his cruelty, still he is entitled
to take away from her the custody of her children. We do not look
upon the parental authority as one to exercise merely for the profit
of the parents, though it may be so abused, but for the advantage
of the child. . . . The substantial reality of the old common law right
has faded almost to fiction, under the ameliorating influences of
modern common law of Pennsylvania."[7] The d'Hauteville case had
been a building block in the construction of these new custody rules.

Ellen and Gonzalve's legal struggles also stoked the engines pro-
pelling companionate marriage. Her charges of husbandly tyranny,
Barton's denunciation of his marital conduct, and the public furor
over their case fueled debate over the legitimacy of mental cruelty
as a ground for divorce. Not surprisingly, Judge Edward King of
the Philadelphia Court of Common Pleas rendered a path-breaking
decision on the issue only nine years after Barton's verdict. King,
who had advised Cadwalader on how to tell Ellen's story, rejected
the orthodox Anglo-American rule that only actual or threatened
physical violence justified a finding of marital cruelty. Using words
that echoed those of both John Cadwalader and David Sears and
seemed to have Gonzalve in mind, King argued that "a husband
may, by a course of humiliating insults and annoyances, practiced
in the various forms which ingenious malice could readily devise,
eventually destroy the life or health of his wife, although such conduct may be unaccompanied by violence, positive or threatened."
On the contrary, the judge insisted, to "hold absolutely that if a husband avoids positive or threatened personal violence, the wife has
no legal protection against any means short of these, which he may
resort to, and which may destroy her life or health, is to invite such a
system of infliction by the indemnity given the wrongdoer."[8] King's
opinion "marked a watershed in the history of matrimonial cruelty."[9] It also rebroadcast Ellen's pleas that companionate marital
ideals and the right to demand freedom from marital tyranny must
govern the law of marriage and divorce. And thus, somewhat para-
doxically as Betty Farrell suggests, the d'Hauteville case "added a
precedent to nineteenth-century law that promoted a more individ-
ualistic and less paternalistic model of the family, at the same time

it demonstrated the power and reach of a family such as the Boston Searses, organized effectively along corporate kinship lines."[10]

The d'Hauteville case had institutional as well as doctrinal consequences. Its broad dissemination reinforced a fundamental yet unarticulated assumption of American family law: Disputes among family members should be resolved in adversarial contests pitting husband against wife, mother against father, and parent against child. This commitment too would be embedded in American family law and like the others would govern families well into the next century.

The d'Hauteville case did not influence family law in these ways because it enunciated binding rules like a regular legal precedent. Instead, its power was experiential. Like other precedents of legal experience, it became a "discourse of legitimacy." As John Louis Lucaites explains, such a discourse establishes ideals that "make it possible to accommodate a wide range of competing interests in a particular community, because the tie that binds the community is not a commitment to the absolute and universal meanings of key values, but to a set of key terms that are rhetorically consistent, but also flexible enough to be adapted to different situations, circumstances, and interests."[11]

The d'Hauteville case acted as a discourse of legitimacy by helping to frame debates about family law problems. Amidst bitter fights over how to conceptualize legal disputes over marriage and parenthood, it publicized particular constructions of family law rules as expressions of primary public values. In particular, it broadcast maternal preference as a legitimate legal expression of the era's dominant social values like the nurturing superiority of mothers, and thus reigning public narrative of custody law.[12] Yet the stories of the case also incorporated resistance to that new legal story line. Gonzalve was far from alone in arguing that family stability and social order depended on male sovereignty in the home. Wide dissemination of the d'Hautevilles' stories not only lengthened the legal life of Barton's words and Ellen's successful legal strategies, it gave renewed publicity to Gonzalve's failed attempt to preserve paternal autonomy and independence even in troubled families. Many lawyers and laypeople rallied to his cause and denounced the verdict as a legal lesson in misdirected judicial governance of the home. Its invocation perpetuated those oppositional voices as well. Their efforts ensured that the dominance of maternal preference in custody law would be neither swift nor complete. Even so, the debate occurred within the doctrinal confines of the best interest of the child doctrine and the other basic legal rules Barton had invoked.

Doctrines like these channeled conflict by dictating the *form* not the *specific result* of custody disputes. As such, the d'Hauteville case served as a discourse of legitimacy because it captured public and professional attention by speaking to all sides in the deepening controversy over how to govern American families, while at the same time framing the very conversations it inspired. In short, it helped craft a new public narrative of custody law.

Though the impact of the d'Hauteville case as a precedent of legal experience was most apparent in family law, when examined through the lens of time it also can be understood as a culture-revealing not just a culture-shaping legal event.[13] As social dramas playing out the fundamental conflicts of an era, cases like this one are prime illustrations of the power of legal authority in American society. Most importantly, they reveal that the meaning of law at any particular moment in time is determined by a complex interaction between the relatively autonomous internal rules and practices of the legal system and the press of external beliefs, concerns, and commitments on that system. They teach us the legal lesson that law is fluid, contested, time-bound, and often contradictory and not the impartial, timeless, and fixed system of rules we assume it is or may want it to be.

The d'Hauteville case also makes us consider the most powerful legal rules – law directing doctrines – as the product of multiple legal experiences not single determining judgments by appellate judges or specific enactments by legislators. In the course of a trial or legislative debate, as Ellen and Gonzalve and all those who experienced their case learned so well, the uncertain meaning of contested rules forced litigants, lawyers, judges, petitioners, legislators, and commentators to battle over their definition. The d'Hautevilles' fierce struggle over the meaning of custody law's best interest of the child doctrine reveals the courtroom to be a place of dominion, resistance, and negotiation, and suggests why some contests over legal meanings spill out of courthouses into the streets, press, coffeehouses, pubs, parlors, and meeting halls. At the same time, Ellen's recurrent attempts to secure statutory rights for married women demonstrate that the legislative chamber is a similar arena for legal conflict. The d'Hautevilles' struggles also dramatically illustrate how American federalism fueled legal conflict by promoting a babel of official legal discourses. Ellen's frantic forum shopping and legislative lobbying exposed the institutional and ideological sources of legal diversity. It arose from the jurisdictional pluralism created by American federalism, and from the divergent beliefs and practices held by professionals and laypeople in various locales across the republic. In these ways, precedents of legal experience like this one are vivid examples of how American courtrooms and legislative chambers serve as critical sites for the creation and imposition of cultural meanings over everything from market duties to family rights. And through its transformation into a precedent of legal experience, the d'Hauteville case displays the pivotal role headline-grabbing trials play in maintaining legal authority. They broadcast the new constructions of legal rules to audiences inside the courtroom and those following the case out in the community.[14]

At the same time, the use of the law by laypeople like the d'Hautevilles documents the hegemonic power of the American legal order to shape conflict without dictating the result of specific legal contests. The couple's private and public pleas disclosed again and again that once disputing individuals stumbled into the law's shadow they became dependent on legal validations of their claims. In their dependency can be seen telling examples of how litigants must "shape their own meanings and public values to conform to a language recognized as legal discourse."[15] For Ellen and Gonzalve, as for all others drawn into the courtroom and the legislature, the law channeled claims into prescribed legal forms first in an inchoate way in private bargaining, and then more directly as lawyers' drafted translations of their stories for the courtroom, the judges reached a verdict, and legislators drafted statutes.

By going to law individuals like the d'Hautevilles not only had their claims translated into the language of the law, they also entered a partially autonomous realm within American society that had its own institutional hierarchy and commitments. These too had a significant impact on the presentation and resolution of problems like theirs. In the law office, the courtroom, and even the legislative chamber, lawyers, judges, and legislators exercised a privileged ability to set the terms of conflict and report the results. In agreeing to listen to and then accept disputes like the d'Hautevilles, they allowed laypeople to participate in the boundary-making ceremonies that helped define legal rules. The bench and bar, however, had the dominant power to mark those boundaries and create a doctrinal language that could then be used in other struggles. As a result, cases like the d'Hautevilles' that erupt in moments of doctrinal discontinuity become the means for imposing new rules that voice some aspirations while silencing others.

The law's dominion ensured that the gradual but certain legalization of their conflict experienced by Ellen and Gonzalve would be felt again and again by countless other women and men who turned to the law to solve their problems. Through their time and into ours, the law's reach has extended over more and more aspects of American life as more and more people made the same journey into the law's shadow as the d'Hautevilles. Even so, their case also reveals the interactive reality of the law's hegemony in America. It demonstrates both the law's power to shape conflict and popular consciousness, while at the same time disclosing how disputes pursued by laypeople help create the forms and substance of the law.[16]

Individual litigants, reporters, editors, and many other laypeople make cases like the d'Hautevilles' precedents of legal experience. They, particularly the litigants, cannot be dismissed simply as passive recipients of legal knowledge from lawyers, judges, and legislators. Instead cases like this one locate the creation of powerful legal doctrines, such as the tender-years rule so important to the d'Hauteville case, in the collision of established legal rules with the multiple life experiences of all those affected by a case at its specific moment in time. Too much of our legal history assumes that such rules are created out of the blinding insights or reflexive reactions of appellate judges and legislators. The d'Hautevilles' multiple legal experiences challenge those assumptions.

The d'Hauteville case did not just happen to Ellen and Gonzalve. They created it, nurtured it, and propagated it. Each spouse, willingly or not, turned to the law for strategic purposes. It provided rules that organized their conflict and public forums for resolving it. But it did more than that for them as for other litigants. The law also gave them a language to express their own sense of themselves as holders of rights and words to articulate their demands. Part of law's appeal is evident in its ability to provide disputing individuals and their many judges such a vocabulary. The range of that language is significant as well. By providing words and stages for a variety of voices, trials and legislative debates are critical sites for contests between contending legal visions.[17]

As such, cases like this one highlight the role of individuals in fostering legal change. Ellen and Gonzalve's determination to fight for Frederick made them solitary legal combatants in the gender wars of their time. Unlike organized groups campaigning for women's rights or defending patriarchal authority, they used the law to seek a specific personal goal. Yet their struggle connected them with those larger movements in two ways: First, they helped create new legal rules of custody law such as maternal preference and tender-years that affected all parents; and second, their stories reinforced the public movements by encouraging some campaigners and discouraging others. In this way the d'Hautevilles made their case a critical front in the conflicts of their era.

Ellen and Gonzalve's explosive trial in particular not only reveals the sources but also some of the consequences of legal dominion over American dispute resolution. Most importantly, it exposes the power of the adversarial ideal lodged in the very marrow of American legalism. Winner-take-all courtroom contests invested this and all other precedents of legal experience with their greatest drama and importance. The adversarial imperatives of the courtroom forced everyone drawn to the case to render a verdict and thus invest themselves in the fate of Ellen, Gonzalve, and Frederick and in the rules of custody and marriage. In doing so, the d'Hauteville case, like other popular trials, added legitimacy to the American tendency to solve problems through gladiatorial contests in the courtroom.

Some of the liabilities of this reliance on adversarial solutions to complex social problems are also revealed in cases like the d'Hautevilles'. Though courts like the Philadelphia Court of General Sessions have proven themselves adept at sifting through contradictory evidence and reaching verdicts, trials also further inflamed passions, first by pitting client against client and lawyer against lawyer, and then, as they spilled out of the courtroom, by instigating fights among spectators and commentators. Equally significant, the very clarity of trial verdicts' dogmatic rhetoric often masks the difficulties of reaching just resolutions for all the parties.

Though much has changed over the years since 1840 when the d'Hautevilles battled each other in the Philadelphia Court of General Sessions, the legal ritual has remained surprisingly stable and so has the commitment to solving private problems through adversarial contests. Just like the family debates of the era, so the institutional questions of those years continue to bedevil us as well. All the more so, because the d'Hauteville case exposes the underside of Tocqueville's insights about the power of law in the new republic. The American tendency to turn critical issues over to the courts that the French traveler discovered just a few years before the d'Hauteville trial produced yet another question that haunts us still: How much power should we give judges to solve our problems?

The very fate of the custody law rules that the d'Hauteville case helped promulgate make it a cautionary tale about the consequences of asking common law judges to solve multifaceted problems like family disputes. In the late twentieth century, when the parenting skills and rights of fathers regained social and legal legitimacy, another moment of doctrinal discontinuity and gender uncertainty made custody cases as difficult to resolve as they had been in Ellen and Gonzalve's troubled time. With maternal preference discredited as a clear legal guide, once again judges had to determine the relative merits of each parent and the interests of their children without an agreed-upon doctrinal yardstick or settled social beliefs. The resulting conflicts demonstrate once again that custody rules are always legal translations of dominant gender beliefs and practices and always unstable and subject to shifting legal and social changes. Equally important, despite suggestions that alternative dispute-resolution techniques like mediation be used to solve custody fights, trials continue to be the final venue for troubled families.[18] Past and present child custody cases, especially precedents of legal experience like the d'Hauteville case that are both sources and examples of the law's adversarial commitments, disclose just how deeply embedded the combative ideals of the adversary system are in the republic's legal culture. They have become fundamental tenets of American legal faith not likely to be dislodged.[19]

The irresistible lure of the courtroom so visible in the d'Hauteville case also reveals a second and equally important part of the law's hold on American society. Just as the legal experiences of previous men and women with troubled marriages influenced them, so Ellen and Gonzalve helped construct legal rules and practices that cast a shadow on other couples who found themselves enmeshed in the law as they fought over their children and their marriages. It affected legal consciousness as well as legal rules. Like other precedents of legal experience, the case sent out clear messages that instructed disputing parents, spouses, and their lawyers about how to bargain and how to tell courtroom stories. Women who wanted to keep their children had to draft stories that Ellen helped script, in which they played the role of the responsible mother. Conversely, men who wanted to keep their families together or gain their children had to take note of Gonzalve's inability to write an effective defense of paternal rights. For some his defeat became a cautionary tale; and for others her victory was a welcomed storyline to legal success. Though people attached different meanings to the stories, as the disparate public verdicts made clear, the tales themselves reverberated through the republic. As they did, the case not only reinforced ongoing trends in American family law, such as its growing maternalism, it dictated how other troubled couples must act as they too felt themselves falling under the law's shadow. In this way, the case helped write the legal stories other women and men would tell.

All precedents of legal experience lengthen the law's shadow over those in conflict. At the same time Tocqueville's shadow imagery underscores the need to understand the interactive reality of legal experiences. Perceiving the influence of the formal legal order, past and present, as a shadow on the rest of society gives the authority of law a compelling visual image without eliminating the role of laypeople in law creation. On the contrary, it compels us to use a broad working definition of law. Instead of relying solely on positiv-

ist conceptions of law simply as rules created by courts and legislatures and then imperially imposed on society, the shadow imagery
alerts us to other forms of legalism and other creators of law. Cases
like this one become examples of how law inspired popular notions
of rights, status, and duties; and at the same time how popular legal
behavior by litigants, newspaper editors, and many others influenced the formal rules of law. As such it returns a degree of power
to individuals – it recognizes their legal agency – without denying
the dominant authority of the legal system. Only by recognizing law
in shadows can we begin to understand the full meaning of procla-
mations like Abraham Lincoln's that law must be America's civil
religion.

By helping to extend the law's shadow over more men and
women caught in troubled marriages, the d'Hauteville case reveals
the ultimate meaning of a precedent of legal experience. Such cases
become embedded in the legal culture as fables and in doing so
influence popular and professional legal consciousness not just at
the time in which they occur but through time as well. In all such
cases, law and rhetoric fuse to send out influential messages through
compelling stories that help set the pattern for subsequent legal
battles. These stories become the ways individuals comprehend and
argue about their own problems. Even as the memory of a trial like
the d'Hautevilles' fades, a residue remains as it does after every
popular trial. In this way such cases enter the collective memory as
precedents of legal experience. Their influence comes from their
control over the memory and consciousness of audiences. They encourage and empower some; they threaten and weaken others. But
as such cases enter popular and professional memory, they become
part of the process of legal change itself.

Coda

While the d'Hauteville case entered American legal culture as a precedent of legal experience, it remained as it had begun, an individual legal experience for its principal characters. The case had been a defining moment for each of them. For the rest of their lives, Ellen and Gonzalve felt its effects. They continued to perform the roles scripted for them in the Philadelphia Court of General Sessions. Gonzalve became the patriarch he had so desperately wanted to be by creating a new life and new family at Hauteville. Ellen fulfilled the role of responsible mother that she and her lawyers had created in the Philadelphia courtroom. And their fight for Frederick continued as well.

In 1858 Ellen and Frederick sailed for Europe and one last struggle with Gonzalve. It would be, though, a clash of hearts not law. Unlike a previous visit when they slipped in and out of the continent without telling Gonzalve, Ellen notified her former husband of their voyage. He immediately invited Frederick to Hauteville. Gonzalve staged a lavish welcome for the boy. Peasants showered him with flowers and pulled his carriage up the hill to the chateau. Down in the village of Vevey, Ellen worried that her son would resent her for what he had lost, and feared losing him to Hauteville's splendor. Watching the unfolding drama, Ellen's sister Anna reported to her husband back in Boston, "Mr. d'Hauteville is evidently doing his utmost to please [Frederick], and the boy would be more than mortal not to be dazzled. He is evidently looking at it all through rose colored glasses, and is astonished at the beauty of Hauteville, the wealth he sees, and aristocratic manners – but I think his love for his mother will soon make him forget all this, though from my heart, I pity the poor lad."[1] After a few days Frederick returned to Ellen. He regretted nothing. Mother and son sailed home for Boston.

Twenty years after Ellen's fateful decision to leave Gonzalve, the d'Hauteville case finally ended. The final victory had not come in a courtroom or a legislative chamber, though the influence of both had been immense. Frederick's choice to return to his mother had in many ways been determined years before when John Cadwal-ader's crafty courtroom calculations, George Washington Barton's sweeping judicial vindication, and Rhode Island and New Hamp-shire's creation of secure maternal havens gave the boy to Ellen. Nevertheless, powerful as the law had been, it could not render the ultimate verdict that each parent sought. Only Frederick had the power to give either his mother or his father what they wanted. In the summer of 1858, he finally had to choose. Ellen won the fight for Frederick.

Ellen's victory was fateful in many ways. In 1862, while dutifully caring for Frederick stationed in Washington, D.C., as an officer in the union army, she contracted hepatitis. She died on November 30th at the age of forty-three. In an evocative epitaph, the *Daily Advertiser* eulogized Ellen as "[s]ympathetic by nature, she was ten-derly careful of the feelings of all, and never by thoughtlessness or design wounded the self-love of the most humble or sensitive, but graciously and even gratefully received the smallest favor or atten-tion from the most unpretending and obscure. To feminine gentle-ness of disposition, and the most perfect simplicity and refinement of character, she united an excellent understanding and an almost masculine resolution and energy, fitting her – through the experi-ence and discipline of life – for any emergency or trial that could befall her. A devoted mother of an only son, at the sacrifice of her own feelings, and actuated by that which forgets itself in devotion to the interest, wishes and honor of the object of its devotion, she consented, and even encouraged his wish to do his part on the field of battle, in the great cause of his country."[2]

Ellen and Gonzalve were not alone, of course, in feeling the im-pact of their legal struggles. Shortly after his mother's death, Fred-erick wrote David asking for permission to marry. "My dearest grandfather," he declared, "you have treated me from my birth till now as you would have treated a most beloved child. You alone have been to me a Father – give me now your blessing for without it I can never be happy." David sent his approval accompanied by the assurance, "You have ever been and always will be regarded by me as a beloved child, and I have endeavored to the best of my judg-ment to be to you a father."[3]

David continued his fatherly role for another decade until his death in January 1871. Miriam had died a few months earlier. Gon-zalve followed them to the grave in 1890. After burying his first wife but one year after their wedding, Frederick remarried and eventu-ally fathered three children. He died in 1918 at the age of eighty. Frederick Sears d'Hauteville was buried next to his mother.[4]

A Note on Sources and Citations

The Report of the d'Hauteville Case published by Samuel Miller a few weeks after the trial is the primary source for the case. The original trial records no longer exist. In later phases of the case, Ellen criticized the *Report* as an incomplete version of the trial that tried to tilt public opinion in Gonzalve's favor. I have tried to address her complaint in my critical evaluation of the volume, use of supplemental sources, and attempt to recover each actor's story as fully as possible. Ultimately, however, the limits of the *Report* are far outweighed by its utility in reconstructing the case. All of the italicized words and phrases in my text are in the *Report*. For stylistic reasons, I have changed the transcript's third person to first person and altered archaic legal phrasings. In the numbered notes, I have identified it simply as the "*Report*."

In addition to the *Report*, I have used manuscript collections in Boston and Philadelphia. The Massachusetts Historical Society holds the Sears Family Papers and the Amory Family Papers. In the notes, citations to these materials include: the "Sears Papers," "Sears Letterbook," and "Amory Letters." The Historical Society of Pennsylvania has an extensive collection of Cadwalader Papers. I have used John Cadwalader's case materials cited as the "d'Hauteville File."

Finally, the Rhode Island State Archives contains a file on Gonzalve's failed petition to have himself exempted from the 1841 Act limiting the custody rights of foreign fathers. I have cited it as "Rhode Island Petition."

Notes

Preface

1. *Keywords, A Vocabulary of Culture and Society,* rev. ed. (New York, 1985), 126–9.
2. For useful discussion about historicizing experience, see Joan Scott, "The Evidence of Experience," *Critical Inquiry* 17(1991): 773–97; Kathleen Canning, "Feminist History After the Linguistic Turn: Historicizing Discourse and Experience," *Signs,* 19(1994): 374–8; and for an anthropological view on the issue, see Roger D. Abraham, "Ordinary and Extraordinary Experience," in Victor W. Turner and Edward M. Bruner, eds., *The Anthropology of Experience* (Urbana, IL, 1986), 49.
3. For the most helpful synthesis of family change in this era, see Steven Mintz and Susan Kellogg, *Domestic Revolutions, A Social History of American Family Life* (New York, 1988), chap. 3.
4. My understanding of the power of law in American society has been greatly influenced by work on Gramsci's concept of hegemony. Beyond Gramsci's own writings, I have found particularly compelling the work of T. Jackson Lears, "The Concept of Cultural Hegemony: Possibilities and Problems," *American Historical Review,* 90(1985): 567–93; and Jean Comaroff and John Comaroff, *Of Revelation and Revolution, Christianity, Colonialism, and Consciousness in South Africa* (Chicago, 1991), 12–32.
5. Roscoe Pound, *The Formative Era of American Law* (Boston, 1942); James Willard Hurst, *Law and the Conditions of Freedom in the Nineteenth-Century United States* (Madison, WI, 1956); Morton Horwitz, *The Transformation of American Law* (Cambridge, MA, 1976). For the most recent survey of American legal history, see Kermit Hall, *The Magic Mirror, Law in American History* (New York, 1989).
6. "Intimacy on Trial, Cultural Meanings of the Beecher-Tilton Affair," in Richard Wightman Fox and T. J. Jackson Lears, *The Power of Culture, Critical Essays in American History* (Chicago, 1993), 131.
7. For an introduction to the method, see Giovanni Levi, "Micro History," in Peter Burke, ed., *New Perspectives in Historical Writing* (Cambridge, 1991), 107; and for an example of a microhistory of a trial, see Edward Berenson, *The Trial of Madame Caillaux* (Berkeley, 1992).
8. For a discussion of these points, see Carlo Ginzburg, "The Judge and the Historian," *Critical Inquiry,* 18(1991): 79–92.
9. "The Braided Narrative: Substance and Form in Social History," in A. Fletcher, ed., *The Literature of Fact* (New York, 1976), 109–34, esp.

120–1. And for a helpful discussion of narrative styles, see Peter Burke, "The History of Events and the Revival of the Narrative," in Burke, ed., *New Perspectives on Historical Writing*, 233–48.

10. For an insightful discussion of narrative forms, see Margaret R. Somers, "Narrativity, Narrative Identity, and Social Action: Rethinking Working-Class Formation," *Social Science History*, 16(1992): 591–630. And see also the general issue of *Social Science History* devoted to a discussion of the narrative and introduced by William H. Sewell, Jr., "Narratives and Social Identities," *Social Science History*, 16(1992): 479–88. Also very helpful are Edward M. Bruner, "Ethnography as Narrative," in Turner and Bruner, eds., *The Anthropology of Experience*, 139–55, and the general discussion of narrative methods in Natalie Davis's brilliant *The Return of Martin Guerre* (Cambridge, MA, 1983).

11. My approach to narrative analysis has been influenced by Lawrence Stone, "The Revival of Narrative: Reflections on an Old New History," *Past and Present*, 85(1979): 3–24; and Alan Megill, "Recounting the Past: 'Description,' Explanation, and Narrative in Historiography," *American Historical Review*, 94(1989): 627–53.

12. For a compelling argument about the importance of narratives in legal analysis, see Kathryn Abrams, "Hearing the Call of Stories," *California Law Review*, 79(1991): 971.

13. I intentionally use the term "recounting" in agreement with Megill that it "helps us appreciate that 'description' is not a neutral preliminary to the *real* work of explanation, not mere data collection. It leaves us better able to see that the two cannot be given a differential importance in abstraction from the aims and audiences of particular historical works." I also concur with his assertion that narrative "blends recounting and explanation," "Recounting the Past," 637, 638.

1. Entering the Law's Shadow

1. *Report*, 52–3.

2. *Democracy in America, In Two Volumes with a Critical Appraisal of Each Volume by John Stuart Mill* (New York, 1970), trans. Henry Reeve, 1:151–2. Emphasis added.

3. For a critical evaluation of the shadow of the law, see Herbert Jacob, "The Elusive Shadow of the Law," *Law & Society Review*, 26(1992): 565–90.

4. For a useful discussion of this point, see Sally Falk Moore, *Law as Process: An Anthropological Approach* (London, 1978), 55.

5. Karen Lystra, *Searching the Heart, Women, Men, and Romantic Love in Nineteenth-Century America* (New York, 1989), 223; Merril D. Smith, *Breaking the Bonds, Marital Discord in Pennsylvania, 1730–1830* (New York, 1991), 46–7.

6. "Obituary of David Sears," *New England Historical and Genealogical Register*, 26(1872): 207.

7. Richard Hildreth, *"Our First Men": A Calendar of Wealth, Fashion, and Gentility, Containing Lists of Those Persons Taxed in the City of Boston, Cre-*

dibly Reported to Be Worth One Hundred Thousand Dollars, With Biographical Notices of the Principal Persons (Boston, 1846).

8. Robert Charles Winthrop, Jr., "Memoir of David Sears," *Massachusetts Historical Society Proceedings*, 2(1886): 23, footnote 1. The stanza is from Byron's poem, "The Bride of Abydos."

9. One of the uncertainties of the story is whether the most appropriate English translation of the d'Hauteville rank should have been baron or count. The family apparently preferred count, and as it seems to have been the most widely used, I have followed that practice in these pages. Ellen eventually even challenged the legitimacy of any title.

10. For the significance of studying the upper class, particularly Boston Brahmins, see Betty Farrell, *Elite Families, Class and Power in Nineteenth-Century Boston* (Albany, NY, 1993), esp. Introduction, chap. 1.

11. Ibid., 83–4; and see Lee Virginia Chambers-Schiller, *Liberty, A Better Husband, The Single Woman in America: The Generations of 1780–1840* (New Haven, CT, 1984), 35–6; William H. Pease and Jane H. Pease, *The Web of Progress, Private Values and Public Values in Boston and Charleston, 1828–1843* (New York, 1985), 106, 117; Lystra, *Searching the Heart*, 157–9.

12. *Report*, 66–81.

13. Ibid., 73.

14. For a discussion of the significance of breach of marriage promises and the law that governed them, see Michael Grossberg, *Governing the Hearth, Law and the Family in Nineteenth Century America* (Chapel Hill, NC, 1985), chap. 2.

15. Burke cited in John F. Kasson, *Rudeness and Civility, Manners in Nineteenth Century America* (New York, 1990), 60, and see generally 62.

16. For a description of marital trauma, see Chambers-Schiller, *Liberty*, 38, and see generally chap. 1. For a discussion of the introspective nature of courtship during these years, see Lystra, *Searching the Heart*, 31–7.

17. *Report*, 74–80.

18. Ibid., 69.

19. Ibid., 119–20.

20. A copy of the marital agreement can be found in the Sears Papers as well as in an abbreviated form in the *Report*, 200–2.

21. *Report*, 122–8, 145–6, 199.

22. James Fennimore Cooper, *Excursions in Switzerland* (Paris, 1836), 285.

23. *Report*, 162, 163, 86, and for conflicting versions, see generally 86–8, 162–6.

24. *Ibid.*, 164, 165.

25. For a description of the ceremony, see Cordelia Sears to Anna Amory, 23 August 1837, Amory Papers.

26. Ellen Rothman, *Hearts and Hands, A History of Courtship in America* (New York, 1984), 56–7.

27. Anna Amory to Miriam Sears, 12 August 1837, Amory Papers.

28. Lystra, *Searching the Heart*, 192–3.

29. For a compelling discussion of the nature of troubled American marriages, see ibid., chap. 7.

30. For contemporary descriptions of the area, see Thomas Roscoe, *The*

Tourist in Switzerland and Italy (London, 1830), 1–39; William Beattie, *Switzerland, Illustrated* (London, 1836), 2:148–9; Cooper, *Excursions,* 284–6.

31. *Report,* 89.
32. Smith, *Breaking the Bonds,* 51.
33. Lystra, *Searching the Heart,* 215–21.
34. *Report,* 90, 91, 90.
35. Rothman, *Hearts and Hands,* 117; and for a discussion of the primal role of women in maintaining Brahmin kin networks, see Farrell, *Elite Families,* chap. 4.
36. *Report,* 91–9
37. Ibid., 92–9.
38. Ibid., 168.
39. Ibid., 170, 171.
40. Ibid., 93.
41. Ibid., 205–6.
42. Ibid., 172–3.
43. Ibid., 95.
44. Ibid., 173, 174.
45. For discussions of Cass's ministry, see Andrew C. McLaughlin, *Lewis Cass* (Boston, 1891), chap. 6; Frank B. Woodford, *Lewis Cass, The Last Jeffersonian* (New Brunswick, NJ, 1950), chap. 10. For a description of Cass's apartment, see Edward L. Pierce, ed., *Memoir and Letters of Charles Sumner* (London, 1878), 1:253.
46. *Report,* 174.
47. Ibid., 96.
48. Quoted in Woodford, *Lewis Cass,* 36.
49. *Report,* 99. For discussions of nostalgia, see George Rosen, "Nostalgia: A 'Forgotten' Psychological Disorder," *Clio Medica,* 10(1975): 28–51; Leon Grinberg and Rebecca Grinberg, "A Psychoanalytic Study of Migration: Its Normal and Pathological Aspects," *Journal of Psychoanalytic Association,* 32(1984): 13–38; and Roderick Peters, "Reflections on the Origin and Aim of Nostalgia," *Journal of Analytical Psychology,* 30(1985): 135–48.
50. *Report,* 174.
51. Lystra, *Searching the Heart,* 51–2, and see 207–8; see also Smith, *Breaking the Bonds,* 51–65.
52. Karen Halttunen, *Confidence Men and Painted Women, A Study of Middle-Class Culture in America, 1830–1870* (New Haven, CT, 1982), 119, 120, and see generally 118–22.
53. *Report,* 26–7.
54. Ibid., 27, 28, 29; and see 217–19.
55. Ibid., 29–30.
56. Ibid., 25.
57. Ibid., 107.
58. Ibid., 220.
59. *Report,* 37. For a discussion of this customary practice, see Hendrik Hartog, "Mrs. Packard on Dependency," *Yale Journal of Law & the Humanities,* 1(1988): 90–1.
60. *Report,* 55, 38.

61. For a discussion of the relationship between the shadow of the law and the way a dispute is framed, see Jacobs, "The Elusive Shadow of the Law," 568–9.
62. Ibid., 40ff.
63. Ibid., 38, 39.
64. Ibid., 221.
65. Lystra, *Searching the Heart*, 9.
66. *Report*, 183.
67. Ibid., 47.
68. Ibid., 12.
69. Ibid., 55.
70. Ibid., 12, 133.
71. *New England Genealogical Register,* 35(1881): 192–3.
72. *Report*, 257, 259.
73. Ibid., 221–2.
74. Ibid., 131–3.
75. Ibid., 201.
76. For a description of innovations at the Tremont, see Daniel Boorstin, *The Americans, The National Experience* (New York, 1965), 136–40.
77. David B. Tyack, *George Ticknor and the Boston Brahmins* (Cambridge, MA, 1967), 156.
78. The Searses' mansion is now part of the Somerset Club. For a description of the mansion and its construction, see Allen Chamberlain, *Beacon Hill, Its Ancient Pastures and Early Mansions* (Boston, 1925), 176–8. Tocqueville and Beaumont dined at the Searses' mansion during their visit to Boston and praised the sumptuous meal they had there. For their description, see George W. Pierson, *Tocqueville and Beaumont in America* (New York, 1938), 364.
79. One Who Knows Them, *The Aristocracy of Boston* (Boston, 1848), 30; "David Sears," *New England Historic, Genealogical Society,* 26(1872): 207–8; Reverend Philip Brooks, "The Episcopal Church," in Justin Winsor, ed., *The Memorial History of Boston* (Boston, 1881), 3:445; Winthrop, "Memoir," 10–14. For a vivid description of Boston in 1840, see Pease and Pease, *The Web of Progress*, 2–4; and for a study of the Boston Associates, see Robert F. Dalzell, Jr., *Enterprising Elite: The Boston Associates and the World They Made* (Cambridge, MA, 1987).
80. Francis J. Grund, *Aristocracy in America, From the Sketch-Book of a German Nobleman* (London, 1839), 2:30–1, 51–2; and see Roland N. Stromberg, "Boston in the 1820's and 1830's," *History Today,* 11(1961): 593–4.
81. *Report*, 147–8, 148.

2. Bargaining in the Shadow of the Law

1. For a general discussion of the changes in the family during this era, see Steven Mintz and Susan Kellogg, *Domestic Revolutions* (New York, 1989), chaps. 1–4.
2. The reactions attributed to Ellen and Gonzalve in this chapter are based on their correspondence and subsequent legal actions as is evident in the second part of this chapter.

3. Martin Shapiro, "On the Regrettable Decline of Law French, or Shapiro Jette le Brickbat," *Yale Law Journal*, 90(1981): 1,201.
4. For insightful analyses of lawyer–client relations, see Austin Sarat and William L. F. Felstiner, "Law and Social Relations: Vocabularies of Motive in Lawyer/Client Relations," *Law & Society Review*, 22(1988): 738; and idem, "Enactments of Power: Negotiating Reality and Responsibility in Lawyer-Client Interactions," *Cornell Law Review*, 77(1992): 1,447–98.
5. Hendrik Hartog, "Marital Exits and Marital Expectations in Nineteenth Century America," *Georgetown Law Journal*, 80(1991): 109.
6. *Report*, 132, 132–3, 133.
7. *Marshall v. Rutton*, 101 Eng. Reps. 1538, 1539 (1800).
8. Nelson Blake, *The Road to Reno* (New York, 1962), 14–15, 31–3.
9. Ibid., 61.
10. Revised Statutes of 1836, 480; Tapping Reeve, *The Law of Baron and Feme* (Conn), 91–7, 166, 213–15; George E. Howard, *A History of Matrimonial Institutions* (Chicago, 1904), 3:6–7; Marylynn Salmon, *Women and the Law of Property in Early America* (Chapel Hill, NC, 1986), chap. 4.
11. Revised Statutes of 1827–8, 2:1,44–7; Howard, *Matrimonial Institutions*, 3:102–4.
12. Sir William Blackstone, *Commentaries on the Laws of England* (London, 1765–9), 1:468; and see Norma Basch, "Invisible Women: The Fiction of Marital Unity in Nineteenth-Century America," *Feminist Studies*, 5(1979): 436–66.
13. *Rogers v. Rogers*, 4 Paige's Chancery Reports 516 (New York, 1834).
14. Jane H. Pease and William H. Pease, *Ladies, Women, and Wenches: Choice and Constraint in Antebellum Charleston and Boston* (Chapel Hill, NC, 1990), 114.
15. Rhode Island Petition, 125–6.
16. Hartog, "Marital Exits," 114–15; Roderick Phillips, *Putting Asunder, A History of Divorce in Western Society* (New York, 1988), 242–5
17. Phillips, *Putting Asunder*, 141–58.
18. Howard, *Matrimonial Institutions*, 3:5–7; see for specifics Blake, *Road to Reno*, 50
19. Revised Statutes of 1827–28, 2:144–7; Howard, *Matrimonial Institutions*, 3:103–5; Blake, *Road to Reno*, 66–7.
20. Calvin quoted in Phillips, *Putting Asunder*, 53, 54, and see generally 52–62, 84–94, 208–9, 405; see also Jean Kellerhals, Jean Francois Perrin, and Laura Vaneche, "Switzerland," in Robert Chester, *Divorce in Europe* (Leiden, Netherlands, 1977), 195–210; Antoine Rochat, *Le Régime Matrimonial du Pays de Vaud à la Fin de l'Ancien Régime et Sous le Code Civil Vaudois* (Lusanne, 1987).
21. Phillips, *Putting Asunder*, 89
22. For a early example of such claims, see the discussion of the 1734 Thrall divorce in Alison Duncan Hirsch, "The Thrall Divorce Case: A Family Crisis in Eighteenth Century Connecticut," in Linda Speth and Alison Duncan Hirsch, *Women, Family, and Community in Colonial America: Two Perspectives* (New York, 1983), 43–75; and the case in Glenda Riley, *Divorce: An American Tradition* (New York, 1991), 20–1.

23. *Brainard v. Brainard*, 1 *Brayton* 55 (Vermont, 1816).
24. Stowell cited in Robert Griswold, "The Evolution of the Doctrine of Mental Cruelty in Victorian American Divorce, 1790–1900," *Journal of Social History*, 20(1986): 132; and see idem, "Divorce and the Legal Redefinition of Victorian Manhood," in Mark C. Carnes and Clyde Griffen, eds., *Meanings for Manhood, Constructions of Masculinity in Victorian America* (Chicago, 1990), 96–110.
25. See for example, *Hill v. Hill*, 2 Mass. Reps. 150 (1806); and *Warren v. Warren*, 3 Mass. Reps. 321 (1807).
26. *Thornberry v. Thornberry*, 25 Ky. Reps. 323 (1829)
27. For a discussion of these issues, see Thomas Haskell, "Capitalism and the Origins of the Humanitarian Sensibility," *American Historical Review*, 90(1985): 339–61, 547–66; and Myra C. Glenn, *Campaigns Against Corporal Punishment, Prisoners, Sailors, Women, and Children in Antebellum America* (Albany, NY, 1984).
28. Riley, *Divorce*, 55–9. For examples of gendered approaches to property right, see Richard Chused, "Married Women's Property and Inheritance by Widows in Massachusetts: A Study of Wills Probated Between 1800 and 1850," *Berkeley Women's Law Journal*, 2(1986): 65–85; and Suzanne Lebsock, *The Free Women of Petersburg* (New York, 1984), 136–7.
29. William O'Barr and John M. Conley, "Small Claims Court Narratives," in David Papke, ed., *Narrative and Legal Discourse, A Reader in Storytelling and the Law* (Liverpool, 1991), 76–7.
30. *Report*, 133, 134. See Karen Lystra, *Searching the Heart, Women, Men, and Romantic Love in Nineteenth-Century America* (New York, 1989), 236–7 for a discussion of the impact of husbandly concern about marital happiness on patriarchal power; and see Hartog, "Marital Exits," 110–15.
31. For a valuable discussion of religion and law as alternative sources of authority, see Carol Weisbrod, "Family, Church, and State," *Legal History Program, Working Papers*, Working Paper #2, Institute for Legal Studies, University of Wisconsin, Madison, School of Law.
32. *Report*, 134ff.
33. For a discussion of the issue, see Lystra, *Searching the Heart*, 241–2. And for a discussion of Boston Brahmin anti-Calvinism, see William H. Pease and Jane H. Pease, *The Web of Progress, Private Values and Public Styles in Boston and Charleston, 1828–1843* (New York, 1985), 130.
34. *Report*, 137ff.
35. Ibid., 34.
36. Ibid., 11.
37. For a statement of the traditional Anglo-American law of custody, see Blackstone, *Commentaries on the Laws of England*, 1:450, 441.
38. For a contemporary expression of such concerns, see Mary Becker, "Maternal Feelings: Myth, Taboo, and Child Custody," *Southern California Review of Law and Women's Studies*, 1(1992): 143.
39. The one major exception was the English and American practice of making mothers the natural guardians of their children.
40. For an example of the legal recognition of custom, see Blackstone, *Commentaries on the Laws of England*, 2:74–5, 90–1.

41. For a discussion of custom and law, see Stanley Diamond, "The Rule of Law Versus the Order of Custom," in Robert Paul Wolff, ed., *The Rule of Law* (New York, 1971), 115–44.

42. *Rex v. Delaval*, 3 Burr. 1434 (K.B. 1763); *Blisset's Case*, Lofft 748, 98 Eng. Reps. 899 (K.B., 1774).

43. Michael Grossberg, *Governing the Hearth, Law and Family in Nineteenth-Century America* (Chapel Hill, NC, 1985), 235–7; Hendrik Hartog, "John Barry's Rights: Of Power, Justice, and Coverture," presented at the Amherst Seminar on Law & Society, July 1992, 1.

44. *De Manneville v. De Manneville*, 10 Ves. 62, 32 Eng. Reps. 762 (Chan., 1804).

45. *Rex v. Greenhill*, 4 Ad. & E, 624, 111 Eng. Reps. 922 (K.B. 1836). See also the decisions against poet Percy Bysshe Shelley, *Shelley v. Westbrook*, 37 Eng. Reps. 850 (Ch. 1817); and for other cases, see *Wellesley v. The Duke of Beaufort*, 38 Eng. Reps. 236 (Ch. 1827); *Wellesley v. Wellesley*, 4 Eng. Reps. 1078 (H.L. 1828); *Wellesley v. Wellesley*, 4 Eng. Reps. 1,078, 1,080, 1,083 (H.L., 1828); and *Ball v. Ball*, 2 Sim 35. For an overview of these developments, see, Jamil S. Zainaldin, "The Emergence of a Modern American Family Law: Child Custody, Adoption, and the Courts, 1796–1851," *Northwestern Law Review*, 73(1979): 1,060–1; Douglas R. Rendleman, "Parens Patriae: From Chancery to Juvenile Court," *South Carolina Law Review*, 23(1971): 208.

46. Zainaldin, "The Emergence of a Modern American Family Law," 1,053–4, 1,063

47. For a discussion of Norton, see her own works, *Separation of the Mother and Child by the Law of Custody of Infants Considered* (privately printed, 1837), and *A Plain Letter to the Lord Chancellor on the Infant Custody Bill* (London, 1839); and see Mary Lyndon Shanley, *Feminism, Marriage, and the Law in Victorian England, 1850–1895* (Princeton, NJ, 1989), 136–7; Susan Maidment, *Child Custody and Divorce: The Law in Social Context* (London, 1984), 113–16.

48. *Equity Jurisprudence*, (Boston, 1846), 4th ed., chap. 25, sec. 775–6; Rendleman, "Parens Patriae," 220.

49. Grossberg, *Governing the Hearth*, chap. 7.

50. Ibid., 240

51. Cited in Norma Basch, *In the Eyes of the Law: Marriage and Property in Nineteenth-Century America* (New York, 1982), 40.

52. Ibid., 248–50.

53. *Report*, 137.

54. Grossberg, *Governing the Hearth*, 240.

55. *Report*, 148.

56. David to Lewis Cass, 15 November 1839, Sears Papers. For an example of David's legal advice, see his letter to McKeon, Hoffman, and Gerard, 19 October 1839, Sears Papers.

57. William T. David, *Bench and Bar of the Commonwealth of Massachusetts* (New York, 1974, reprint), 1:426; *The National Cyclopaedia of American Biography* (New York, 1929), 6:381.

58. "Gerard, James Watson," *Dictionary of American Biography*, ed. Allen Johnson and Dumas Malone (New York, 1931), 7:217.

59. *The People, ex relatione Barry v. Mercein*, Paige (New York, 1839), 57, 61,

65–8; and for the most insightful analysis of the case, see Hartog, "John Barry's Rights: Of Power, Justice, and Coverture."

60. *The Barry Case, A Review of, and Strictures on the Opinion of His Honor the Chancellor of the State of New-York, Delivered 26th August, 1839, in the Late Case of The People, ex relatione John A. Barry versus Thomas R. Mercein* (New York, 1839).

61. However, there was a growing clamor against private legislative acts, especially bills of divorce. For a thorough dicussion of the issue, see Richard Chused, *Private Acts in Public Places, A Social History of Divorce in the Formative Era of American Family Law* (Philadelphia, 1994).

62. *Report*, 185, 34; and for David Sears's explanation of the effort, see ibid., 260.

63. Basch, *In the Eyes of the Law*, 28–9, 137; idem, "Equity vs. Equality, Emerging Concepts of Women's Political Status in the Age of Jackson," *Journal of the Early Republic*, 3(1983): 306–8; and Paula Baker, "The Domestication of Politics: Women and American Political Society, 1780–1920," *American Historical Review*, 89(1984): 622–32.

64. Ibid., 132.

65. *Report*, 47ff.

66. *New York Sun*, Friday, 13 March 1840, p. 2.

67. *Report*, 13, 14, 111; and for the continued lobbying in New York, see David Sears to John McKeon, 13 April 1840, Sears Papers.

68. In drawing the distinctions between hegemony and ideology and between agentive and nonagentive forces, I have been greatly influenced by John Comaroff and Jean Comaroff's, *Of Revelation and Revolution, Christianity, and Colonialism, and Consciousness in South Africa* (Chicago, 1991), 24, 22.

69. Ellen to Anna Amory, 7 November 1839, Amory Letters.

3. Out of the Shadow

1. *Nancy Shippen, Her Journal Book*, ed. Ethel Armes, (Philadelphia, 1935), 273, 273–4, and see 291–2. For other accounts of the incident, see Mary Beth Norton, *Liberty's Daughters, The Revolutionary Experience of American Women, 1750–1800* (Boston, 1980); Linda Kerber, *Women of the Republic, Intellect & Ideology in Revolutionary America* (Chapel Hill, NC, 1980). For a similar story of another woman trapped by the patriarchal biases of the law during these revolutionary years, see the discussion of the property rights battle of Grace Galloway in Joan R. Gunderson, "Independence, Citizenship, and the American Revolution," *Signs*, 13(1987): 70–3.

2. For a discussion of this point, see Michael Grossberg, *Governing the Hearth, Law and Family in Nineteenth-Century America* (Chapel Hill, NC, 1985), chap. 8; and idem, "Crossing Boundaries: Nineteenth-Century Domestic Relations Law and the Merger of Family and Legal History," *American Bar Foundation Research Journal*, (1985), 819–32.

3. Thomas R. Meehan, "'Not Made Out of Levity' Evolution of Divorce in Early Pennsylvania," *Pennsylvania Magazine of History and Biography*, 92(1968): 441–64; George E. Howard, *A History of Matrimonial Institu-*

tions (Chicago, 1904), 2:315–27, 3:96–160; Roderick Phillips, *Putting Asunder, A History of Divorce in Western Society* (New York, 1988), 142–3, 149–52, 154–5.

4. *Commonwealth v. Addicks*, 5 Binney 520, 522 (Pa. 1813).

5. *Commonwealth v. Addicks*, 2 Searge and Rawle, 174, 176, 177 (Pa. 1816).

6. Merrill D. Smith, *Breaking the Bonds, Marital Discord in Pennsylvania, 1730–1830* (New York, 1991), 42.

7. For general discussions of the status of women in antebellum Pennsylvania, see Ira W. Brown, "Women's Rights Movement in Pennsylvania, 1848–1873," *Pennsylvania History*, 23(1965): 154; G. S. Rowe, "Women's Crime and Criminal Administration in Pennsylvania, 1763–1790," *Pennsylvania Magazine of History and Biography*, 109(1985): 335–68; Meehan, "Divorce in Early Pennsylvania," 198–9; Carol Shammas, Marylynn Salmon, and Michele Dahlin, *Inheritance in America, From Colonial Times to the Present* (New Brunswick, 1987). And for a discussion of divorce in Pennsylvania, see Smith, *Breaking the Bonds*, esp. chaps. 1, 2, and 4.

8. For general discussions of the status of children in antebellum Pennsylvania, see Sister Monica Kiefer, "Early American Childhood in the Middle Atlantic Area," *Pennsylvania Magazine of History and Biography*, 68(1944): 3–37; Jacqueline S. Reinier, "Rearing the Republican Child: Attitudes and Practices in Post-Revolutionary Philadelphia," *William and Mary Quarterly*, 39(1982): 150–61; and Barry Levy, *Quakers and the American Family, British Settlement in the Delaware Valley* (New York, 1988).

9. See, for example, Michael Hindus, *Prison and Plantation: Crime, Justice, and Authority in Massachusetts and South Carolina, 1767–1878* (Chapel Hill, NC, 1978).

10. *The Making of Pennsylvania* (Philadelphia, 1896), 60, 209–10, 212. For a discussion of Fisher, see E. Digby Baltzell, *Puritan Boston and Quaker Philadelphia* (Boston, 1979), 304–5. And for a recent argument about the link between the state's population diversity and its liberalism, see Sally Schwartz, *A Mixed Multitude* (New York, 1992).

11. Baltzell, *Puritan Boston and Quaker Philadelphia*, 283, 54, and see 283–4. Emphasis in the original.

12. *Aristocracy in America, From the Sketch-Book of a German Nobleman* (London, 1839), 2:167–8.

13. André Jardin, *Tocqueville, A Biography* (New York, 1988), trans. Lydia Davis with Robert Hemenway, 157–60.

14. The term is Louis Hartz's, see *Economic Policy and Democratic Thought, Pennsylvania 1776–1860* (Cambridge, MA, 1948), 242.

15. See Gibson's dissent in *Eakin v. Raub*, 12 Sergent & Rawle 330 (Pa. 1825).

16. *Ex parte Crouse*, 4 Wharton 9, 11 (Pa. 1838).

17. *Report*, 148.

18. Quoted in Gary Nash, "The Philadelphia Bench and Bar, 1800–1861," *Comparative Studies in Society and History*, 7(1965): 205.

19. Ibid.

20. On the Philadelphia bar generally, see J. Thomas Scharf and Thomas Westcott, *History of Philadelphia, 1609–1884* (Philadelphia, 1884), vol.

2, chap. 39; E. Digby Baltzell, *Philadelphia Gentlemen, The Making of a National Upper Class* (Glencoe, IL, 1958), 145–7; idem, *Puritan Boston and Quaker Philadelphia*, chap. 17.

21. Baltzell, *Philadelphia Gentlemen*, 249.

22. *The Cloth Cases*, 5 Federal Cases 1068, Case No. 2,902, E.D. Pennsylvania (1840).

23. *Dictionary of American Biography* (New York, 1935), 3:398–9.

24. John Samuel, *John Cadwalader's Office* (Law Association of Philadelphia, undated) 7,8.

25. *Proceedings of the Constitutional Convention and Obituaries and Addresses on the Occasion of the Death of the Honorable William M. Meredith, of Philadelphia, September 16, 1873* (Philadelphia, 1873): 6, and see generally 6–20, 53; Scharf and Westcott, *Philadelphia*, 2:1,541; Ellis P. Oberholtzer, *Philadelphia, A History of the City and Its People* (Philadelphia, 1911), 2:120; R. L. Ashurst, "William Morris Meredith," *Pennsylvania Bar Association*, 26 June 1901; *Dictionary of American Biography*, 12:548–9.

26. *Proceedings of the Constitutional Convention, 1873*, 16.

27. Scharf and Westcott, *Philadelphia*, 2:1541.

28. Ashurst, "William Morris Meredith," 38.

29. Ibid.

30. Quoted in ibid.

31. Scharf and Westcott, *Philadelphia*, 2:1542; Robert Ferguson, *Law and Letters in American Culture* (Cambridge, 1984), 68.

32. Undated letter quoted in Charles Chauncy Binney, *The Life of Horace Binney, with Selections from His Letters* (Philadelphia, 1903), 71–2.

33. *Ibid.*, 202; and see *Dictionary of American Biography*, 2:280–2.

34. William B. Reed, *Memories of Familiar Books, with a Memoir of the Author*, ed. Manton Marble (New York, 1876), v–xv; Ellis P. Oberholtzer, *A Literary History of Pennsylvania* (Philadelphia, 1906), 358–9; *Dictionary of American Biography*, 15:461–2; Philip P. Auchampaugh, "James Buchanan, The Squire from Lancaster," *Pennsylvania Magazine of History and Biography*, 56(1932): 26–7.

35. David Paul Brown, *Eulogium of the Life and Character of the Late Honorable Joseph Reed Ingersoll, Delivered September 28, 1869* (Philadelphia, 1869); Scharf and Westcott, *Philadelphia*, 2:1532; "The Second Troop Philadelphia City Calvary," *Pennsylvania Magazine of History and Biography*, 52(1928): 379–80, footnote 609.

36. *The Letters of John Morin Scott and His Wife Mary Emlen Scott* (Philadelphia, 1930), 11–16; Henry Simpson, *The Lives of Eminent Philadelphians, Now Deceased* (Philadelphia, 1859), 867–72.

37. Nicholas Wainwright, "The Age of Nicholas Biddle," in Russell Weigley et al., eds., *Philadelphia, A 300-Year History* (New York, 1982), 300; and see Nash, "The Philadelphia Bench and Bar," 204–9. For a general assessment of the Philadelphia bar and a comparison with lawyers in Boston, see Baltzell, *Puritan Boston and Quaker Philadelphia*, 336–52.

38. For an introductory discussion of nineteenth-century legal communities, see Michael Grossberg, "Institutionalizing Masculinity: The Law as a Masculine Profession," in Mark Carnes and Clyde Griffen, eds., *Meanings for Manhood, Constructions of Masculinity in Victorian America* (Chicago, 1990), 133–51, and see esp. 133–5.

39. "Statement of the Case of Mr. Gonzalve Grand D'Hauteville," (New York, 1840), 5–6, 29–31.

40. *Report*, 5ff.

41. Samuel Pennypacker, *Congress Hall, An Address by Honorable Samuel Pennypacker, LL.D., at the Last Session of the Court of Common Pleas, No. 2, in Congress Hall* (Philadelphia, 1895). And see Allan Steinberg for a description of the run-down condition of the building by midcentury, *The Transformation of Criminal Justice, Philadelphia, 1800–1880* (Chapel Hill, NC, 1989), 22–3.

42. John Hill Martin, *Bench and Bar of Philadelphia* (Philadelphia, 1883), 81–2, and see 40 for a general description of the development of county courts in Philadelphia.

43. *The Biographical Encyclopaedia of Pennsylvania of the Nineteenth Century* (Philadelphia, 1874), 447–8.

44. *The Biographical Encyclopaedia of Pennsylvania*, 76–7, 173; Simpson, *The Lives of Eminent Philadelphians*, 246–7; Oberholtzer, *Literary History of Philadelphia*, 246–8; Sam Bass Warner, *The Private City, Philadelphia in Three Periods of Its Growth* (Philadelphia, 1968), 130–1; Steinberg, *The Transformation of Criminal Justice*, 22.

45. Scharf and Westcott, *Philadelphia*, 2:1,545.

46. *Report*, 8.

47. Statement dated 13 July 1840, d'Hauteville File.

4. Into a Court of Law

1. Quoted in E. Digby Baltzell, *Puritan Boston and Quaker Philadelphia* (Boston, 1979), 69.

2. For a discussion of social dramas, see Victor Turner, *Dramas, Fields, and Metaphors* (Ithaca, NY, 1974), chap. 1. And for a description of the theatrical aspects of the Philadelphia criminal courts, see Allen Steinberg, *The Transformation of Criminal Justice, Philadelphia, 1800–1880* (Chapel Hill, NC, 1989), 16–24.

3. "Introduction," in Robert Hariman, ed., *Popular Trials, Rhetoric, Mass Media, and the Law* (Birmingham, AL, 1990), 5.

4. Edward M. Bruner, "Experience and Its Expressions," in Victor W. Turner and Edward M. Bruner, eds., *The Anthropology of Experience* (Urbana, IL, 1986), 9–10.

5. "Reflexivity as Evolution in Thoreau's *Walden*," in Turner and Bruner, eds., *The Anthropology of Experience*, 79.

6. *Public Ledger*, 13 July 1840, 2.

7. Nicholas B. Wainwright, "The Age of Nicholas Biddle," in Russell Weigley et al., eds., *Philadelphia, A 300-Year History* (New York, 1982), 300; Daniel A. Cohen, "The Murder of Maria Bickford: Fashion, Passion, and the Birth of a Consumer Culture," *American Studies*, 31(1990): 5–10; Dan Schiller, *Objectivity and the News, The Public and the Rise of Commercial Journalism* (Philadelphia, 1981), esp. chaps. 1–2.

8. Daniel A. Cohen, *Pillars of Salt, Monuments of Grace, New England Crime Literature and the Origins of American Popular Culture, 1674–1860* (New York, 1993), 251.

9. Elwyn B. Robinson, "The Public Ledger: An Independent Newspa-

per," *Pennsylvania Magazine of History and Biography*, 64(1940): 43–55; Nicholas B. Wainwright, "History of the *Philadelphia Inquirer*," Supplement to *Philadelphia Inquirer*, 16 September 1962, 1–23; idem, "The Age of Nicholas Biddle," 300; Ellis Paxon Oberholtzer, *Philadelphia, A History of the City and Its People*, (Philadelphia 1911), 2:219–24; J. Thomas Scharf and Thomas Westcott, *Philadelphia of Philadelphia, 1609–1884* (Philadelphia, 1884), 2:2,001–2.

10. Bruce Kapferen, "Performance and the Structuring of Meaning and Experience," in Turner and Bruner, eds., *The Anthropology of Experience*, 191.

11. Norman Rosenberg, "Law Noirs," *Law and History Review*, 12(1994): 341–5; and see, generally, David Ray Papke, ed., *Narrative and the Legal Discourse, A Reader in Storytelling and the Law* (Liverpool, 1991).

12. Undated letter from David Sears to Cadwalader, d'Hauteville File. The file also includes copies of Ellen's version of events in her marriage and various drafts of Cadwalader's briefs. Unfortunately, similar files compiled by Gonzalve's counsel could not be located.

13. Lawrence M. Friedman, "Law, Lawyers, and Popular Culture," *Yale Law Journal*, 98(1989): 1,559; and Laura Hanf Korobkin, "The Maintenance of Mutual Confidence: Sentimental Strategies at the Adultery Trial of Henry Ward Beecher," *Yale Journal of Law & the Humanities*, 7(1995): 14.

14. *Report*, 8.

15. Ibid., 9.

16. Ibid., 10.

17. Ibid.

18. Ibid., 11ff.

19. Ibid., 15, 16.

20. Ibid., 16–17.

21. Ibid., 18, 30–1.

22. Ibid., 31.

23. Ibid., 35.

24. Ibid.

25. Ibid., 36–50.

26. Ibid., 14, 15, 51.

27. Ibid.

28. For a useful discussion of women in Pennsylvania courts, see G. S. Rowe, "The Role of Courthouses in the Lives of Eighteenth Century Pennsylvania Women," *Western Pennsylvania Historical Magazine*, 68(1985): 5–23.

29. *Report*, 52.

30. *Public Ledger*, 18 July 1840, 2. For a similar story, see the *Pennsylvania Inquirer*, 20 July 1840, 2.

31. *Report*, 52–3.

32. Ibid., 54–5, 56.

33. *Germantown Telegraph*, 22 July 1840, 2; *New York Sun*, 22 July 1840, 1; *Boston Post*, 25 July 1840, 1; *Boston Courier*, 27 July 1840, 4; and for a general discussion of Boston newspapers, see Charles A. Cummings, "The Press and the Literature of the Last One Hundred Years," in Justin Winsor, *The Memorial History of Boston* (Boston, 1881), 3:627–33.

34. McKeon to D. Sears, 22 July 1840, d'Hauteville File.

35. Wednesday, July 23, 1840, *Diary of Samuel Breck*, Historical Society of Philadelphia, vol. 8, April 1838 to January 1841.
36. Drafts of Cadwalader's brief, including pages containing pinned clippings and his argument, can be found in the d'Hauteville File. And see undated letter from Cadwalader to Binney about the brief in the same collection.
37. *Report*, 61ff.
38. Ibid., 82ff.
39. Ibid., 85.
40. Ibid., 89–93.
41. Ibid., 96, 97.
42. Ibid., 104.
43. Ibid., 108.
44. Ibid., 112, 113.
45. Ibid., 138ff.
46. *The Public Ledger*, 31 July 1840, 1.
47. *Inquirer*, 1 August 1840, 2; and see 20 July 1840, 2 and 31 July 1840, 2. For another local account, see *The Pennsylvanian*, 1 August 1840, 2.
48. John Cadwalader to Ingersoll, 3 August 1840; Miriam Sears to John Cadwalader, 2 August 1840; Miriam Sears to John Cadwalader, 5 August 1840, d'Hauteville File.
49. David Sears to John Cadwalader, 19 August 1840, d'Hauteville File.
50. Park Benjamin to John Cadwalader, 3 August 1840, d'Hauteville File.
51. *Germantown Telegraph*, 5 August 1840, 2.
52. *Report*, 142–4.
53. Ibid., 151–5.
54. Ibid., 155.
55. Ibid., 155ff.
56. Ibid., 165, 166.
57. Ibid., 186ff.
58. Ibid., 189.
59. *Philadelphia Inquirer*, Tuesday, 3 September 1840, 2.
60. Quoted in Robert R. Bell, *The Philadelphia Lawyer, A History, 1735–1945* (Selinsgrove, PA, 1993), 116.
61. *The Forum; or, Forty Years Full Practice at the Philadelphia Bar* (Philadelphia, 1856), 1:lxxiii–lxiv, lxxvi–lxxvii.
62. For a compelling presentation of this view of the law's relative autonomy, see Bruce Ackerman, *We the People: Foundations* (Cambridge, MA, 1990), 37–9.
63. The following paragraphs are based on a reading of Cadwalader's extensive notes retained in his files on the case now lodged at the Historical Society of Pennsylvania.
64. For a discussion of the act, see Susan Maidment, *Child Custody and Divorce: The Law in Social Context* (London, 1984), 110–16.
65. Ruth Bloch, "American Feminine Ideals in Transition: The Rise of the Moral Mother, 1785–1815," *Feminist Studies*, 2(1978): 100; Elizabeth Badinter, *Mother Love, Myth and Reality, Motherhood in Modern History* (New York, 1981); Ann Dally, *Inventing Motherhood: The Consequences of an Ideal* (New York, 1982).
66. Alexis de Tocqueville, *Democracy In America*, trans. Henry Reeve (New

York, 1970), 2:212; Peter Burke, "History of Events," in idem, *New Perspectives on Historical Writing* (Cambridge, 1991), 245. For a discussion of forms of feminism, see Ellen DuBois's comments in the round-table discussion published as "Feminist Discourse," *Buffalo Law Review*, 24(1985): 64–5; and see Linda Kerber, "Separate Spheres, Female Worlds, Woman's Place: The Rhetoric of Women's History," *Journal of American History*, 75(1988): 9–39.

67. All of the information and statements in these paragraphs are drawn from the undated and unnumbered memos in Cadwalader's d'Hauteville File.

68. See for example, Gardiner to Cadwalader, 27 July 1840; Gardiner to Meredith, 23 August 1840; Gardiner to Cadwalader, 23 August 1840; see Gardiner to Cadwalader, 25 August 1840. McKeon to Cadwalader, 20 August 1840; McKeon to David Sears, 22 August 1840; McKeon to Cadwalader, 21 August 1840; all the letters are in the d'Hauteville File.

69. Gerard to Cadwalader, 13 July 1840; and for further advice, see Gerard to Cadwalader, 8 August 1840, d'Hauteville File. For accounts of Gerard's courtroom reputation, see Charles Edwards, *Pleasantries About Courts and Lawyers of the State of New York* (New York, 1867), 81–2, 101, 146–8.

70. R. M. Lee to Cadwalader, 2 September 1840; and Judge Randall to Cadwalader, 12 September 1840, d'Hauteville File.

71. David Sears to Cadwalader, 11 August 1840, d'Hauteville File.

72. Quoted in Barbara Welter, "The Cult of True Womanhood," in Thomas R. Frazier, ed., *The Underside of American History* (New York, 1978), 237.

73. Daniel Webster to David Sears, July 10, 1840, Sears Letterbook.

74. William B. Reed, *Among My Books* (New York, 1871), 128.

75. Gallatin's assistance to Gonzalve was noted in *The Public Ledger*, July 22, 1840, 2.

76. *The Letters of John Morin Scott and His Wife Mary Emlen Scott* (Philadelphia, 1930), 297. The letter collection can be found at the Historical Society of Pennsylvania.

77. Undated memorandum, d'Hauteville File.

78. For a compelling analysis of the nature and purpose of opening statements, see Kathryn Holmes Snedaker, "Storytelling in Opening Statements: Framing the Argumentation of the Trial," *American Journal of Trial Advocacy*, 10(1986): 15–45, and see esp. 17–18, 44–5; and idem, "Storytelling in Opening Statements: Framing the Argumentation of the Trial," in David Ray Papke, ed., *Narrative and the Legal Discourse* (Liverpool, 1991), 132–57.

79. *Report*, 193, 194.

80. The editor of the *Report* explained that he omitted Reed's version of Gonzalve's story "because the facts of the case, as alleged by the relator, have already appeared, in more minute detail, in his petition and suggestions." Ibid., 194.

81. Ibid., 195.

82. *The Ledger*, 5 September 1840, 2. *The Pennsylvanian*, 5 September 1840, 2.

83. Trial notes, d'Hauteville File.
84. Ellen d'Hauteville to Anna Amory, 4 September 1840, 114–16. And see Cordelia Sears to Anna Amory, 17 September 1840, Amory Letters.
85. The editor of the published report of the case decided not to reprint all of the letters. He explained why in a footnote: "The petition, returns and suggestions, filed by the parties, have already been given in full. They contain the most important parts of the correspondence; and, not to swell this volume beyond reasonable limits, we shall not here give the whole testimony, but merely referring to that before spread on the record, abridge the rest, in such a way, however, that nothing of importance shall be omitted. Some of the copies of letters thus to be referred to, were taken from imperfect drafts, and the translation of others are incorrect. Not feeling at liberty to alter records, we have made literal transcripts from them; but shall here, wherever necessary, point out corrections and supply their defects, on a careful comparison with the originals or accurate copies." *Report*, 196.
86. *The Forum*, lxxix.
87. *Report*, 198–9.
88. Ibid., 199–222. Most of the letters read by Reed have already been cited in previous chapters.
89. Ibid., 224–9.
90. Ibid., 229ff.
91. Ibid., 231, 232.
92. Ibid., 232.
93. Ibid., 233, 233–4. For Locke's distinction between paternal and parental power, see John Locke, *Two Treatises of Government*, ed. Peter Laslett (Cambridge, 1963), sec. 52, 345.
94. As he had done in Reed's opening statement, the editor of the *Report* deleted these sections and justified the exclusion by noting: "Here the counsel went into a review of the history of the case, which we omit, because that history has been so fully exhibited, in the different documents put on record." *Report*, 235.
95. Ibid.
96. Ibid., 236, 237.
97. Ibid., 237.
98. Ibid., 239.
99. Baltzell, *Puritan Boston and Quaker Philadelphia*, 358–9.
100. *Report*, 240.
101. Ibid., 241.
102. For a discussion of nonagentive forces, see Jean Comaroff and John Comaroff, *Of Revelation, Christianity, Colonialism, and Consciousness in South Africa* (Chicago, 1991), 22.
103. *Report*, 246, and see generally 246–9.
104. Ibid., 251–2.
105. Ibid., 252–4. And see Charles Knowles Bolton, "Memoir of Francis Calley Gray," *Proceedings of the Massachusetts Historical Society*, 47(1913–14): 529–34.
106. *Report*, 255.

107. Ibid.
108. Ibid., 256–60.
109. Ibid., 260–9.
110. Ibid., 268–73.
111. Ellen d'Hauteville to Anna Amory, 25 September 1840, Amory Letters.
112. *The Public Ledger,* 26 September 1840, 2.
113. *Report,* 276ff.
114. Trial notes, 28 September 1840, d'Hauteville File.
115. *The Public Ledger,* 3 October 1840, 2.
116. *Report,* 278, 278–9, 279–80, 280, 280–1, 281.
117. *The Evening Signal,* 13 October 1840, 1–2; for the exchange of letters between Barry and Cadwalader, see d'Hauteville File. Cadwalader's correspondence also contains copies of a letter from Barry to McKeon asking to see the original letter from Judge Inglis and McKeon's refusal.
118. *Report,* 281, 282, 283.
119. 5 October 1840, "Diary of Sidney George Fisher," 144, Fisher Papers, Historical Society of Pennsylvania.
120. For a analysis of the connections between trials and sentimenal fiction, see Cohen, *Pillars of Salt, Monument of Grace,* esp. 31–2; and Korobkin, "The Maintenance of Mutual Confidence."
121. *Report,* 283, 284, 284–5, 285.
122. For a discussion of judges as patriarches, see Michael Grossberg, *Governing the Hearth, Law and Family in Nineteenth-Century America* (Chapel Hill, NC, 1985), 290–304; and idem, "Institutionalizing Masculinity," in Mark Carnes and Clyde Griffen, eds., *Meanings for Manhood* (Chicago, 1990), 139–43.
123. "How Judges Think," in Gregory Leyh, ed., *Legal Hermeneutics: History, Theory, and Practice* (Berkeley, 1991), 228.
124. "Narrative Models in Legal Proof," in David Ray Papke, ed., *Narrative and the Legal Discourse, A Reader in Storytelling and the Law* (Liverpool, 1991), 167.
125. William M. O'Barr and John Conley, "Small Claims Narratives," in ibid, 68.
126. Richard Weisberg, *Poetics and Other Strategies for Law and Literature* (New York, 1992), 17.
127. *Report,* 287.
128. Ibid., 288.
129. Robert L. Griswold, "Divorce and the Redefinition of Victorian Manhood," in Carnes and Griffen, eds., *Meanings for Manhood,* 99.
130. Barton acknowledged only one possible contrary ruling, "the equivocal exception of the *King v. Smith* . . . in which the judgment of the court is pronounced in terms which leave it somewhat ambiguous, whether the right of disposing of the custody of the infant by the court is admitted or denied." *Ibid.,* 289.
131. Ibid., 289–90.
132. *Mercein v. People ex relazione Barry,* 19 Wendell 16, 72, 73, 74 (NY, 1840).
133. *Report,* 291.

134. Ibid., 291, 292.
135. Ibid., 292.
136. Ibid., 292, 292–93.
137. Ibid., 293.
138. For a compelling account of the power of legal fictions, see Lon Fuller, *Legal Fictions* (Stanford, CA, 1967).
139. *Report*, 293, 294.
140. Ibid., 293.
141. Ibid., 294, 294–5.
142. For a discussion of long-term trends in custody law and the rise of a maternal preference, see Grossberg, *Governing the Hearth*, chap. 7.
143. *Report*, 295.

5. Into the Court of Public Opinion

1. Edward M. Bruner, "Ethnography as Narrative," in Victory M. Turner and Edward M. Bruner, eds., *The Anthropology of Experience* (Urbana, IL, 1980), 153.
2. Jergen Habermas, *The Structural Transformation of the Public Sphere, An Inquiry into a Category of Bourgeois Society*, trans. Thomas Burger with Frederick Lawrence (Cambridge, 1989), 27.
3. For a critical evaluation of Habermas' s notion of the public sphere, see Craig Calhoun, ed., *Habermas and the Public Sphere* (Cambridge, MA, 1992). See also Robert C. Holub, *Jergen Habermas, Critic in the Public Sphere* (New York, 1991). And for the idea of women's virtual representation, see Larzer Ziff, *Writing in the New Nation* (Yale, 1991), 106. Despite male dominance, women editors did raise their voices in the public sphere. For example, the editor of *Godey's Lady's Book* prefaced a published excerpt from a rejected manuscript with the comment: "We will give a short extract from this last article, partly because it is such an excellent specimen of the Rosa Matilda style, and partly to show that M. d'Hauteville is not the only forsaken husband who should excite our sympathy." *Godey's Lady's Book*, March 1841, 142.
4. See, for example, *The Philadelphia Ledger*, 16 November 1840, 1; *The Philadelphia Gazette*, 16 November 1840, announced the verdict and on the same page reprinted the opinion in the *Barry* case; *The Philadelphia Inquirer*, 15 November 1840; *The Germantown Telegraph*, 18 November 1840; *The New York Sun*, 17 November 1840; *The American Sentinel*, 16 November 1840, and reprinted the verdict the next day; *The Boston Post*, 19 November 1840.
5. For a compelling analysis of this shift in public discourse, see Daniel A. Cohen, *Pillars of Salt, Monuments of Grace, New England Crime Literature and the Origins of American Popular Culture, 1774–1860* (New York, 1993).
6. Dan Schiller, *Objectivity and the News: The Public and the Rise of Commercial Journalism* (Philadelphia, 1981), 15
7. Robert Hariman, "Introduction," 4, and see generally 4–5, and idem, "Performing the Laws," 21–6 in Robert Hariman, ed., *Popular Trials, Rhetoric, Mass Media and the Law* (Birmingham, AL, 1990).

8. *The Philadelphia Gazette*, 18 November 1840, 2.

9. *The Public Ledger*, 30 November 1840, 2.

10. *The Philadelphia Monthly Album*, 1(December 1840): 185.

11. *Report*, the advertisement is the third unnumbered page of the volume. For a notice of the book, see *North American Review*, 52(1841): 269; and for an enthusiastic review that read like a promotional ad for the report, see *The Philadelphia Inquirer*, 1 December 1840, 2. For a discussion of the rise of trial reports in the era, see Cohen, *Pillars of Salt, Monuments of Grace*, chaps. 8–9.

12. *Philadelphia Gazette*, 27 November 1840, 2; and see ibid., 24 November 1840, 2. For another favorable review of the d'Hauteville decision by a Philadelphia paper, see *The American Sentinel*, 9 December 1840, 2.

13. For a discussion of the use of gender stereotypes in press accounts of trials, see Daniel A. Cohen, "The Murder of Maria Bickford: Fashion, Passion, and the Birth of a Consumer Culture," *American Studies*, 31(1990): 5–30.

14. *The New York Herald*, 3 December 1840, 1–2. For a quite different view of the Philadelphia press, see Lord B, *A Moral Picture of Philadelphia, The Virtues and Follies of the City Delineated* (Philadelphia, 1845), 7

15. *The Boston Post*, 31 December 1840, 2.

16. *Niles' National Register*, 19 December 1840, 244.

17. John Forney, *Anecdotes of Public Men* (New York, 1873), 428–9.

18. The *Ledger* continued its campaign for women's rights throughout the decade, see Elizabeth M. Geffen, "Industrial Development and Social Crisis, 1841–1854," in Russell Weigley et al., eds., *Philadelphia, A 300-Year History* (New York, 1982), 336.

19. For a discussion of Wright in these terms, see Glenna Matthews, *The Rise of Public Woman, Woman's Power and Woman's Place in the United States, 1630–1970* (New York, 1992), 108–11.

20. *The Public Ledger*, 29 December 1840, 2.

21. William Kent, ed., *Memoirs and Letters of James Kent, LL.D.* (Boston, 1898), 158.

22. *Public Ledger*, 1 January 1841, 2.

23. Edwin C. Surrency, *A History of American Law Publishing* (New York, 1990), 190.

24. For a glimpse of Chandler's practice, see his collected papers at the Massachusetts Historical Society.

25. "Preface," *The Law Reporter*, 1(1839): iii–iv.

26. Ibid.

27. *Review of the D'Hauteville Case: Recently argued and determined in the Court of General Sessions, for the City and County of Philadelphia, by a Member of the Boston Bar* (Boston, 1841), 2,8.

28. Ibid., 17, 19.

29. Ibid., 21, 22.

30. Ibid., 22, 23.

31. Ibid., 23.

32. Ibid., 23, 24.

33. Ibid., 24, 25.

34. Ibid., 26, 29, 30.

35. Ibid., 31, 34, 35.

36. Ibid., 37, 38, 39.
37. Ibid., 41, 41–2.
38. Ibid., 42, 43.
39. *American Jurist and Law Magazine*, (January 1841): 500, 501, 501–2, 502.
40. Anecdote cited in David Paul Brown, *The Forum, or Forty Years Full Practice at the Philadelphia Bar* (Philadelphia, 1856), 2:369. For a sociological analysis strikingly similar in tone, see E. Digby Baltzell, *Puritan Boston and Quaker Philadelphia* (Boston, 1979), 337.
41. *Proprietors of Charles River Bridge v. Proprietors of Warren Bridge*, 36 U.S. 420 (1937). For a compelling discussion of the case, see Stanley Kutler, *Privilege and Creative Destruction: The Charles River Bridge Case* (Boston, 1971).
42. Joseph Story, "The Value of Legal Studies," in William Wetmore Story, ed., *The Miscellaneous Writings of Joseph Story* (New York, 1852), 548; and see Cohen, *Pillars of Salt, Monuments of Grace*, 29–30.
43. *The Boston Post*, 9 January 1841, 1.
44. *The Boston Courier*, 7 January 1841, 2; ibid., 11 January 1841, 4.
45. *The Boston Post*, 27 January 1841, 1.

6. Back into the Shadow

1. Wilhelm Dilthey, *Selected Writings*, ed. and trans. H. D. Richman (Cambridge, UK, 1976), 210, italics added; and see Victor M. Turner, "Dewey, Dilthey, and Drama," in Victor M. Turner and Edward M. Bruner, eds., *The Anthropology of Experience* (Urbana, IL, 1980), 34–6.
2. Anna to Miriam, 6 December 1840; Miriam to Anna, 9 December 1840, Amory Letters.
3. For a discussion of Boston newspapers in the era, see Justin Winsor, *The Memorial History of Boston* (Boston, 1841), 3:627–35.
4. *Mercien v. People ex relazione Barry*, 25 Wendell 64 (New York, 1840). In a letter to her mother, Anna Sears Amory rejoiced in Eliza's victory: "Father told me yesterday of the decision of the Court of Errors in Mrs. Barry's case, and I am truly thankful that the poor woman may at last rest in peace, and as it has so great an influence upon our situation, feel glad that New York as well as Philadelphia may now offer protection." Anna to Miriam, 4 January 1841, Amory Letters. Though the *Barry* case would continue for several more years, John Barry never succeeded in gaining custody of his daughter. His two judicial triumphs, one in 1840 and the other in 1842, were quickly overturned and the United States Supreme Court rejected his claims as well. For a fully chronology of the verdicts in the case, see Hendrik Hartog, "John Barry's Rights: Of Power, Justice, and Coverture," presented at the Amherst Seminar on Law & Society, July, 1992, footnote 7. It should also be noted that despite the interconnections between the two cases, the dominant issues were not exactly the same. Rather than questions about the separation of spousal roles and considerations of maternal custody that figured so prominently in the d'Haute-

ville case, the *Barry* case centered on whether or not John's acts justified a separation by Eliza even if she could not obtain a full divorce.

5. *Daily Advertizer,* 18 January 1841, 2.
6. David Sears to William Meredith, 13 January 1841, Sears Letterbook.
7. Willis Clark to David Sears, 30 March 1841, Sears Letterbook. The letter includes a note by Sears authorizing two payments to Clark.
8. David Sears to Messr. Hottingner & Co., 15 April 1841, Sears Letterbook.
9. David Sears to Messr. Hottingner & Co, 14 May 1841, Sears Letterbook.
10. David Sears to Nathaniel Chapman, June 1841, Sears Letterbook.
11. Statute reprinted in the *Providence Daily Journal,* July 8, 1841, 2.
12. Ellen d'Hauteville to Mr. De Rham, 29 June 1841, Appendix, *Remonstrance of Ellen Sears d'Hauteville to the Rhode Island Assembly,* Rhode Island Petition.
13. David Sears to John Whipple, 2 August 1841, Sears Letterbook.
14. *The Petition of Henry C. De Rham to the General Assembly of Rhode Island to Exempt Paul Daniel Gonzalve Grand d'Hauteville from the Operation of the Law, "To Secure the Fulfillment of Certain Contracts, and for the Relief of Married Women in Certain Cases," Together with the Remonstrance of Ellen S. d'Hauteville and Accompanying Documents, To Which is prefixed the Debate upon a Motion to Repeal that Law* (Providence, RI, 1841), 3.
15. David Sears to Richard Randolph, 4 October 1841, Sears Letterbook.
16. Ibid., 6 October 1841.
17. *The Petition of Henry C. De Rham to the General Assembly of Rhode Island,* 5–8, 13, 16, 18.
18. *The Providence Journal,* 1 November 1841, 2.
19. Ibid., 30 October 1841, 2.
20. Ibid., 1 November 1841, 2.
21. *Laws of the State of New Hampshire: June Session, 1837–1842* (Concord, NH, 1837–42), 533–5.
22. *Gospel Messenger,* 28 August 1841, 3. And for the statute, see *Laws of New Hampshire Passed: June Session 1837–1842* (Concord, NH, 1842).
23. David Sears to Daniel Abbot, 12 October 1841, Sears Letterbook.
24. The manuscript of the appeal was sent to Abbot and is attached to the above letter.
25. Ellen d'Hauteville to Henry De Rham, 5 October 1841, appendix, *Remonstrance of Ellen d'Hauteville,* Rhode Island Petition.
26. David Sears to Thomas H. Perkins, 20 December 1841, Sears Letterbook.
27. *Daily Advertizer,* 30 March 1842; 4 April 1842; 11 April 1842.
28. David Sears to Francois Phillipe Gentor-Doge, 2 April 1842, Sears Letterbook.
29. Ibid., 21 June 1842.
30. David Sears to Frederic Couvreu, 30 November 1842, Sears Letterbook.
31. David Sears to François Phillipe Gentor-Doge, 30 November 1842, and attested to by Ellen Sears d'Hauteville, Sears Letterbook.
32. These conclusions are drawn from letters in the Sears and Amory Collections at the Massachusetts Historical Society.

Afterward

1. *Petition of Henry C. De Rham to the General Assembly of Rhode Island* (Providence, RI, 1841), 14.
2. For a discussion of the importance of the relational setting of a narrative, see Margaret Somers, "Narrativity, Narrative Identity, and Social Action: Rethinking English Working-Class Formation," *Social Science History,* 16(1992): 607.
3. Alexis de Tocqueville, *Democracy in America* (New York, 1970), trans. Henry Reeve, 1:330.
4. Robert Hariman, "Performing the Laws," in idem, ed., *Popular Trials, Rhetoric, Mass Media, and the Law* (Birmingham, AL, 1990), 20.
5. Richard Hildreth, *"Our First Men," A Calendar of Wealth, Fashion and Gentility; Containing Lists of Those Persons Taxed in the City of Boston, Credibly Reported to Be Worth One Hundred Thousand Dollars, With Biographical Notices of the Principal Persons* (Boston, 1846), 40.
6. *Personal Liberty and Habeas Corpus* (Albany, N.Y, 1858), 482; and see Jamil S. Zainaldin, "The Emergence of a Modern American Family Law: Child Custody, Adoption, and the Courts, 1796–1851," *Northwestern University Law Review* 73(1979): 1,071–2.
7. *Commonwealth v. Hunt,* 14 Philadelphia 352, 357 (Pa. 1881).
8. *Butler v. Butler,* 1 Parsons 337, 344 (Pa. 1849).
9. Robert L. Griswold, "The Evolution of the Doctrine of Mental Cruelty in Victorian American Divorce, 1790–1900," *Journal of Social History,* 20(1986): 132.
10. Betty Farrell, *Elite Families, Class and Power in Nineteenth-Century Boston* (Albany, NY, 1993), 91.
11. John Louis Lacaites, "The Impeachment of Henry Sacheverell," in Hariman, *Popular Trials,* 35, and see generally 33–7.
12. For a discussion of public narratives, see Somers, "Rethinking English Working-Class Formation," 604.
13. In making this point I have rephrased Richard Wightman Fox's insight to emphasize the legal elements of such events. See "Intimacy on Trial, Cultural Meanings of the Beecher-Tilton Affair," in Richard Wightman Fox and T. J. Jackson Lears, *The Power of Culture, Critical Essays in American History* (Chicago, 1993), 131.
14. For further discussion of these points, see Sally Merry, "The Discourse of Mediation and the Power of Naming," *Yale Journal of Law & the Humanities,* 2(1990): 1–36.
15. William Forbath, Hendrik Hartog, and Martha Minow, "Introduction: Legal History Symposium," *Wisconsin Law Review,* (1985): 765.
16. For useful discussion of hegemony, see Peter Burke, *History and Social Theory* (Ithaca, NY, 1992), 84–8.
17. Hariman, "Introduction," in idem, *Popular Trials,* 5.
18. For a case that illustrates that continuing reality, see Jonathan Groner, *Hilary's Trial, The Elizabeth Morgan Case, A Child's Ordeal in the American Legal System* (New York, 1991).
19. For a brief but suggestive account of the failed search for alternatives, see Jerold Auerbach, *Justice Without Law?* (New York, 1983).

Coda

1. Anna Amory to William Amory, 27 June 1858, Amory Letters.
2. *The Daily Advertizer,* 2 December 1862, 2.
3. Frederick to David, 21 December 1862; David to Frederick, 2 January 1863, Sears Papers.
4. Information on Frederick's burial is based on information provided by one of her descendants, John Winthtrop Sears.

Index

267